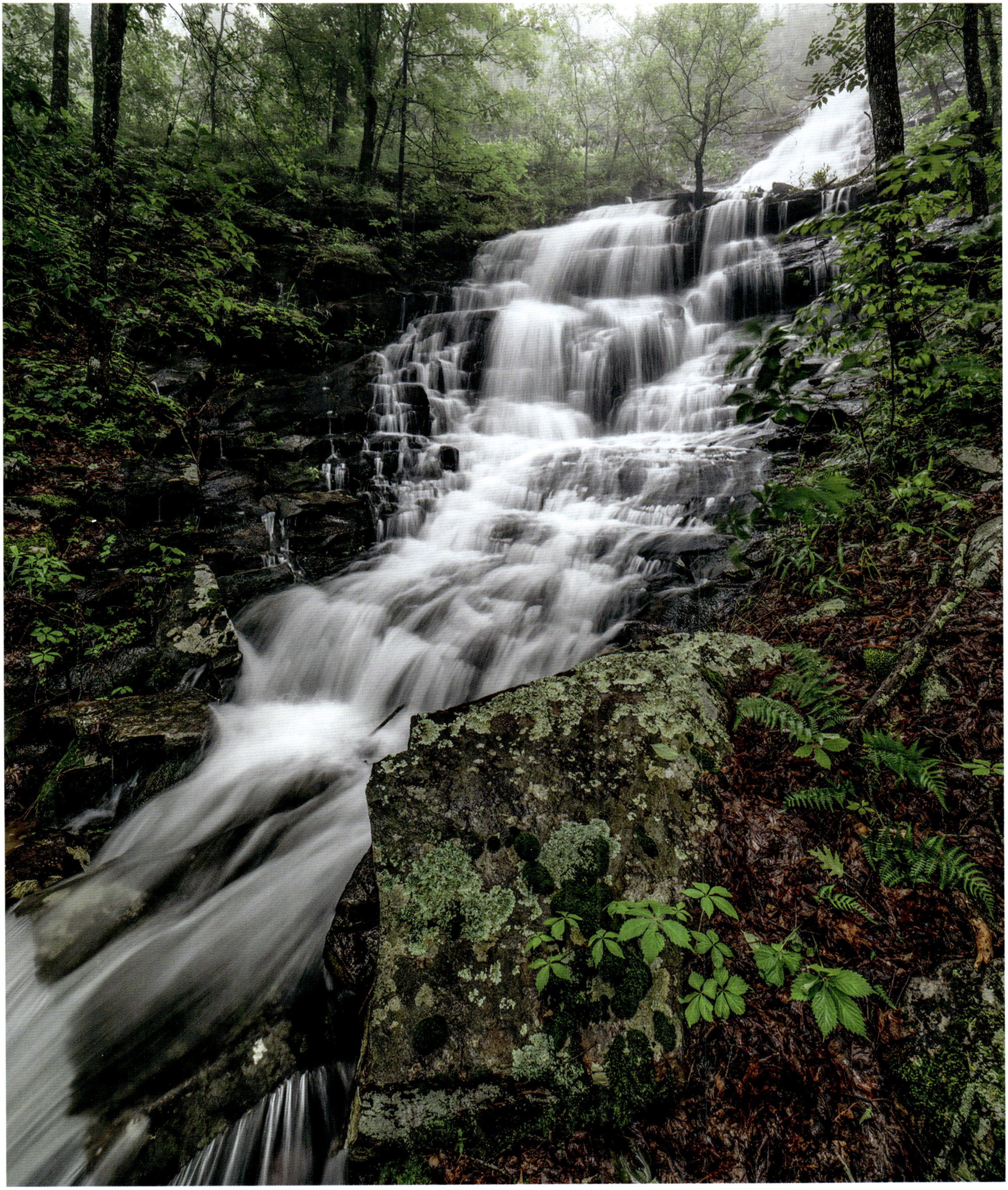

Fringe Falls #2, Mt. Magazine State Park, was a thundering beauty after a week of downpours.
I decided to begin this book with the end—this is the LAST photo that I took for this picture book, just a few weeks before the book was printed. And I'll end with the beginning—the very first photo of mine that was published is on the last page of this book (and is the only photo here that has been in a book before). I hope you ENJOY them all!

ARKANSAS NATURE PHOTOGRAPHER
My 50th Anniversary!

This is Tim's 21st coffee table picture book.

ISBN: 9781882906253

Printed in the USA!!!
Book designed by Tim and Pamela Ernst

All the images in this book are available as fine art canvas, metal or traditional prints in a variety of sizes and prices.
They are printed one at a time per your order by Tim Ernst.
Visit our web site for all the details, and to view other online galleries of Tim's work:

www.TimErnst.com

TIM ERNST PUBLISHING
Jasper, Arkansas 72641

Visit our online store at to see our complete selection
of picture books, guidebooks, and fine art prints.
www.TimErnst.com

Quantity discounts available, and new dealers are always welcome.

Other publications by Tim Ernst:

PICTURE BOOKS

Arkansas: JUST Waterfalls (2025)
Arkansas Greatest Hits (2020, reissued 2025)
Arkansas Splendor (2019)
Arkansas Beauty (2017)
Arkansas In My Own Backyard (2016)
A Rare Quality Of Light: 40 Years of Wilderness Photography (2015)
Arkansas Nightscapes: Wilderness Photos From Twilight 'Til Dawn (2014)
Buffalo River Beauty (2013)
Arkansas Landscapes II (2012)
Arkansas Portfolio III (2011)
Arkansas Autumn: Spectacular Fall Photos Of The Natural State (2010)
Arkansas Wildlife (2009)
Arkansas Landscapes (2008)
Arkansas Waterfalls: Scenic Icons of The Natural State (2007)
Buffalo River Dreams (2006)
Arkansas Portfolio II: Spectacular New Images from The Natural State (2004)
Arkansas Wilderness: My Favorite Photos from The Natural State (2002)
Arkansas Spring: Dogwoods, Waterfalls and Wildflowers (2000)
Buffalo River Wilderness: Photographs by Tim Ernst, Watercolors by William McNamara (1998)
Wilderness Reflections: An Intimate Look at Wild Places in America (1996)
Arkansas Portfolio: Twenty Years of Wilderness Photography (1994)

GUIDEBOOKS

Arkansas Waterfalls (THIRD EDITION 2025)
Arkansas Nature Lover's
Arkansas Hiking Trails
Arkansas Dayhikes For Kids and Families (Pam Ernst)
Buffalo River Hiking Trails
Ozark Highlands Trail
Ouachita Trail

OTHER BOOKS

The Search For Haley (ebook available)
Cloudland Journal (ebook available)

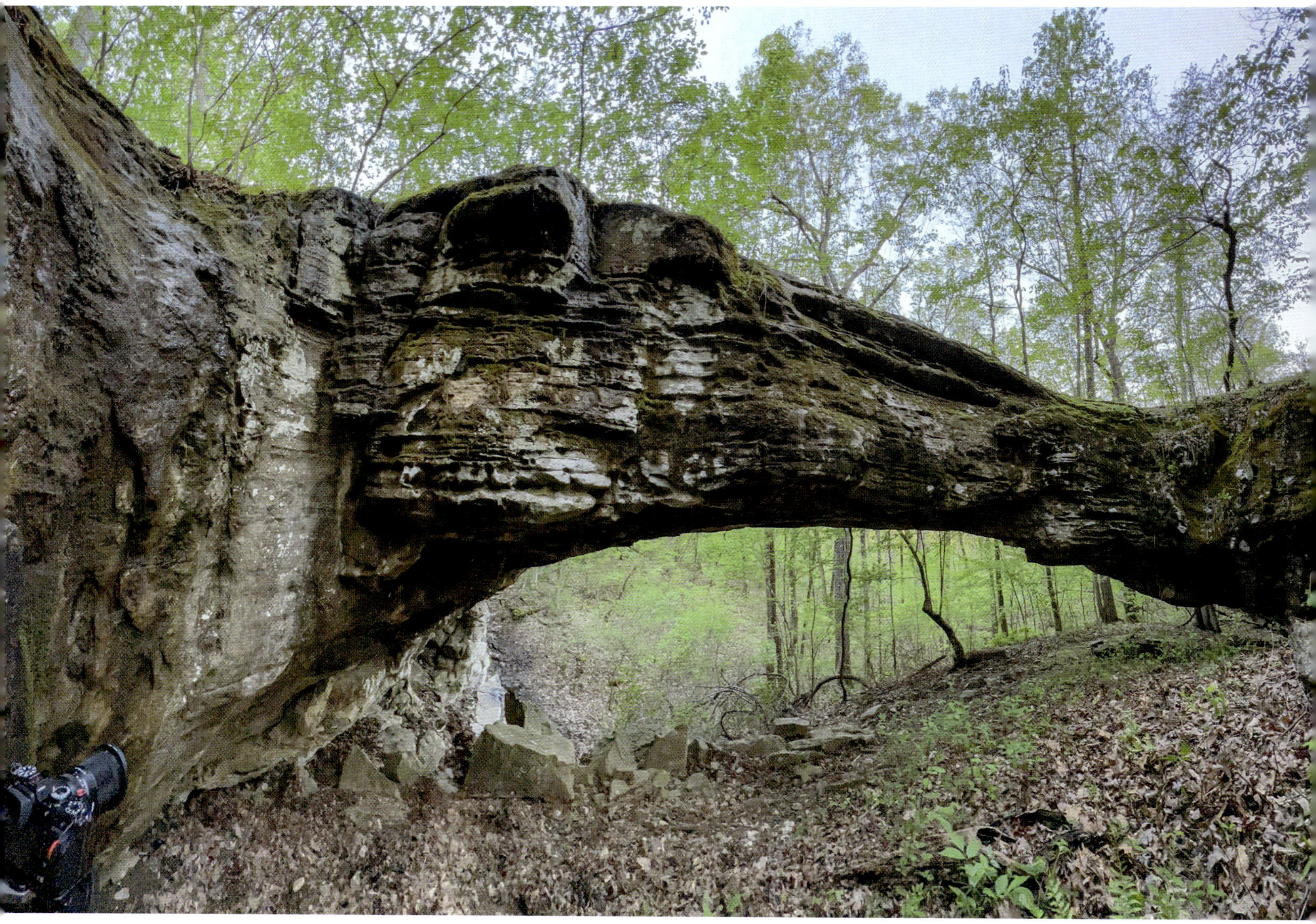

Elephant Head Natural Bridge, Lower Buffalo Wilderness, Buffalo National River

This is one of several photos in this book that were taken with my cell phone. I frequently take snapshots with a phone to get an idea of what a scene might look like as a photo (nature doesn't always look the same in a picture vs. in person). Sometimes I literally can't get the photo with a normal camera and a phone is the only way. This particular natural bridge is so wide, and there is a bluff directly behind me so I could not get far enough back to include the entire rock formation with my normal camera. So I used the panoramic feature of the little phone to get everything in—which I discovered later also included my normal camera on it's tripod.

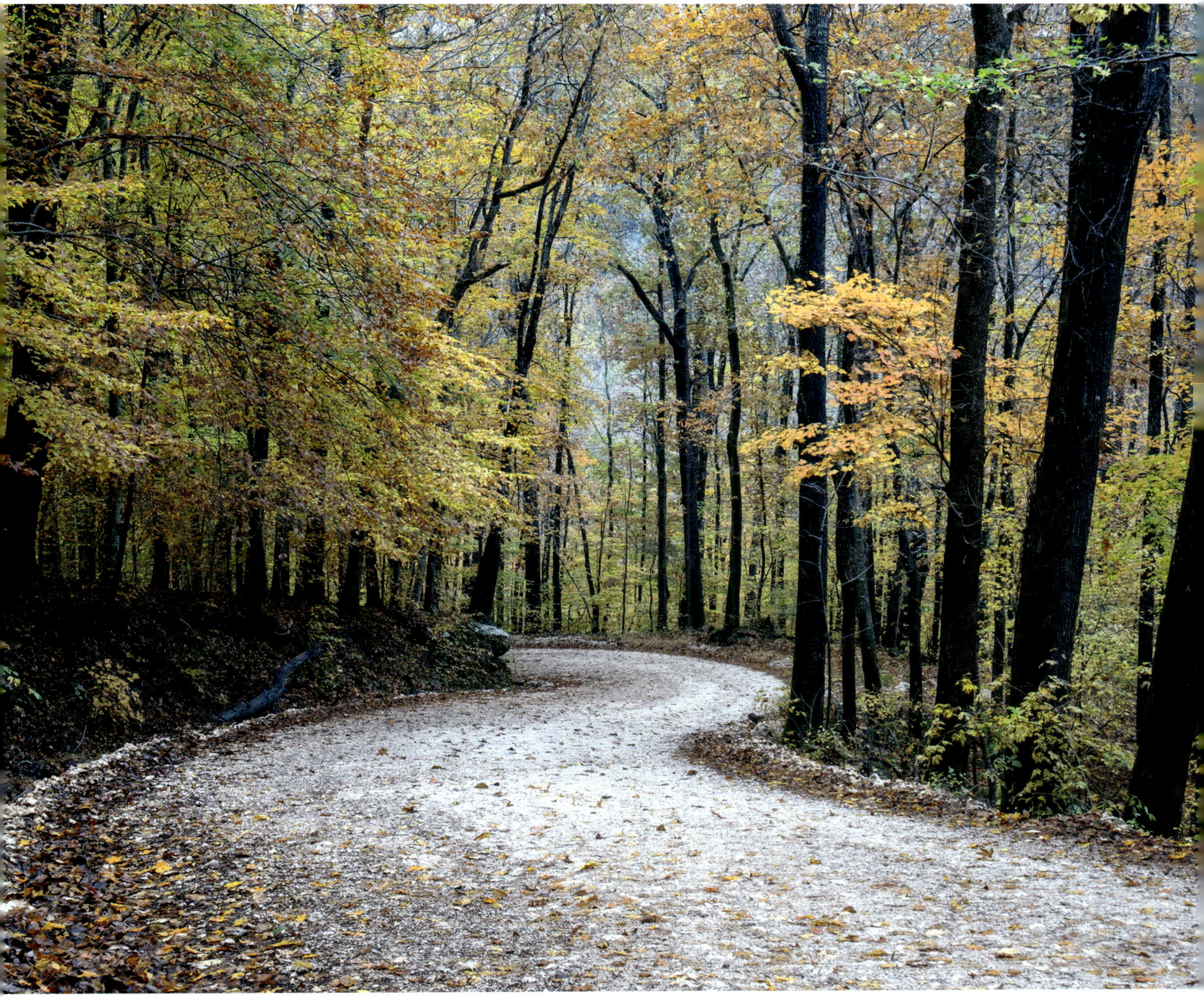

Cave Mountain Road winding its way down the big hill into Boxley Valley

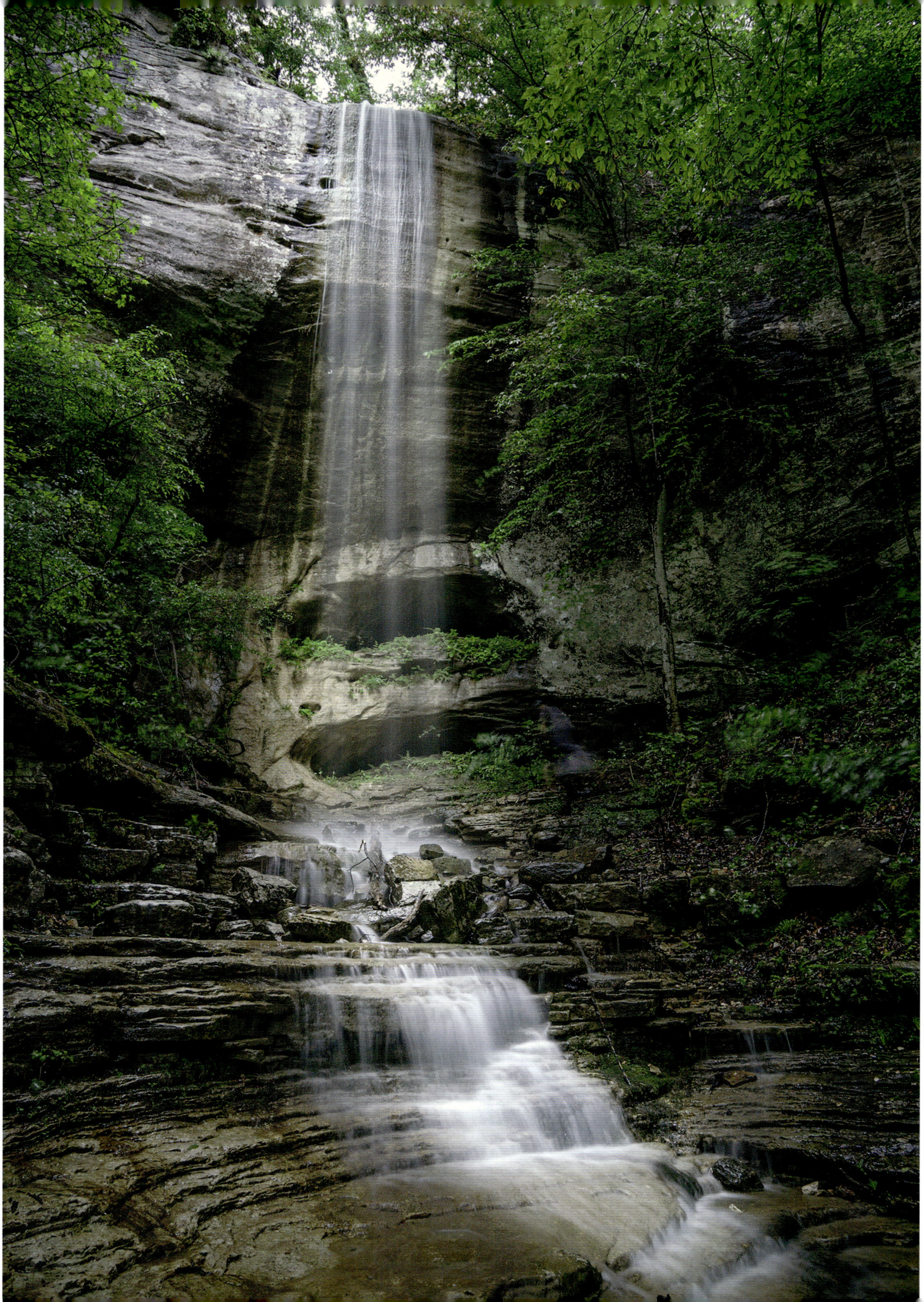

INTRODUCTION

Welcome to my 21st picture book, ***ARKANSAS NATURE PHOTOGRAPHER—My 50th Anniversary***! Inside you will find 169 brand new photos that I've taken since my last picture book came out in 2020—plus a copy on the last page of the very first photo of mine to be published, 50 years ago in 1973! (many have been used in my calendars and other places, but none in a picture book of mine until now) I'm feeling kind of old, but at the same time thrilled that I've been able to survive this long at my dream job of being a nature photographer in the greatest state of them all.

There are no chapters, no order to the layout of this book, and you can open anywhere and go forwards or backwards. I do tend to match up pairs of photos that look good together, and sometimes there will be some sort of relation between the two. But most of the time it's just random, kind of like me!

The photos are a collection of the places I've spent a lot of time in these past few years and find the most interesting photographically—which includes where I live (near Jasper in Newton County and the Buffalo River area). Some places I've been to dozens or even hundreds of times. Others were literally just a moment in time that turned out pretty nice.

Frequent flyer subjects include: waterfalls, stars, naked trees, more waterfalls, historic buildings, the moon, bluffs and the Buffalo River, skies, and many more waterfalls. Sorry about all the waterfalls. I've been neck-deep photographing new waterfalls for a major update to my ***Arkansas Waterfalls Guidebook***—and in fact will soon release an additional picture book with all of the 200 new waterfalls from the guidebook in it (***Arkansas: Just Waterfalls***, my 22nd picture book). And so naturally, many of those same photos appear in this book—I can't get enough of amazing waterfalls and I hope you are OK with that.

All photos have a brief caption but not a lot of additional detail. Some are just random thoughts about the photo, others may be long-winded, trying to explain something, like a bit of history or a photo technique. A few will have a story or two to go with them—I have to watch myself—this is after all a ***picture*** book.

In the end, it's just you and the book and I hope you are able to find a quiet place to sit and ponder and appreciate what a spectacular natural state we have in Arkansas—ENJOY!

Tim Ernst
November, 2025

< Half Moon Falls along the Buffalo River Trail, Buffalo National River

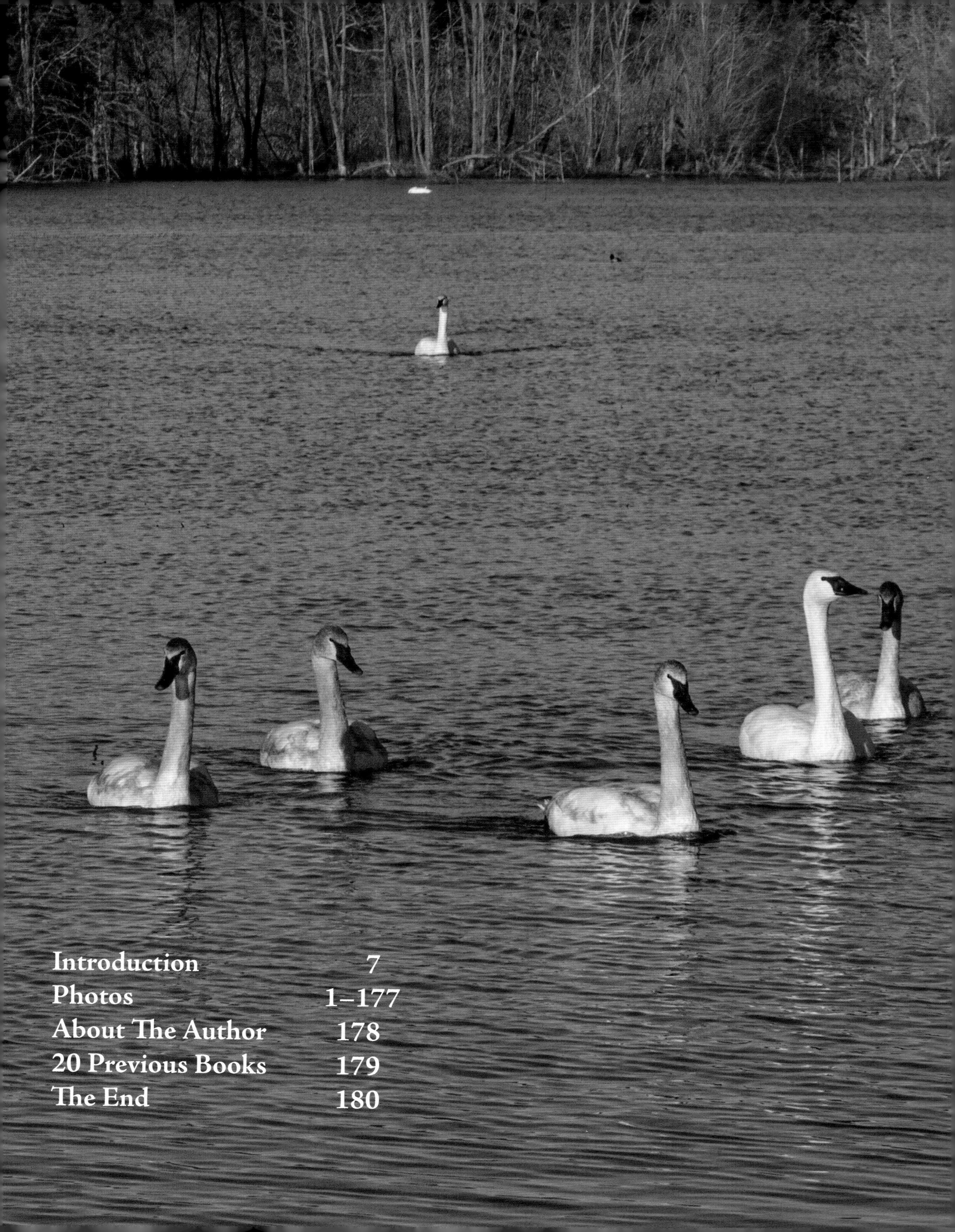

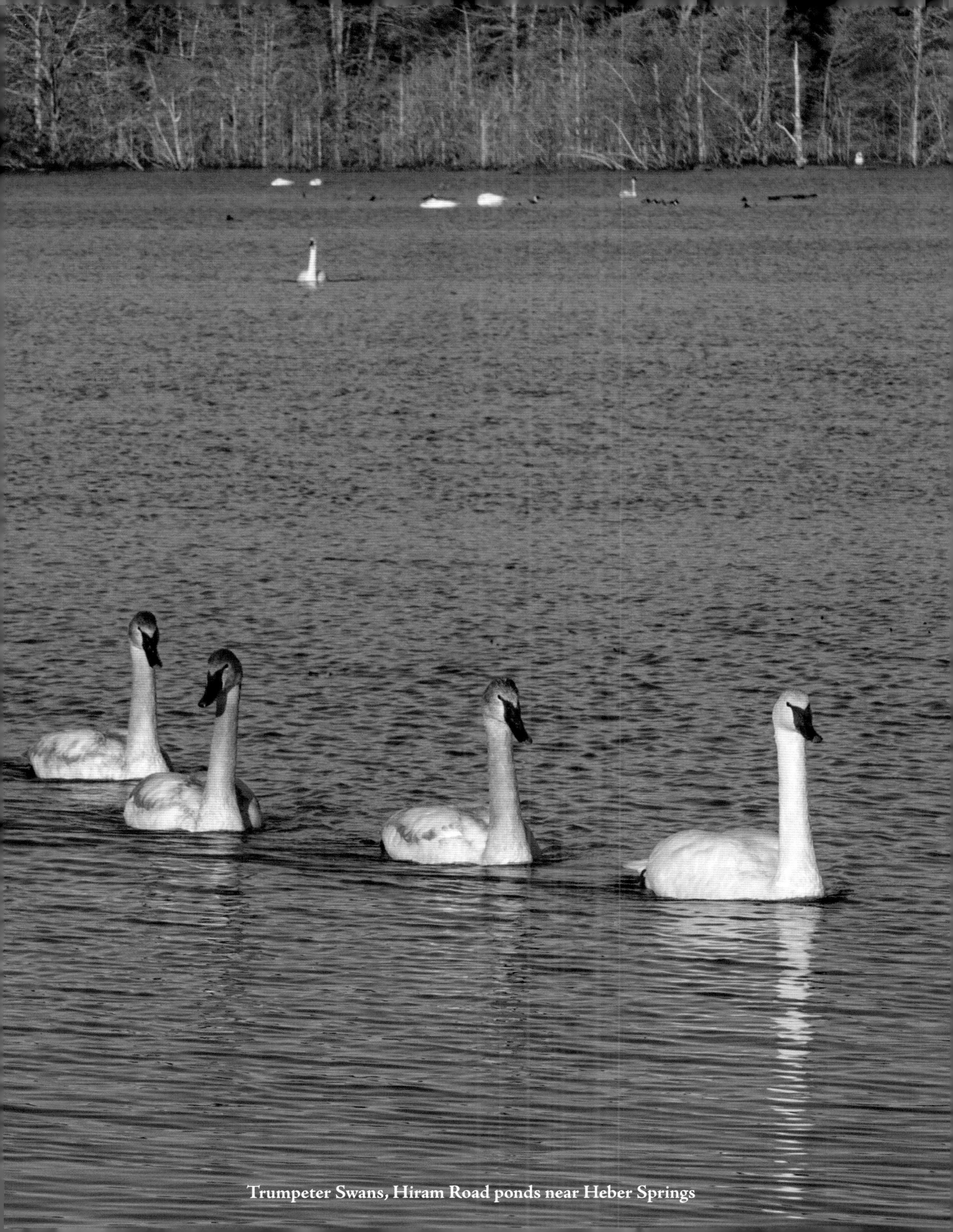

Trumpeter Swans, Hiram Road ponds near Heber Springs

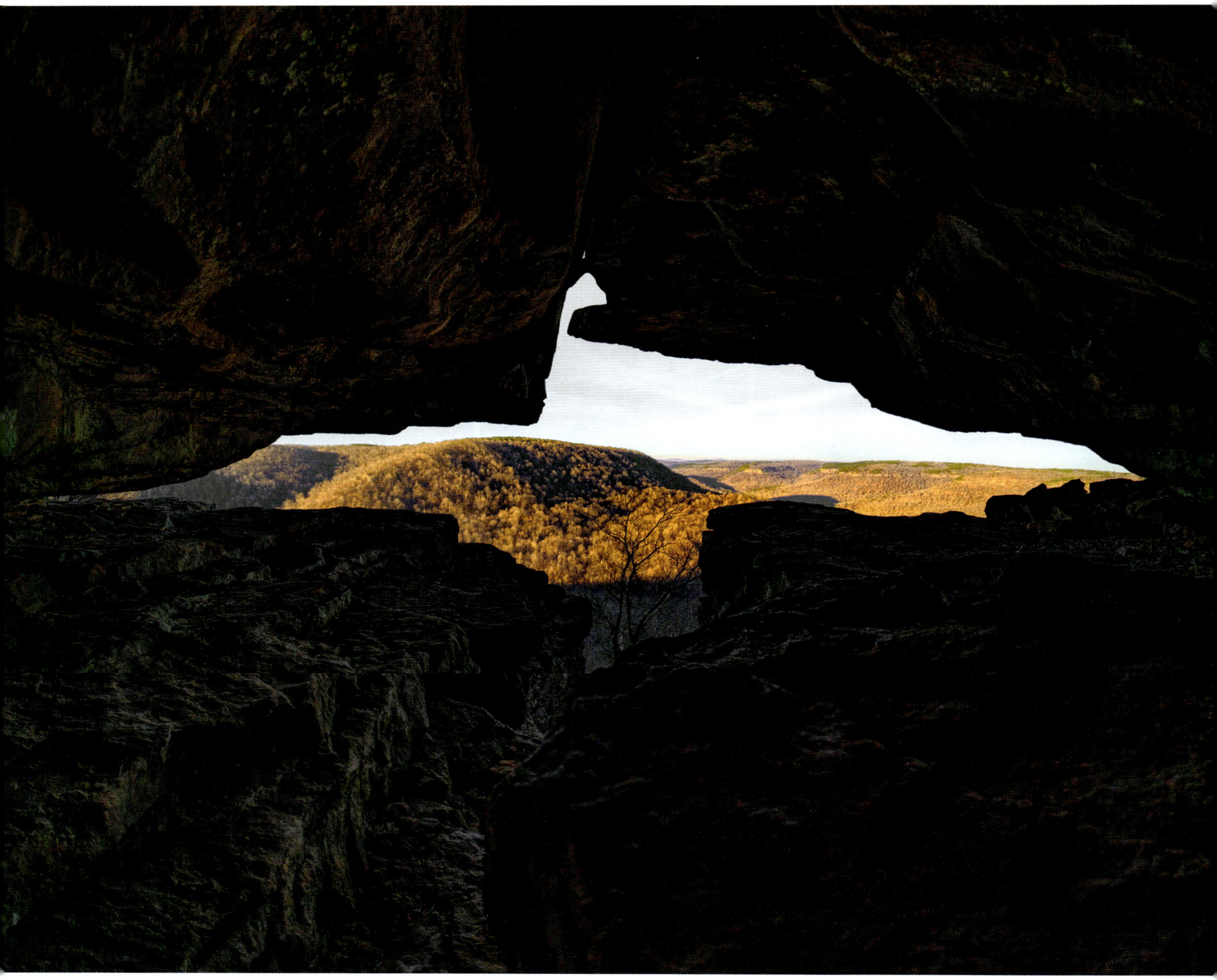

Thunderbird Cave at sunrise, Ozark National Forest (second visit)

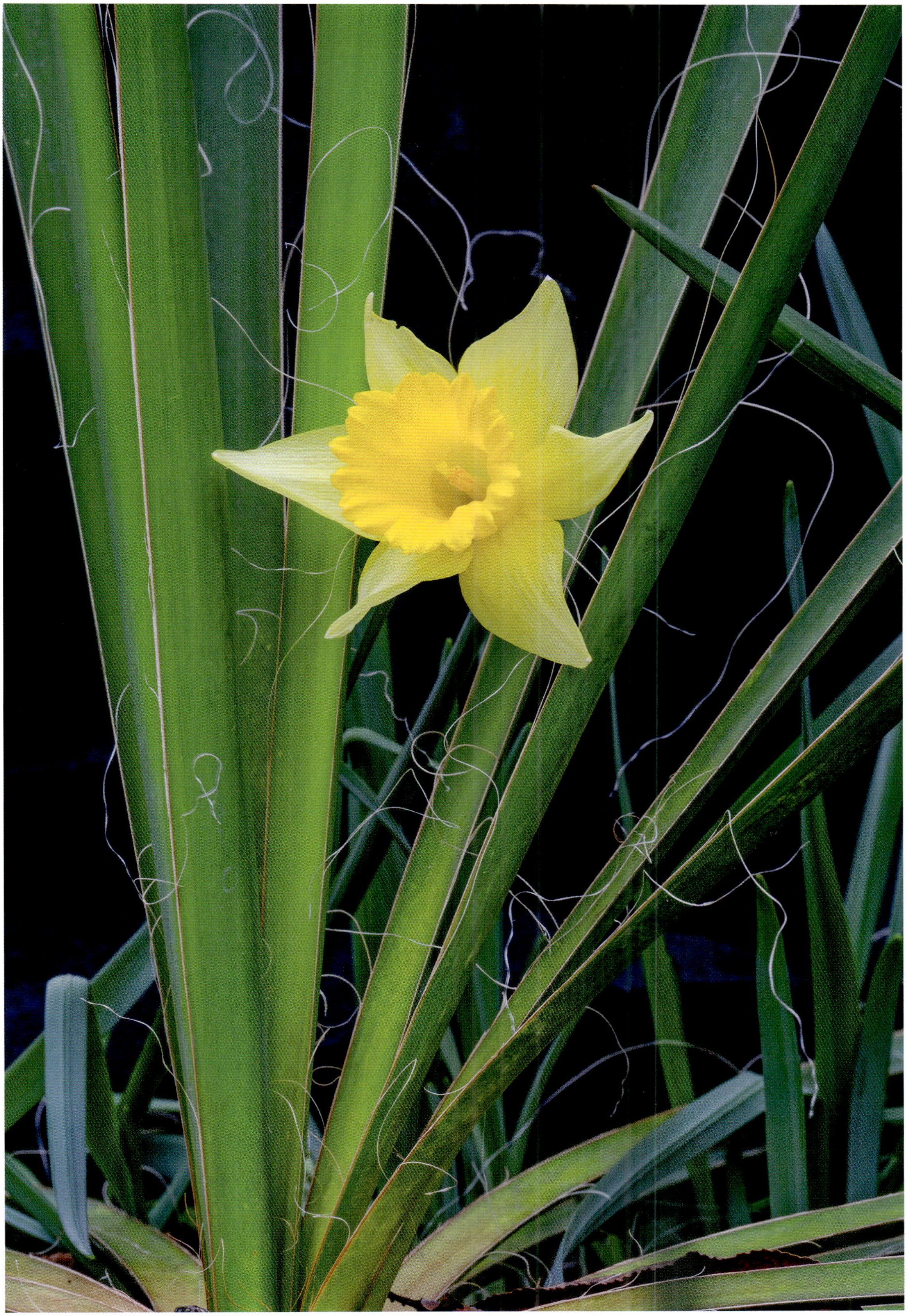

Heirloom Daffodil and yucca plant surviving more than 100 years at our historic homesite

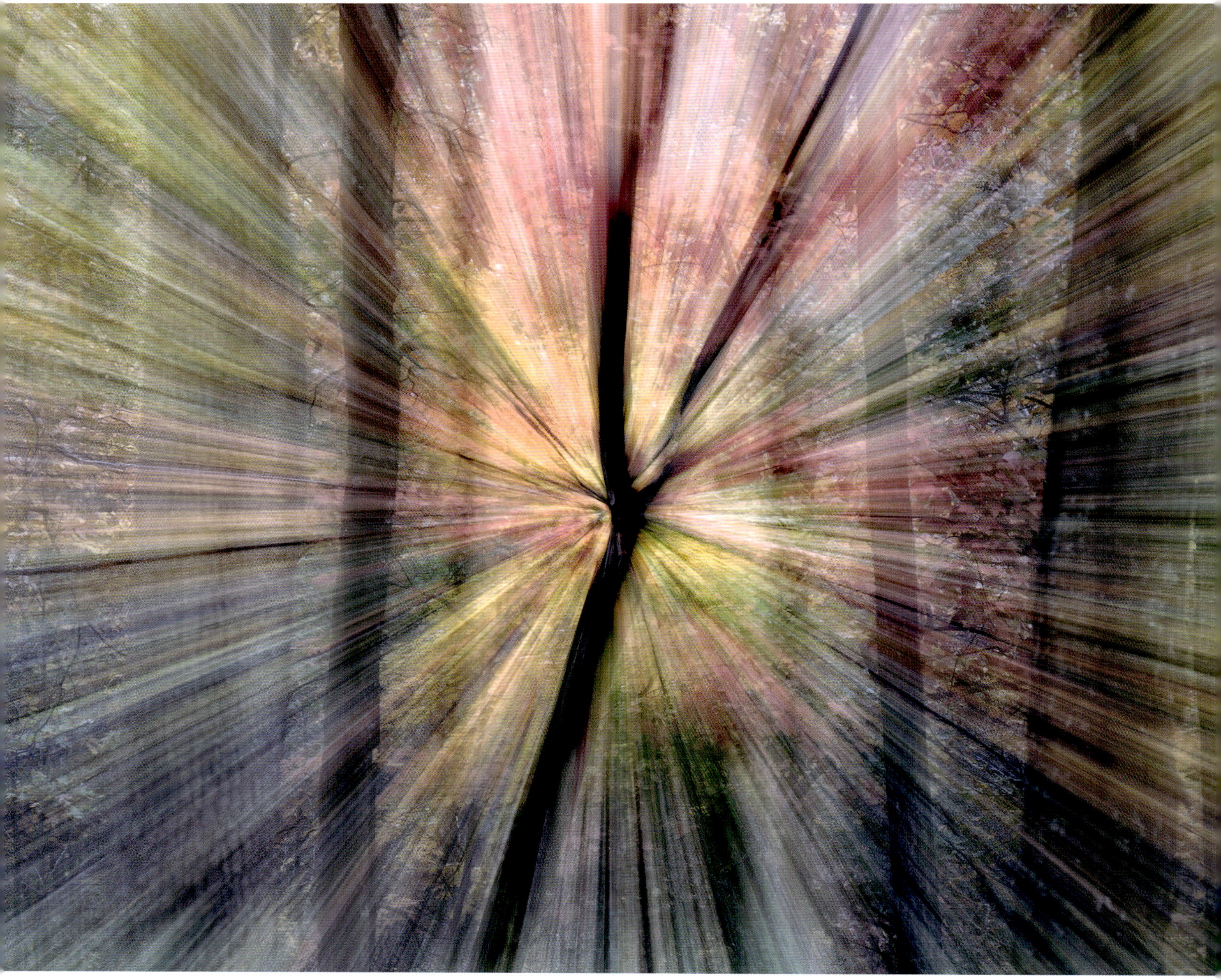

Use a zoom lens and two-second exposure, zoom the lens during the exposure. You never know what it will look like!

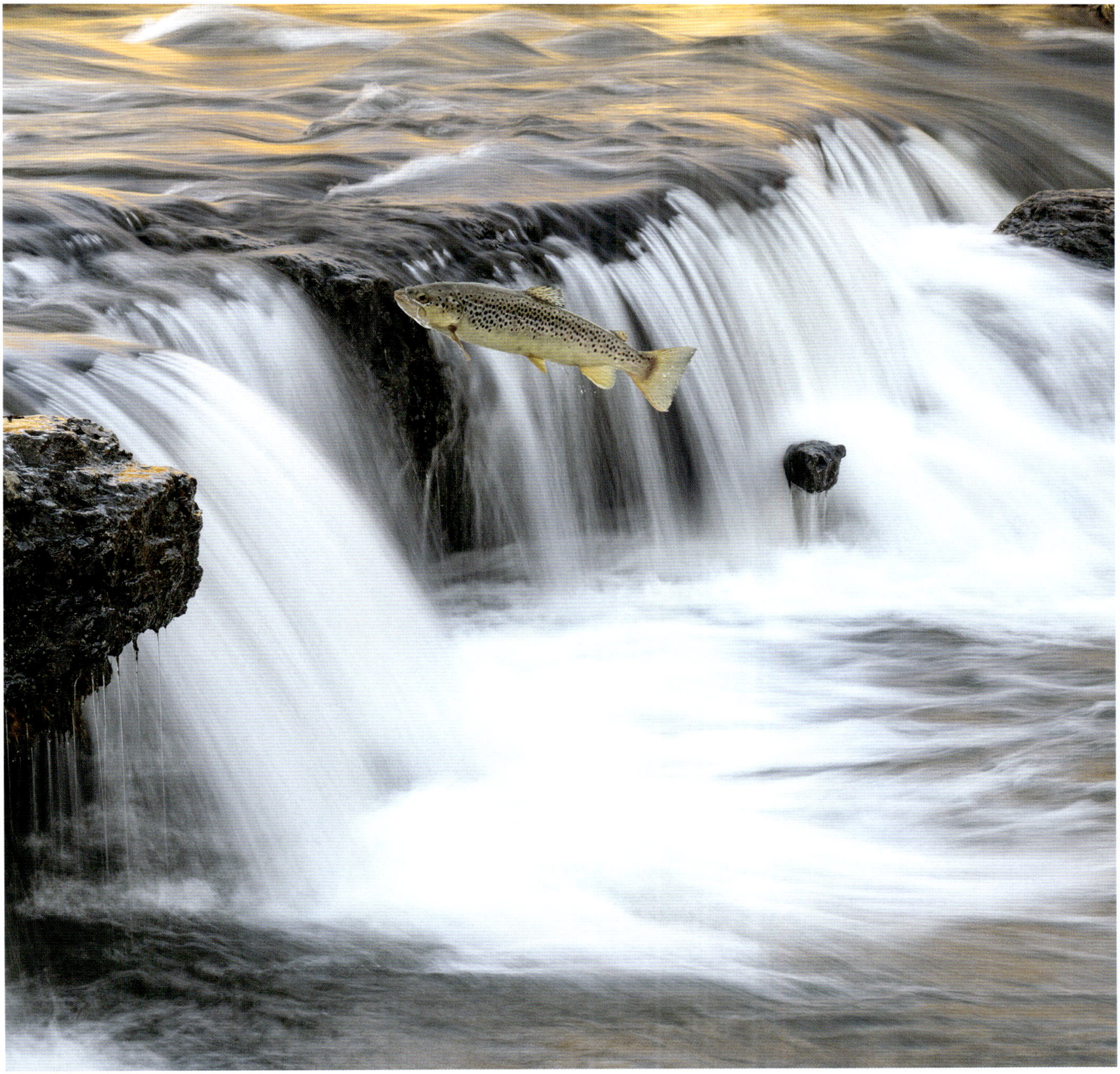

Spawning trout jumping the falls on Running Creek at the base of Norfork Lake Dam

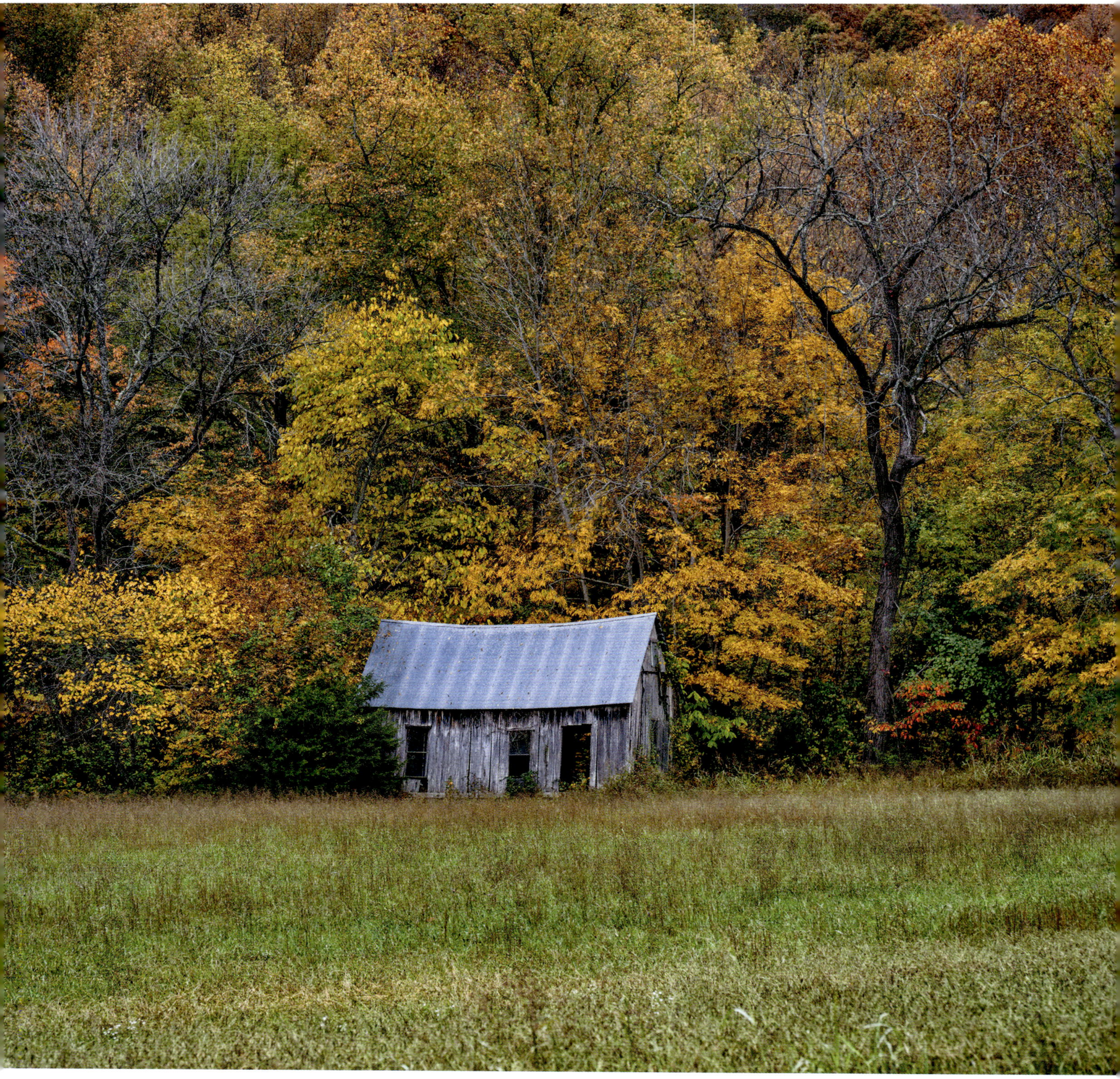

An old cabin/school house at the entrance to Lost Valley

Z Falls on Woods Mountain, Ozark National Forest >

This is one of the more difficult waterfalls to get to the bottom of—I've done it a couple of times and each time I swore I'd never return (of course, I'll make another trip...)

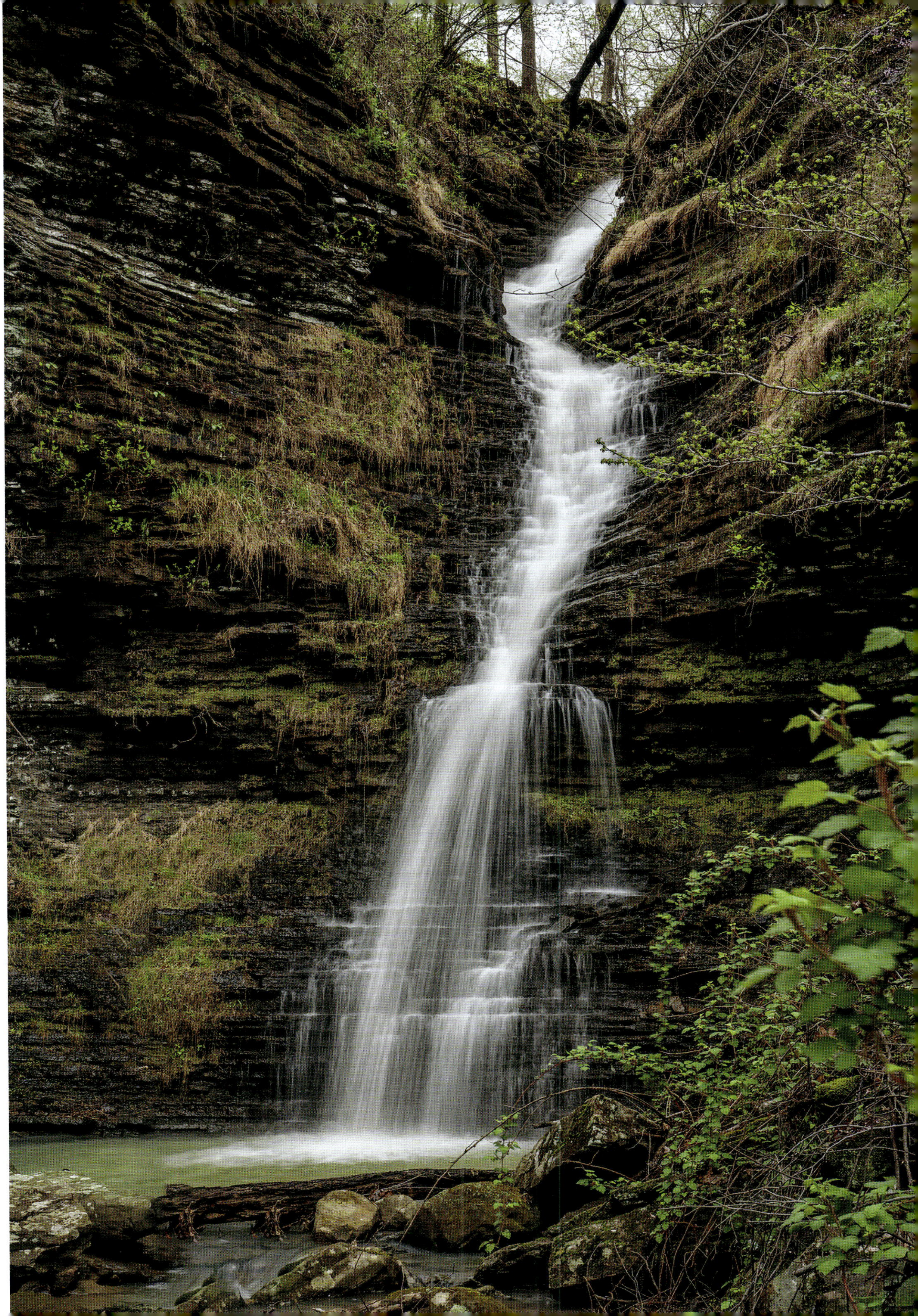

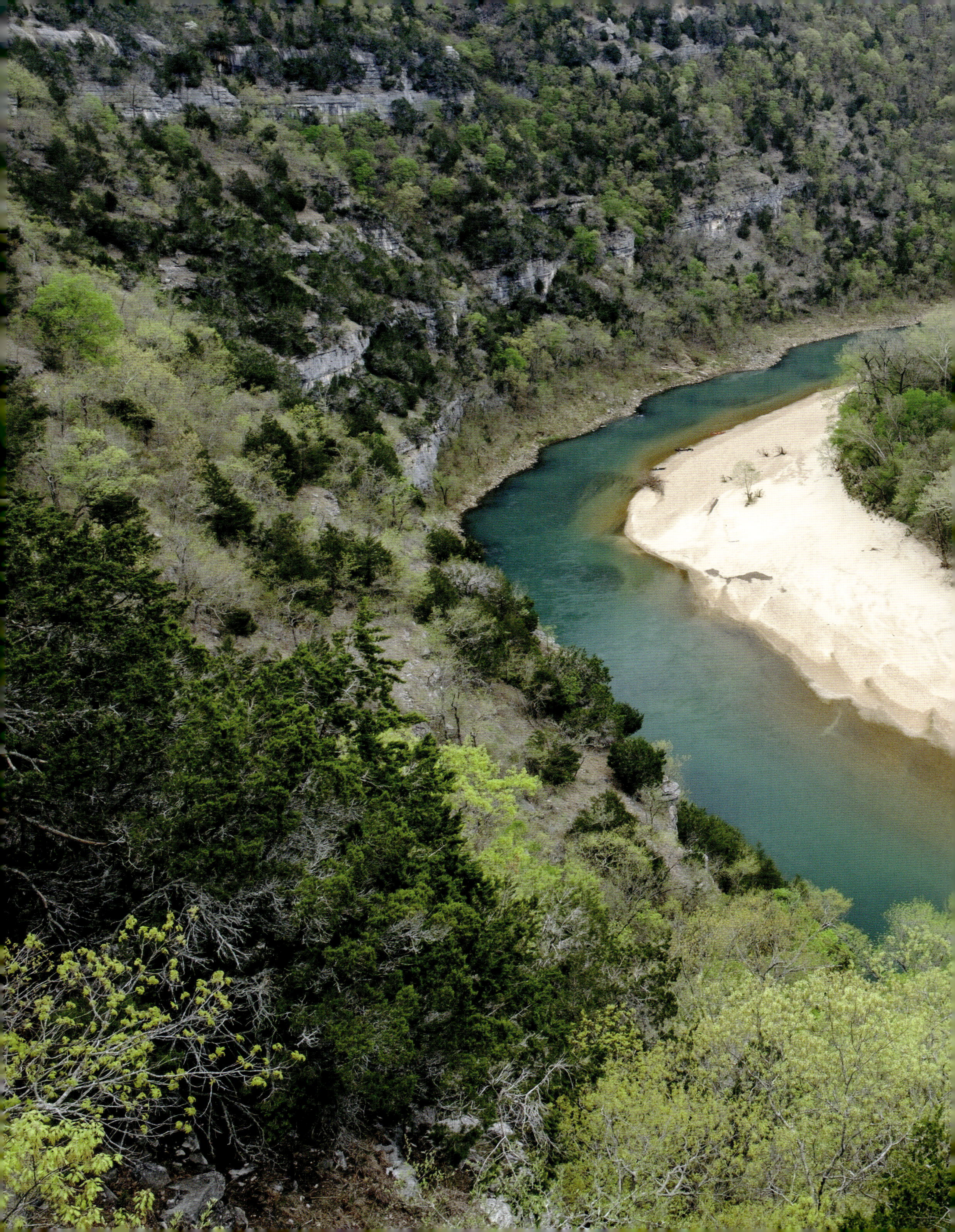

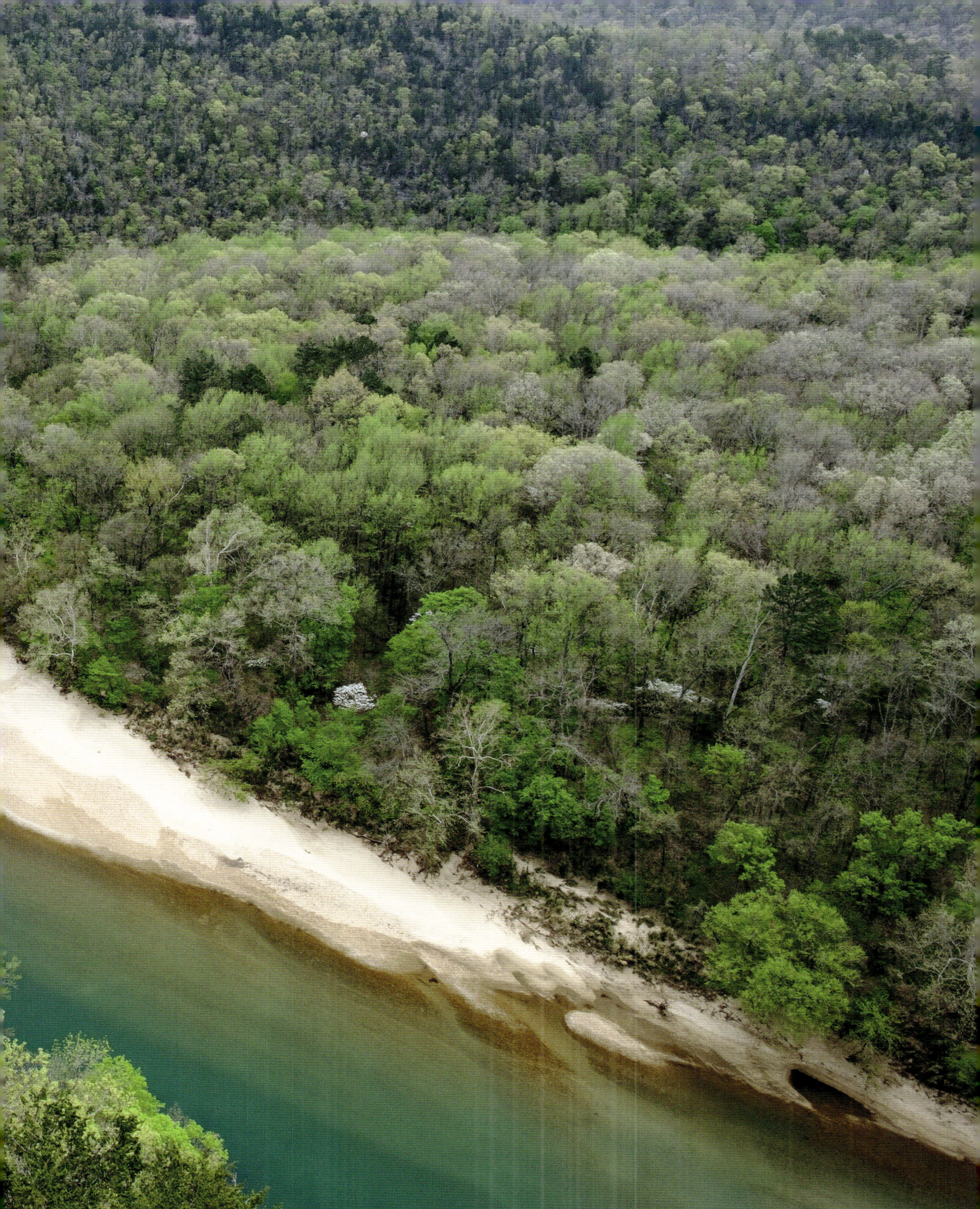

Bice Bend on the Buffalo River, as seen from the top of Ludlow Bluff, the tallest bluff in mid-America at 590'.

The herd gathers, Wilderness Rider Ranch

This is a classic case where my phone saved me. I'd planned to photograph the full moon behind this marvelous naked oak tree. As I was hiking up the hill toward it a herd of cows started gathering at the base of the tree. I loved their silhouettes and thought they made a really nice addition to the scene, but they were starting to leave. I grabbed a quick shot with my phone, and before I could get my real camera set up they had vanished, leaving me with only my phone snapshot. Which camera is the best one? The one you have with you and ready to shoot with!

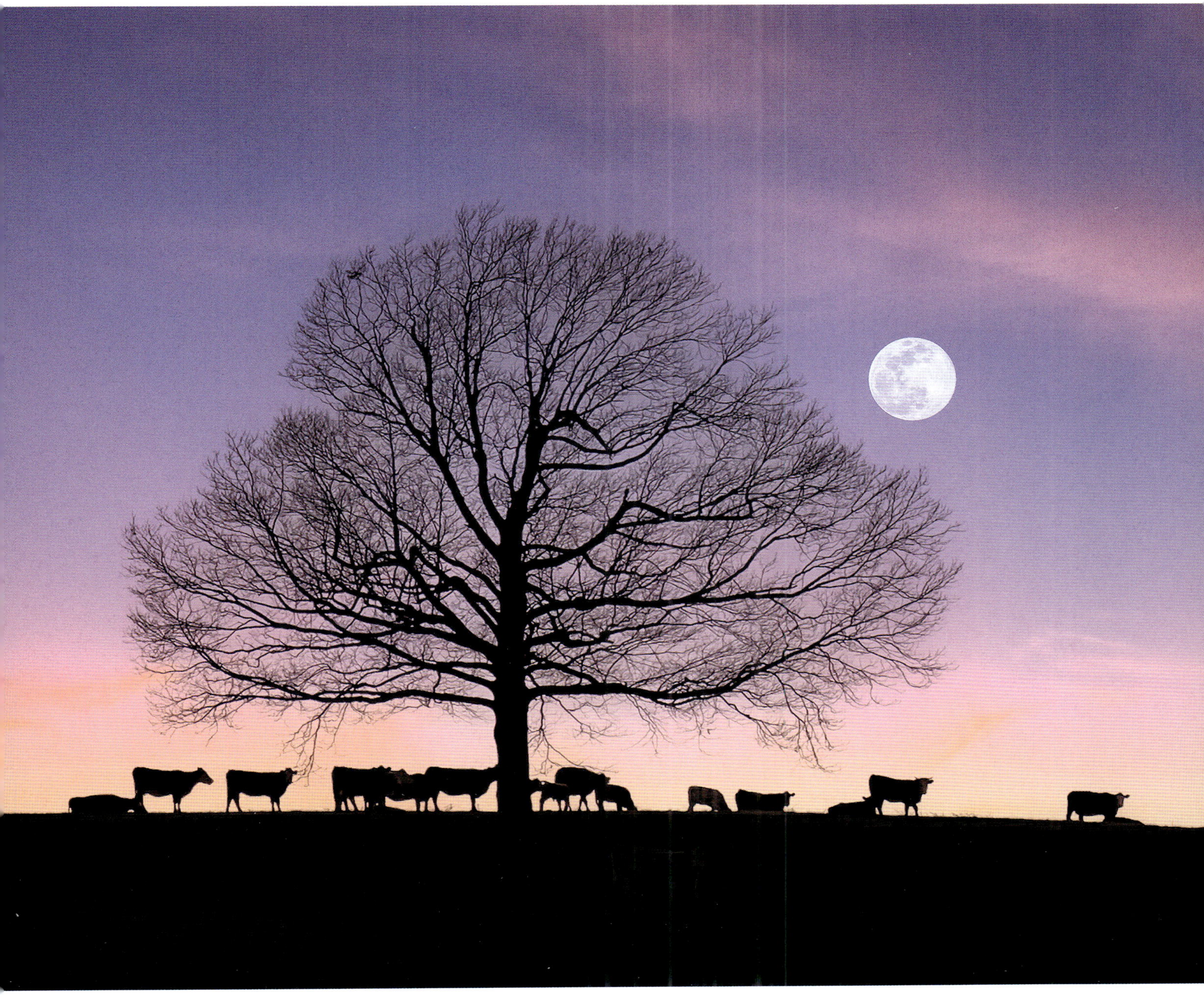

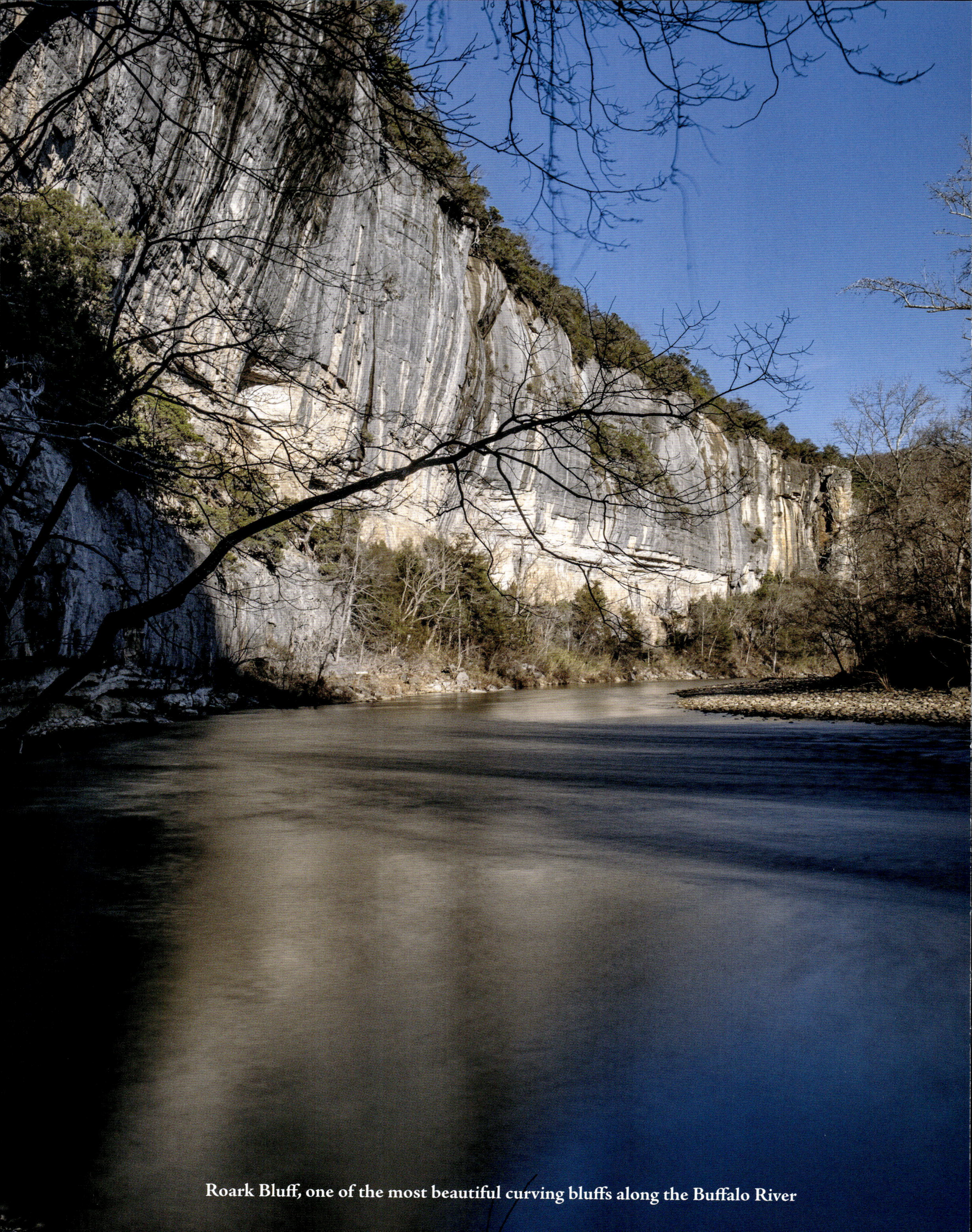

Roark Bluff, one of the most beautiful curving bluffs along the Buffalo River

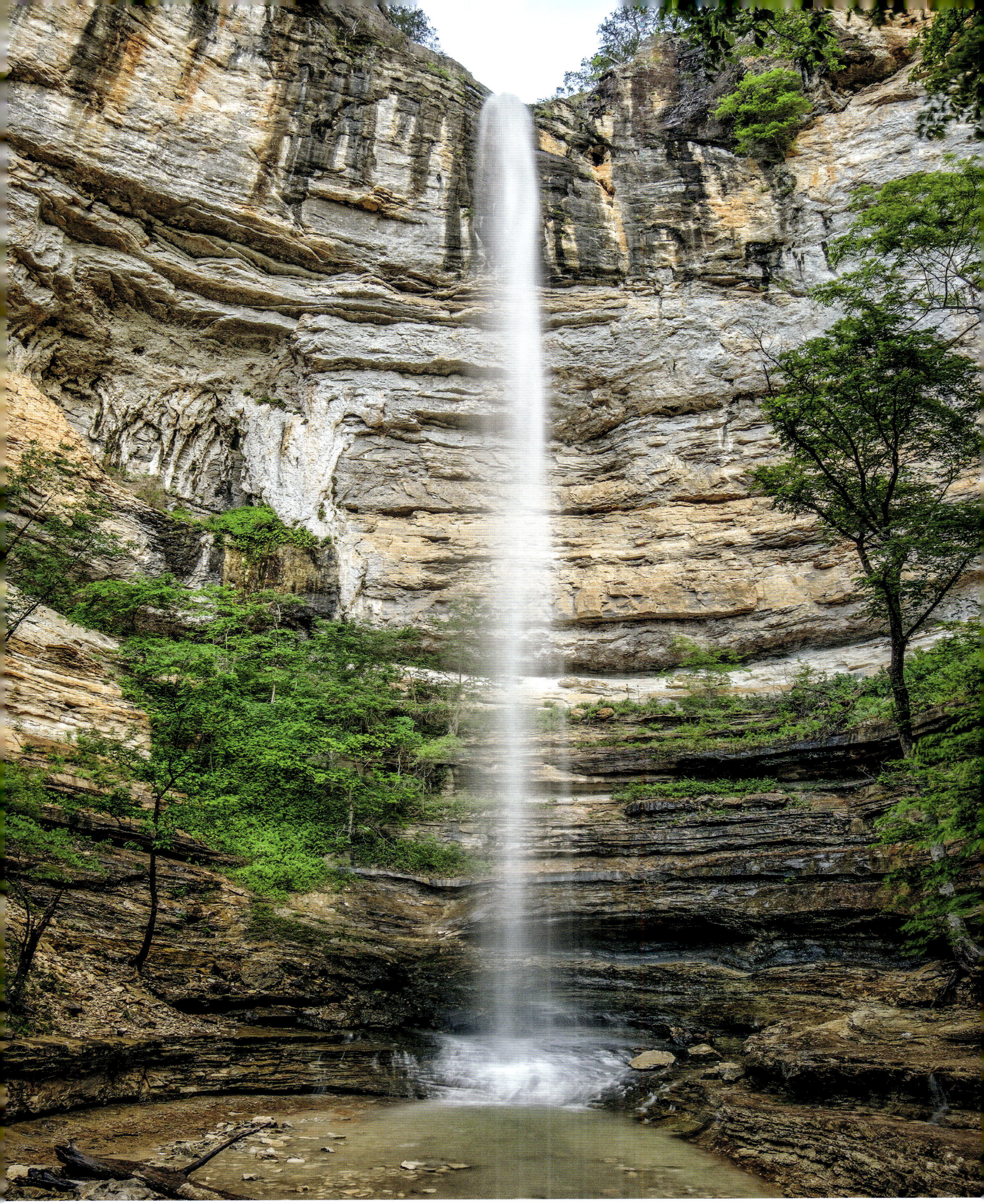

Hemmed-In-Hollow Falls, the tallest waterfall in Mid-America (209'), Buffalo National River.

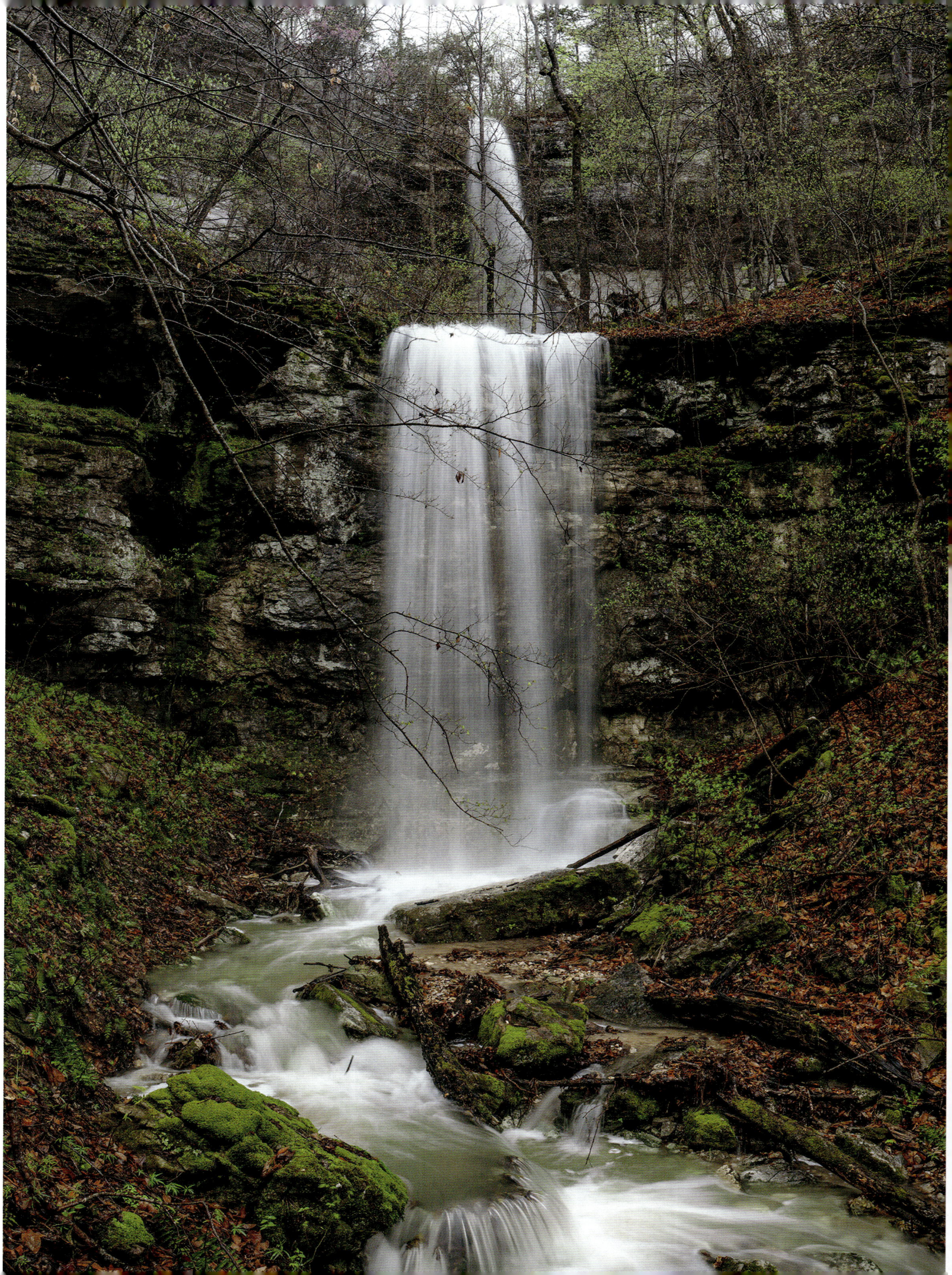

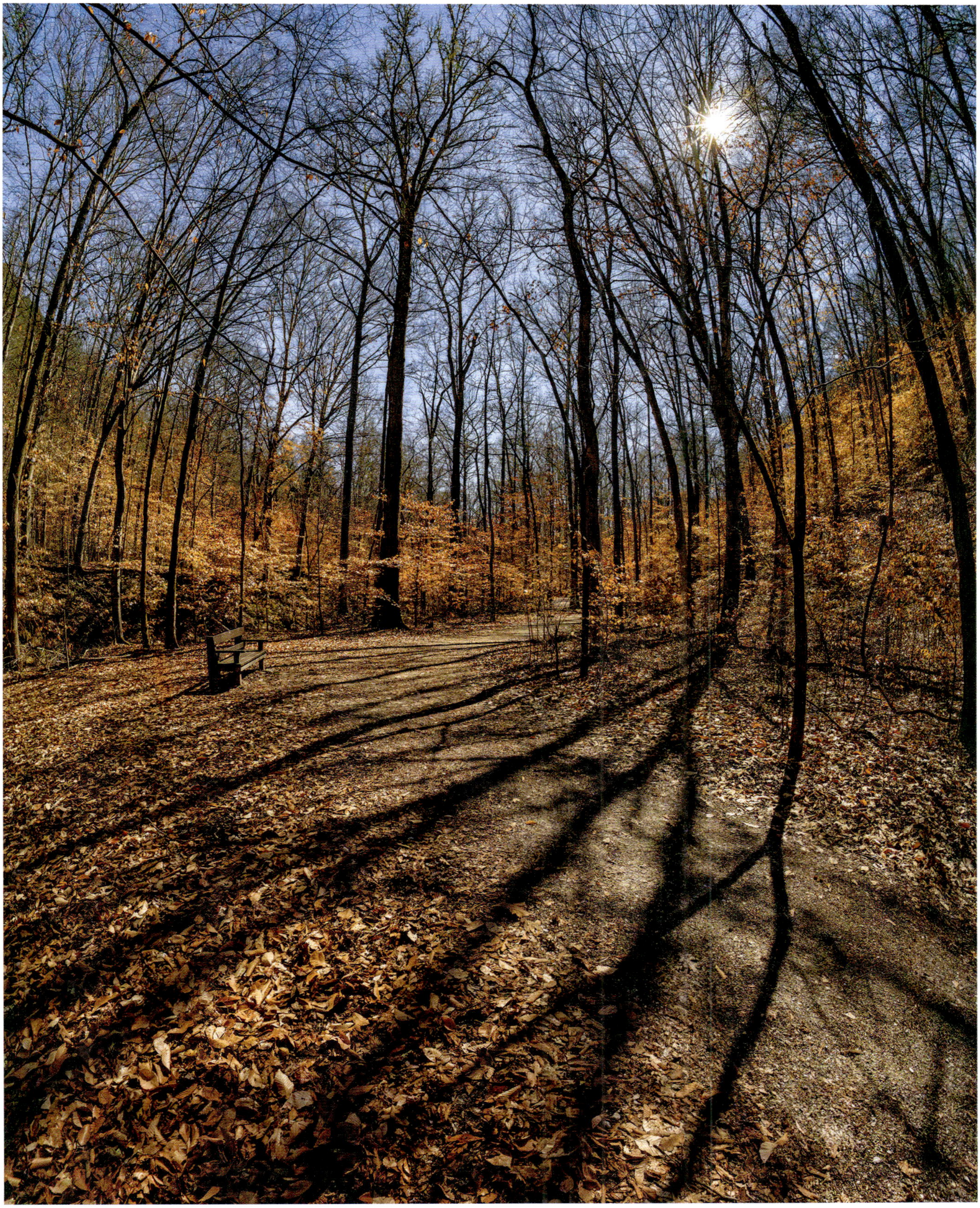

Moonlight and shadows along the Lost Valley Trail.
Young beech trees keep their golden leaves over winter, adding some nice color to the landscape, even at night!

< Littlefoot Falls, with Bigfoot Falls in the background, Ponca Wilderness

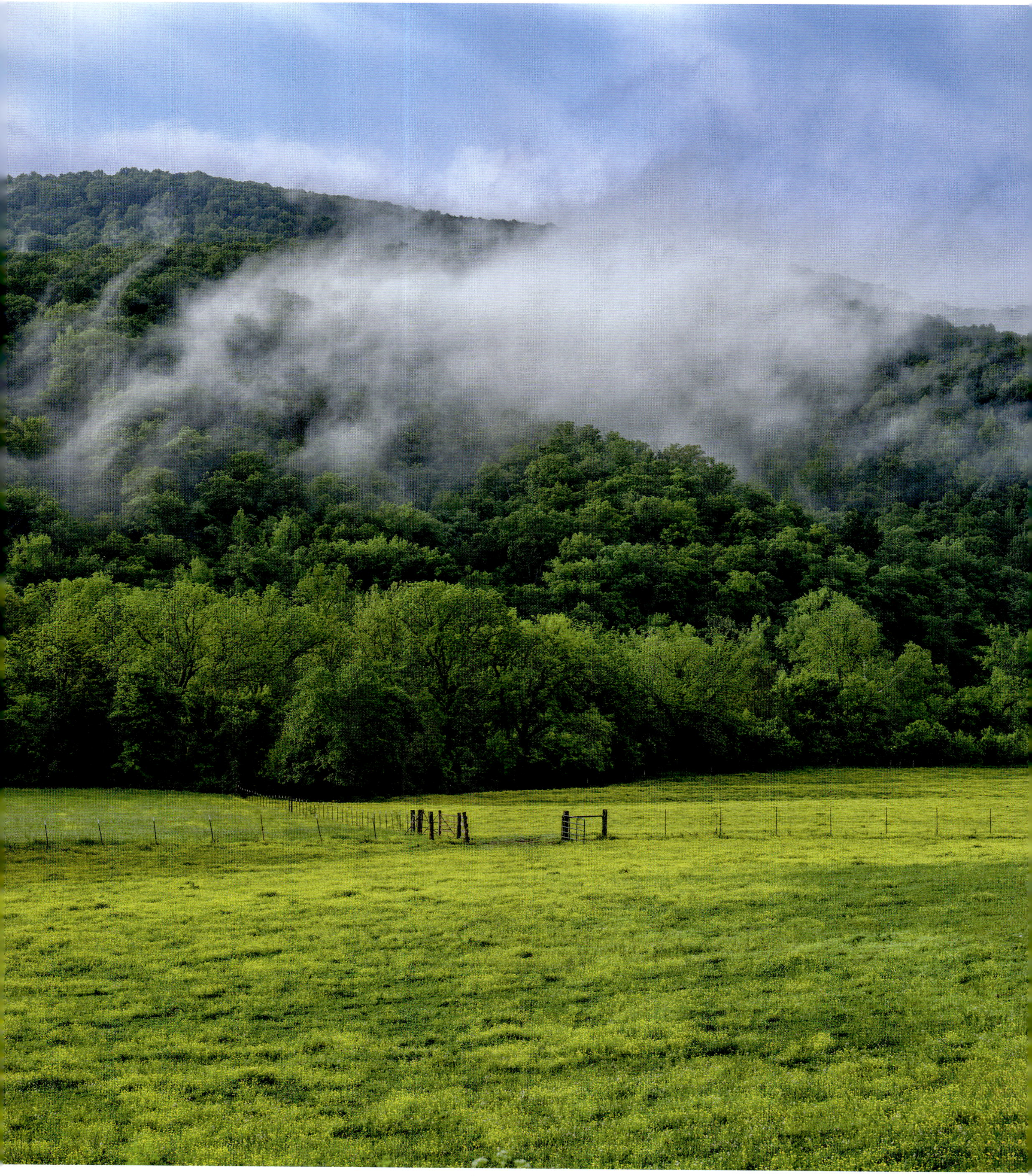

Spring is rising.

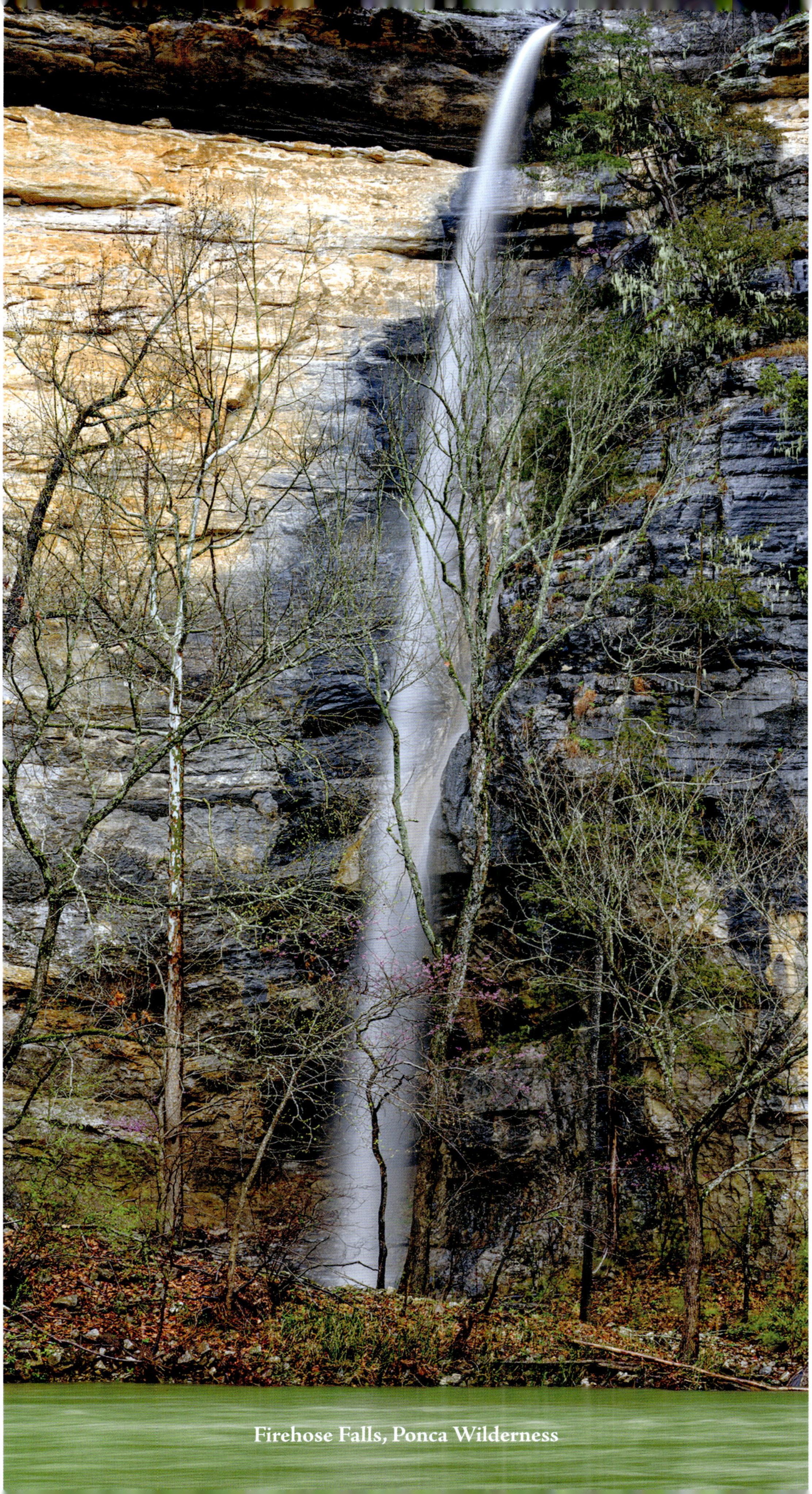

Firehose Falls, Ponca Wilderness

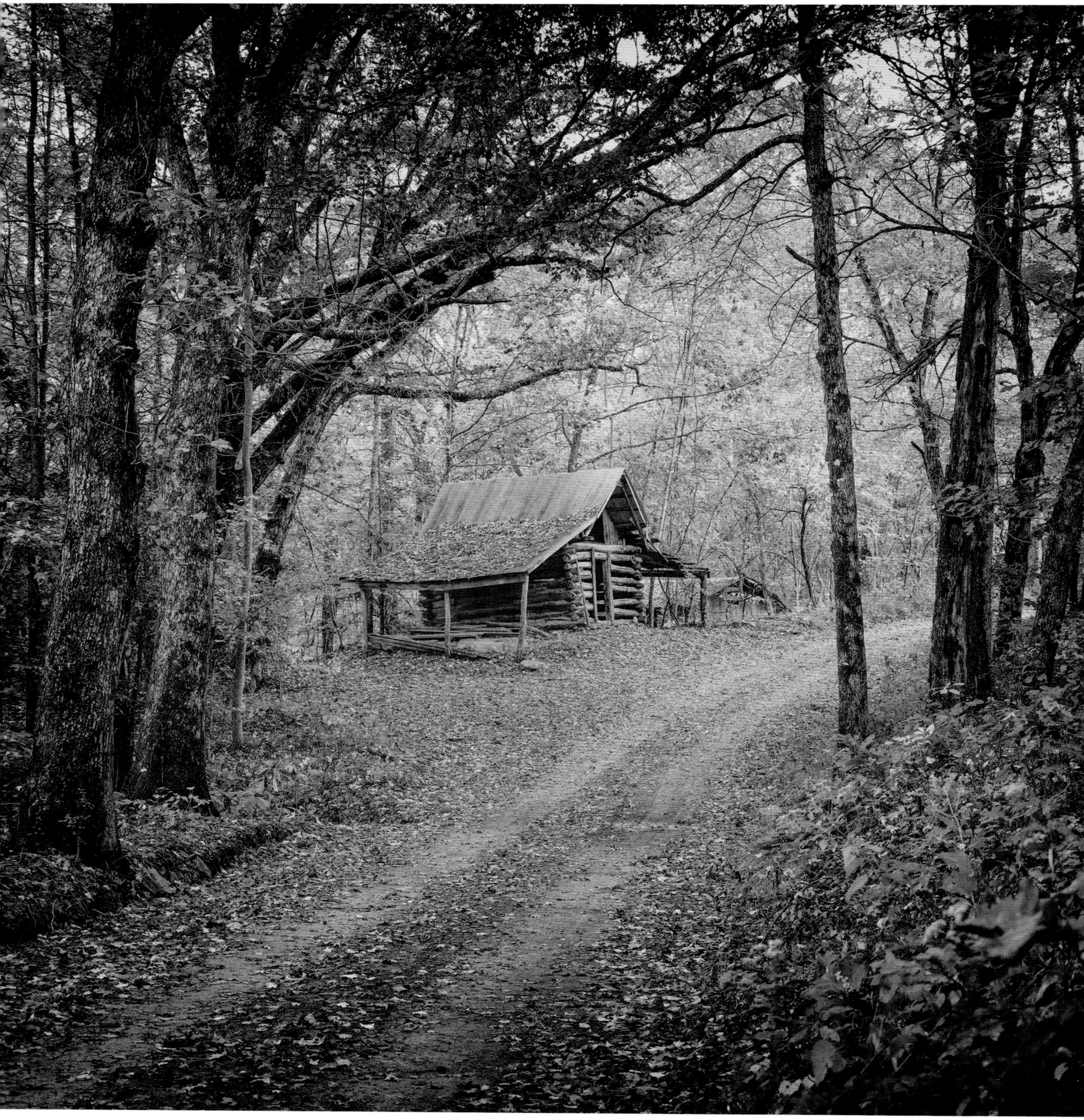

Gregory Blacksmith shop, Johnson County
I first hiked down this old forest road while leading a group of backpackers across Arkansas in late 1980 (no hiking trails back then so we took rural roads). But it wasn't until recently I returned with a camera and found it as a lovely scene.

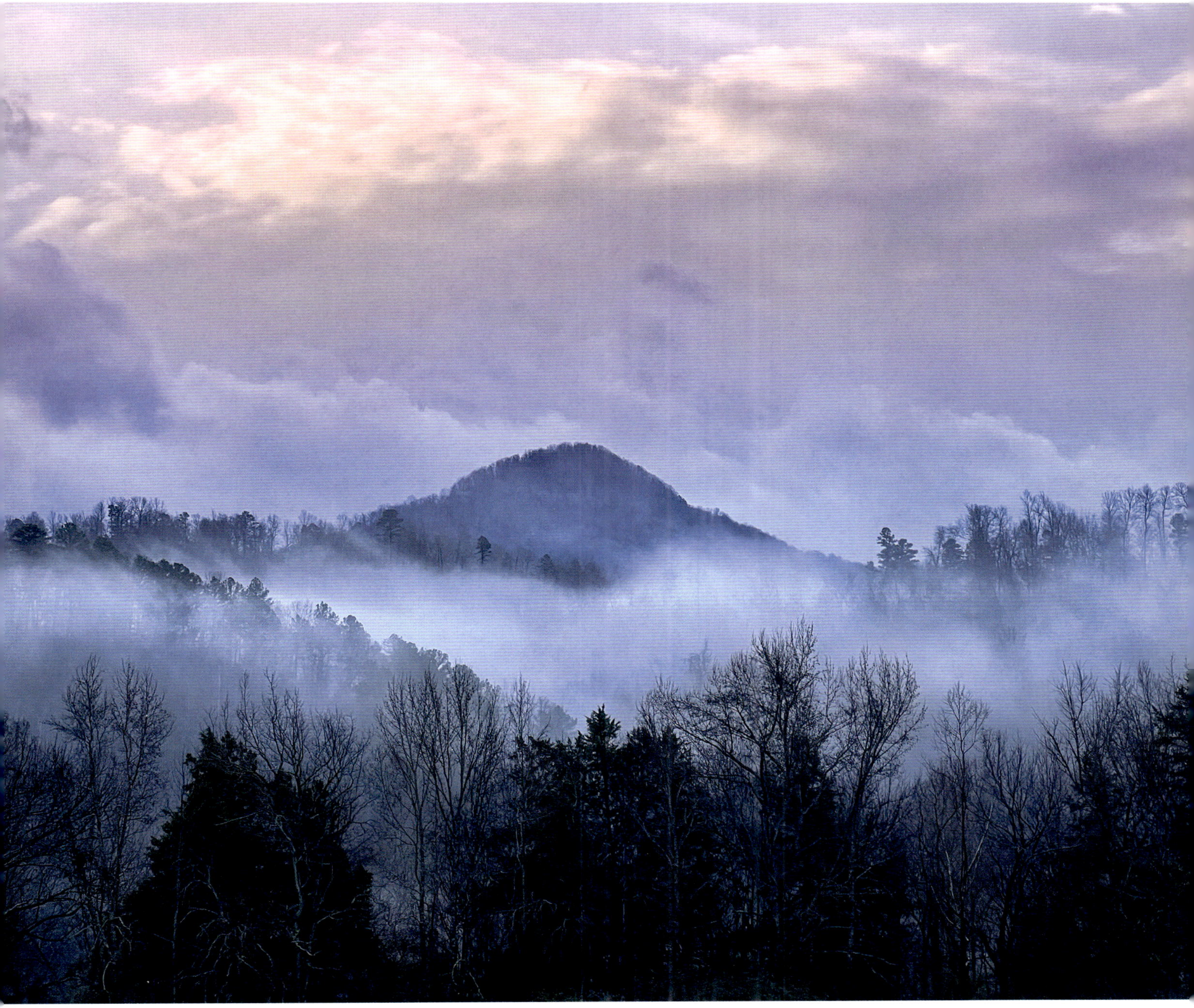

Round Top Mountain as morning fog rises, just south of Jasper.
I literally was stepping out of the Dollar General store in Jasper when I looked up and saw this—another phone snapshot just before the scene disappeared.

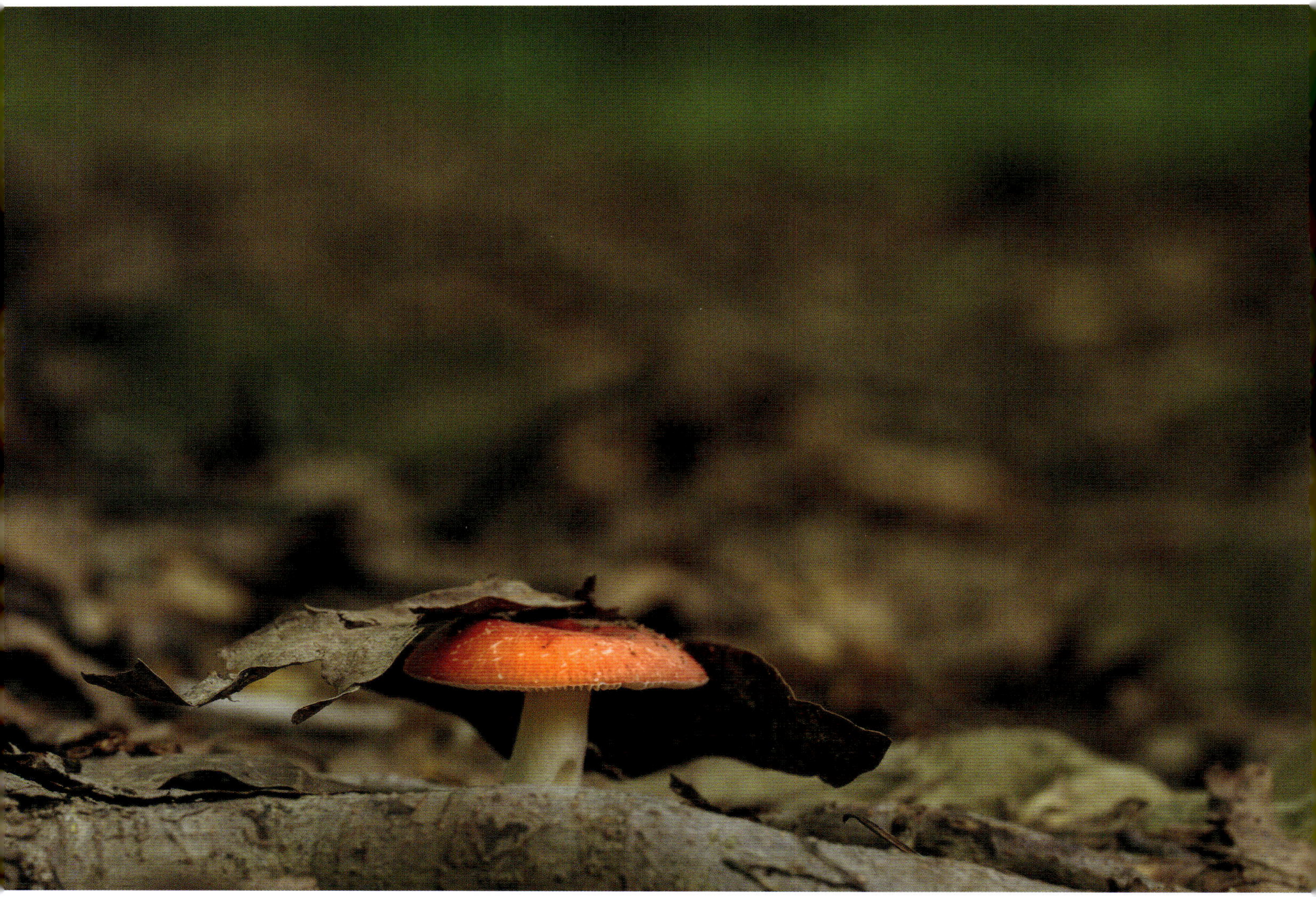

Down on my belly for this shot—I spend a lot of time down low getting a worm's-eye view of the forest.

Jackie Hollow Falls near Compton. >

Directions are easy to find this one—cross the highway and head straight DOWN the steep hillside for half a mile to the falls. Reverse direction to return.

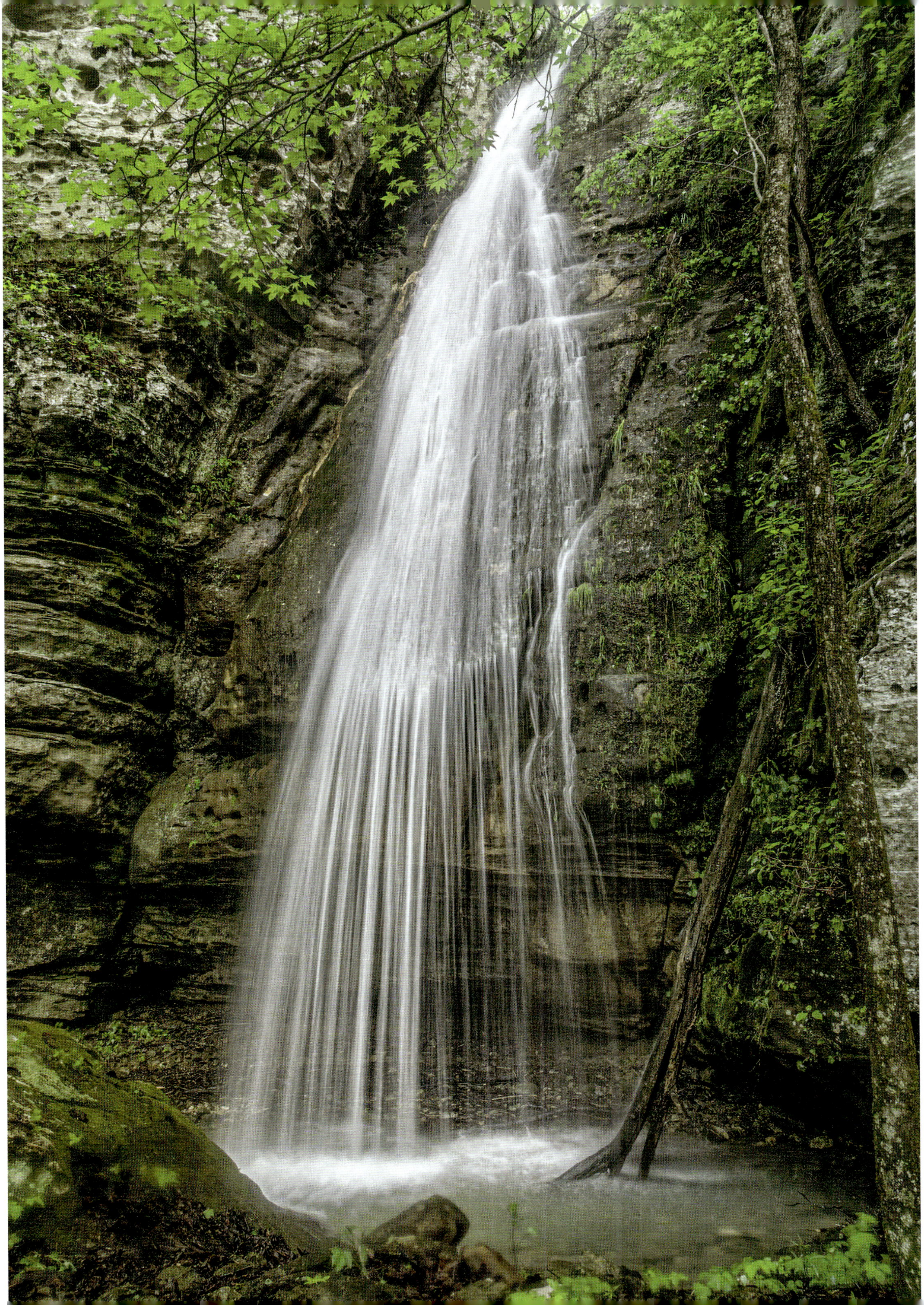

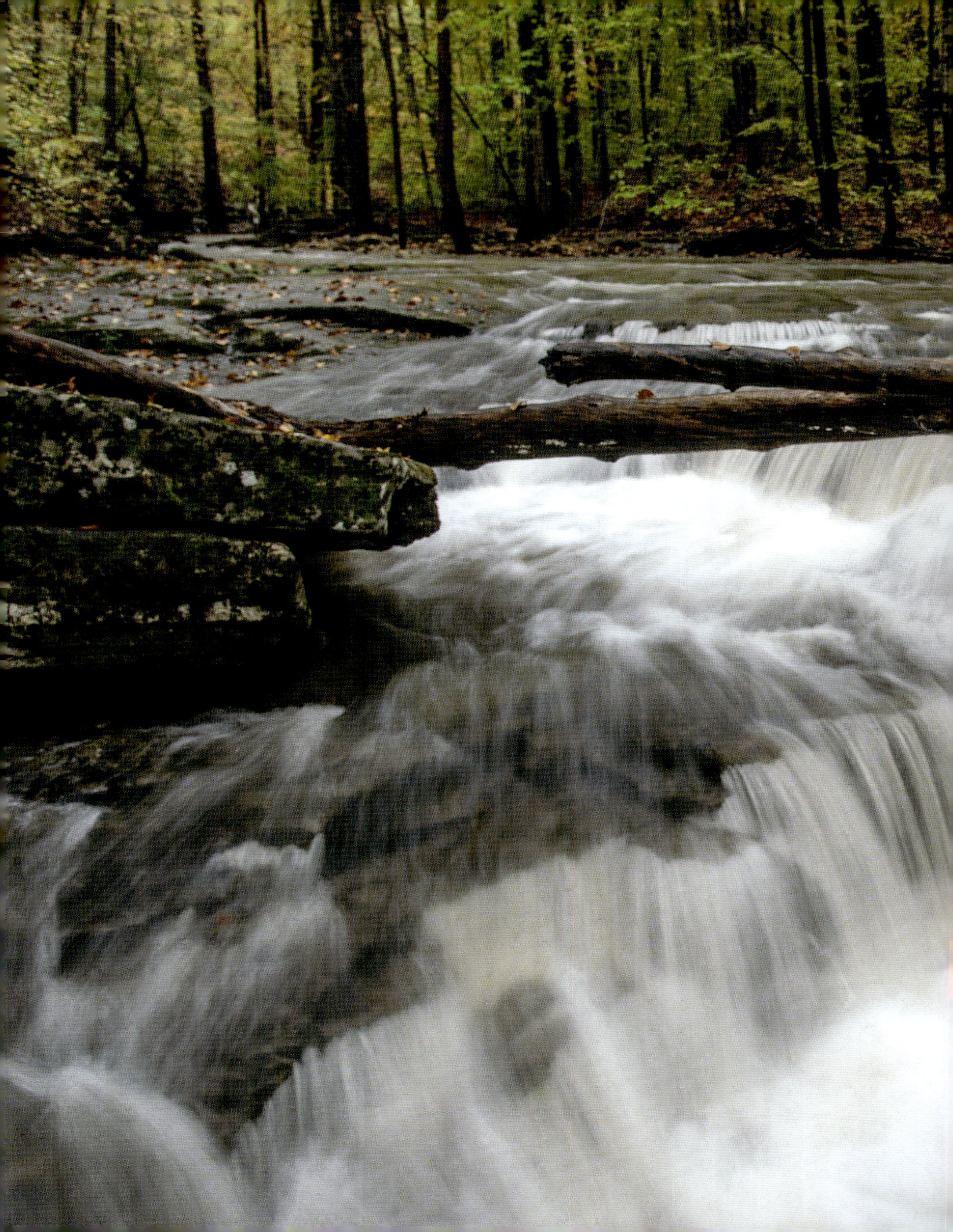

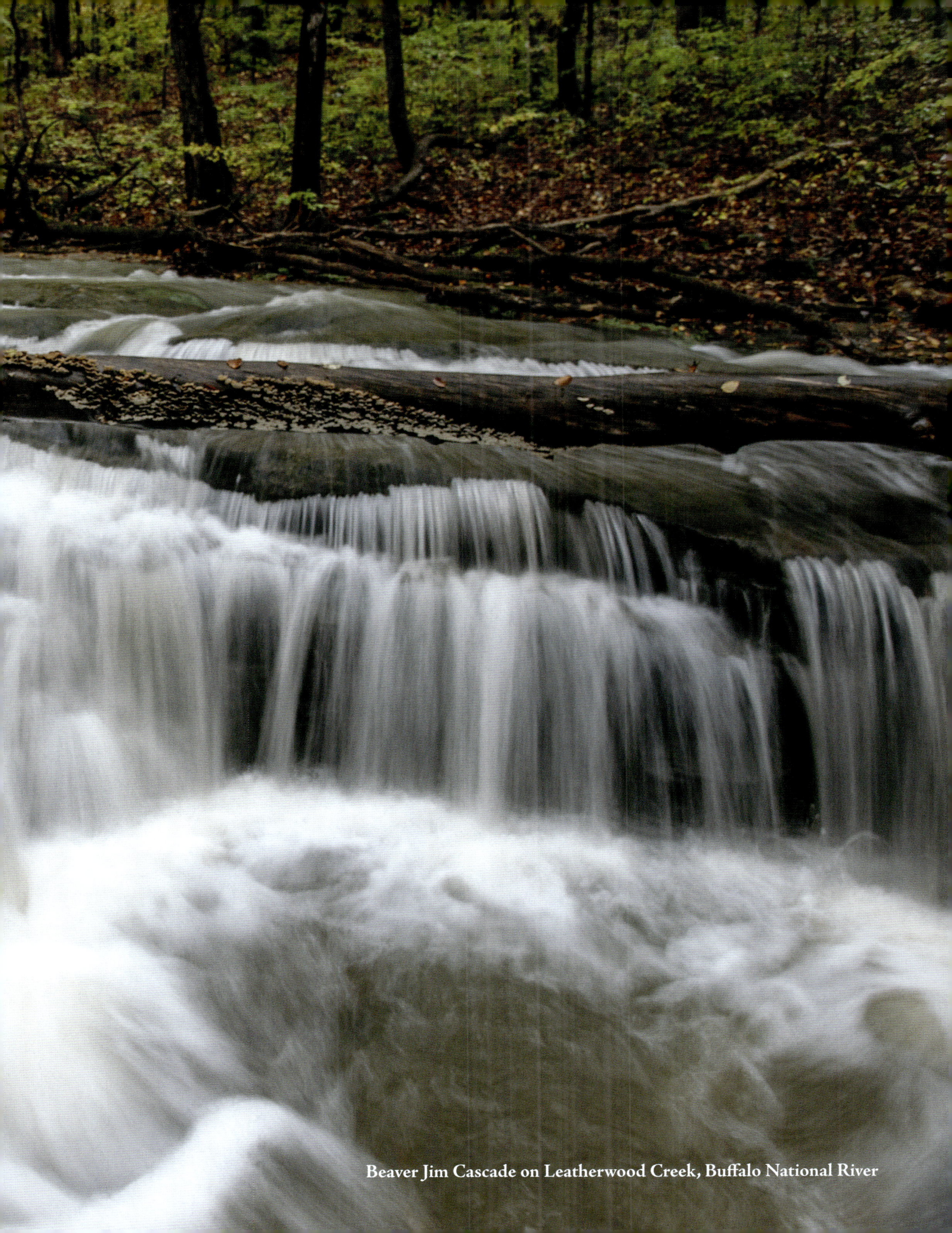

Beaver Jim Cascade on Leatherwood Creek, Buffalo National River

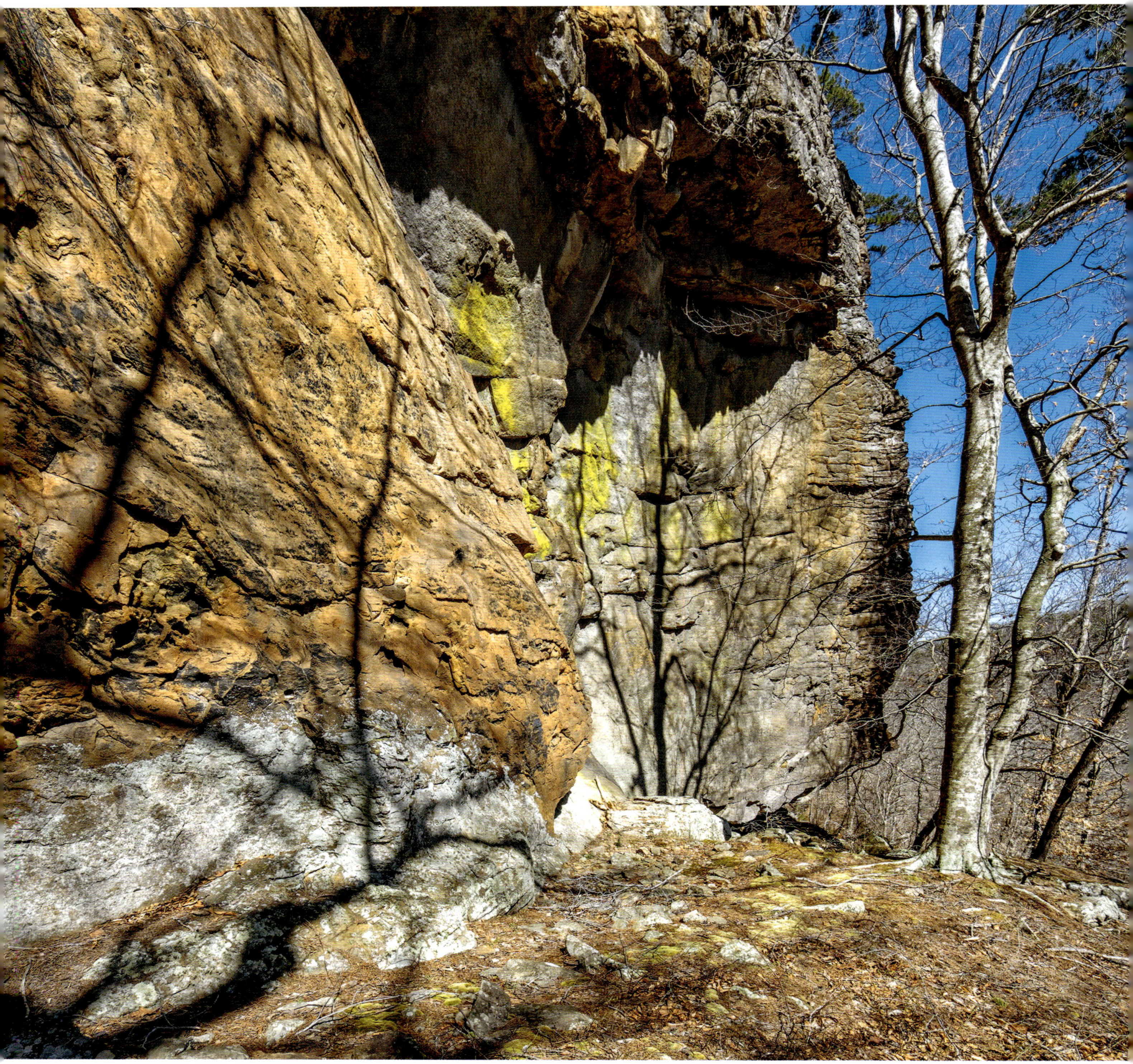

Sandstone bluff covered with lichen and winter shadows, Dismal Creek Scenic Area
I could sit here all day. And sometimes I do.

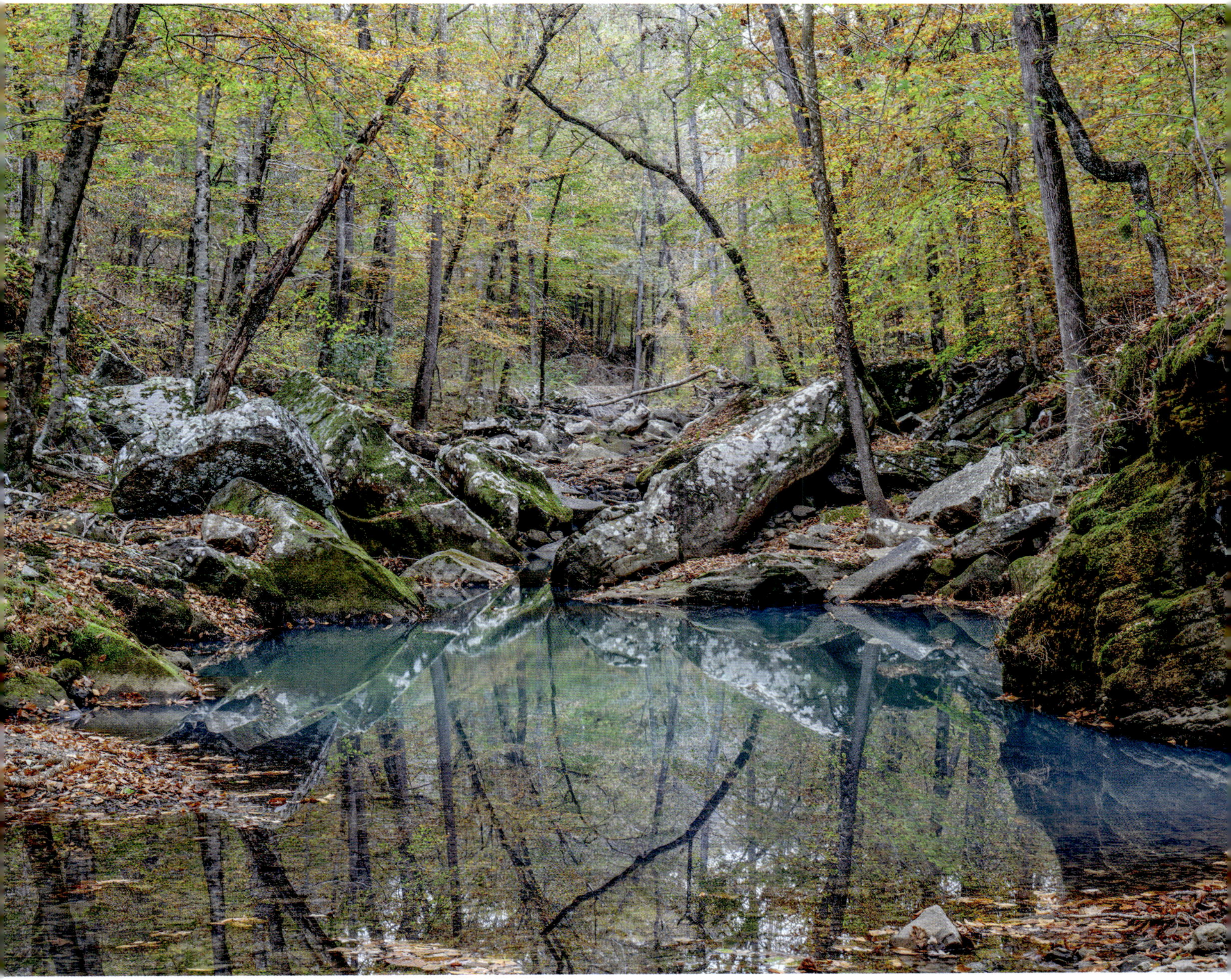

A quiet pool along Lick Branch in the Ozark National Forest.

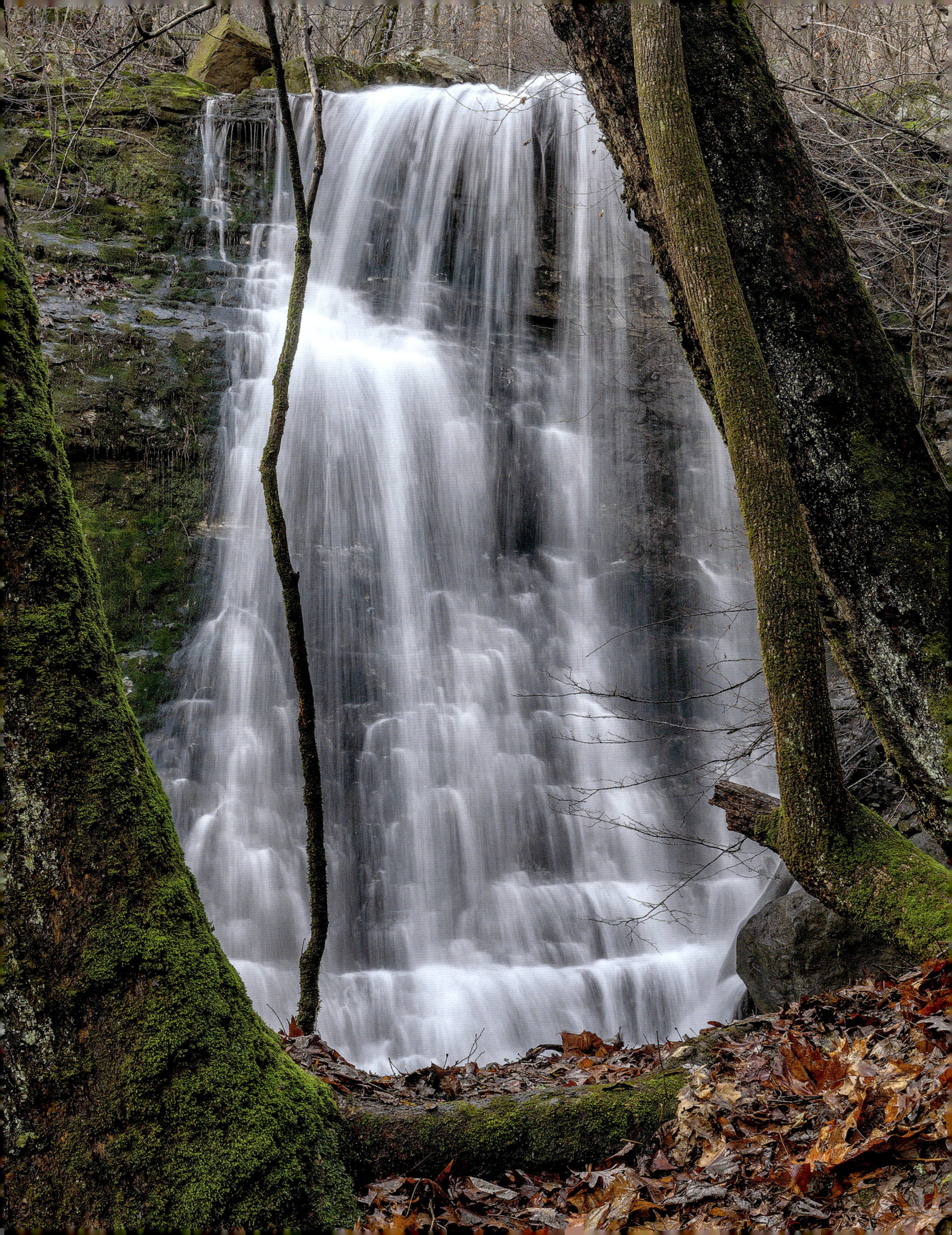

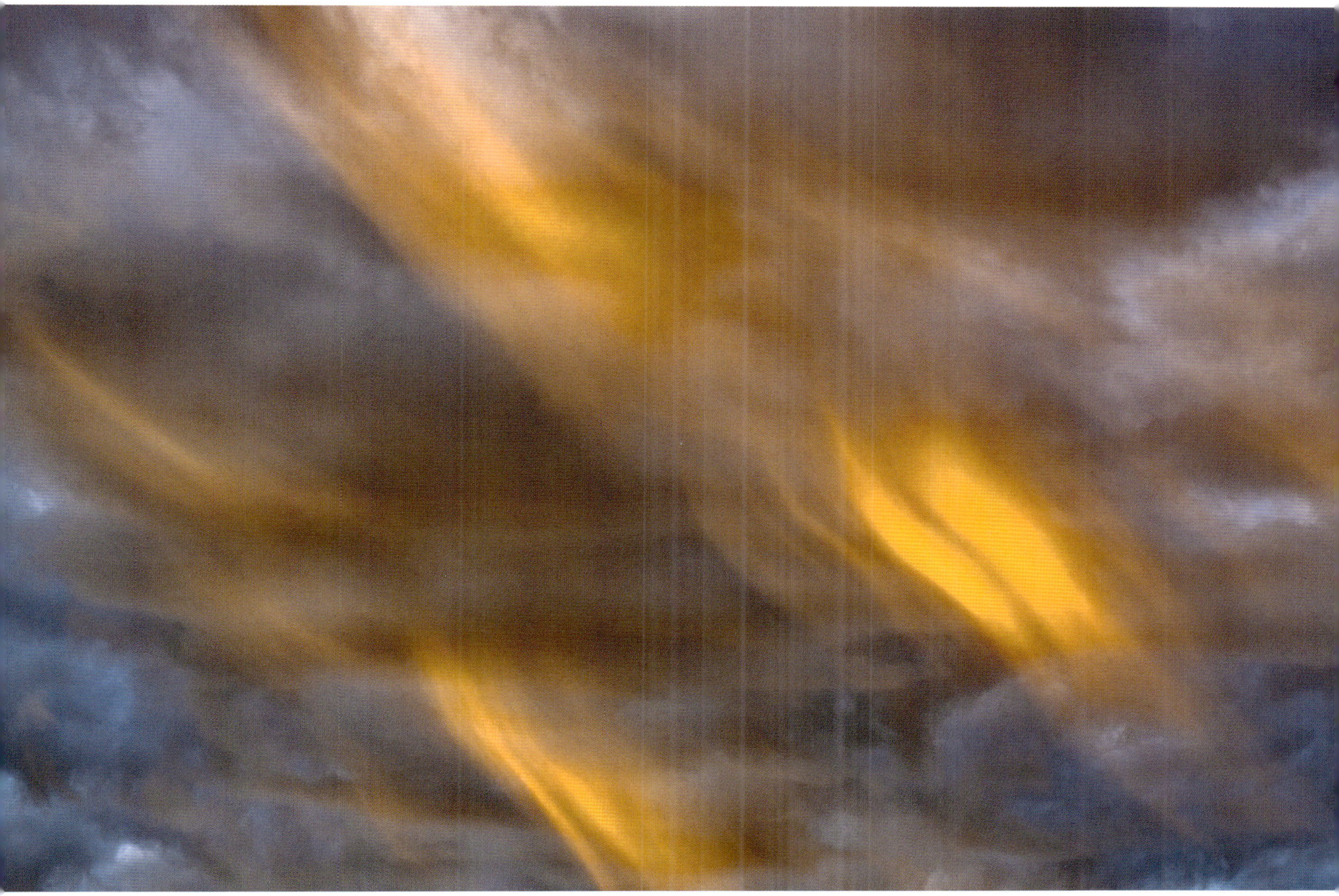

These evening clouds reminded me of angels gathering for sunset.

< Evangeline Archer Falls on Indian Creek, Ponca Wilderness

Evangeline Archer grew up on Markham Hill in Fayetteville and was a staunch supporter of women's rights. She became involved in the battle to protect the Buffalo River in the 1950's, and later joined up with Dr. Neil Compton as a founding member of the Ozark Society. There's a famous photo of her welcoming U.S. Supreme Court Chief Justice William O. Douglas at the Harrison airport for his two day canoe trip down the Buffalo that led to the creation of the Buffalo National River. She had friends in high places and we owe her a great deal for her efforts! She needed a waterfall named in her honor and this is it.

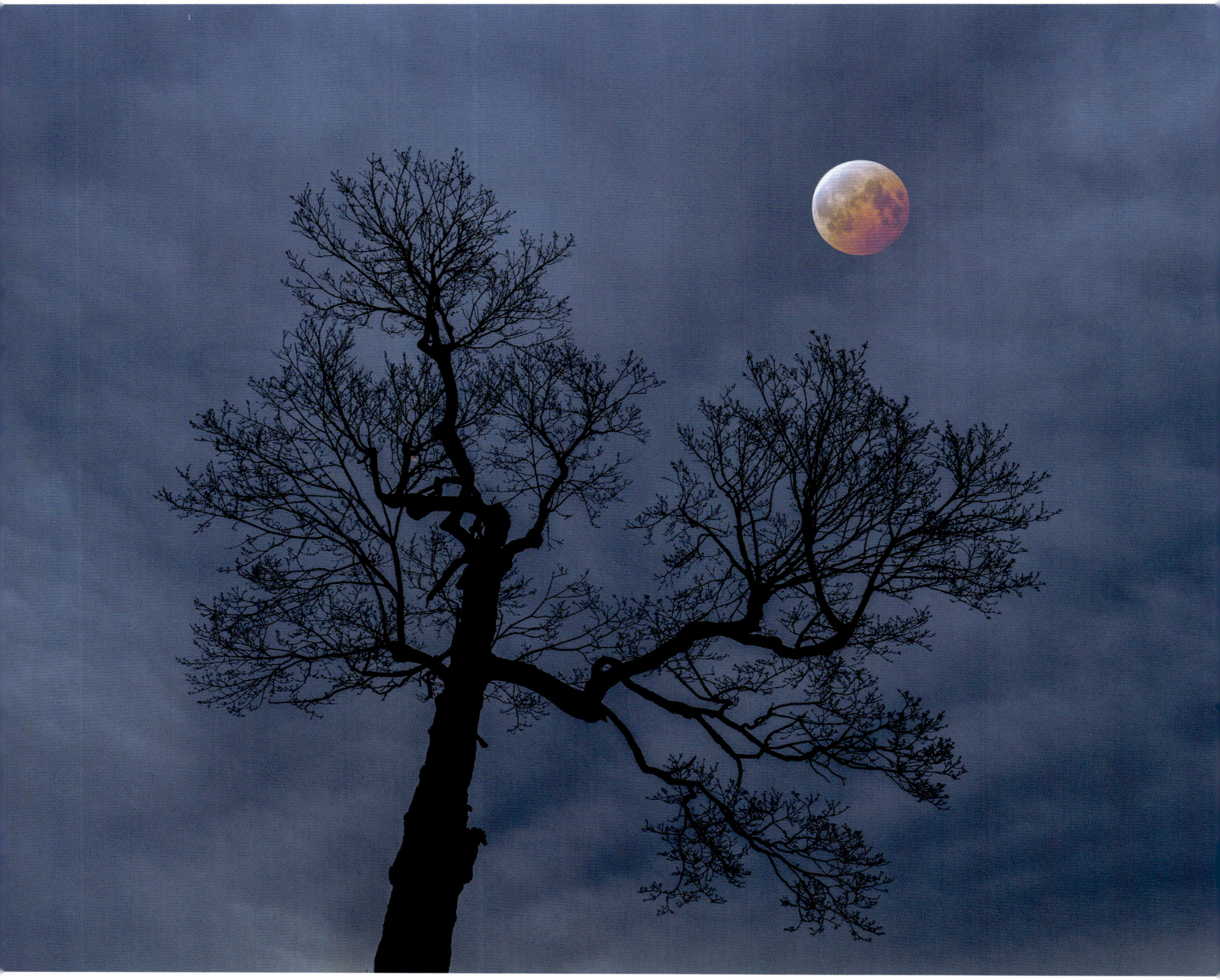

Blood Moon and Oak

I try to keep different scenes in the back pocket of my brain for times like this. I had driven to another county the night of this particular Blood Moon to find clear skies, but I found nothing but clouds there. The current radar showed a small patch of openness 20 miles away, and I remembered THIS tree in that area as something that might look great with the moon. I lucked out with almost-clear skies when I arrived, and the bright moon shone through perfectly. (see a snowy version of this tree on page 102)

Cliff Twin Cascades in Cliff Hollow, Buffalo National River >

Each of these cascades tumbles down more than 100′ from above before pouring into a steep canyon directly behind where I'm standing for this shot.

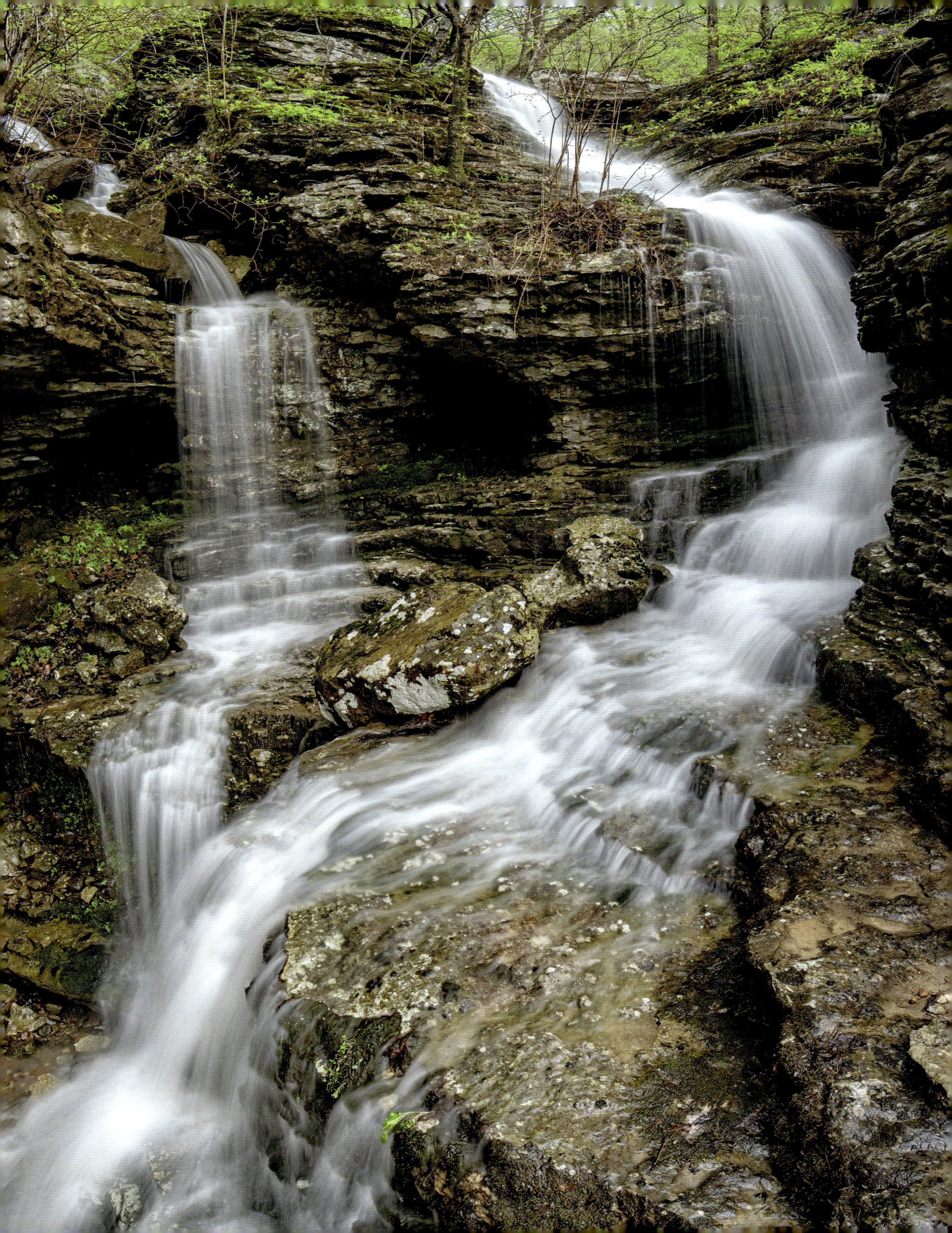

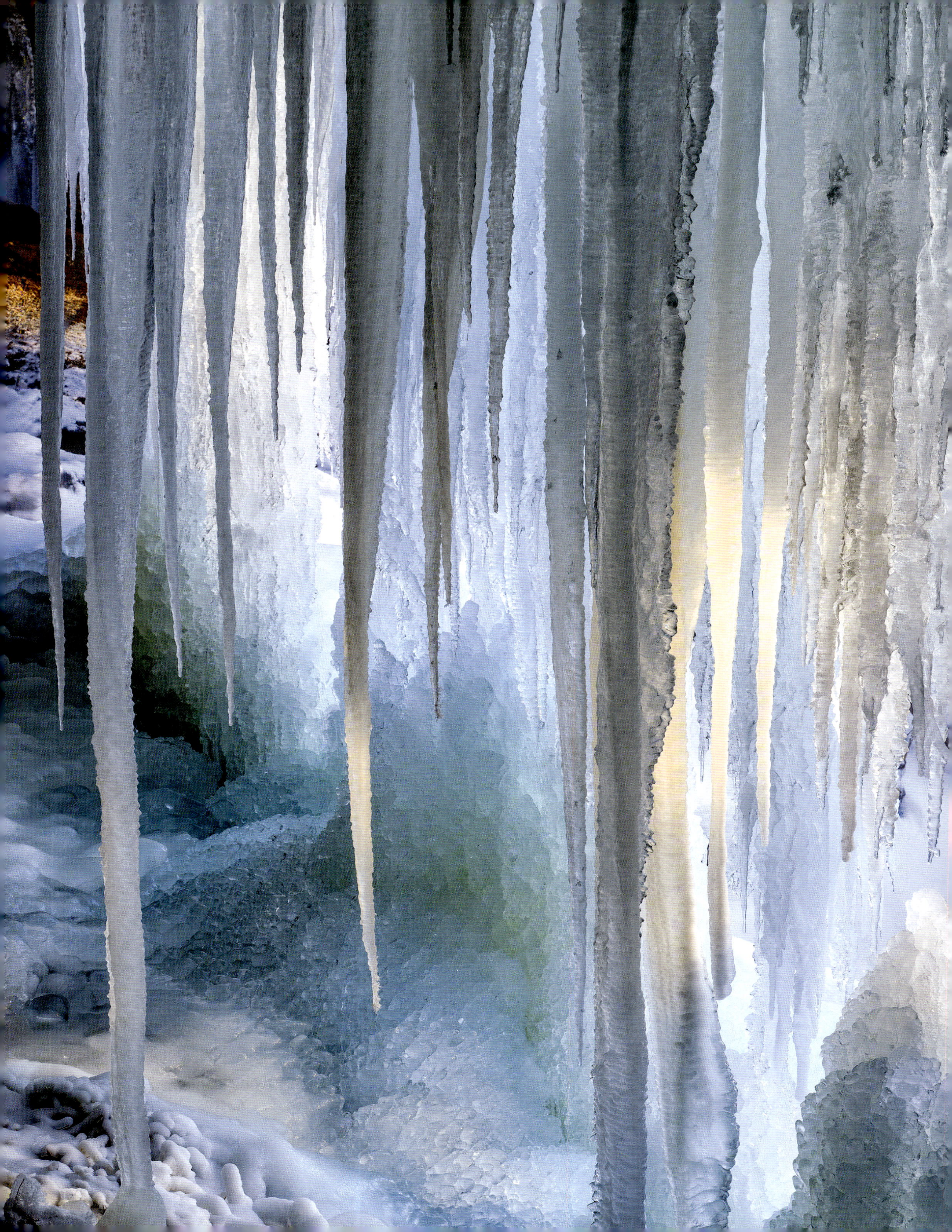

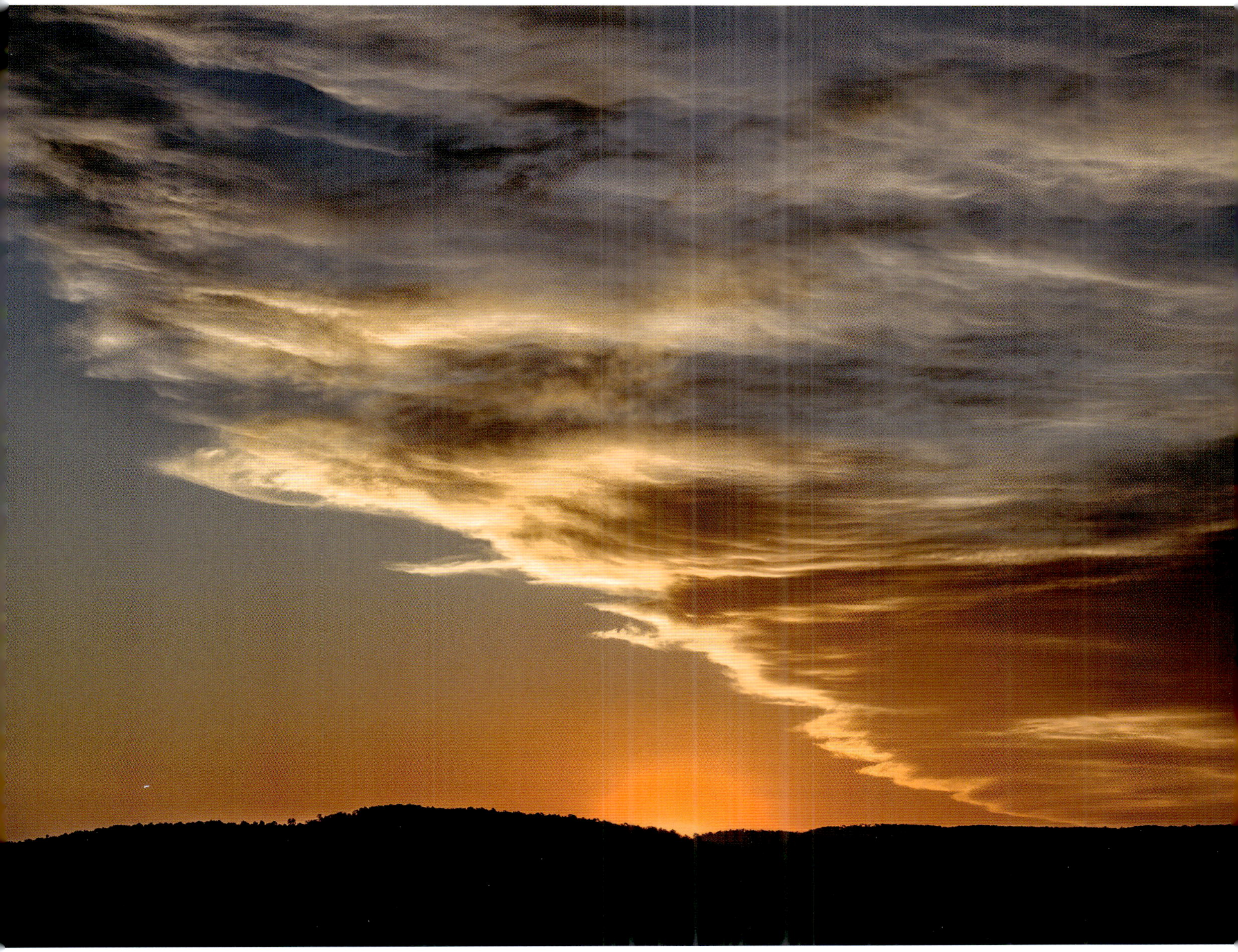

Sunrise, or sunset?

< Inside an ice cave and 5 below zero

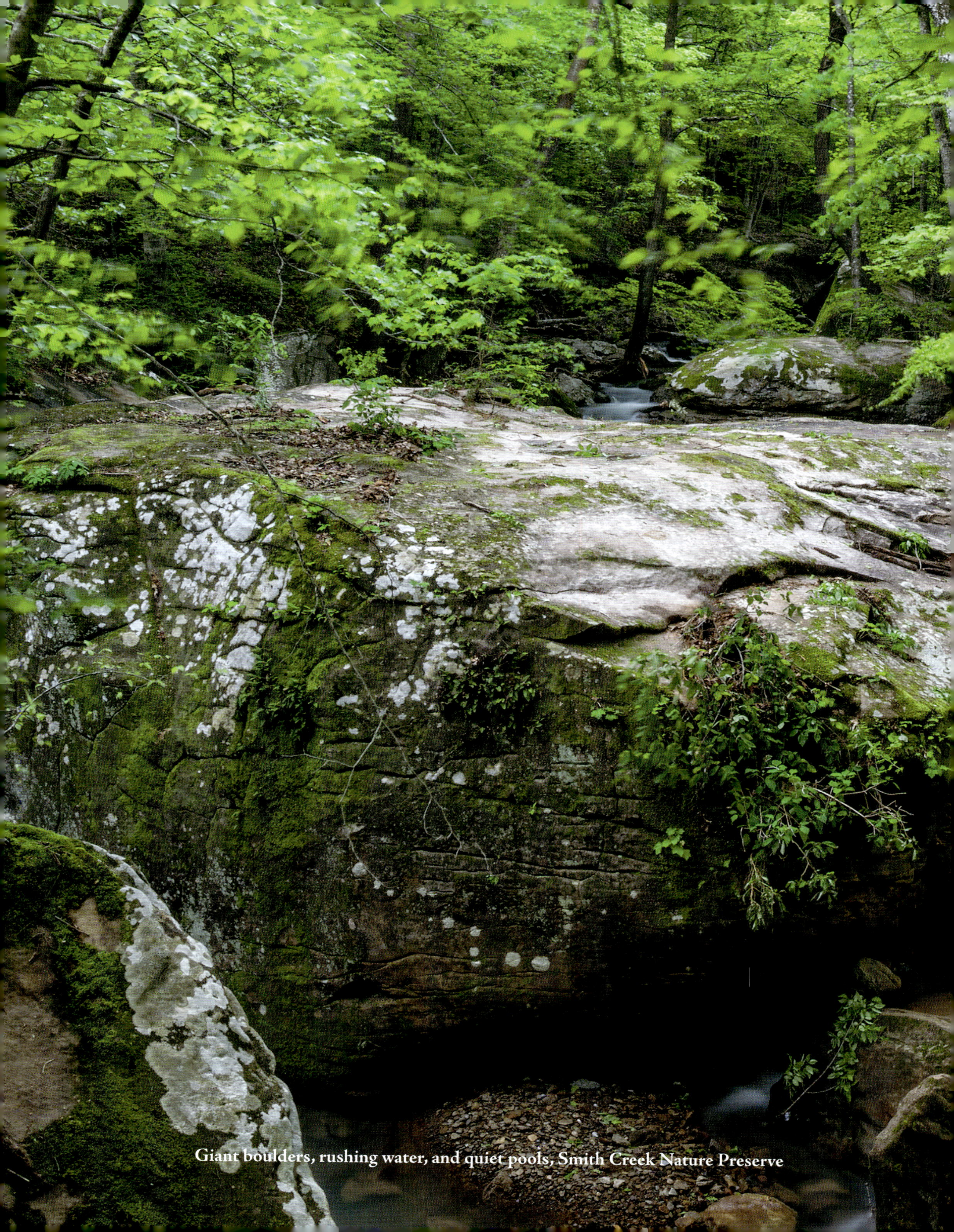

Giant boulders, rushing water, and quiet pools, Smith Creek Nature Preserve

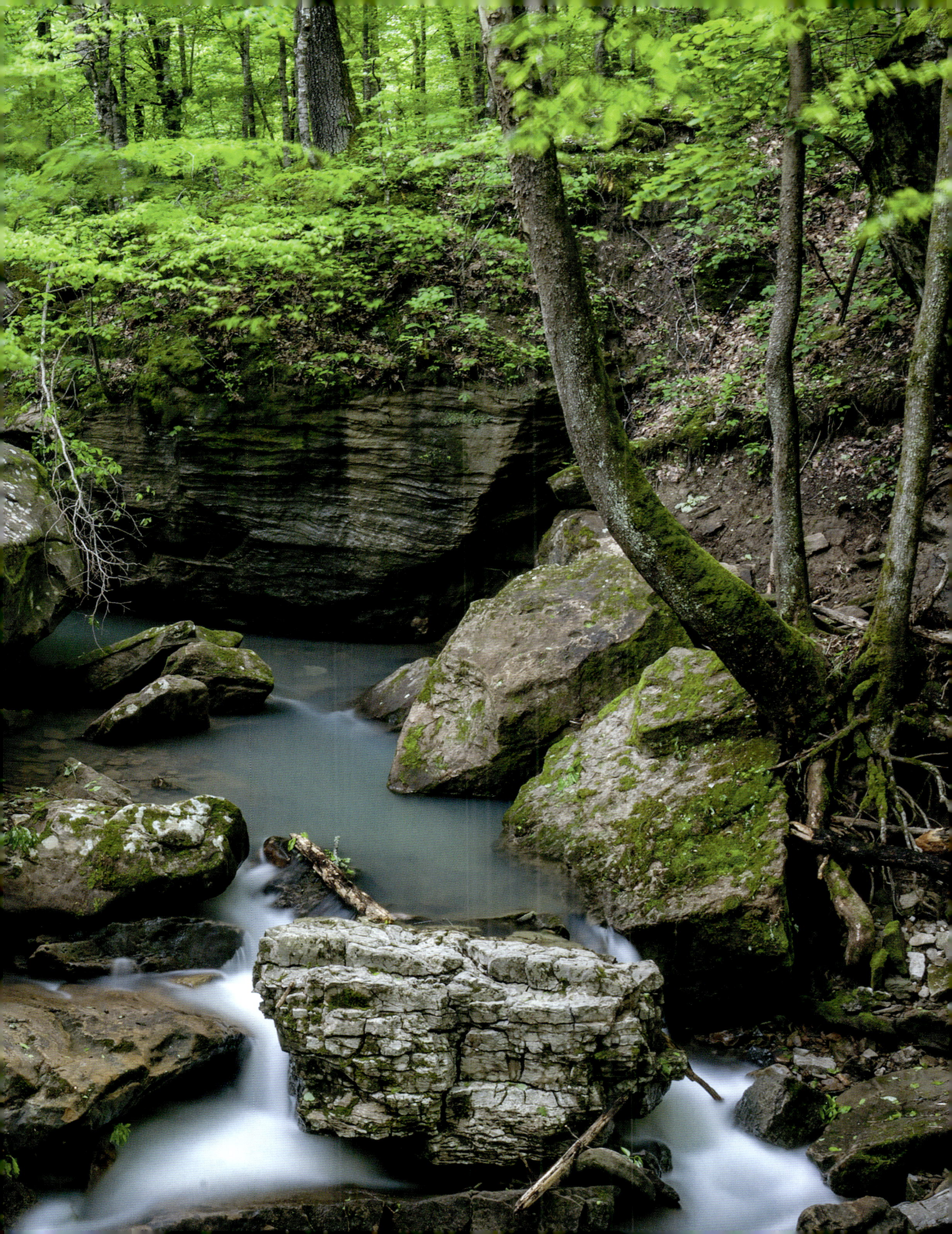

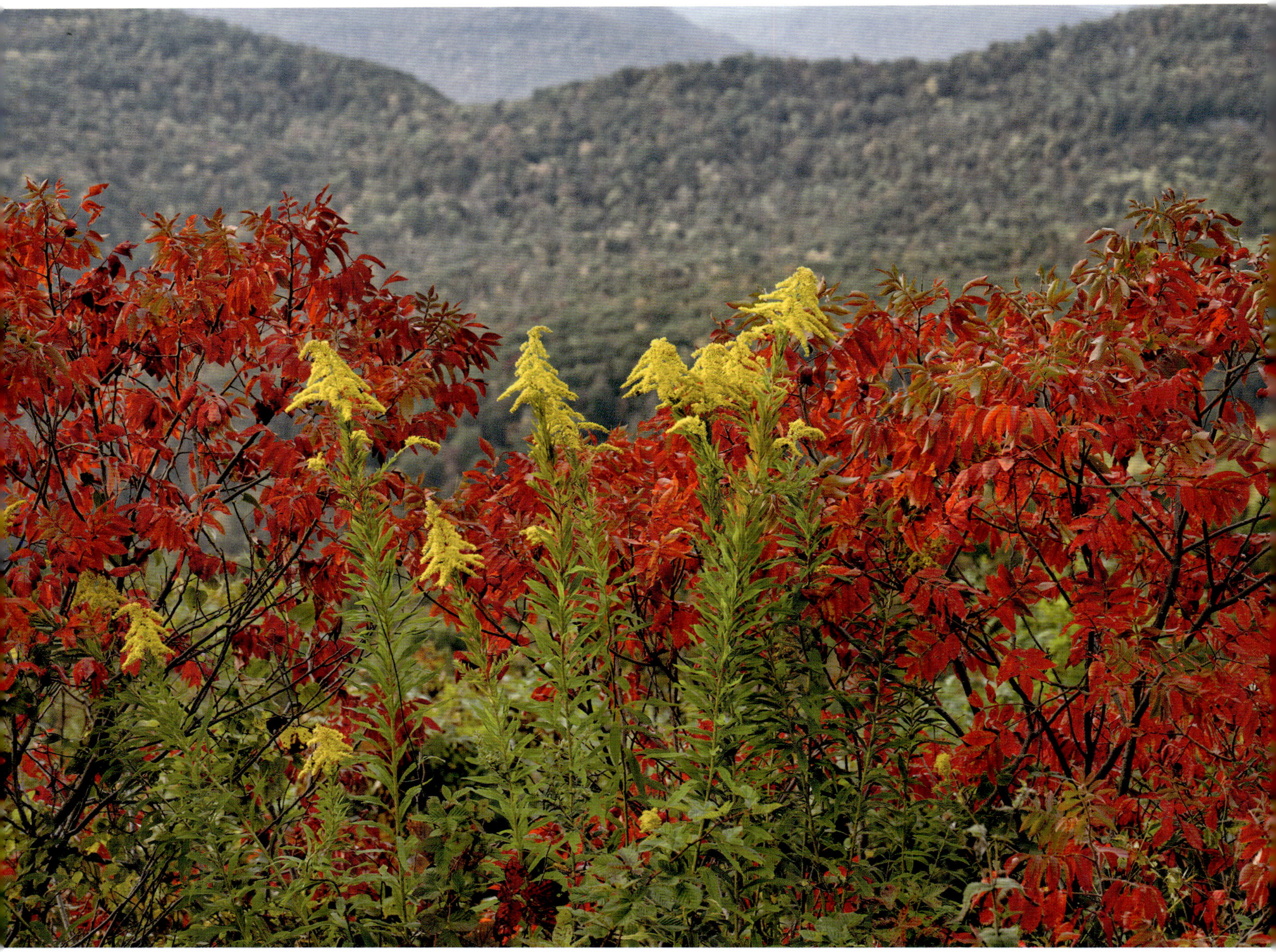

Goldenrod and sumac, early fall color in the Ozarks

Triple Falls (aka Twin Falls) and the Milky Way, Camp Orr Boy Scout Camp >

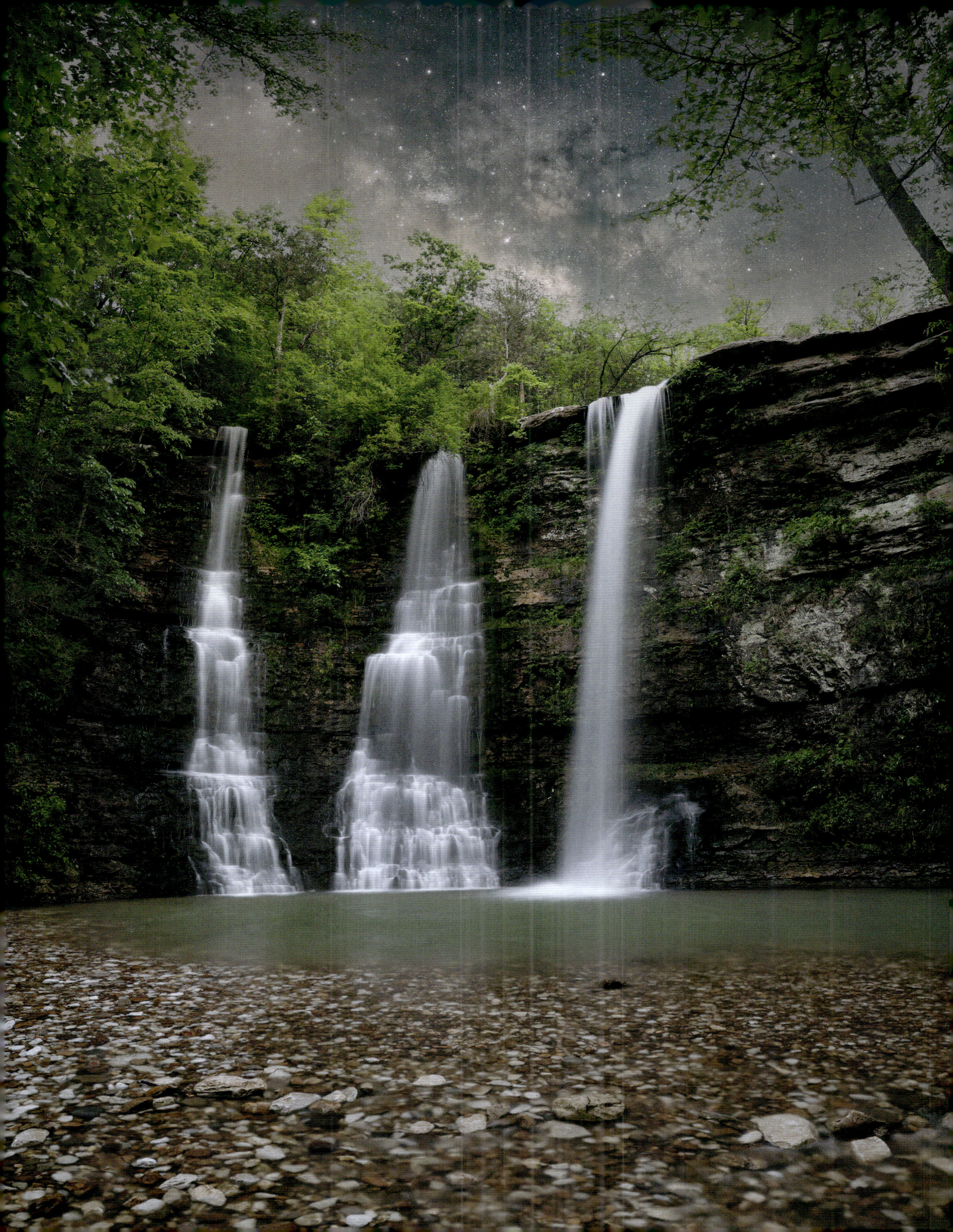

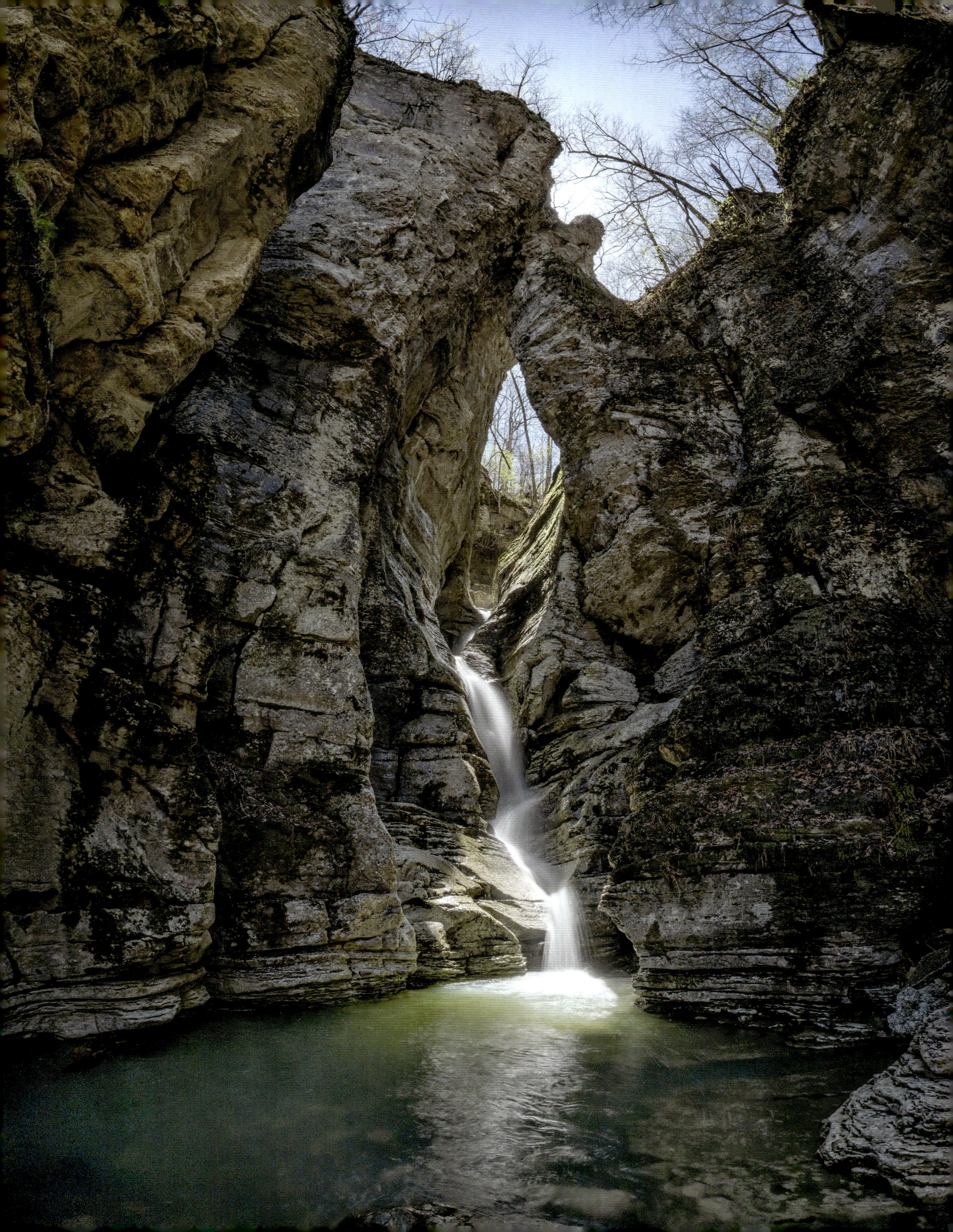

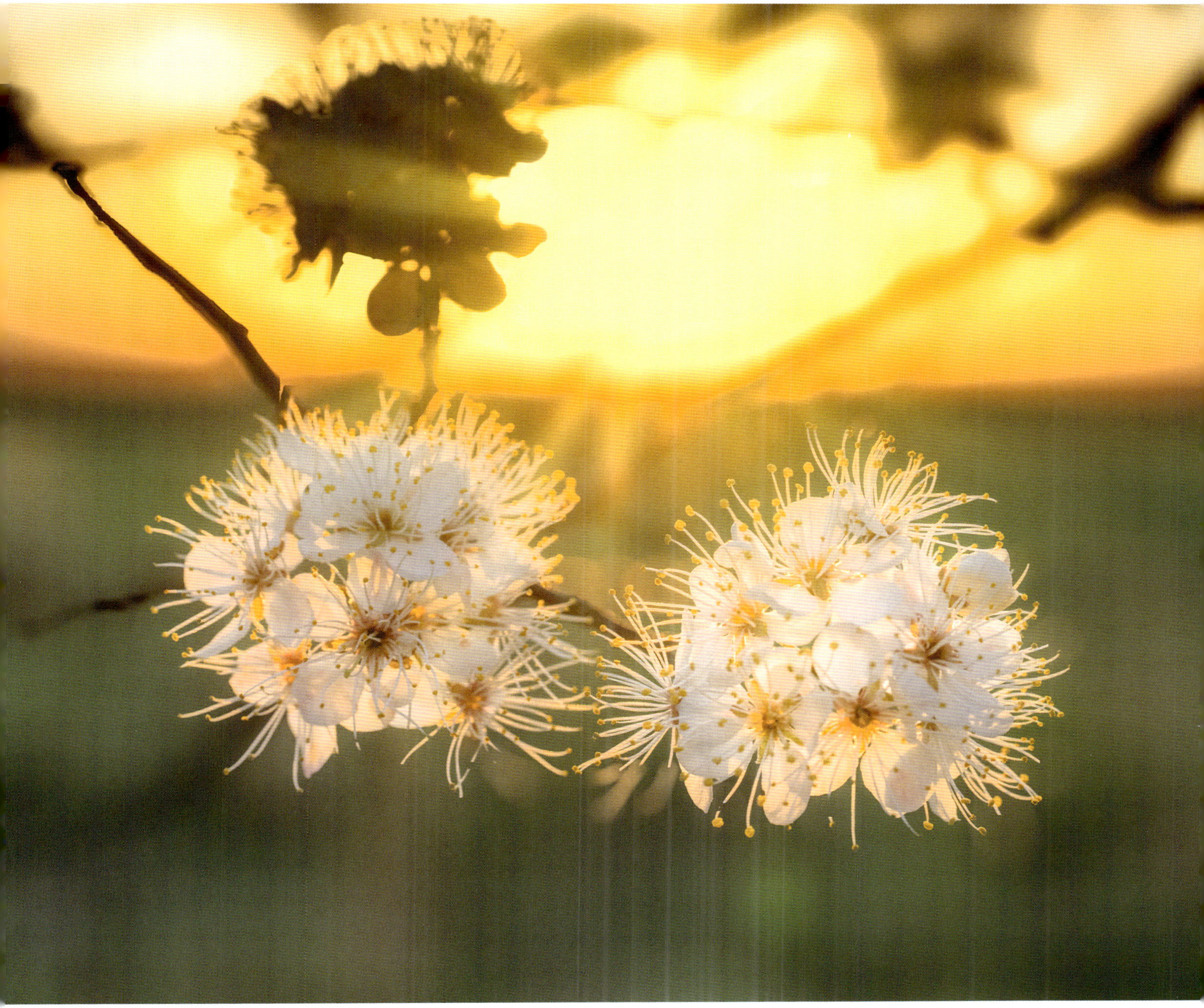

Wild plum blossoms at sunrise.
This is one of the *sweetest* aromas in all of nature!

< Eye Of The Needle on Indian Creek, Ponca Wilderness
I rarely photograph waterfalls during harsh midday sunshine. But there I was, standing right there with a camera—what else could I do?

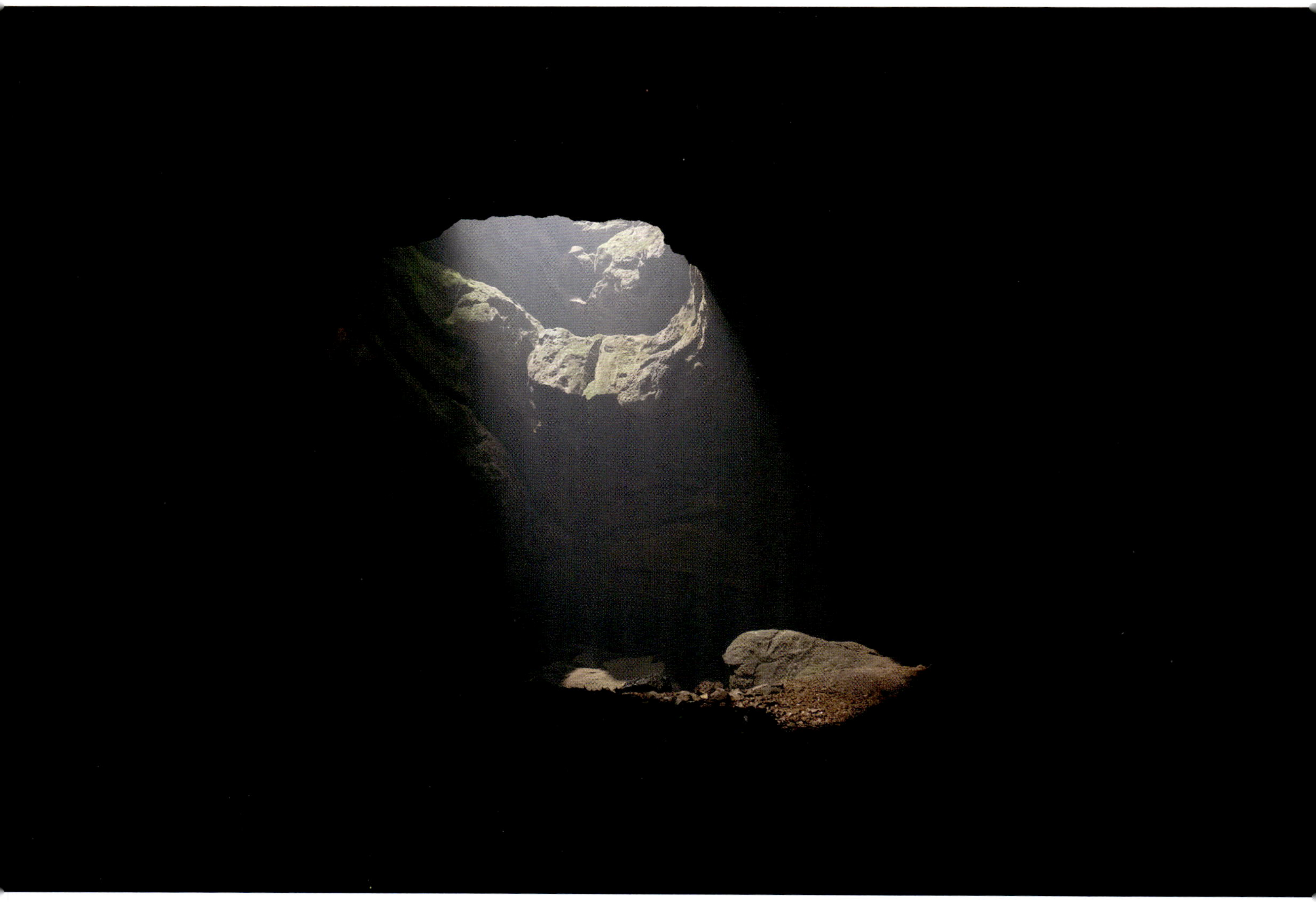

The Mystic Hole in the Duck's Head area of the Lower Buffalo Wilderness

Tombstone Falls on Woods Mountain, Ozark National Forest >

As we were approaching this thundering waterfall for the first time, my buddy Fireman Jeff asked out loud "How do you come up with names for waterfalls anyway?" Three steps later he stopped, looked up, and said "Those rocks look just like tombstones!" Answered his own question. I really like all the rock layers on the bluff behind the falls also—this will always be an interesting waterfall to visit, even when dry.

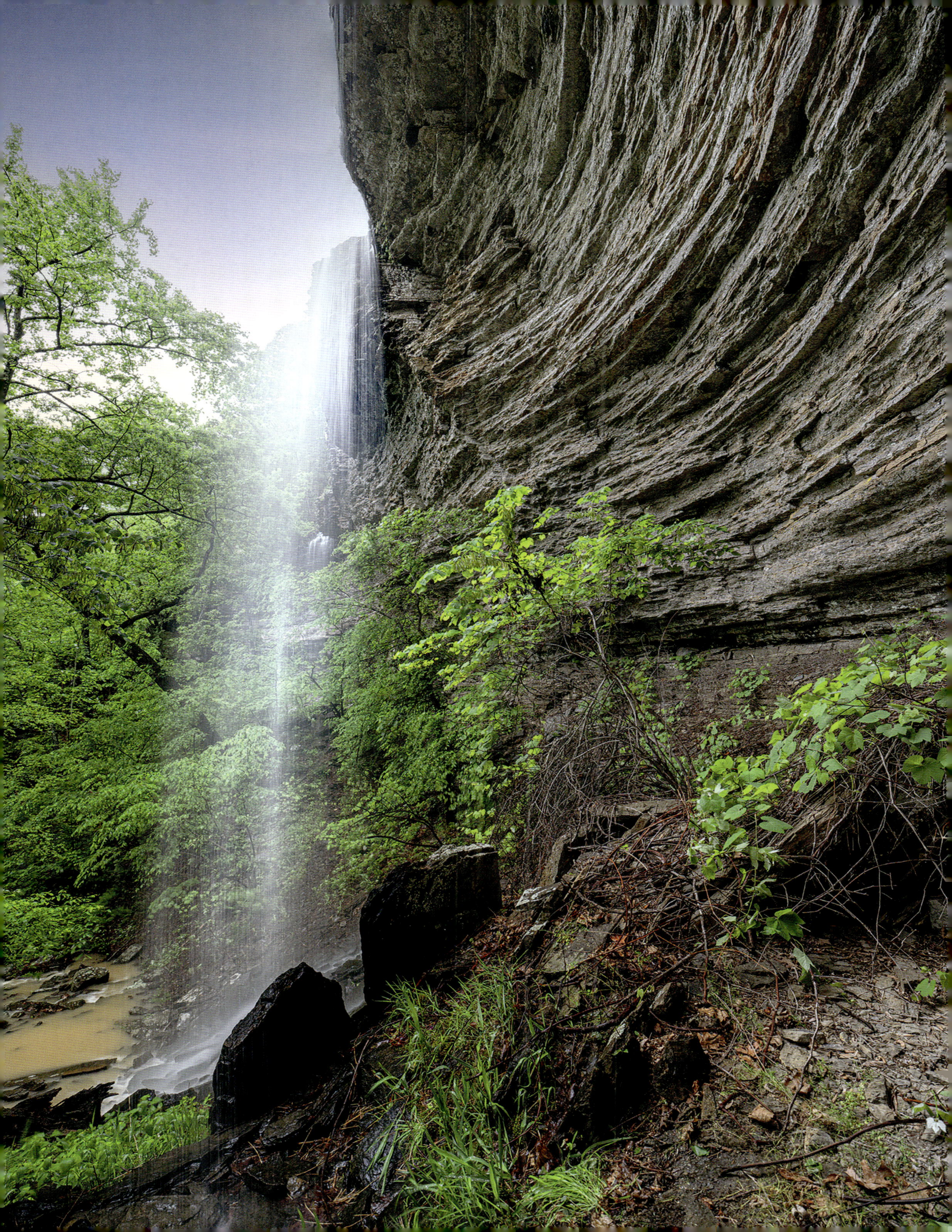

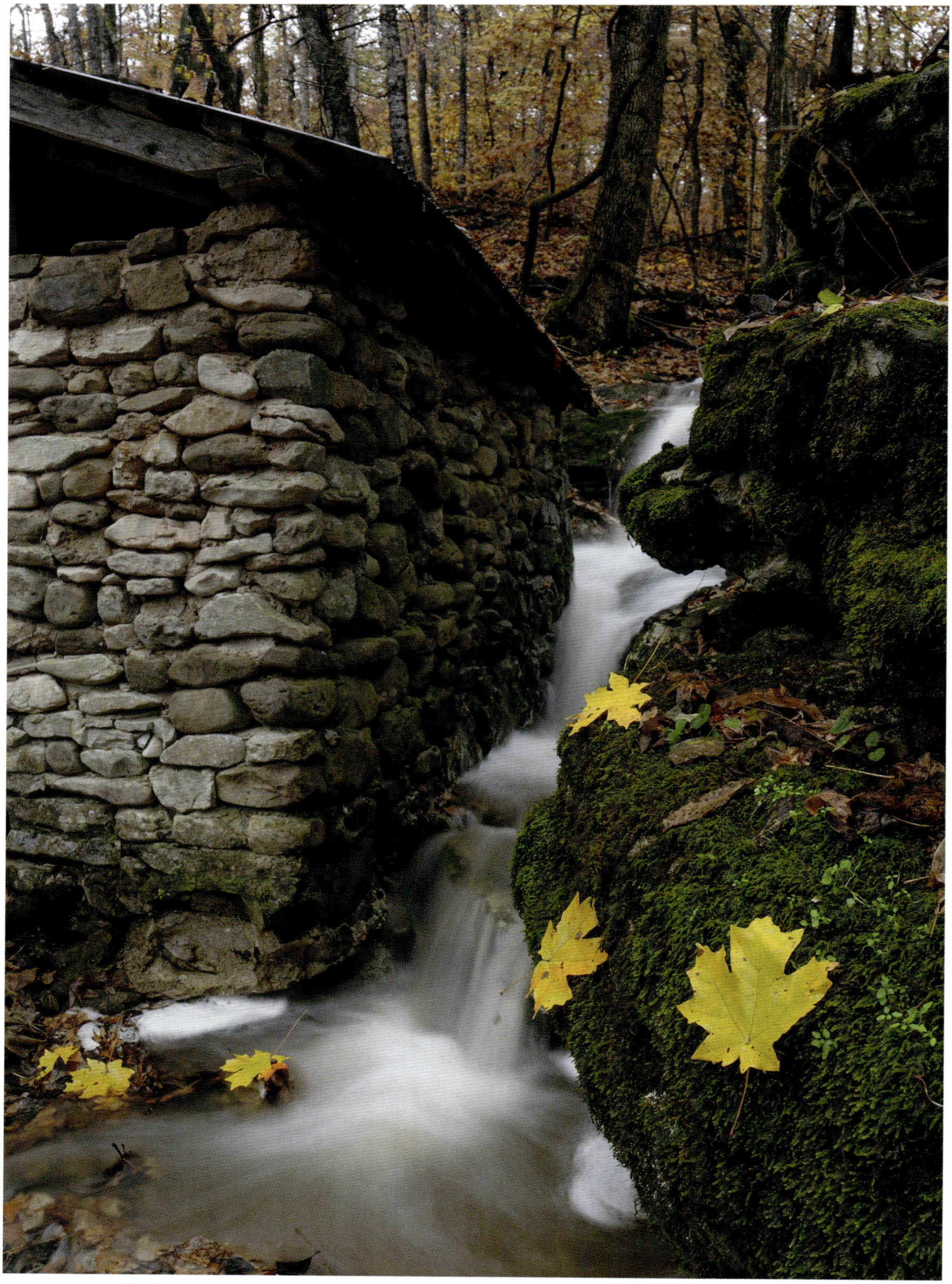

Clyde and Nellie Villines Springhouse, Boxley Valley Historic District

Smith Creek Spring and Nature Preserve, The Nature Conservancy >

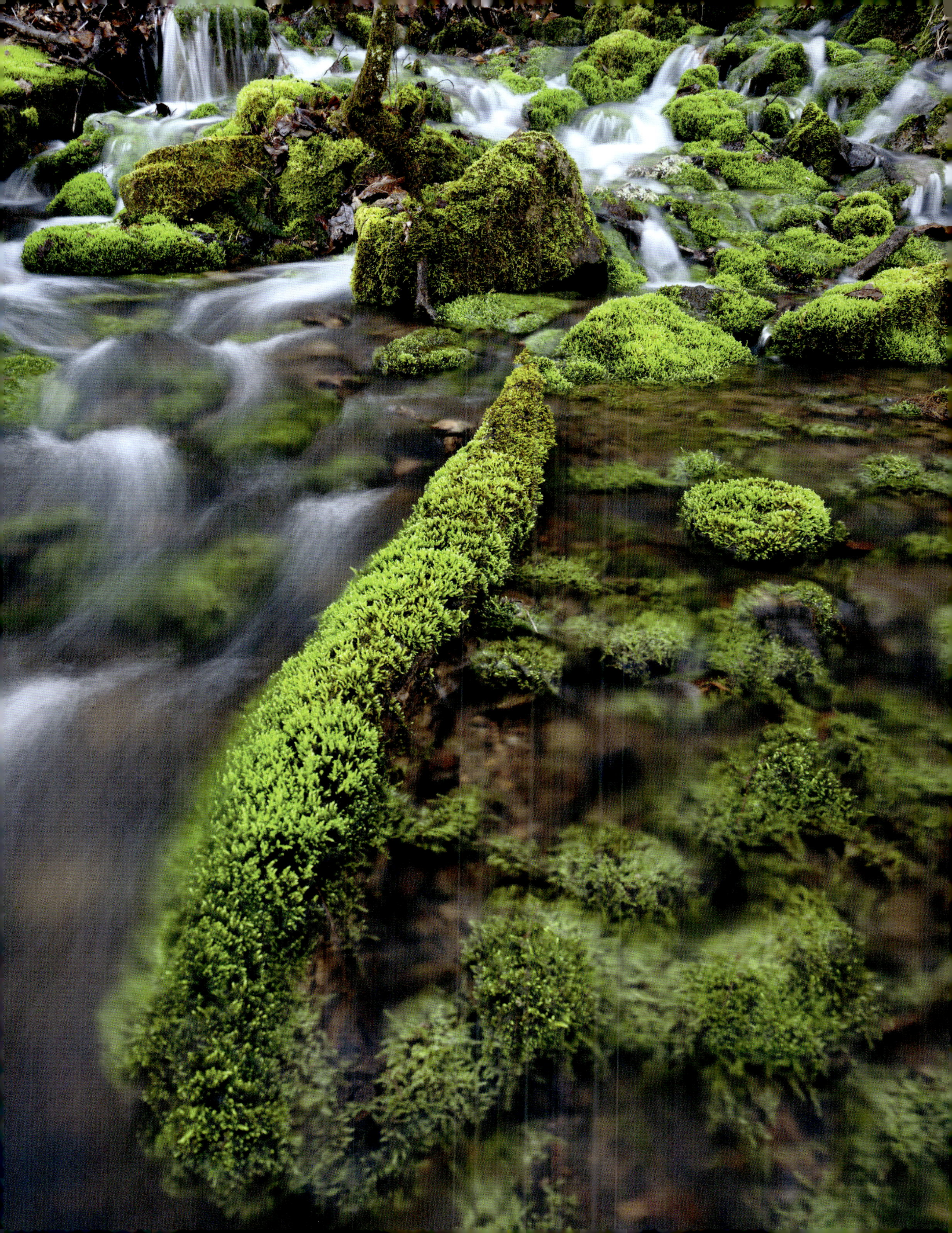

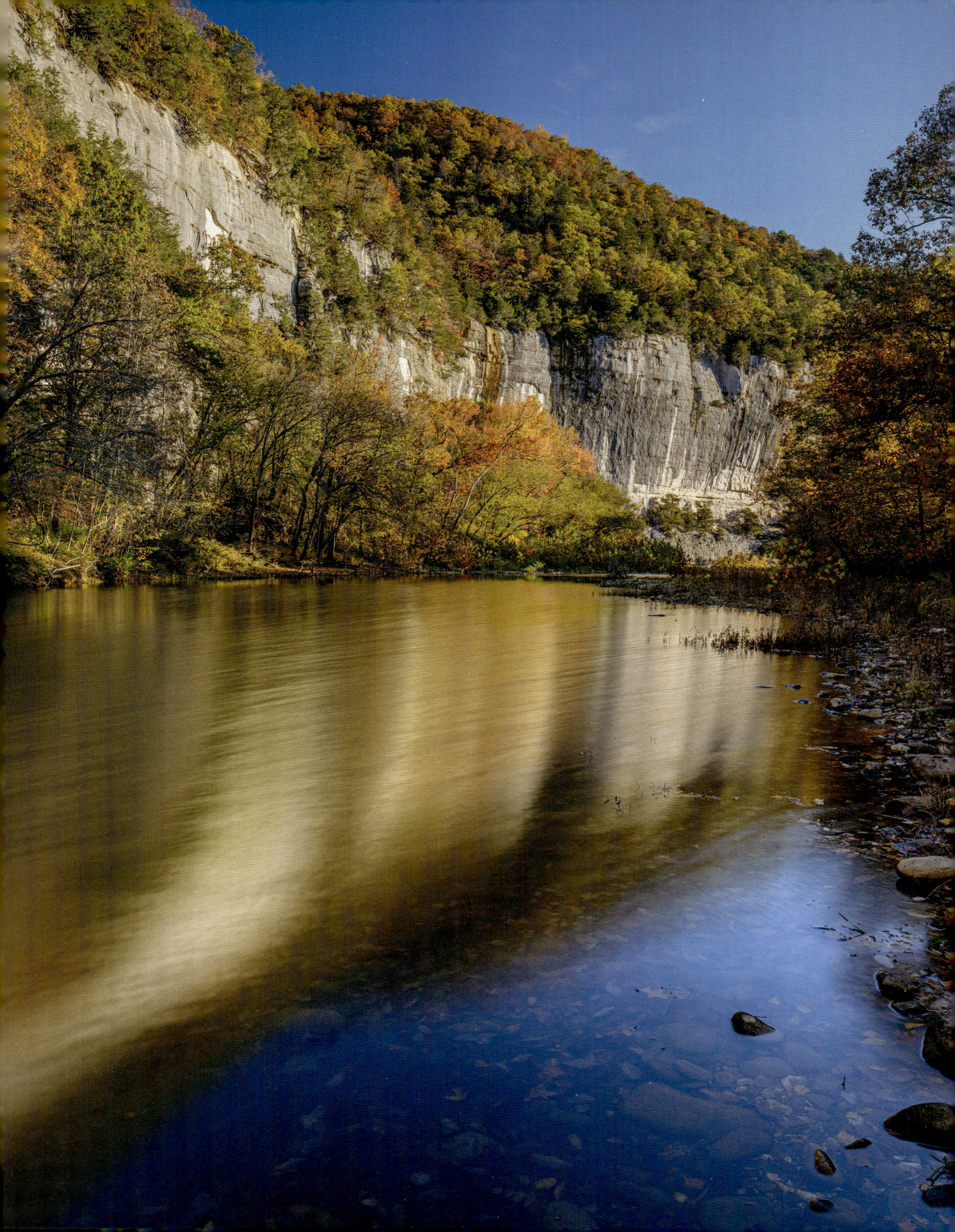

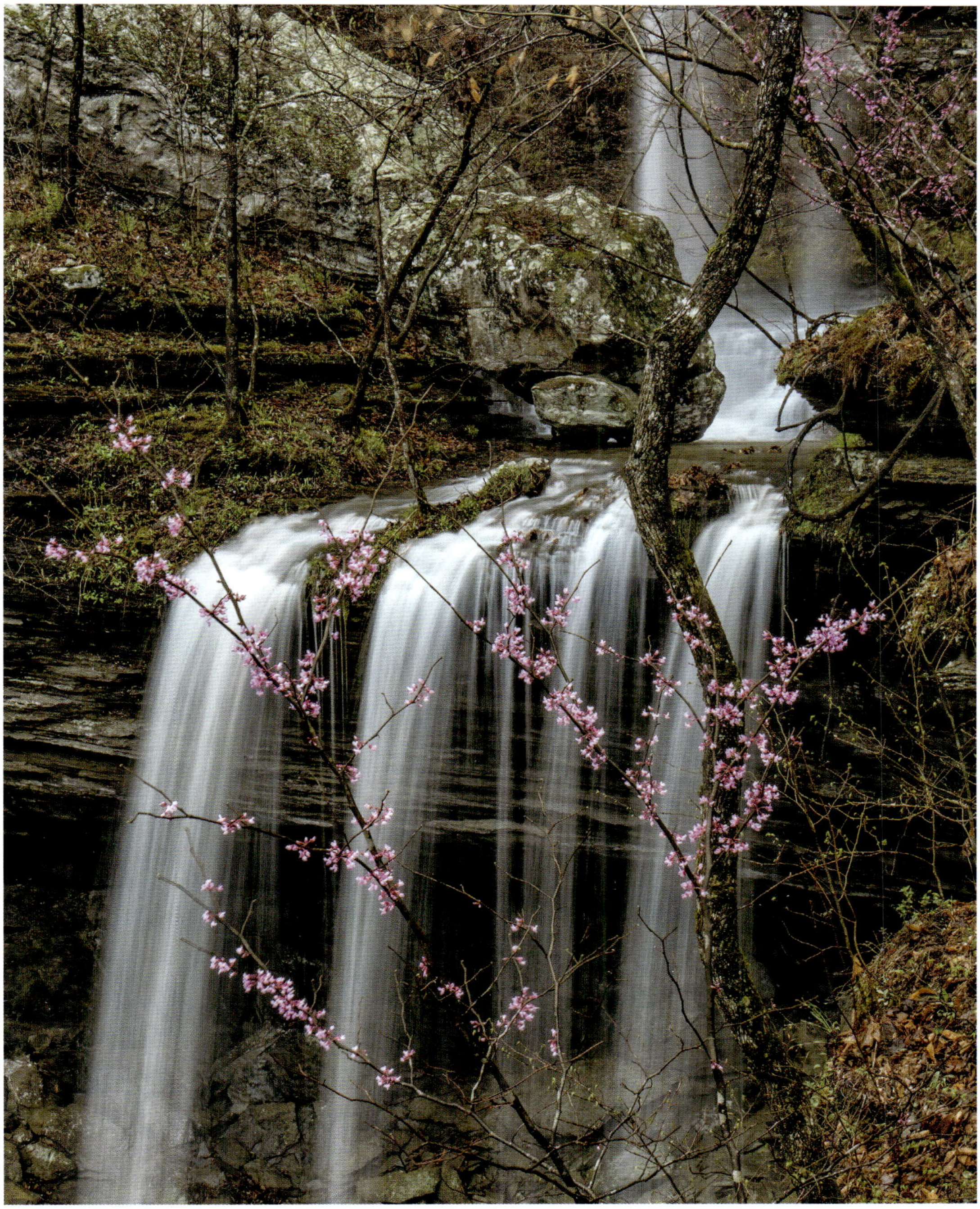

Dismal Double Decker Falls and redbud, Dismal Hollow Research Natural Area, Ozark National Forest

< A long exposure of the wave action on the Buffalo

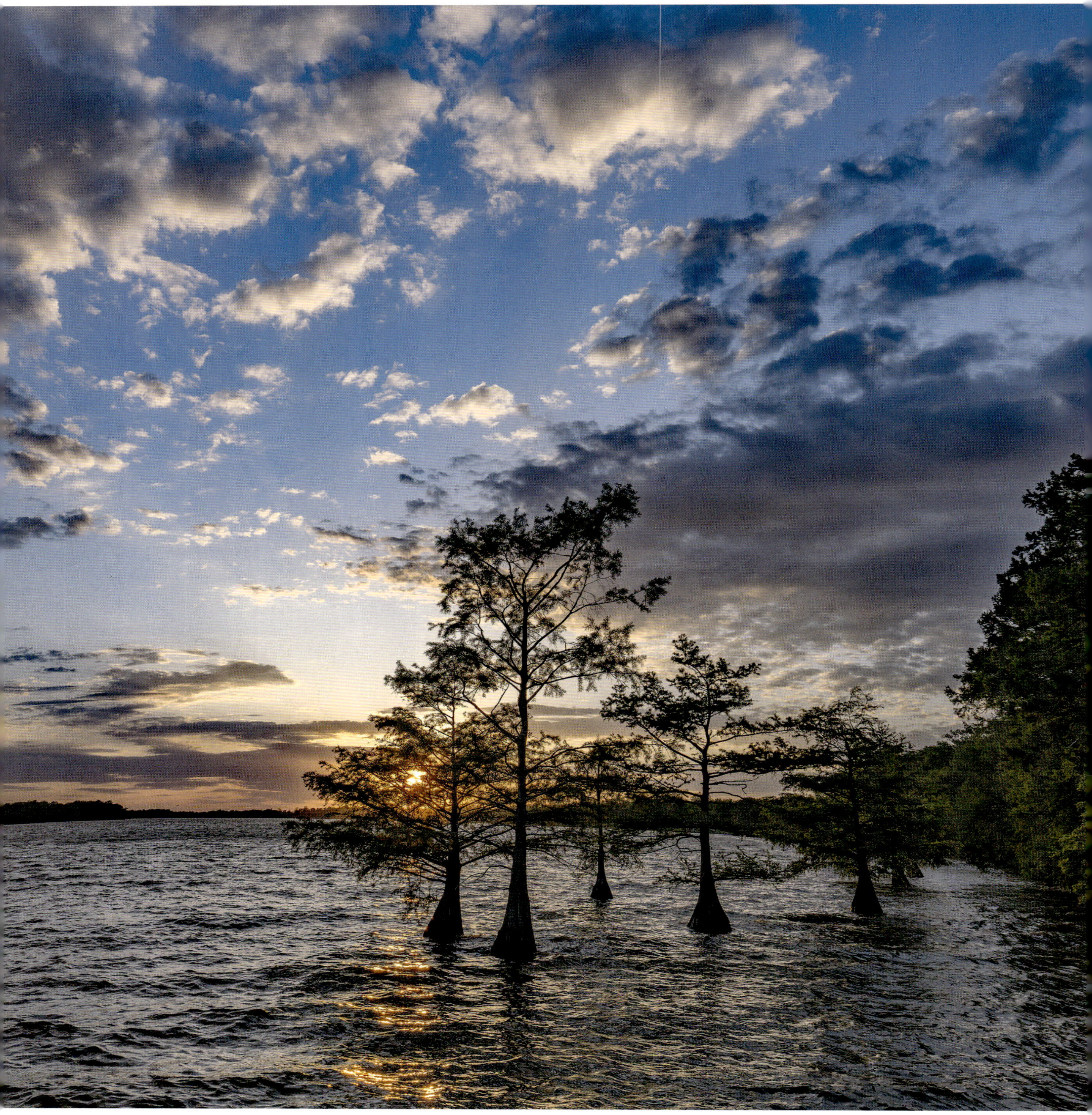

Bald Cypress trees at sunset, Lake Chicot State Park
The wind was blowing so hard I had to strap my tripod to the dock to keep from being blown away.

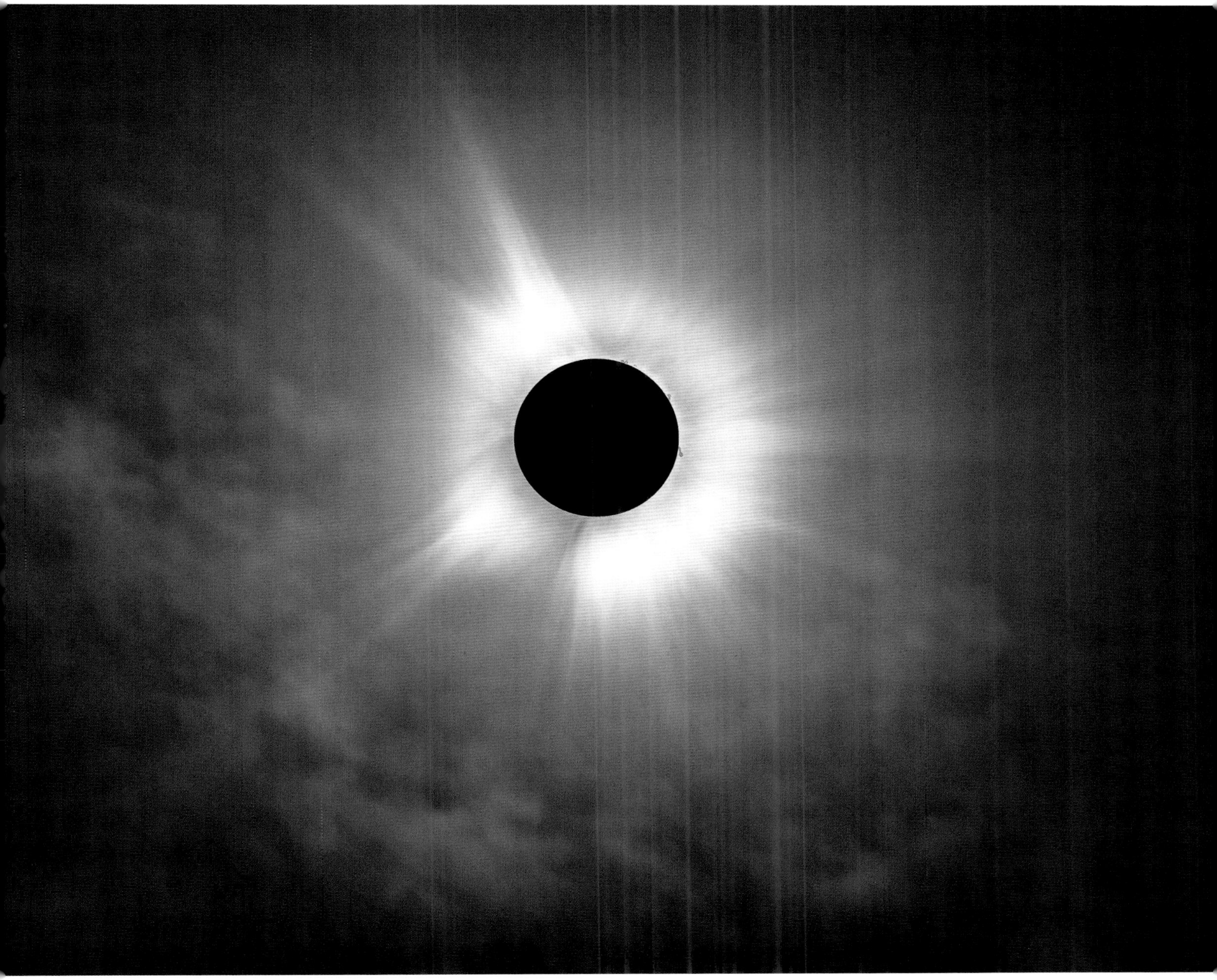

Here's my shot of the Great American Solar Eclipse during totality, April 8, 2024. This shot shows a great bit of detail in the sun's corona (light outer atmosphere), and prominence (the red squiggly clouds of plasma). I did a 24-exposure bracket to help bring out these details.

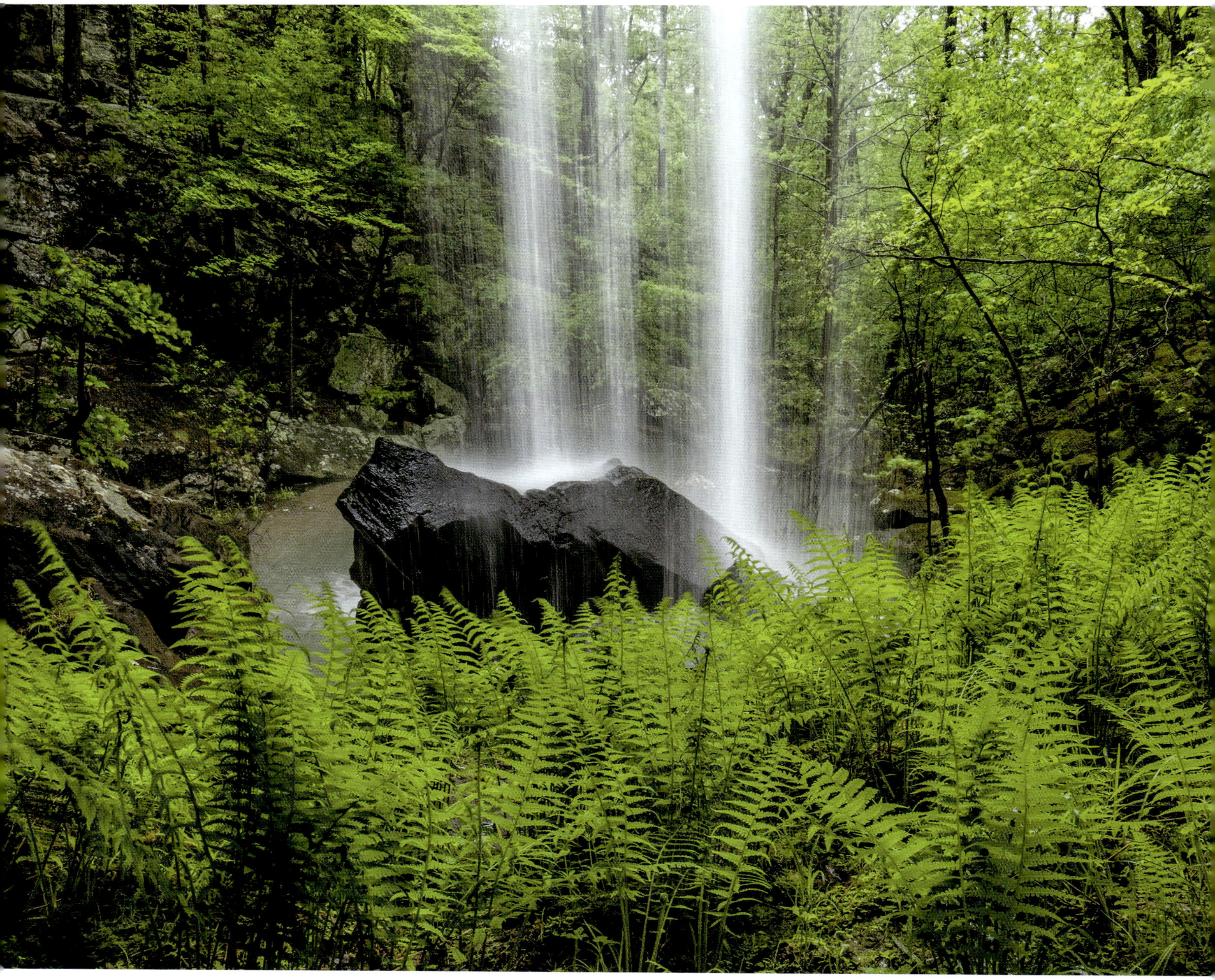

It was fern city at the base of Bearcat Hollow Falls

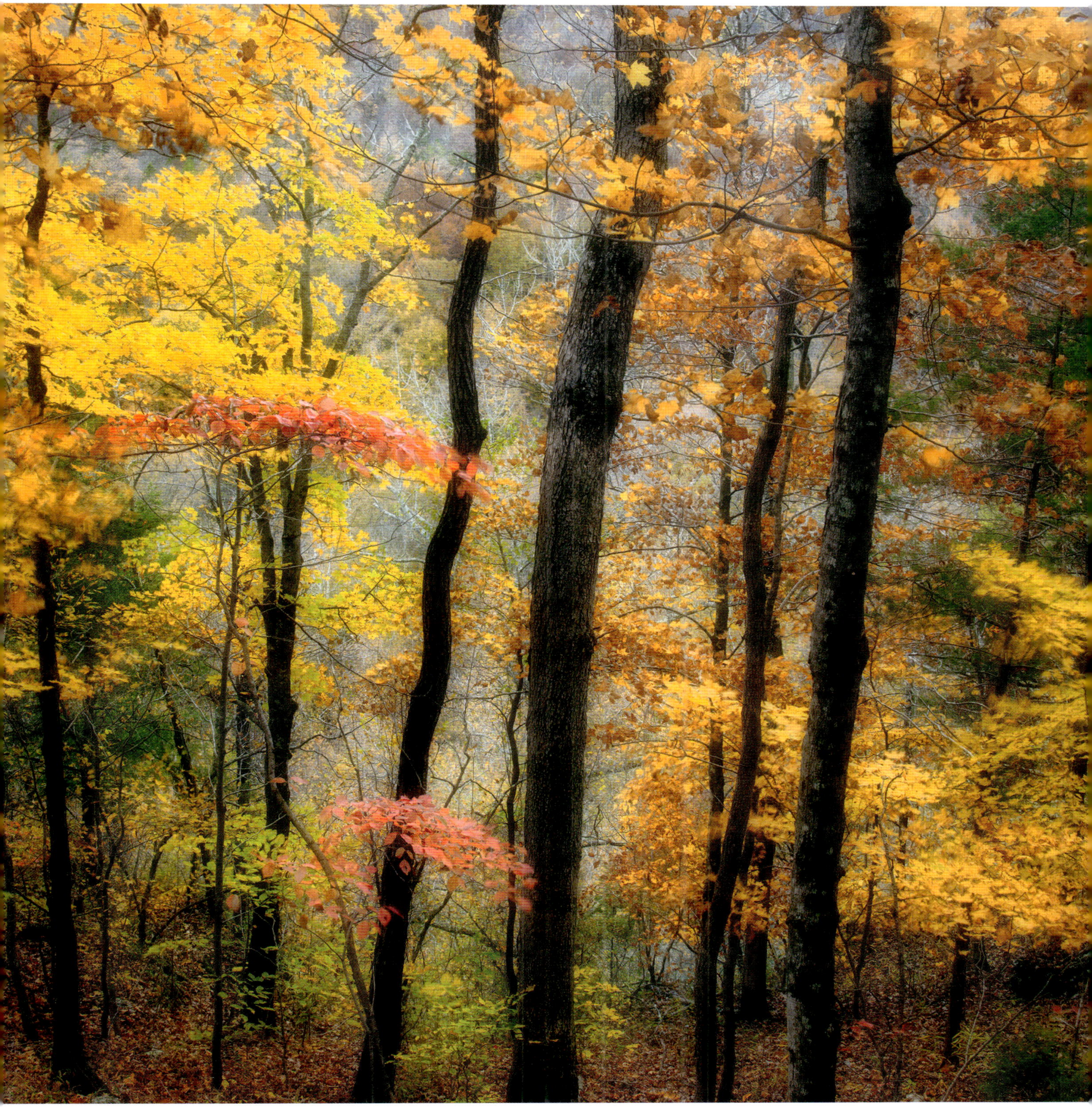

Dogwood, Maple, Oak and Hickory trees gather to show off their brilliant fall color.

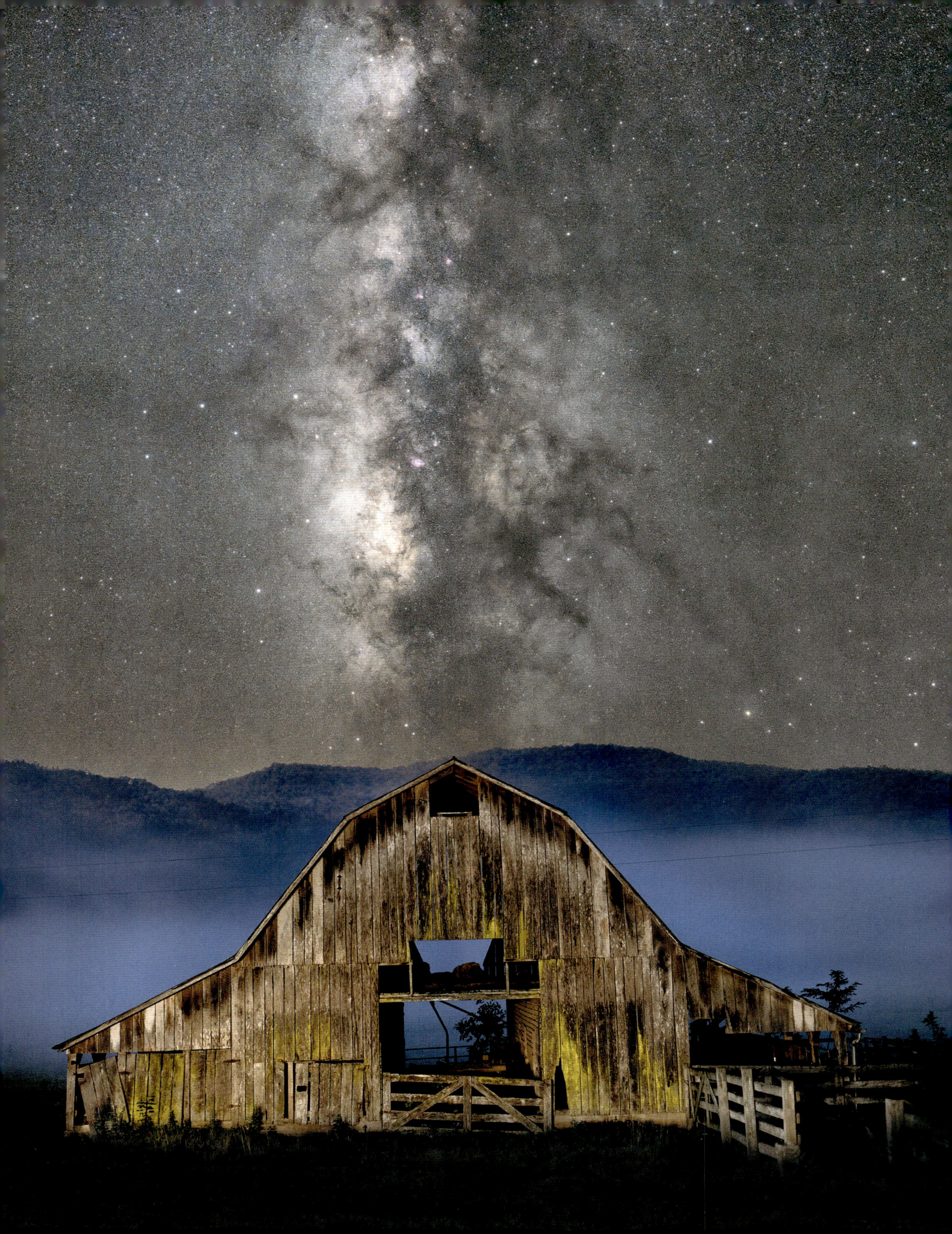

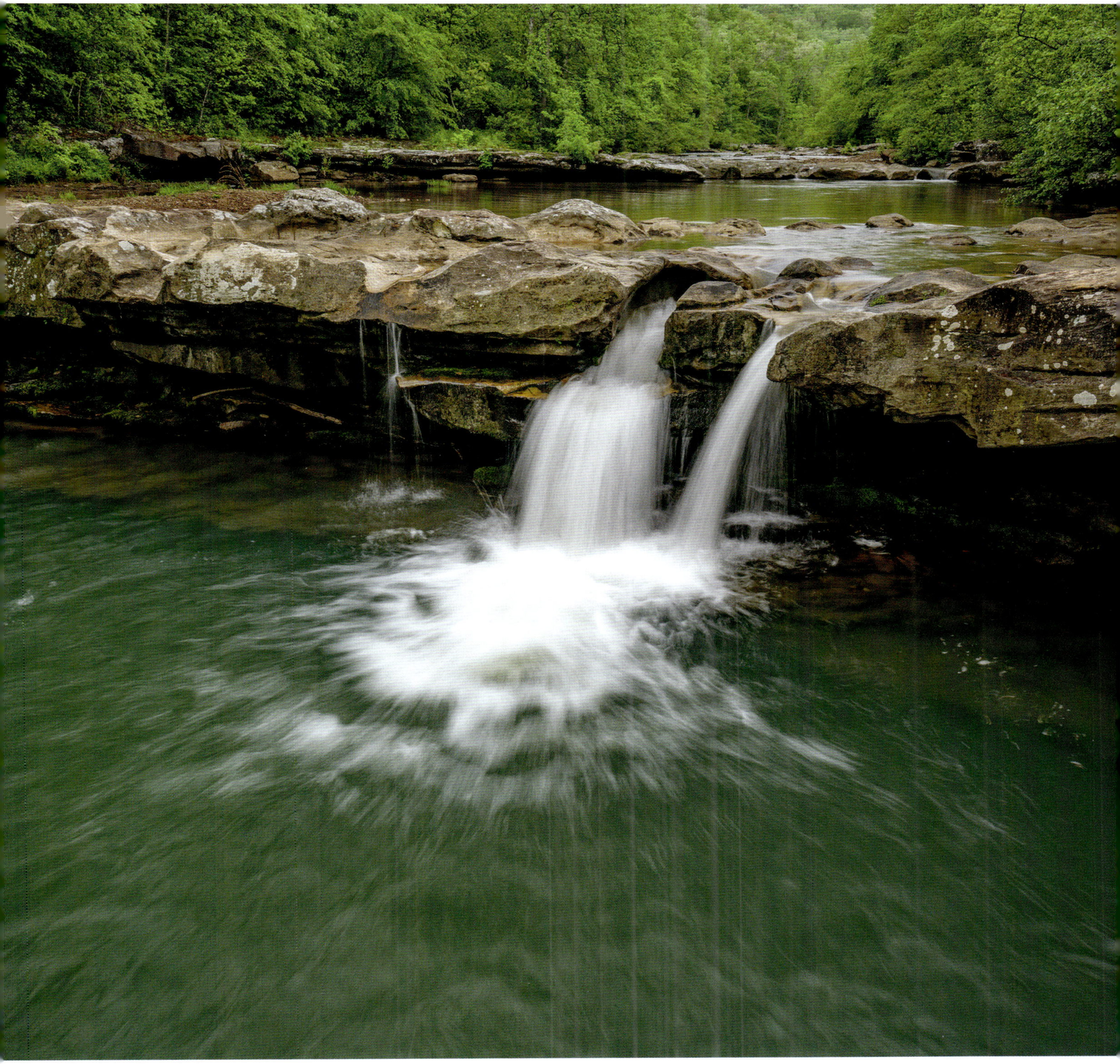

Kings River Falls

< Rustic barn and the Milky Way, Boxley Valley Historic District

It was the middle of the night when I set up to take a photo of what I thought was going to be a silhouetted barn and Milky Way. As I was getting ready to start the long exposure, I noticed a vehicle headed my way. I figured the headlights would be very bright and blow out the barn, so I tried to take the photo before it arrived. When I pushed the shutter button to begin the exposure, I forgot that a two-second delay was active, so the camera hesitated before taking the photo. Turns out that little delay was like magic—the camera did not start the photo until the truck headlights were already past the barn, and while the long exposure was going on only the side lights of the truck illuminated the barn, just enough to make a perfectly-lit barn! My dumb luck strikes again!

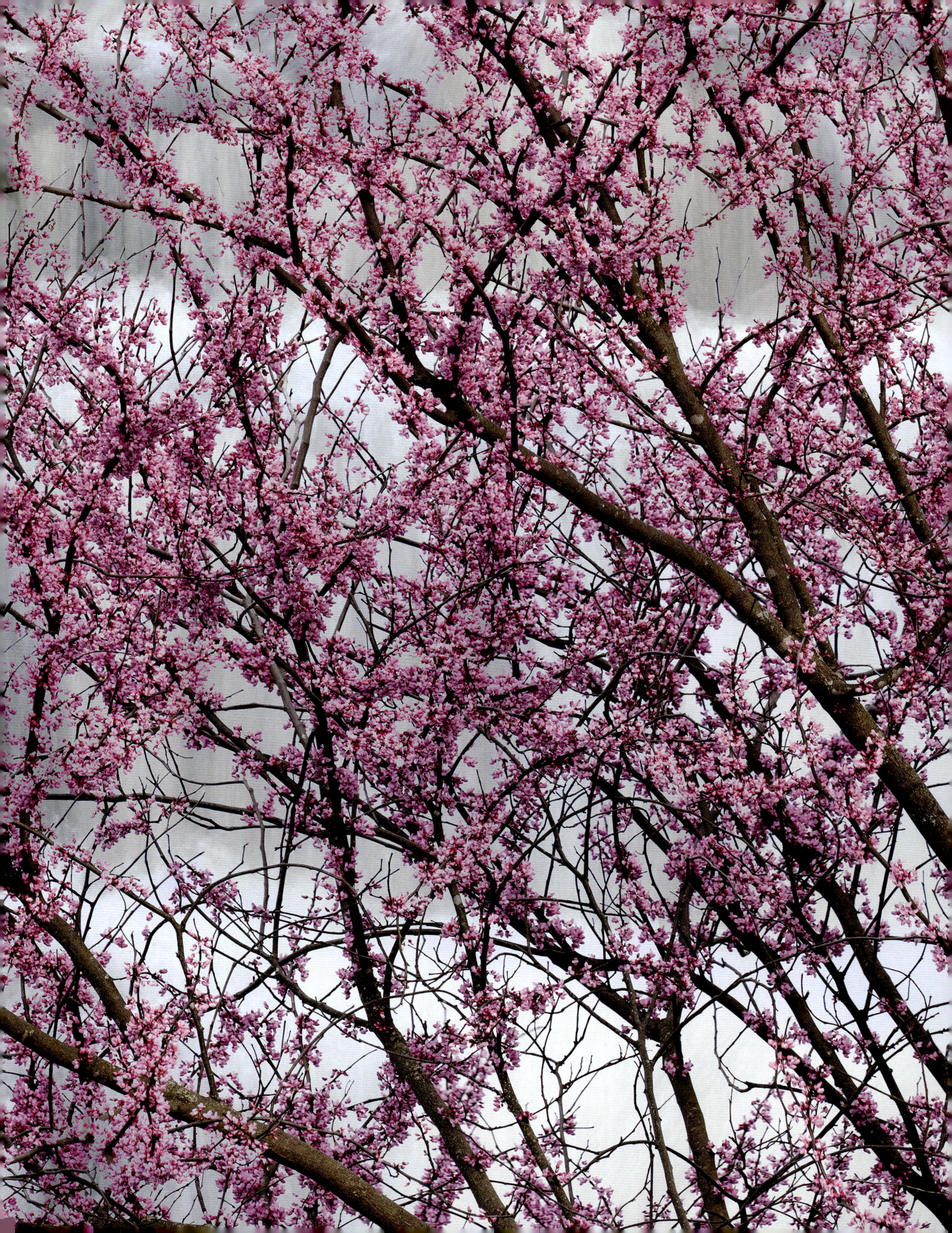

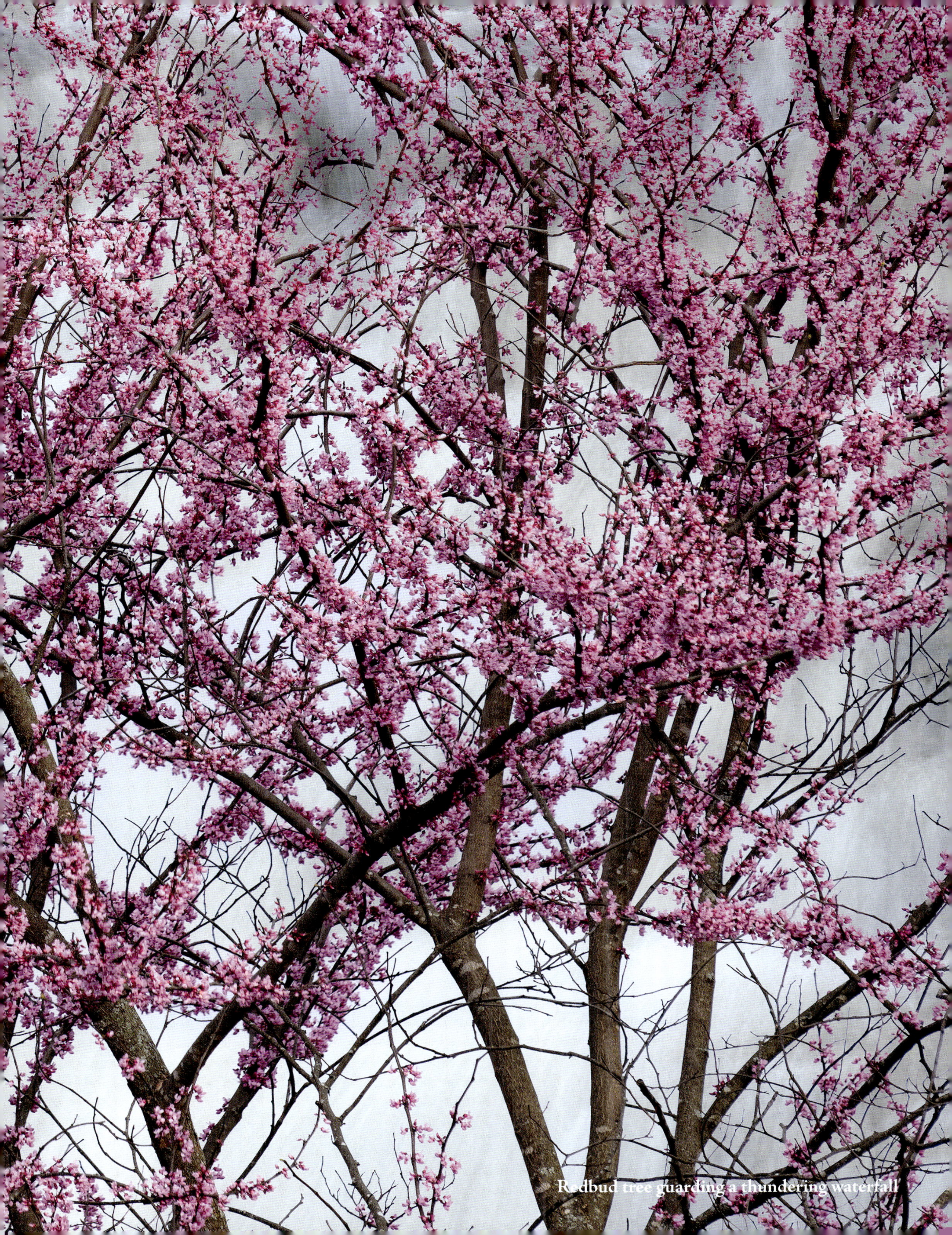

Redbud tree guarding a thundering waterfall

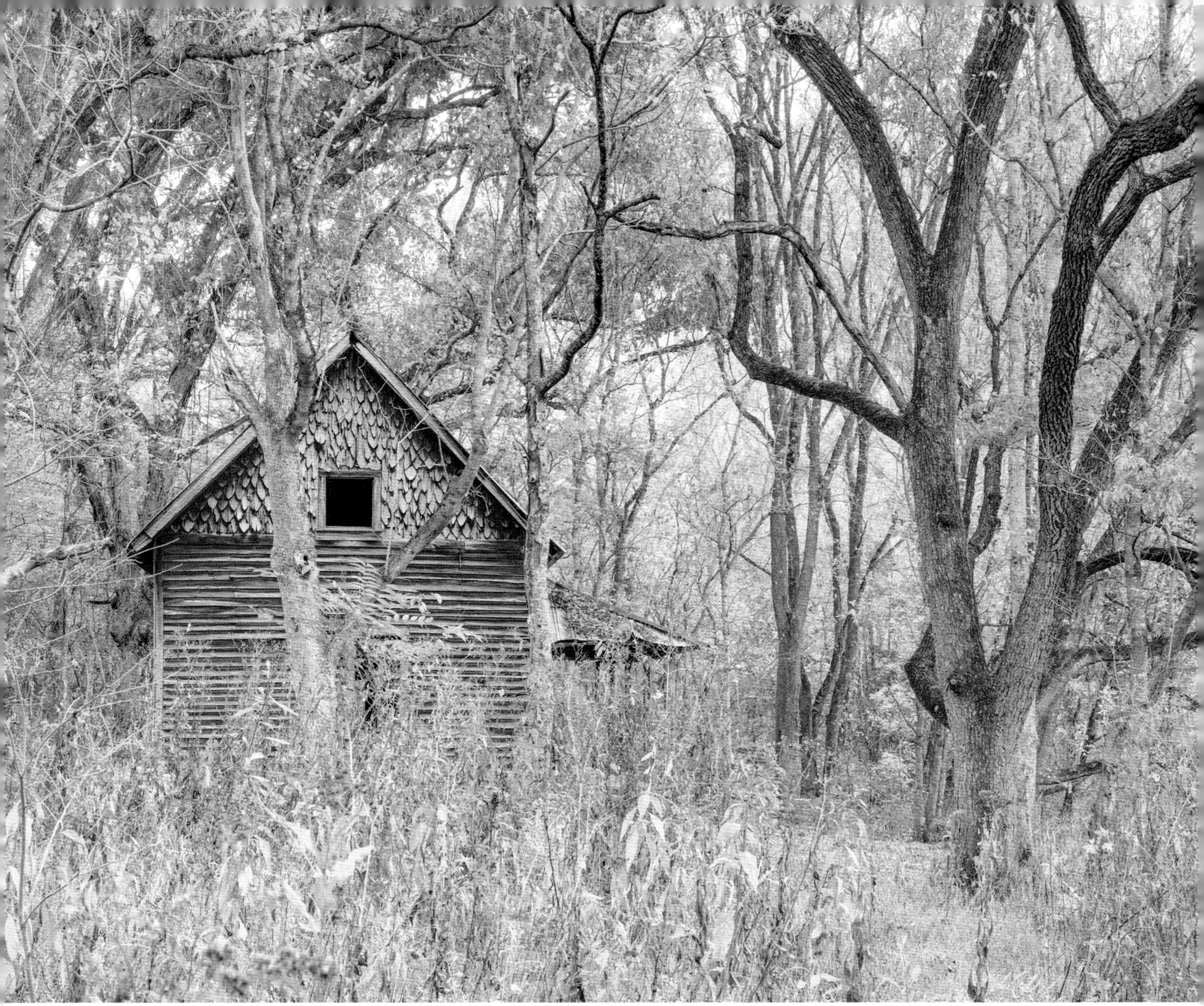

Granny Henderson's Cabin

The mention of "Granny Henderson" can evoke a variety of emotions for different people across Buffalo River country: admiration, nostalgia, anger, sympathy, regret. The fact that her name makes so many feel so strongly is a testament to her resounding legacy across Buffalo National River and the Ozarks.

Since the establishment of Buffalo National River, Eva Barnes Henderson (1892-1979) has become an icon of strength and frontier grit for her rugged self-sufficiency and homesteader lifestyle. For this reason, her old cabin is a popular pilgrimage for hikers, horseback riders, and paddlers in today's Ponca Wilderness.

Built in the early 1900s by Eva and her husband, Frank, the cabin and surrounding homestead gave the newlyweds an immense sense of pride and purpose. Together, the Hendersons maintained agricultural fields, raised cattle, and gathered all of the water they used each day from the river or nearby springs, carrying it back to their cabin in large buckets. When Frank passed away in 1959, Eva did not leave her beloved home. Instead, she continued life as she had always known it, exhibiting the dogged determination to thrive independently and sustain herself well into her eighties without the modern comforts of plumbing, telephone, or electricity. Over the years, as the Buffalo River grew in popularity as a recreation destination, "Granny" welcomed countless paddlers who would camp on her property, and sometimes she even cooked them breakfast before they departed. She was a kind and humble friend to the many strangers who visited her backyard.

Shortly after the National Park Service acquired her property for Buffalo National River, Granny passed away at age 87. If you visit Granny's old place today, take a moment to honor this tenacious and hard working woman who loved every day of her life on the Buffalo. Restoration work on her cabin is set to begin soon... (description is from NPS)

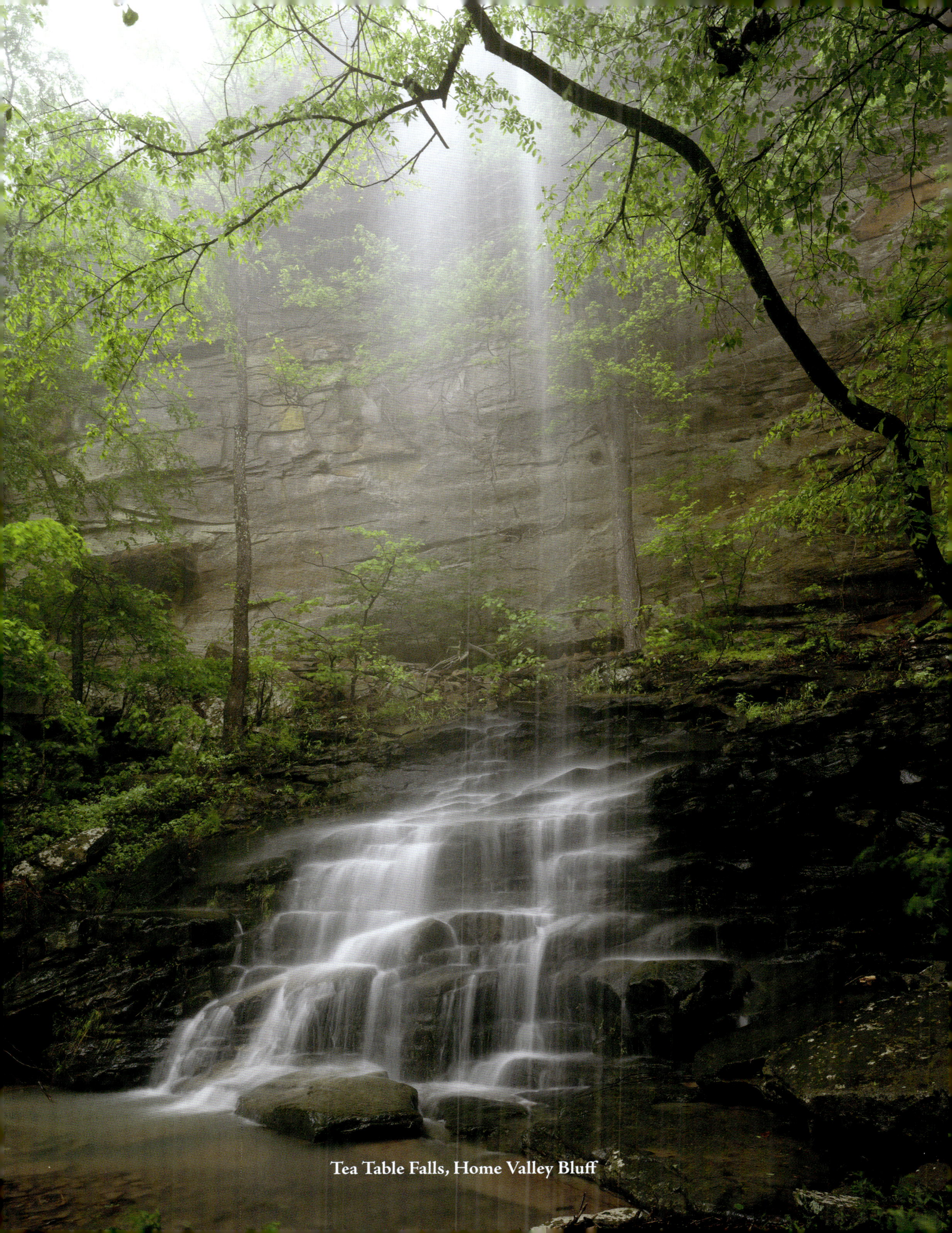

Tea Table Falls, Home Valley Bluff

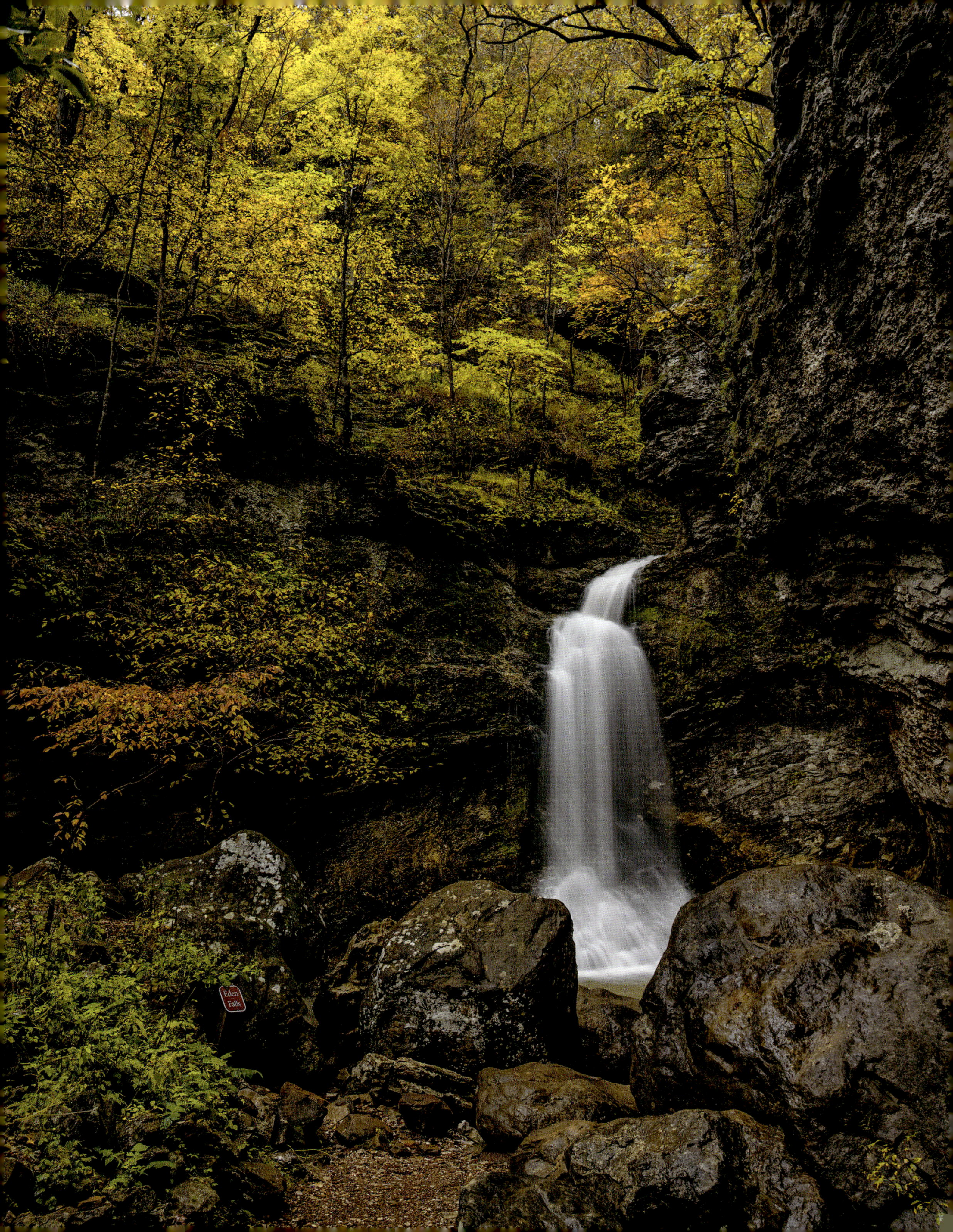
Eden
Falls

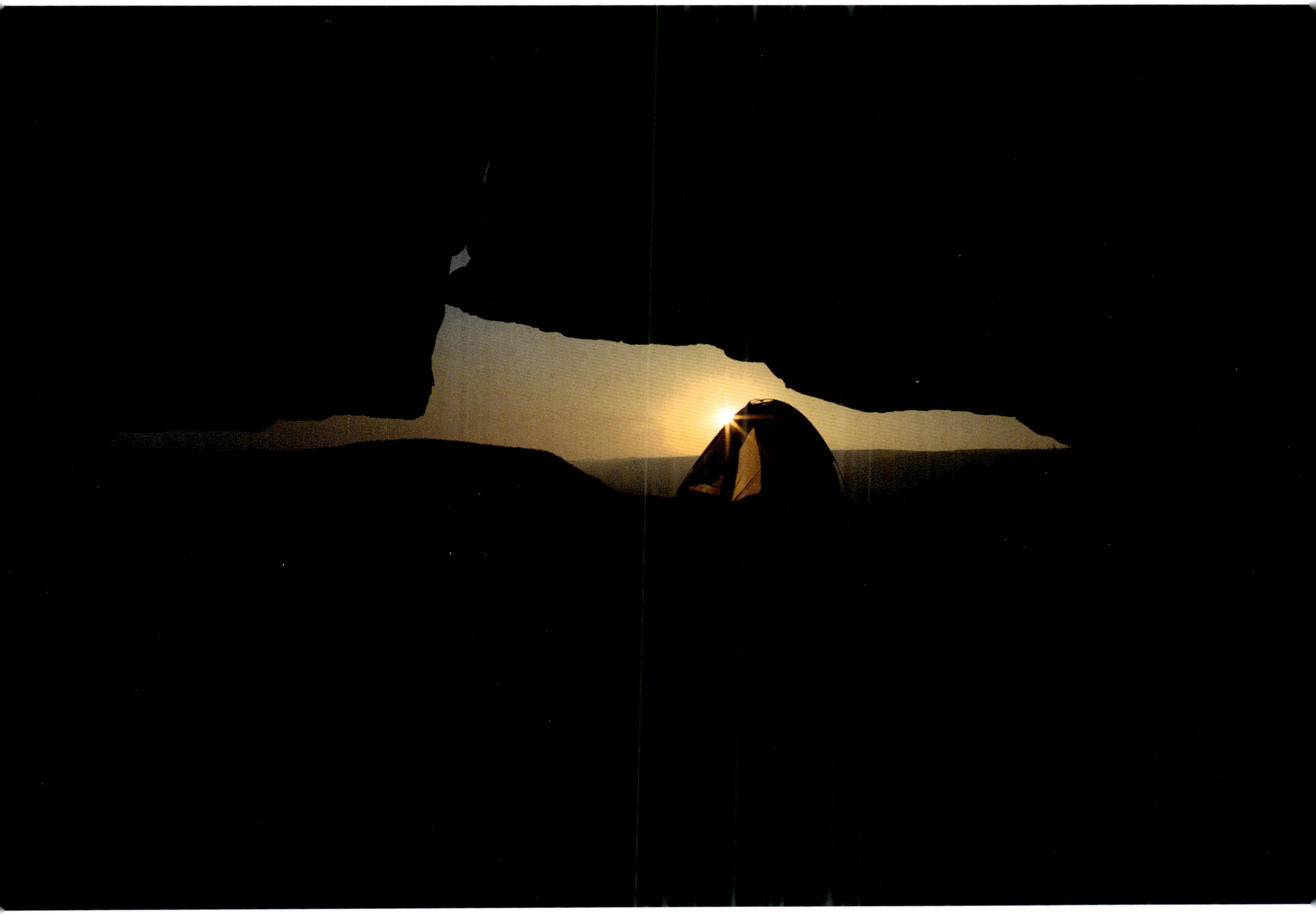

Thunderbird Cave at sunset, Ozark National Forest (4th trip)

< Eden Falls, Lost Valley Trail
This is one of the most visited waterfalls in Arkansas, and always a special treat!

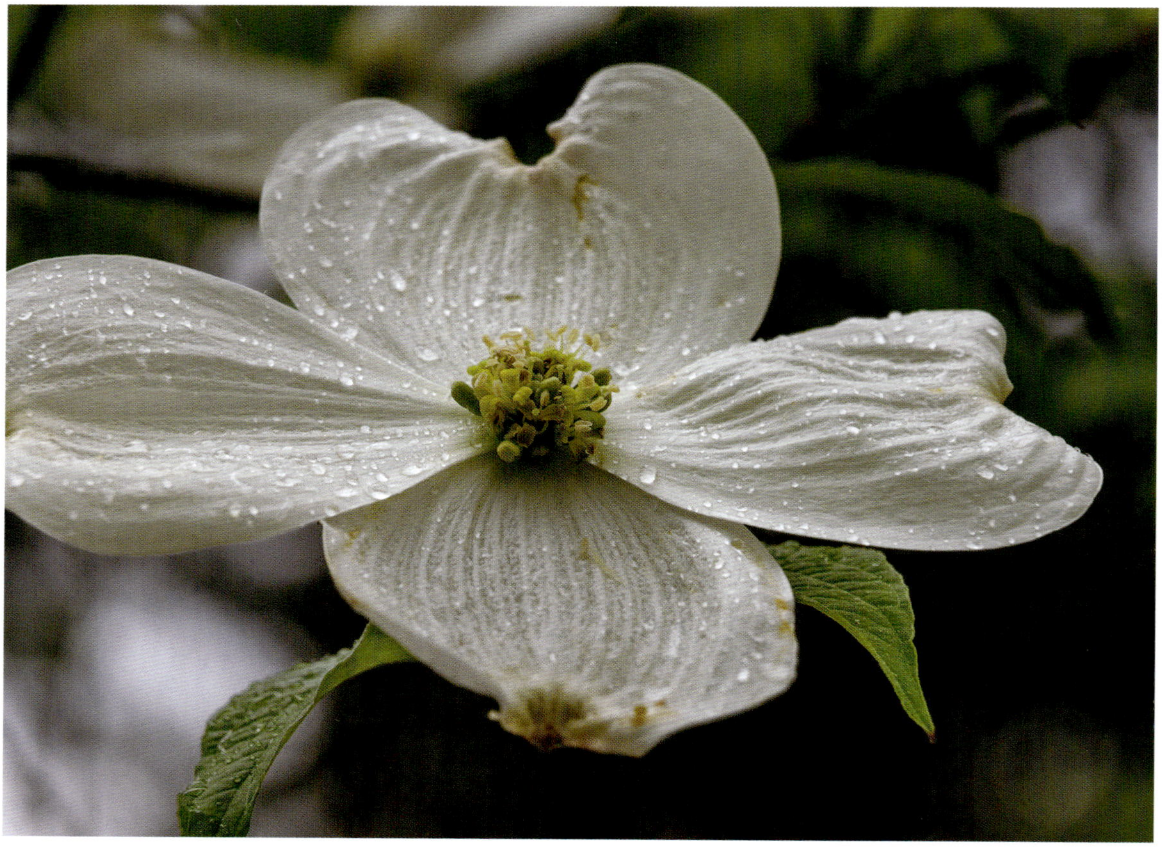

Dogwood

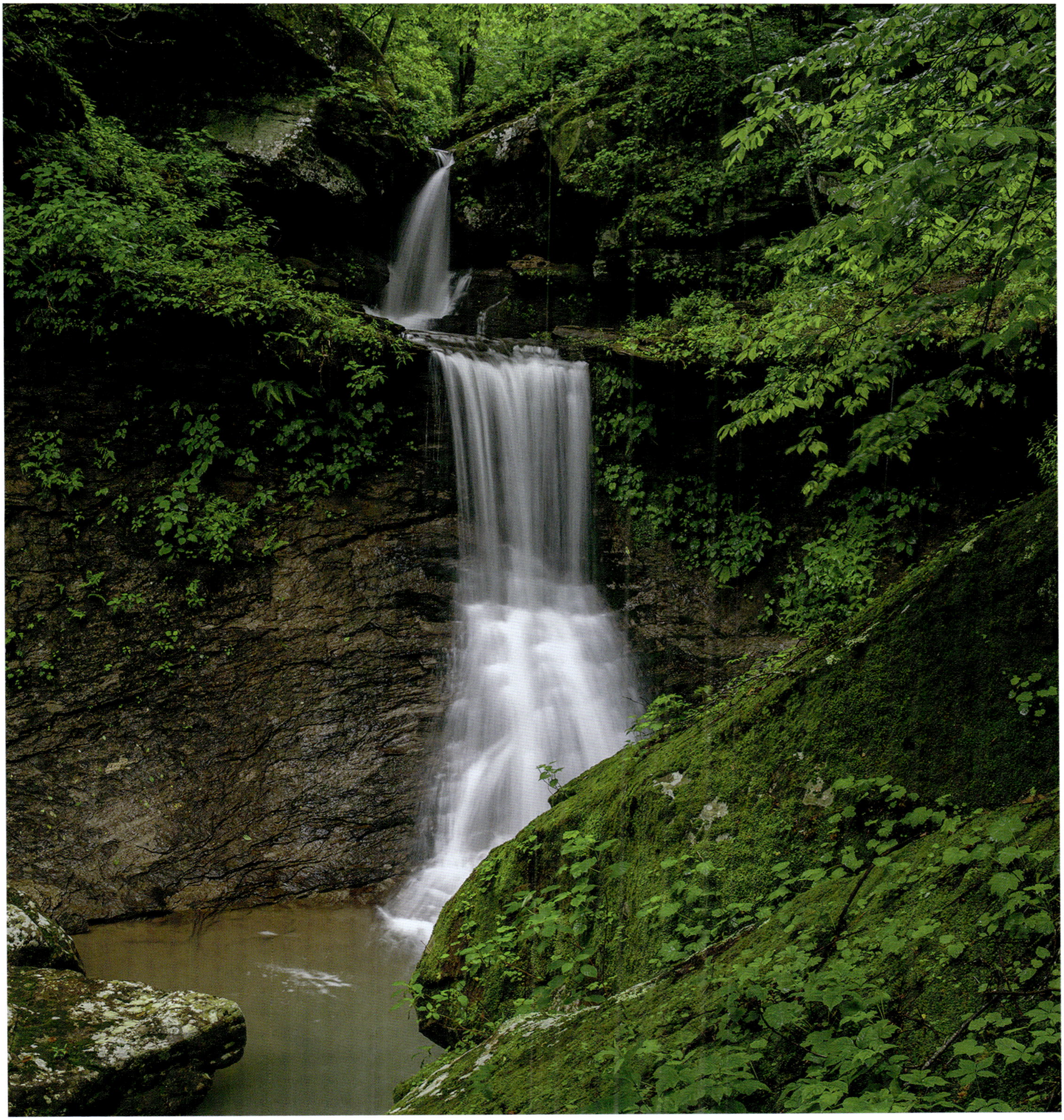

Mossy Falls, Terrapin Branch drainage, Upper Buffalo Wilderness

A tough hike to get to the base of this falls, but each time I arrive all I can do is sit and smile—a lush garden in it's own little private nook.

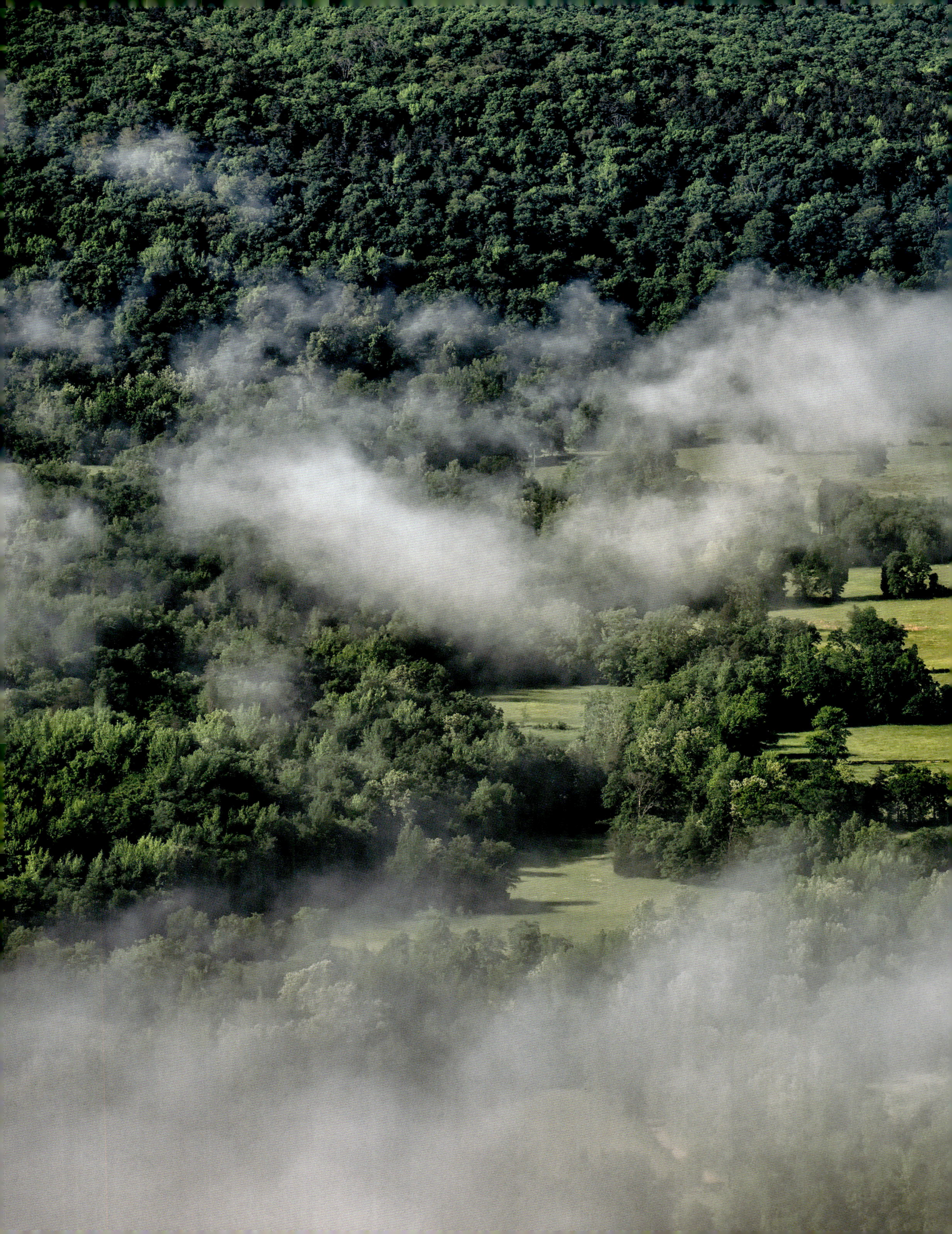

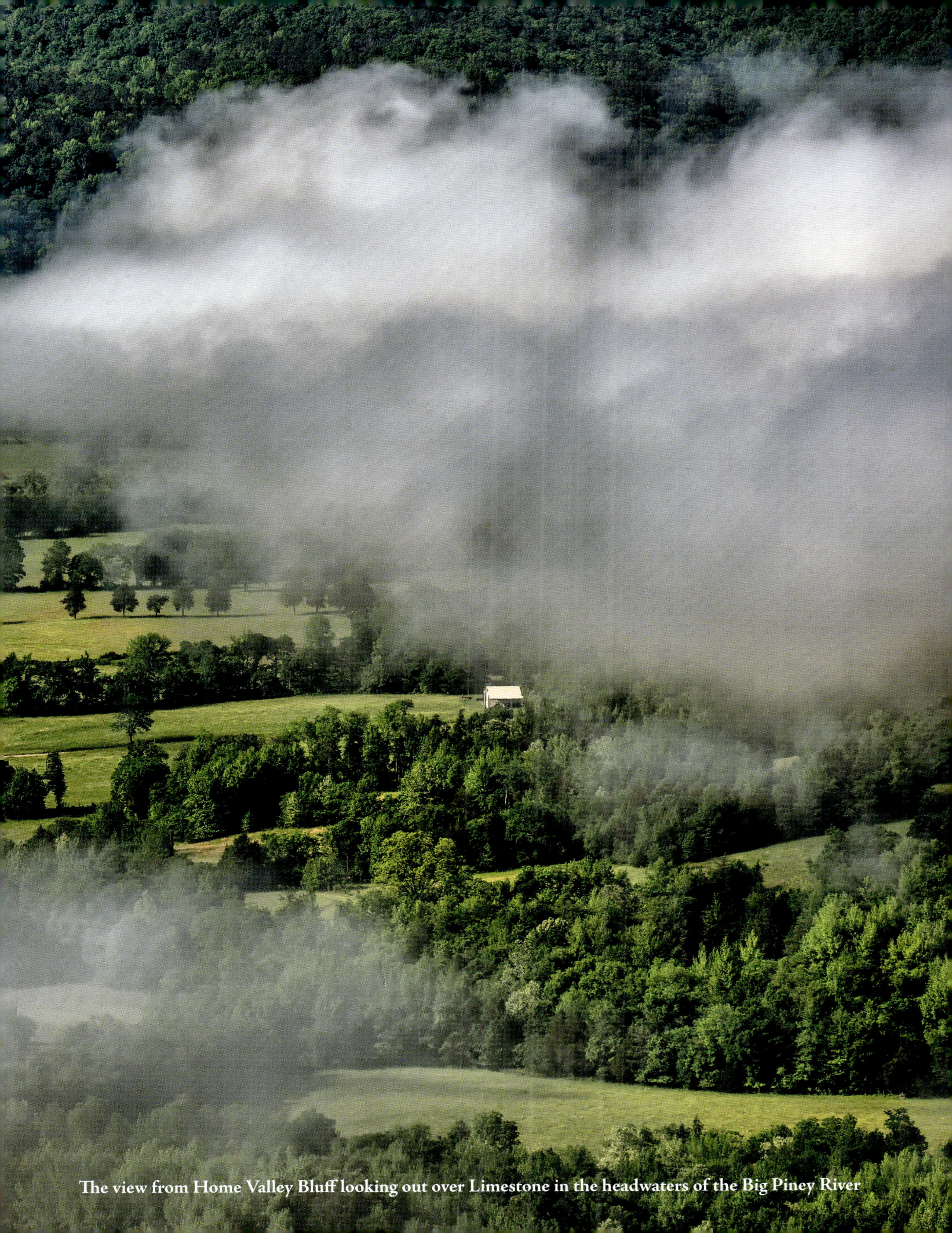

The view from Home Valley Bluff looking out over Limestone in the headwaters of the Big Piney River

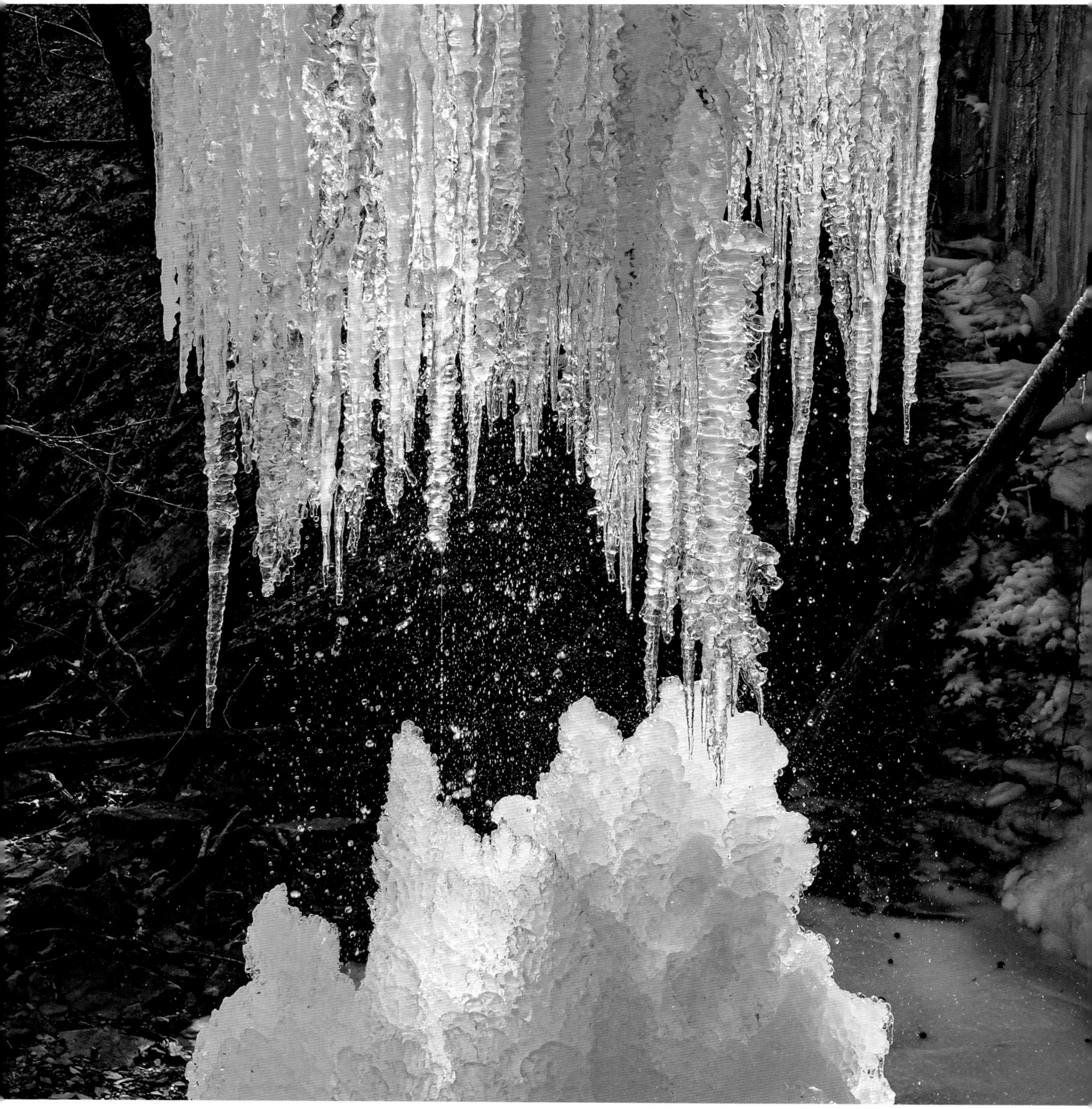

Sunshine arrives at a frozen waterfall and sets a million drops of water free to carry on downstream.

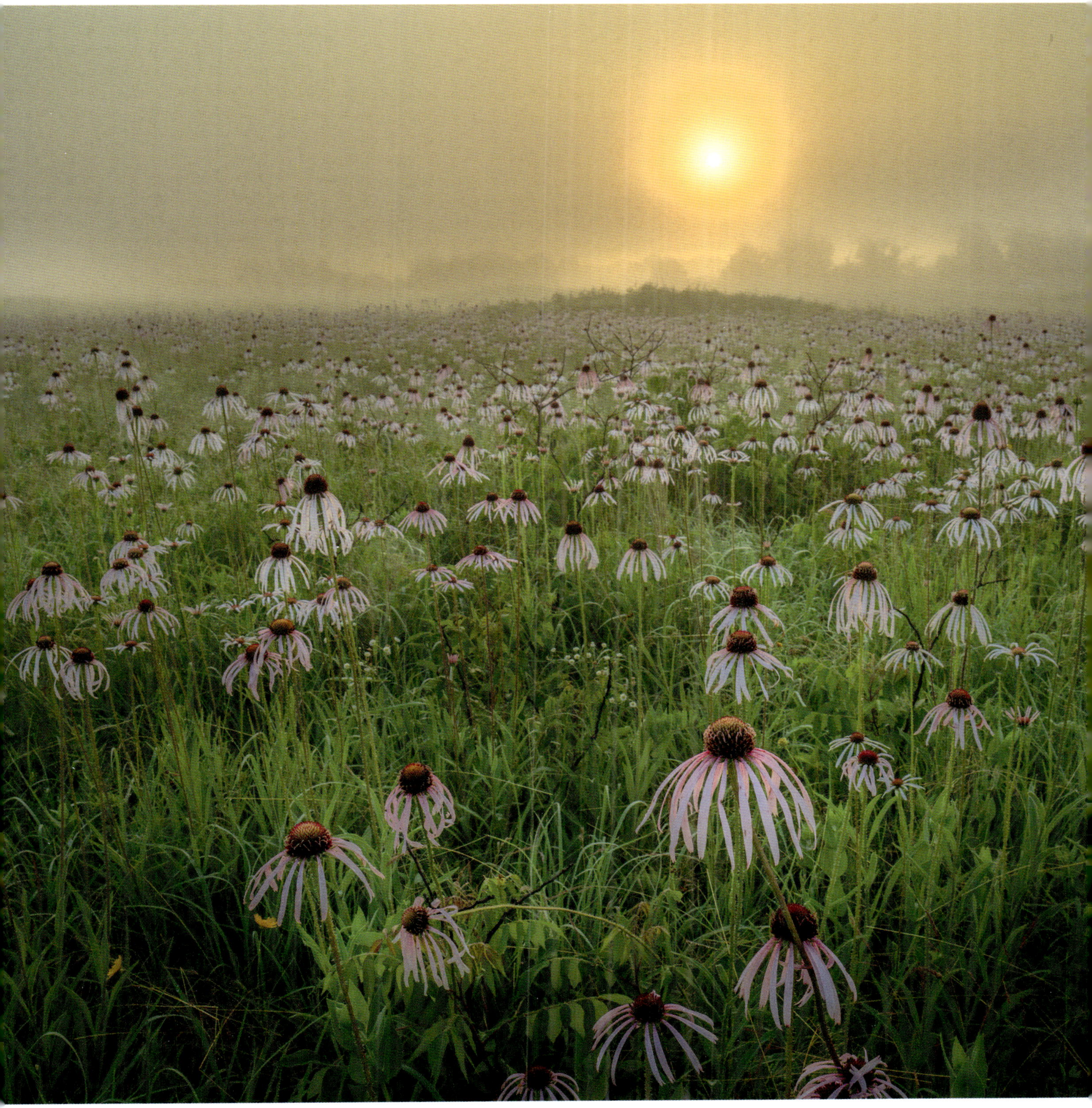

A Pale Purple Coneflower sunrise, Flanagan Prairie Natural Area

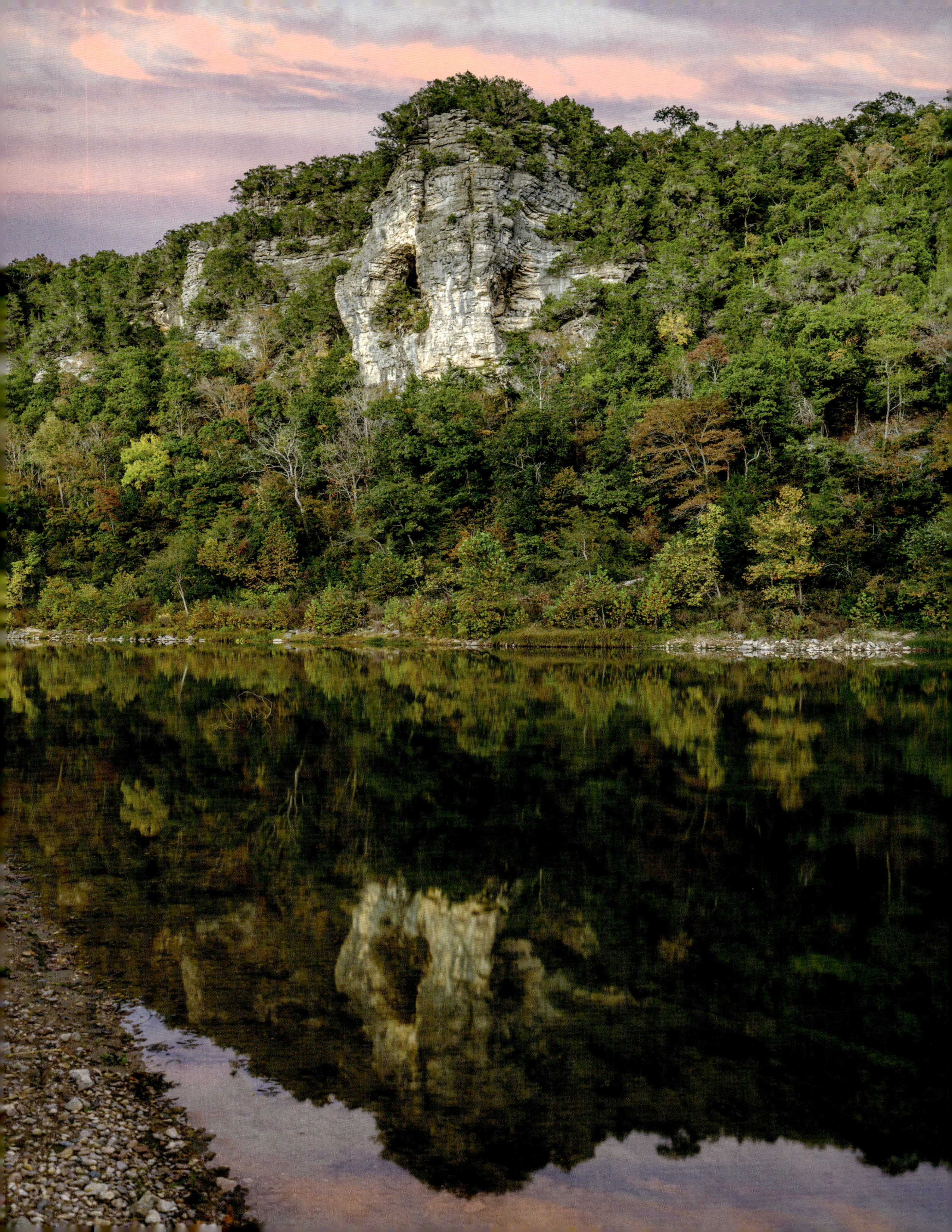

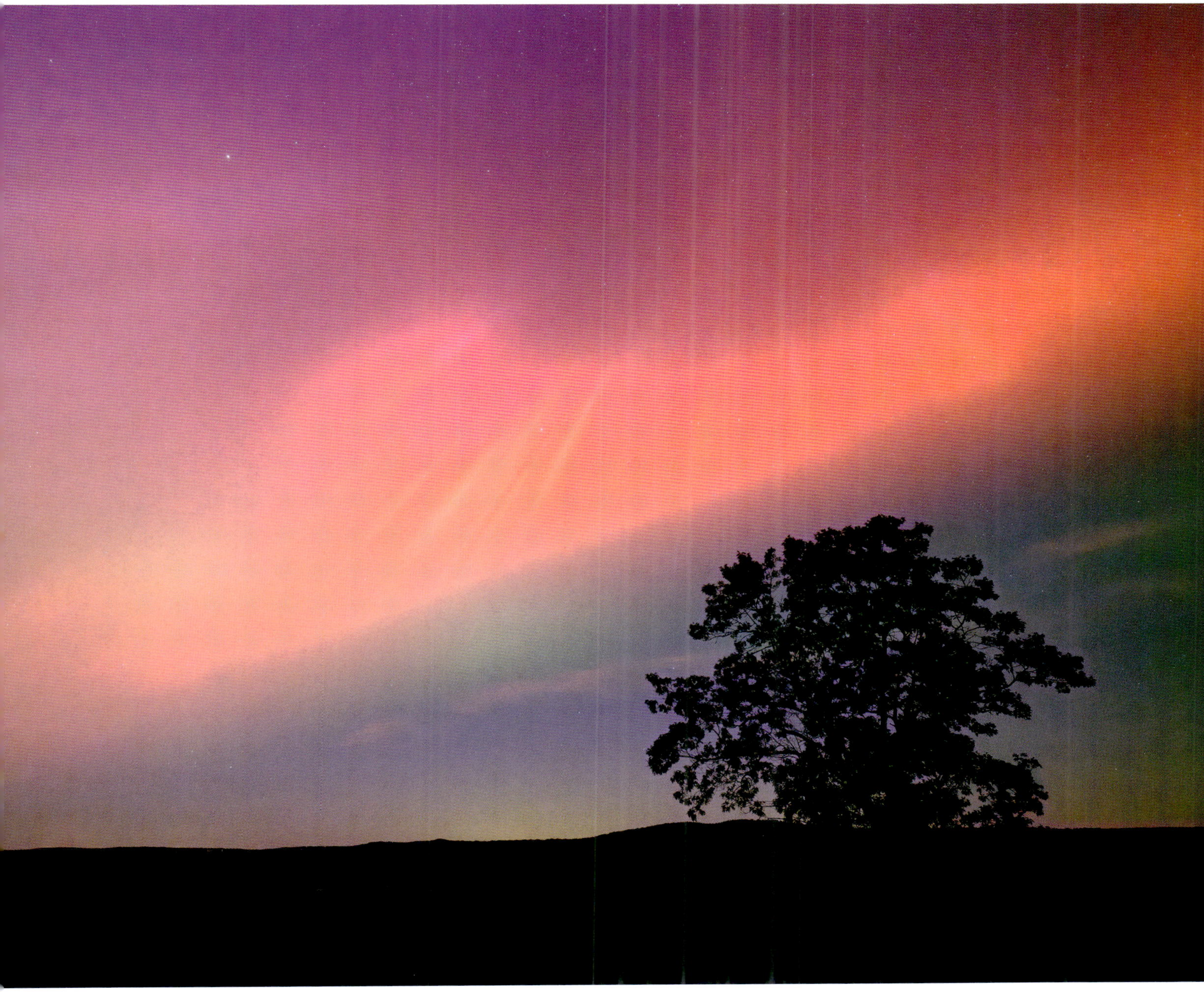

Northern Lights in Arkansas, May 2024

It was an EPIC display of not only color and aurora curtain movement, but this was the most widespread and steady light show of its kind I've ever photographed. AND, while I used my normal camera, lots of folks were able to get a great photo of it with a cell phone!

< Elephant Head Bluff, Lower Buffalo Wilderness (a two-day paddle)

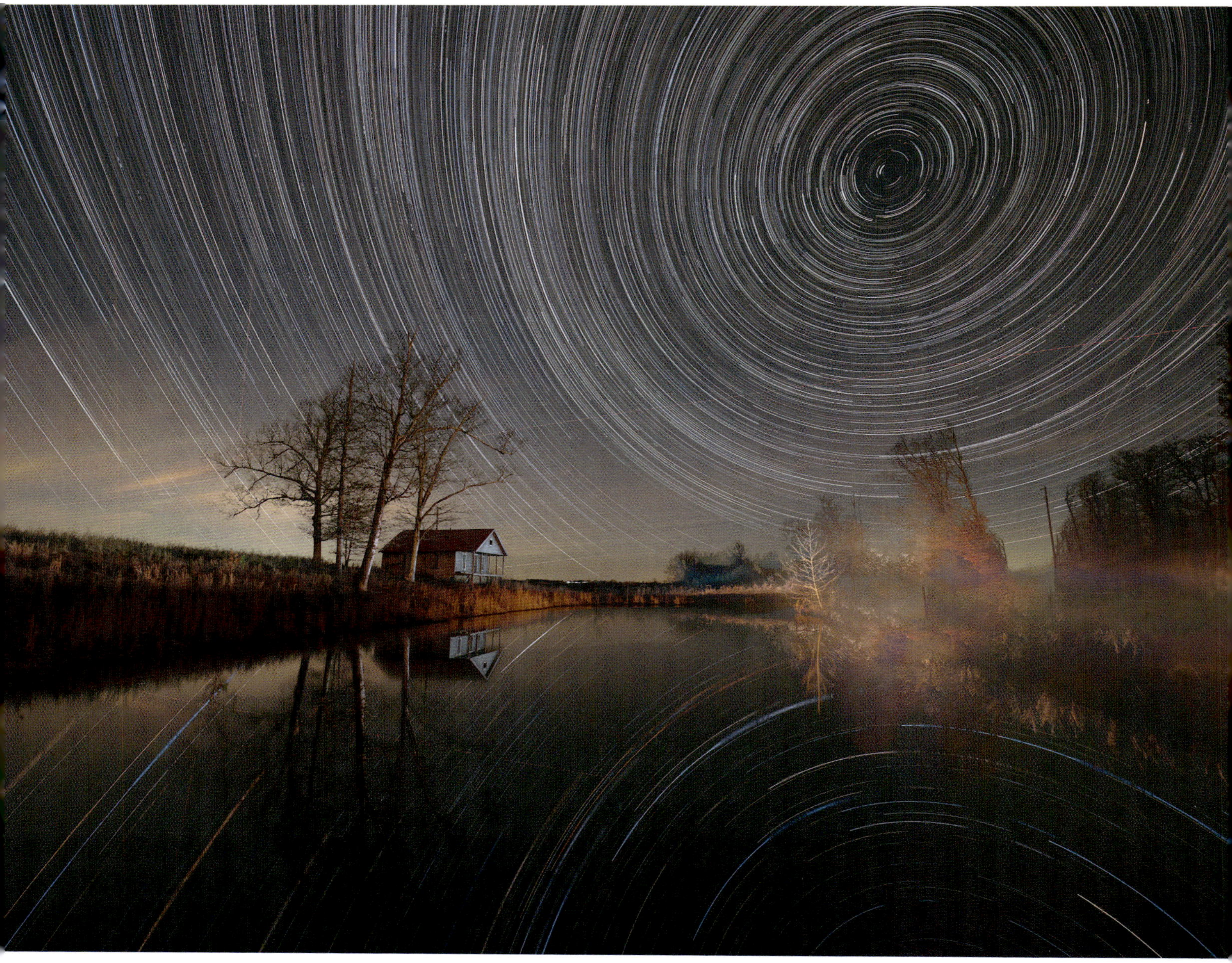

A frozen pond and old cabin along Cave Mountain Road

This star circle took about four hours to complete. I got bored sitting in the car while the camera did all the work, and couldn't sleep, so I simply paced back and forth along the road in the dark - getting as far as a mile away sometimes. I hiked almost ten miles! There were a couple of cars passed during that time—I try to stay out of sight and always hid in the trees so as not to scare them.

Gray Fox Falls, Lower Buffalo River area >

The first time I saw this waterfall I was snowshoeing along the river a day after heavy snowfall, and this was a giant wall of ice. An hour before this, I had come across a gray fox, frozen solid on top of the snow. She was so beautiful, colorful, and seemed at peace.

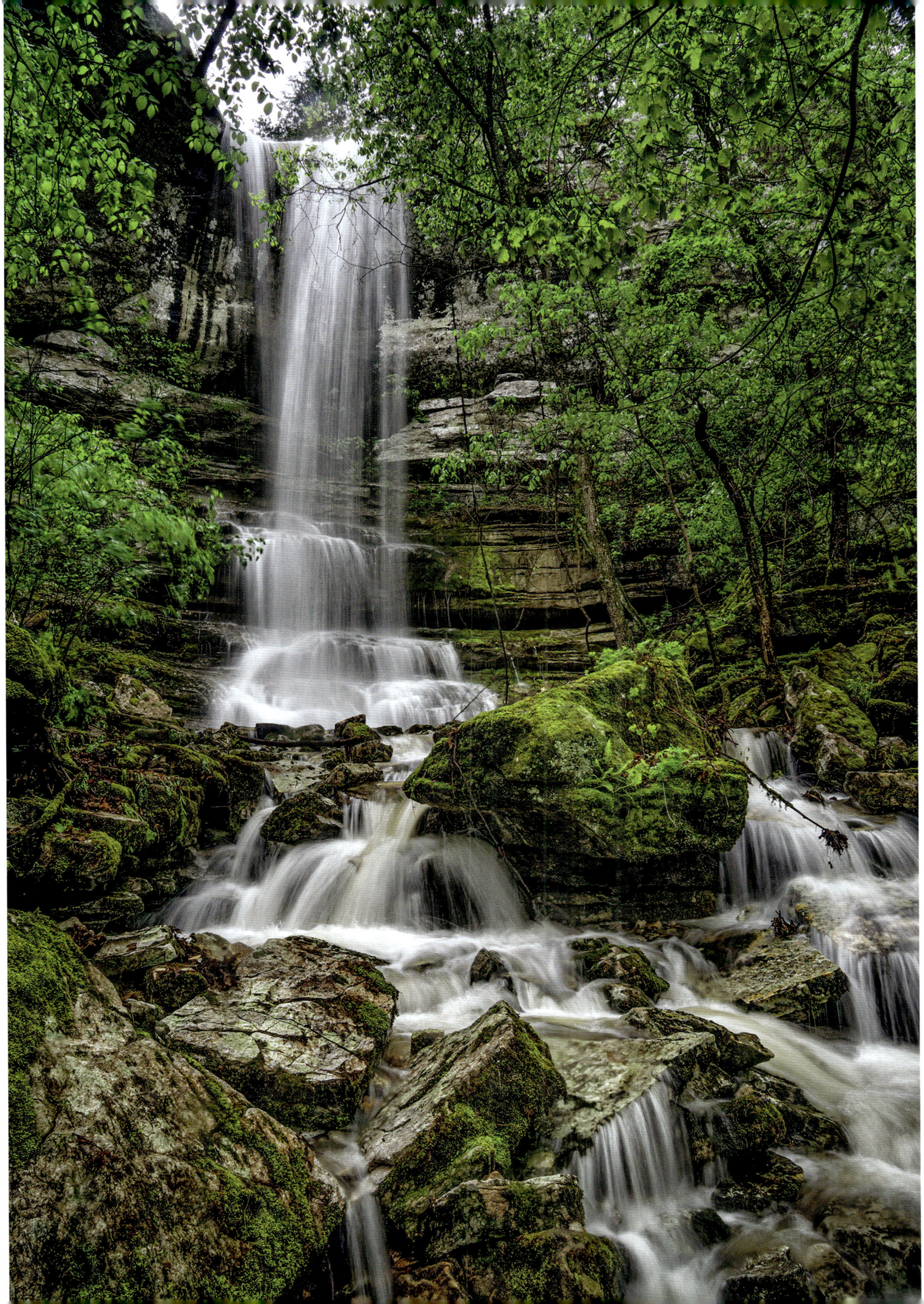

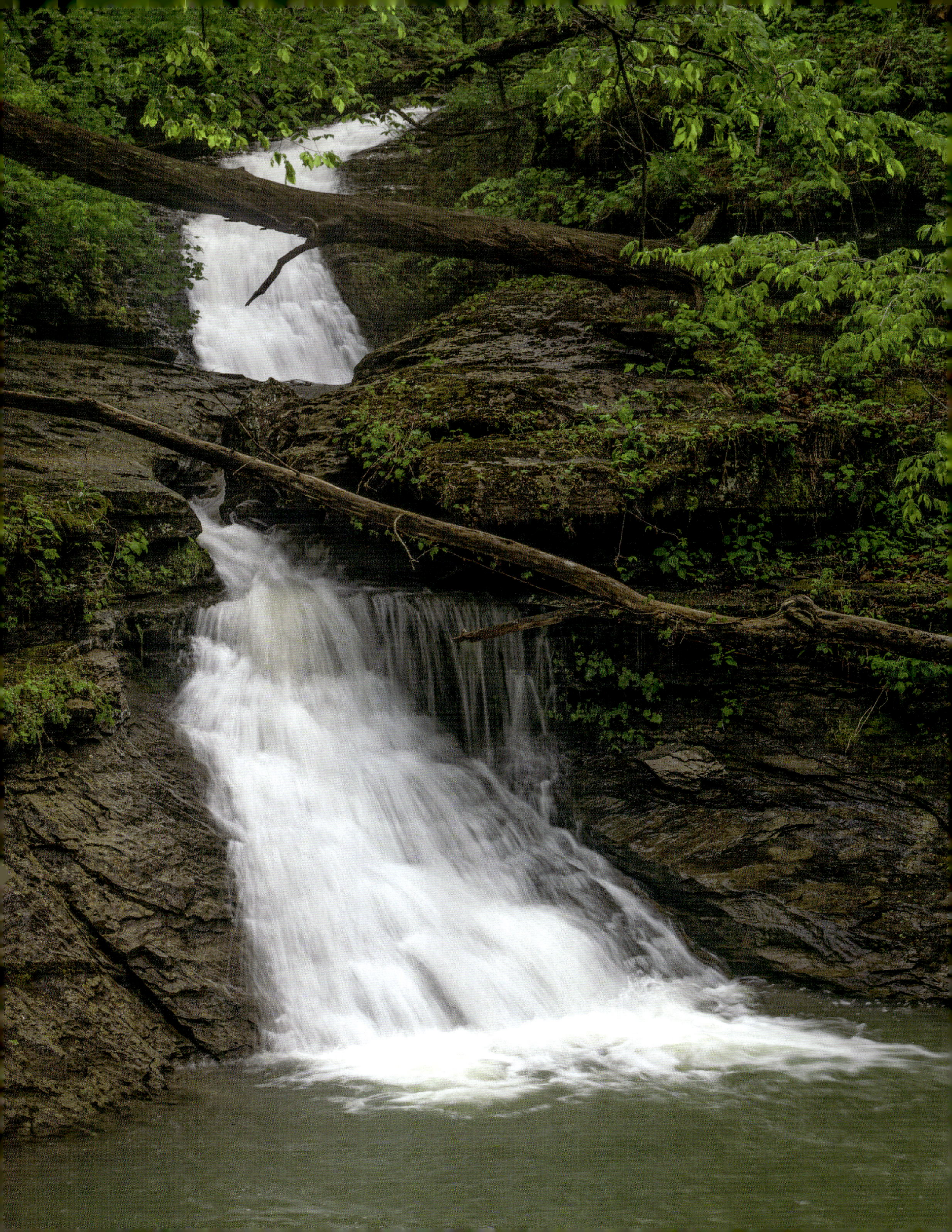

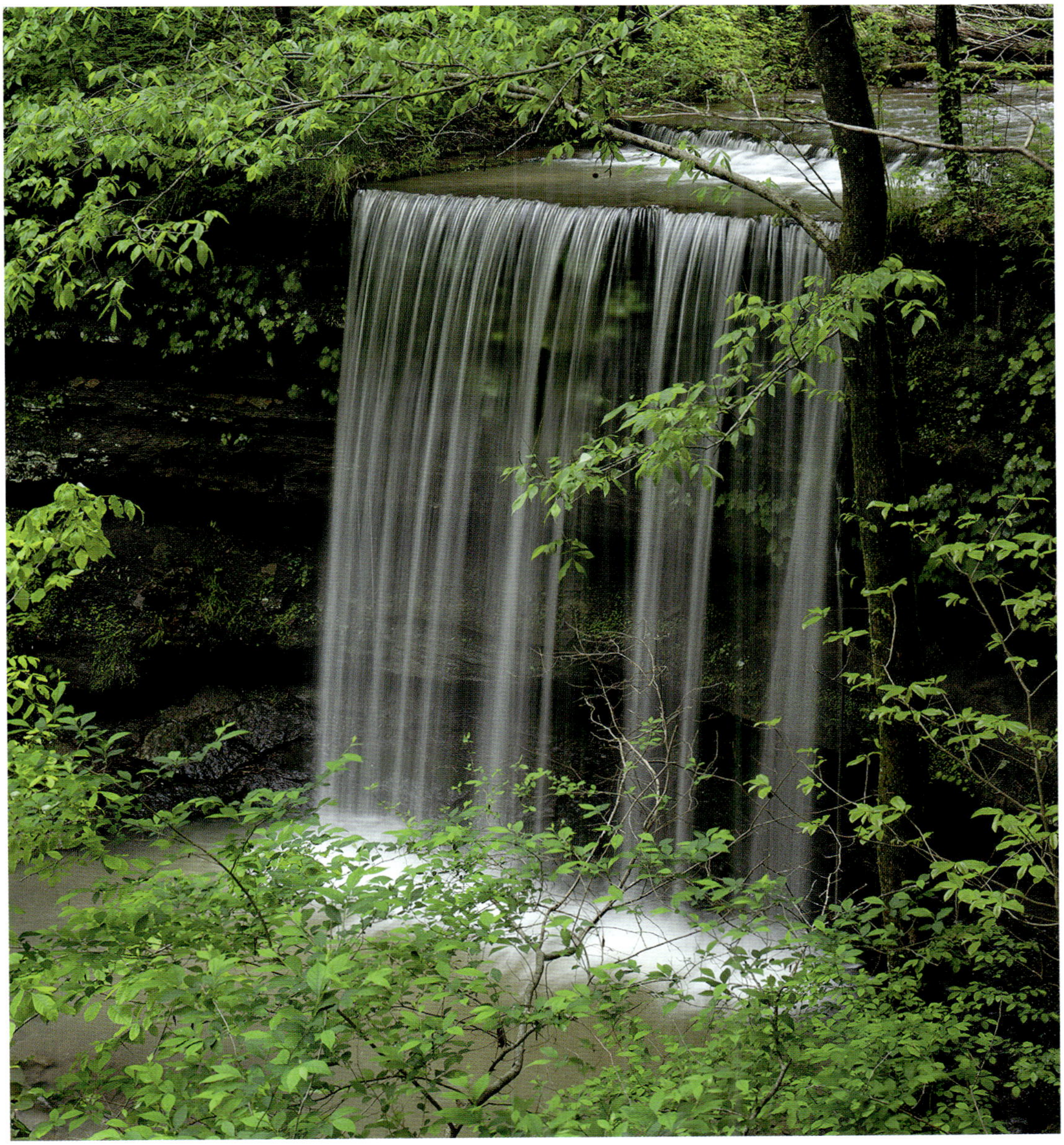

Lucky Falls, Horsehead Creek area near Batson, Ozark National Forest

Lucky is how you feel to be alive if you survive the STEEP trek UP from this waterfall back out to your car!

< Don Kitts Falls, Ozark National Forest

Don was an incredible artist and person who lived nearby at the Heartsong Retreat Center, an interfaith center that he founded in the 1970's. I especially enjoyed his egg tempera painting technique, a traditional method using egg yolk as a binder for pigments.

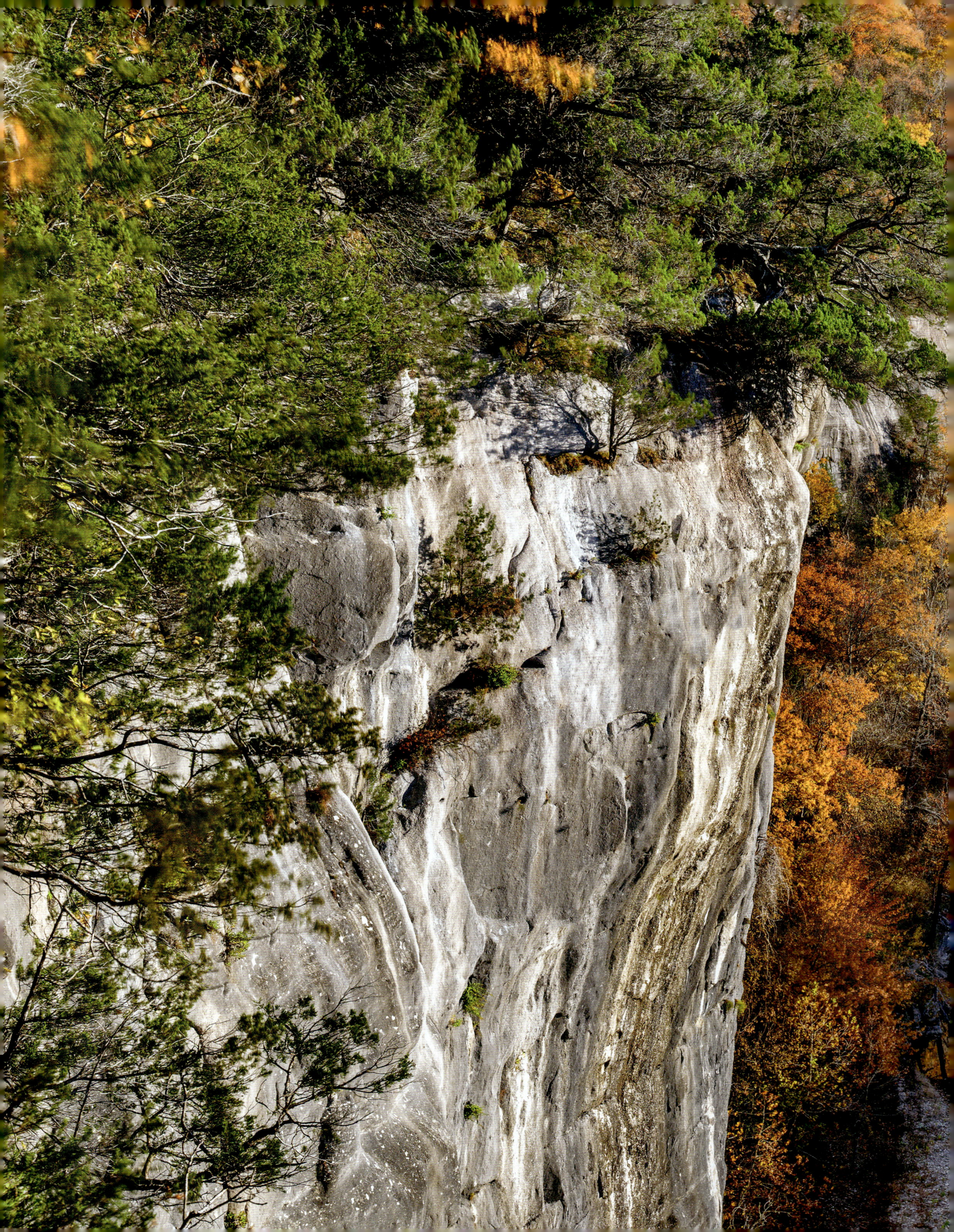

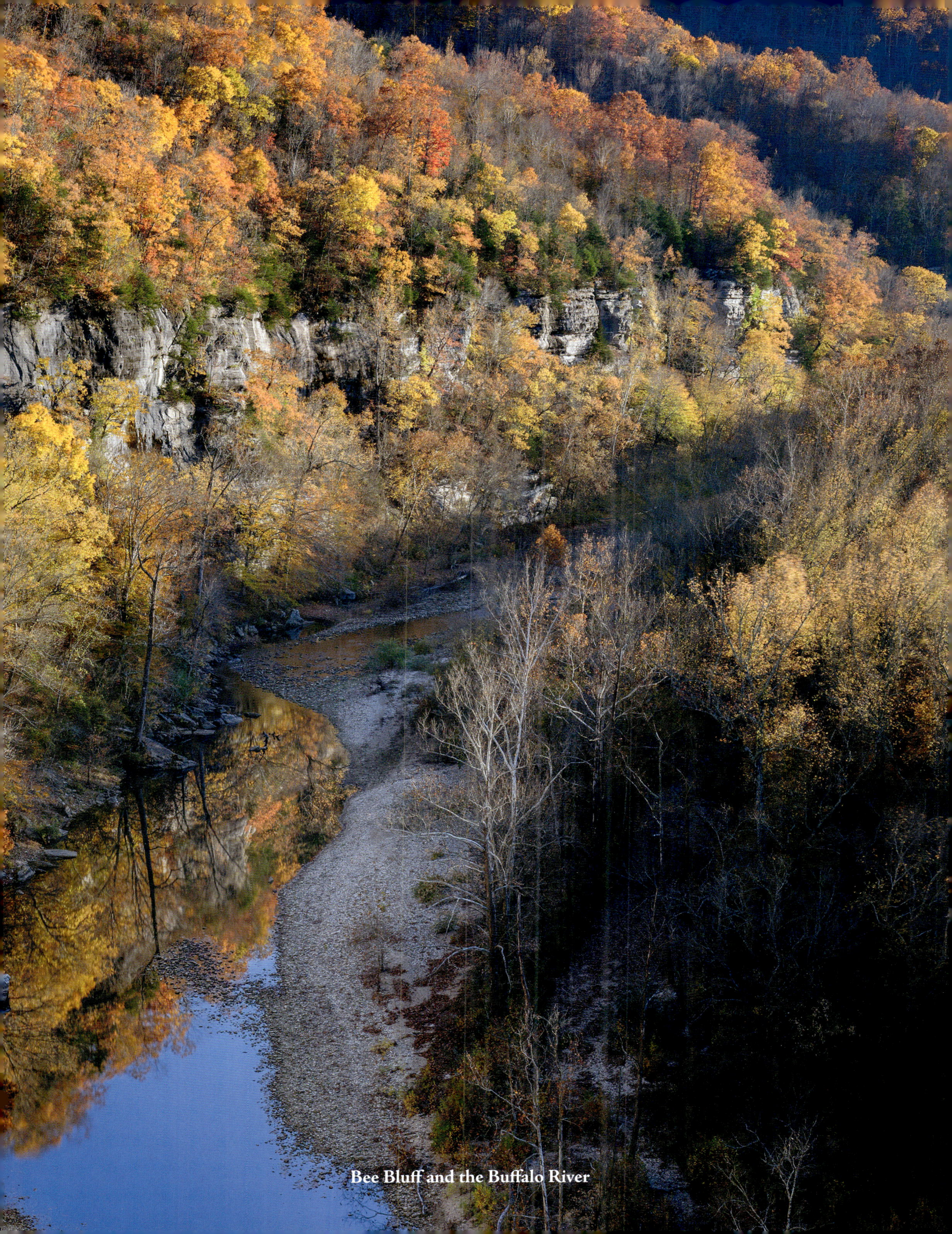

Bee Bluff and the Buffalo River

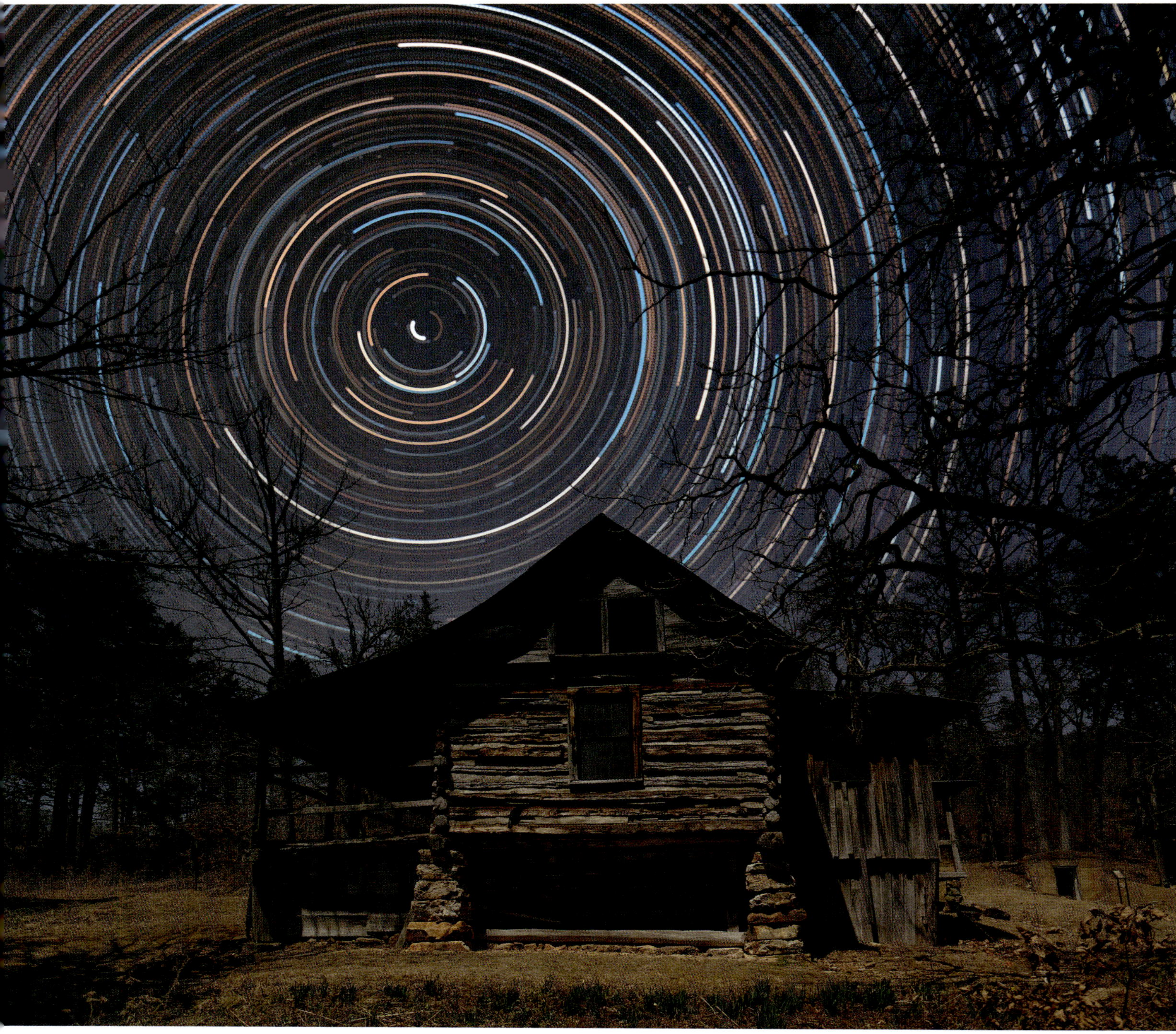

Beaver Jim Villines Cabin lit up with moonlight, and backed by an out-of-focus star circle
The stars were out of focus and this magnified not only the size of their "trails" but also their color.

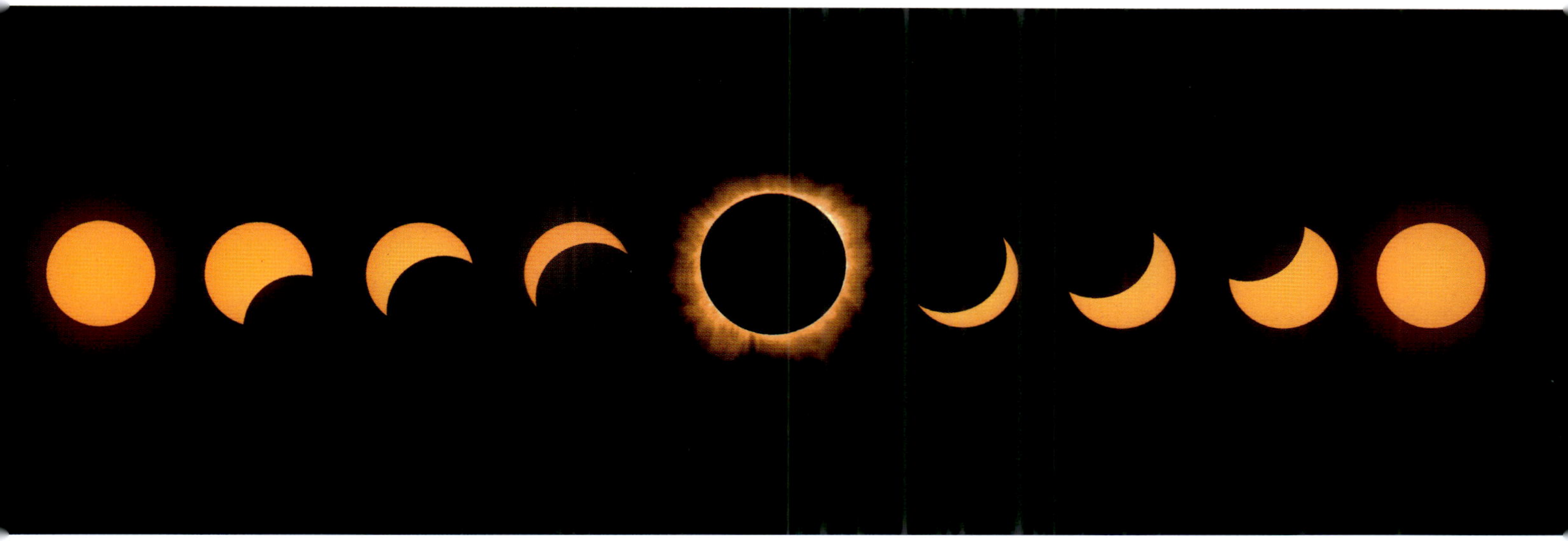

Another collection of eclipse phases from the Great American Solar Eclipse from our back yard in April, 2024.

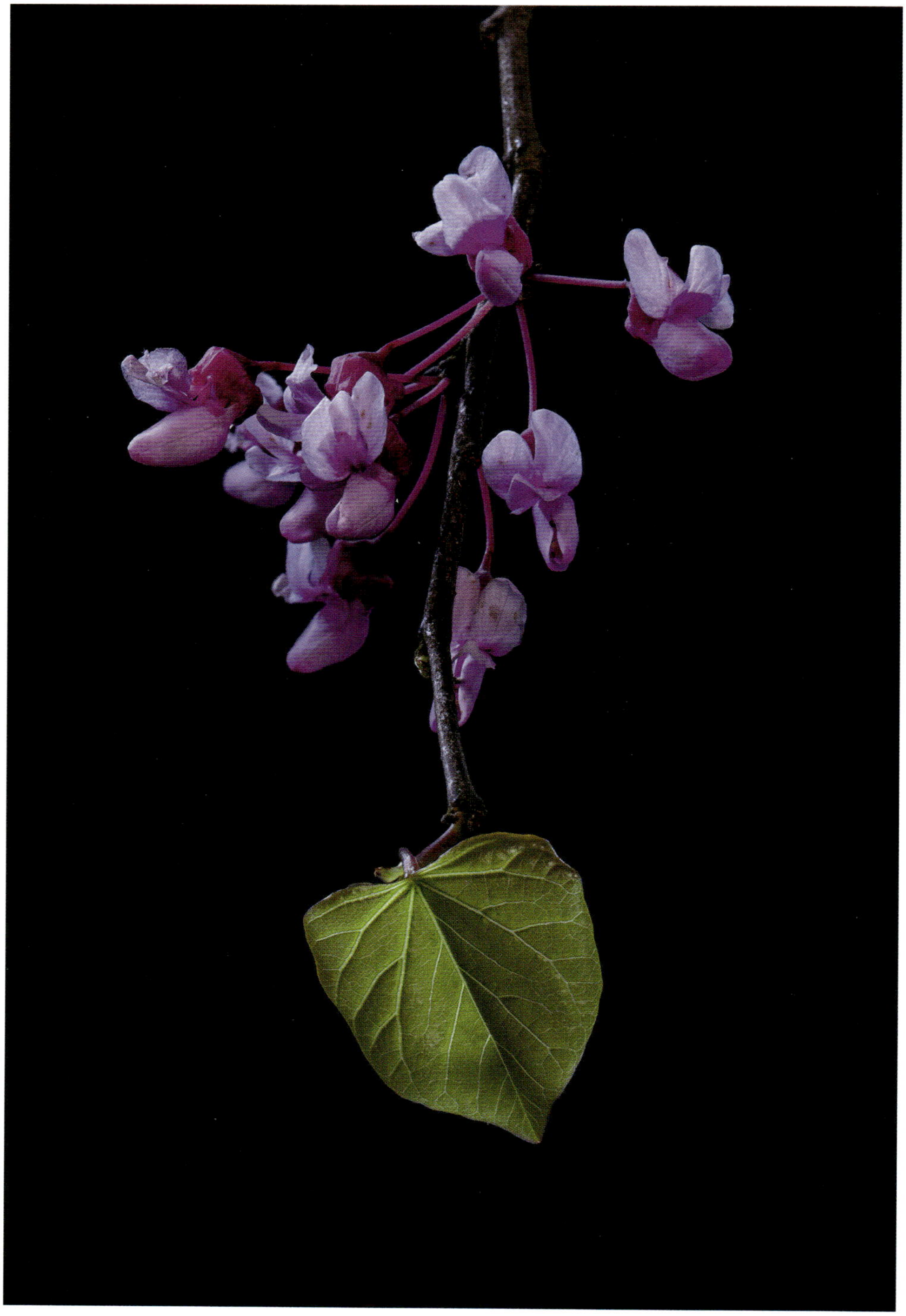

Redbud tree blossom against a dark shadow in the forest.

Trigger Falls, West Horsehead Creek area near Batson >

There are at least nine beautiful waterfalls in this particular drainage that were unnamed by the guy who first documented them, and somehow they all ended up getting named in my waterfall guidebook after famous horses, like Roy Rogers' Trigger.

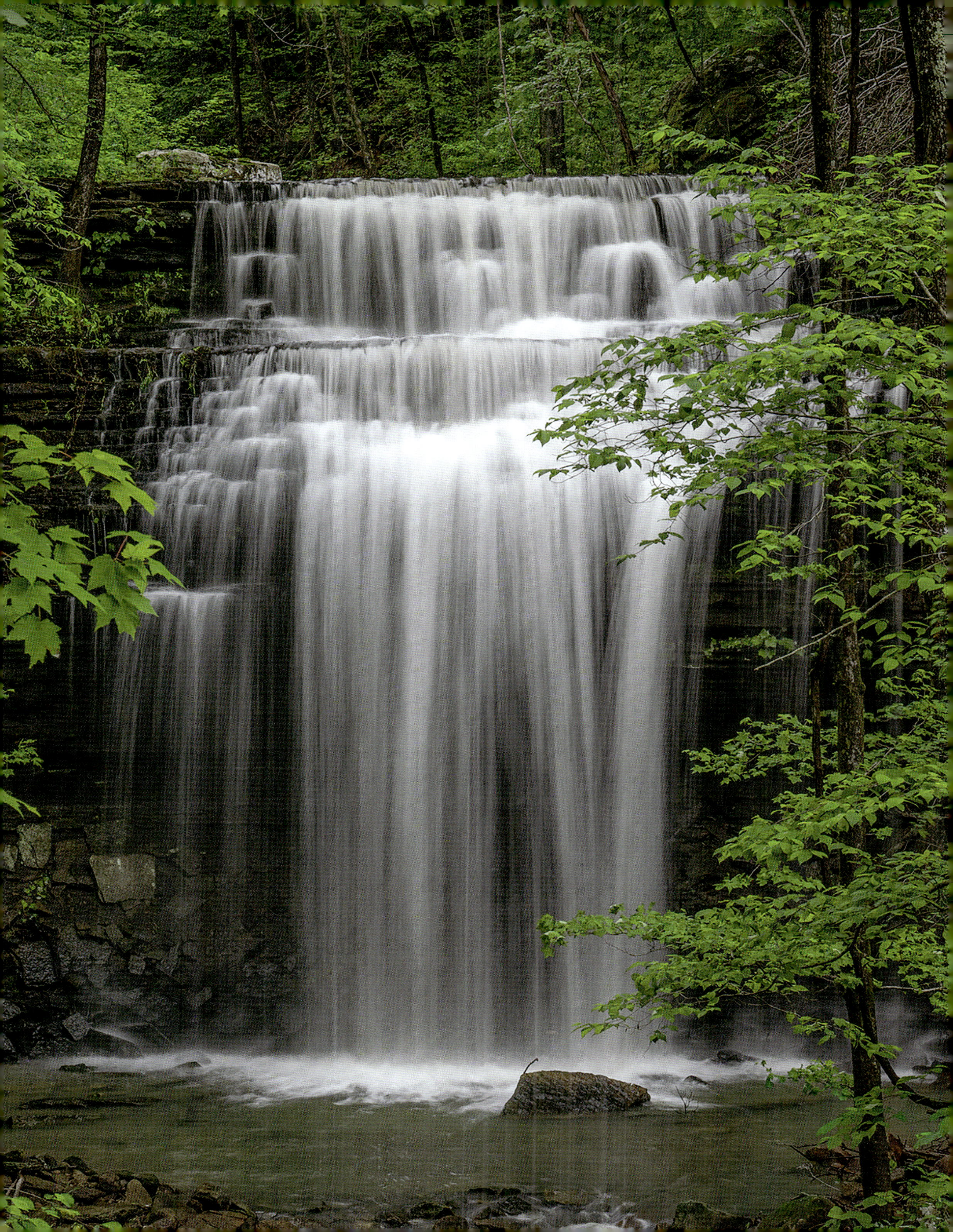

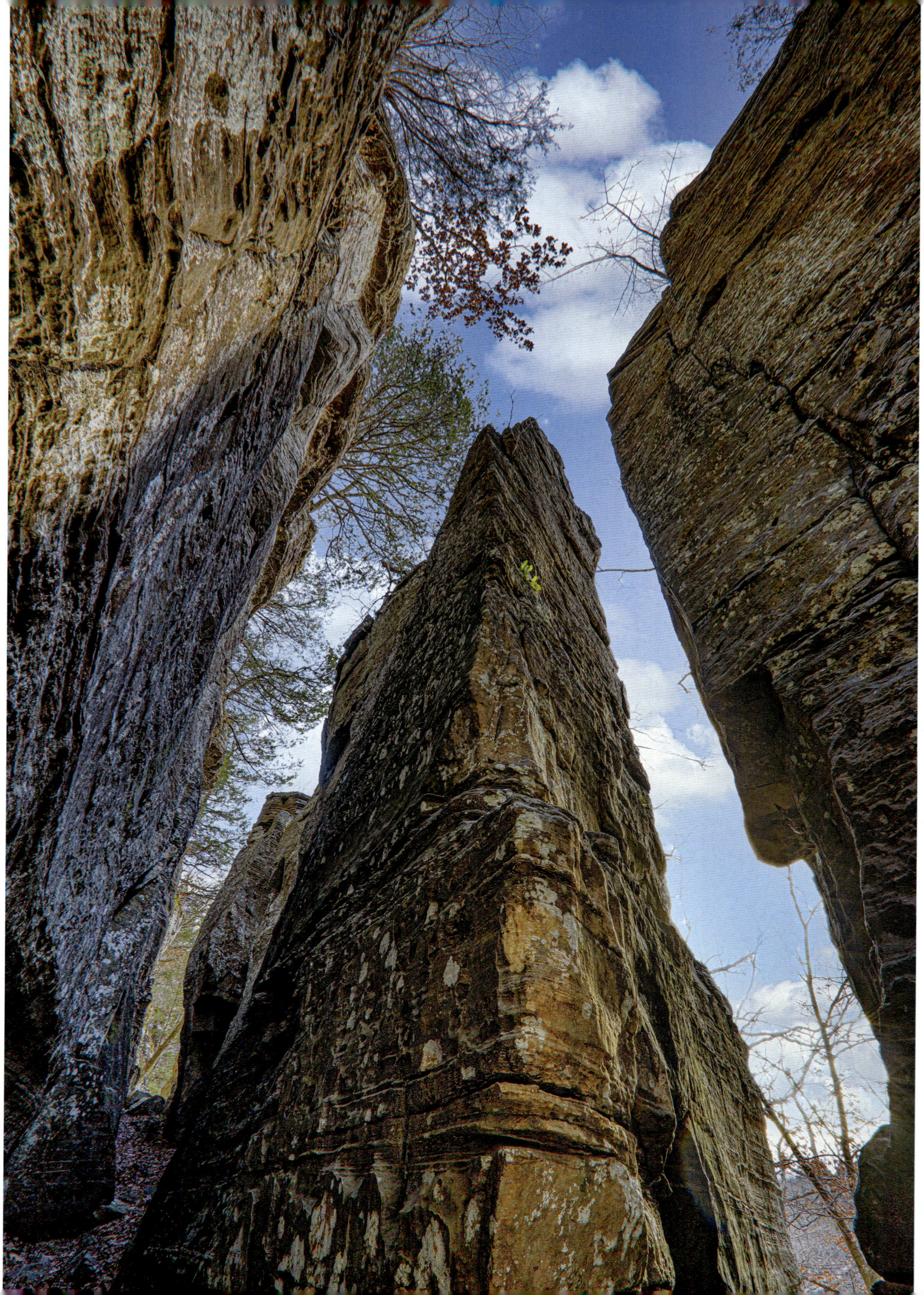

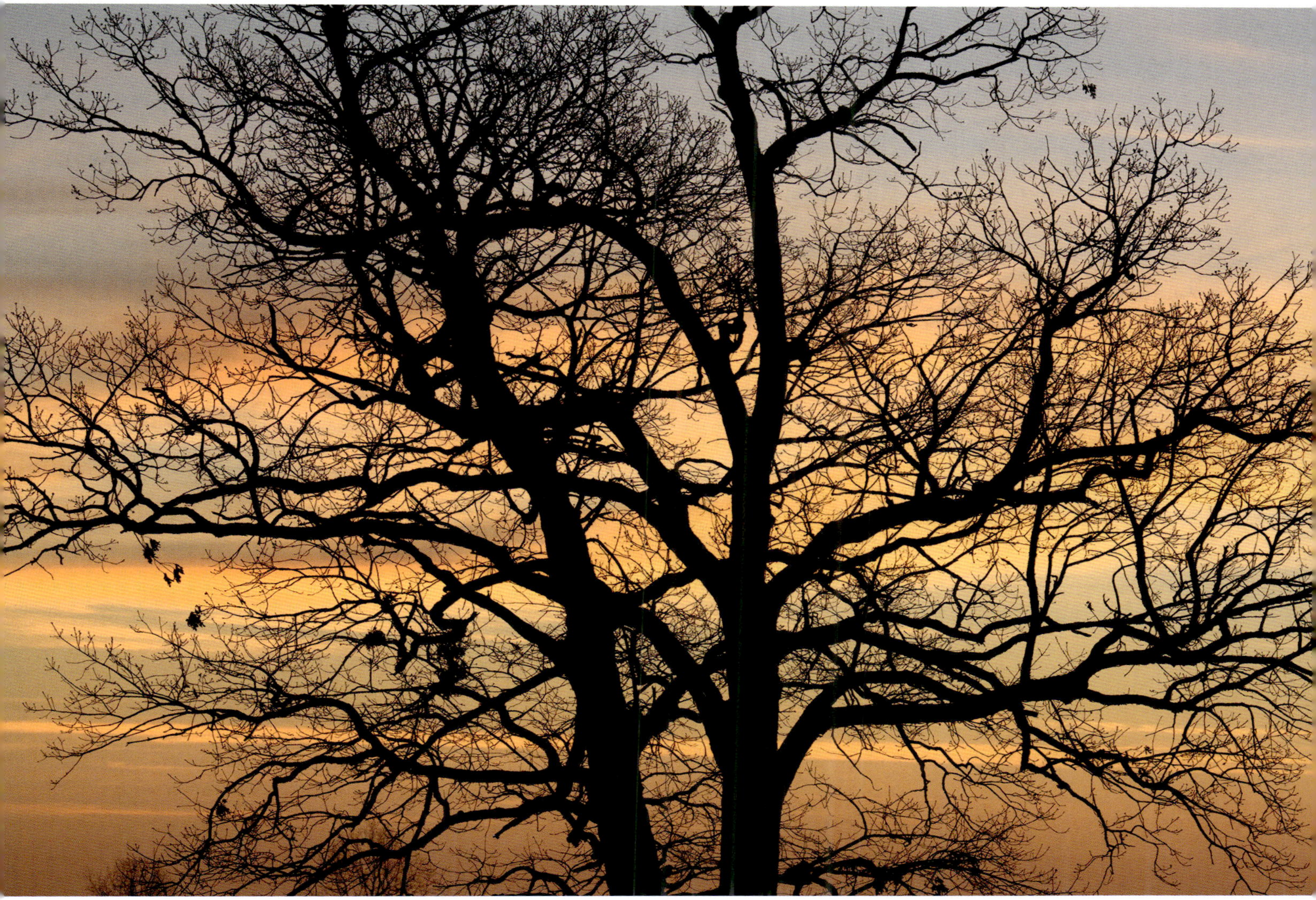

Oak tree at dawn, my favorite time of day to be up and about

< Bee Bluff Pillars, along the Buffalo River Trail near Steel Creek
You can see the top of these from the trail, but to *experience* them you need to visit the bottom.

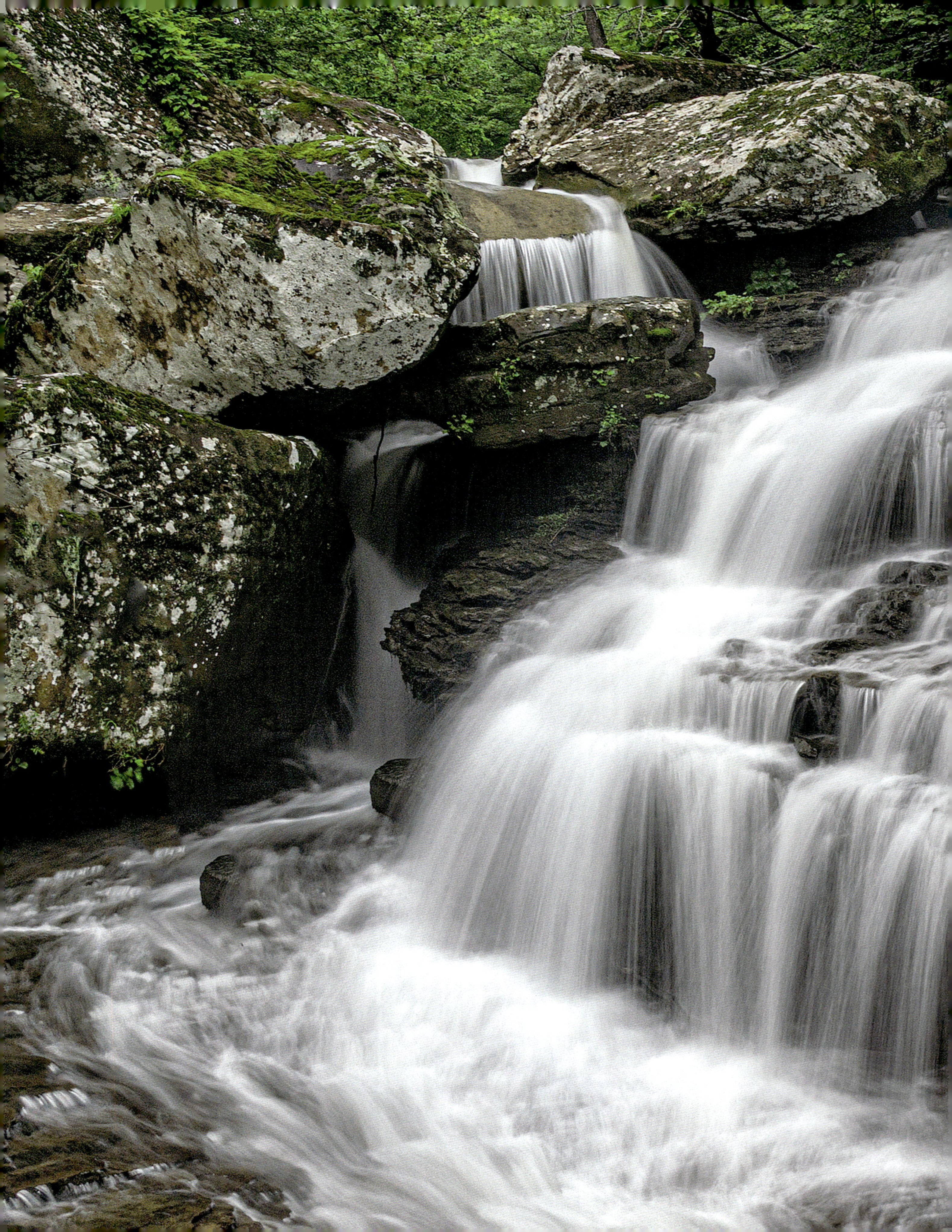

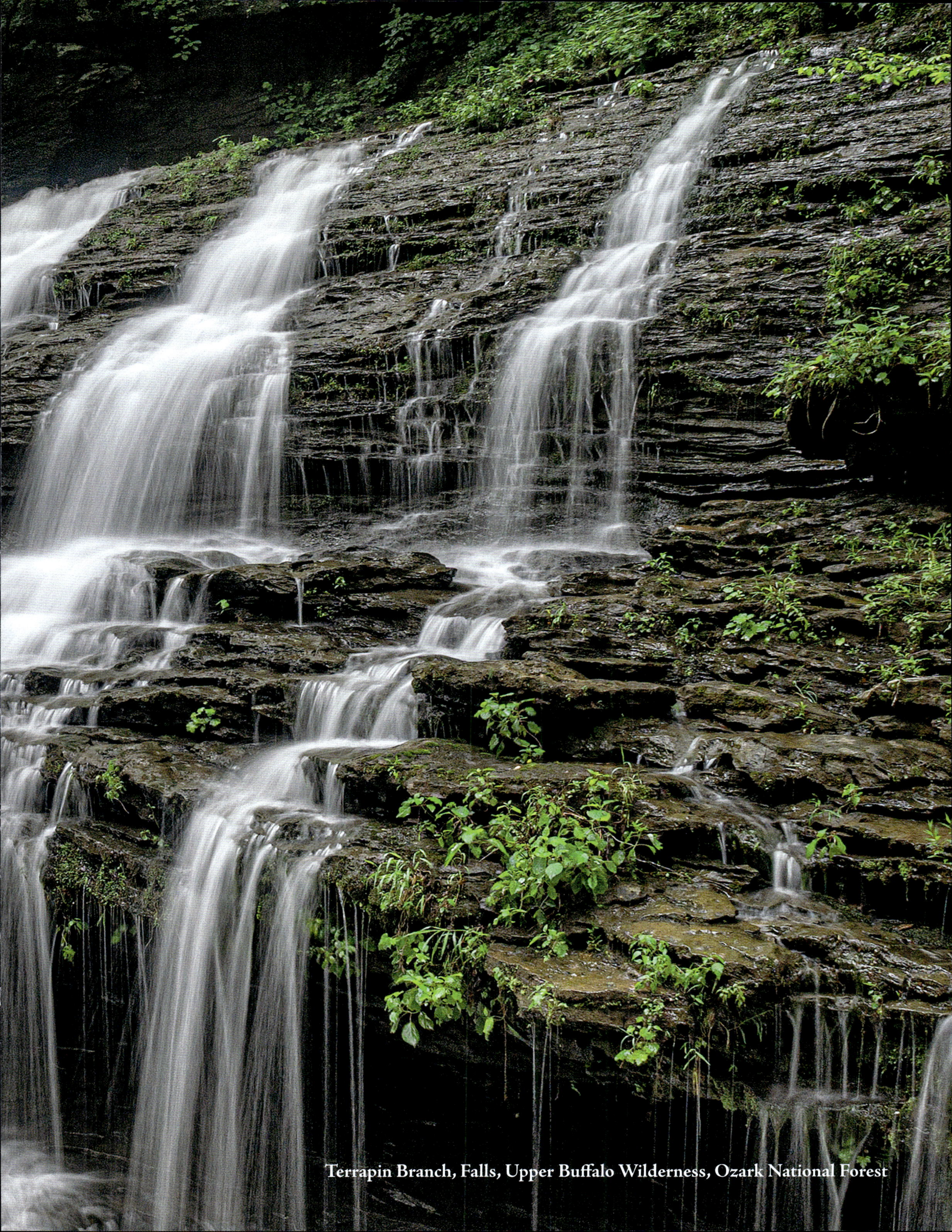

Terrapin Branch, Falls, Upper Buffalo Wilderness, Ozark National Forest

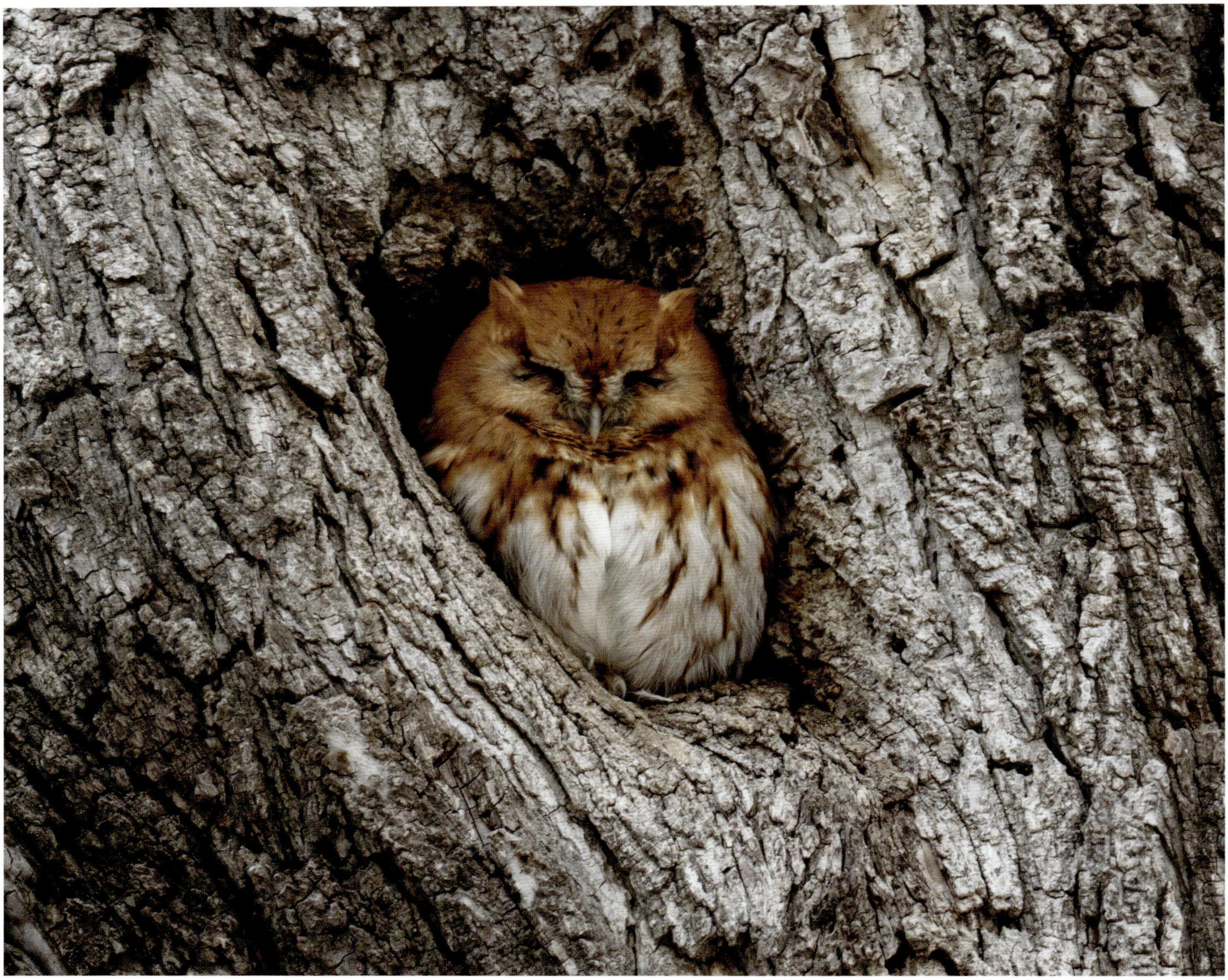

OK, are you getting tired yet with so many photos? OOPS, you are only half way through this book!
This tiny screech owl perched in her spot for months overlooking the Fox & Fern Outdoor Cafe in Jasper.

A bending, twisting oak salutes the full moon >

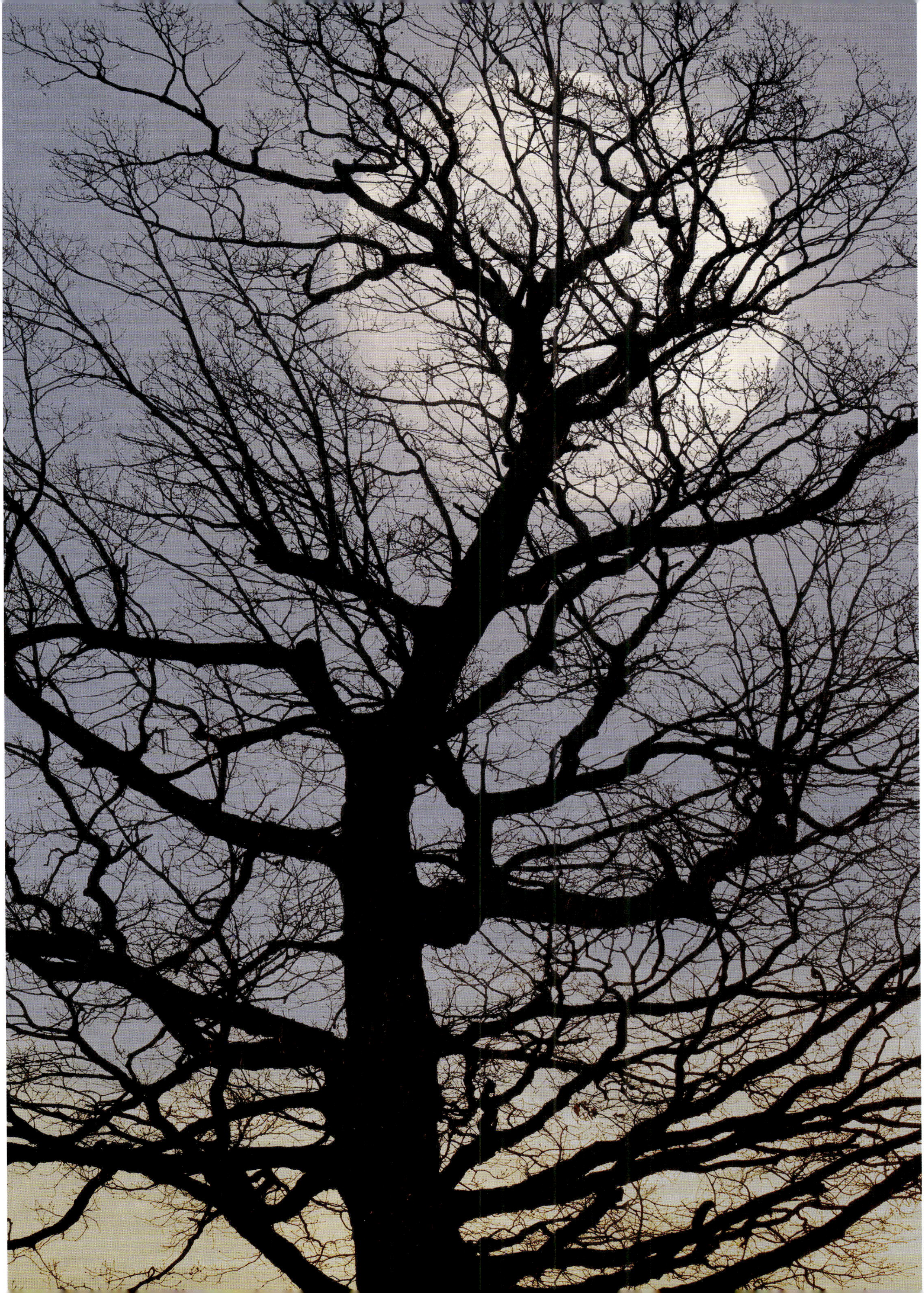

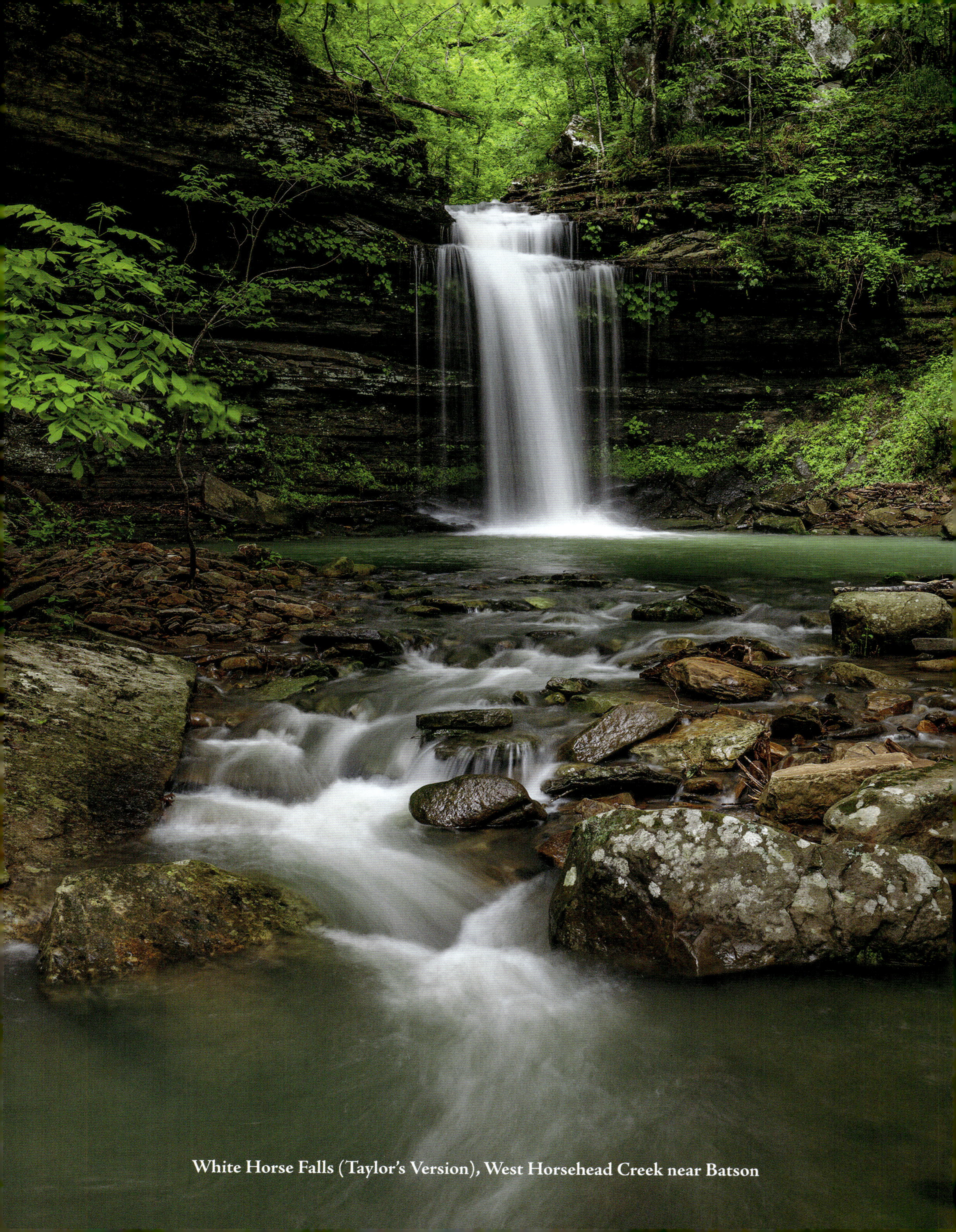

White Horse Falls (Taylor's Version), West Horsehead Creek near Batson

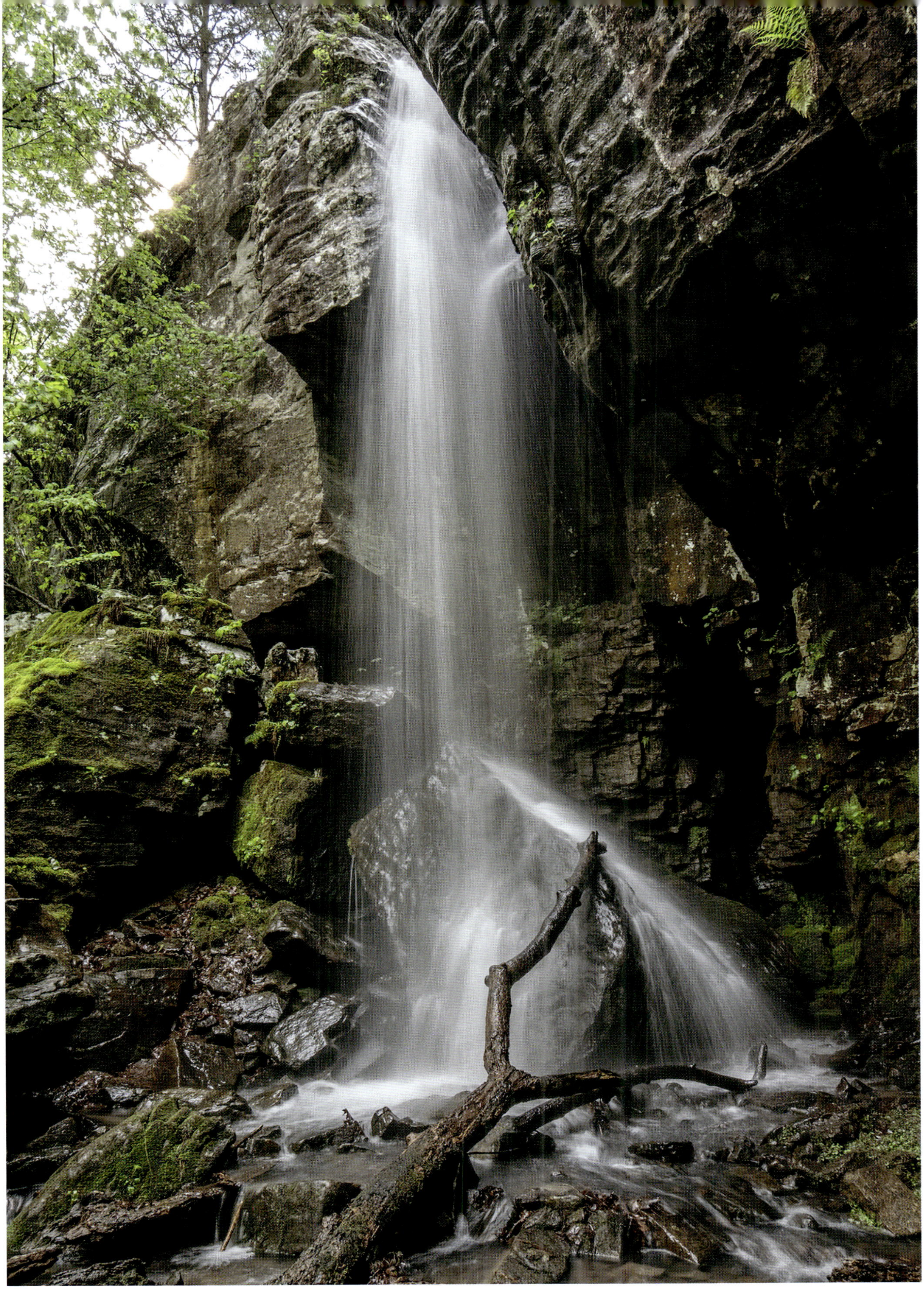

Bear Stair Falls, Bearcat Hollow, Ozark National Forest

IF you happen to encounter a bear here it is possible to climb this rock staircase next to the falls.

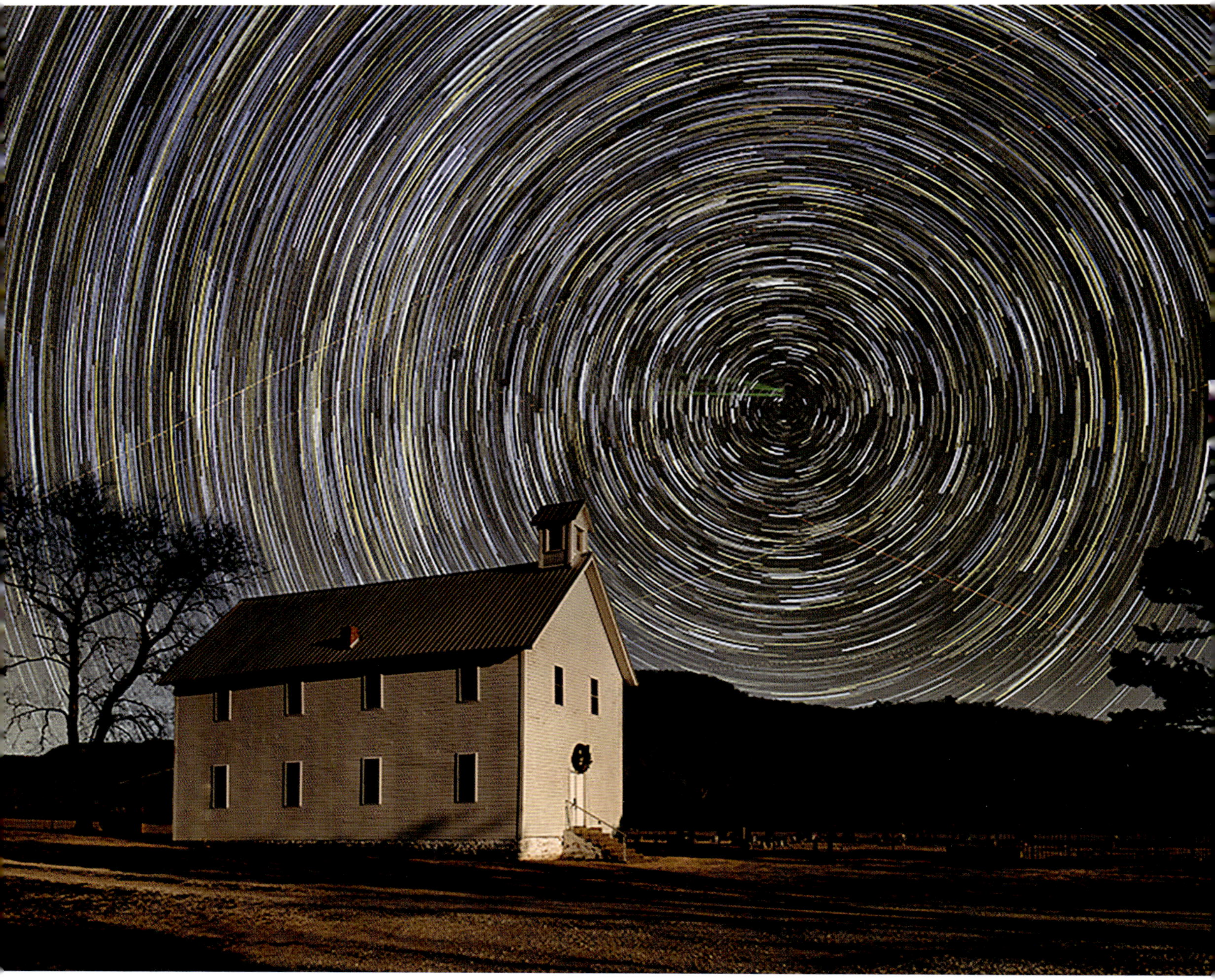

< Boxley Valley Baptist Church and Community Center

There are two parts to this scene. First, it was actually dark when I started taking this photo, and the church was then lit up by a rising moon that was back over my shoulder to the right. Sometimes you just gotta do your homework and figure out these sorts of things, and this time it just happened to work out perfect!

Secondly, I kept the camera running taking a series of one-minute-long exposures for a couple of hours after moonrise to capture the movement of the stars and their "light trails" (caused by the movement of the earth). You may notice that a jet or two, and perhaps the space station, flew through the frame. (also a couple of weird green streaks near the middle that I never did figure out)

I guess there are actually three parts to this. So third, later my computer software combined all the photos into a single exposure, which linked all of the individual star trails into a continuous "trail" or "circle" in the sky. This only works if you point your camera towards the North Star, which is in the middle of the "circle" of stars here. This is the same technique you see used with a couple of other "star trail" photos in the book. I'm a sucker for a good star trail!

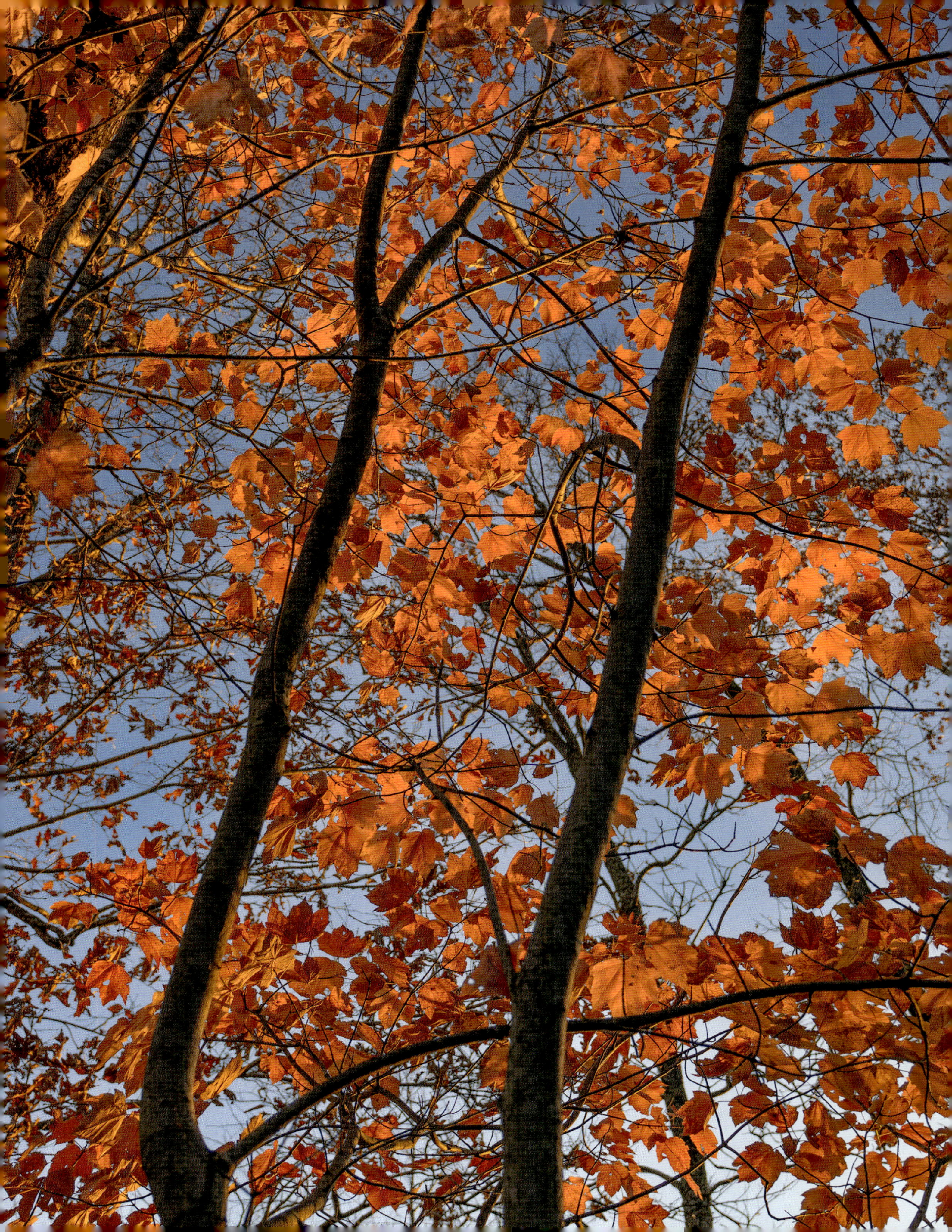

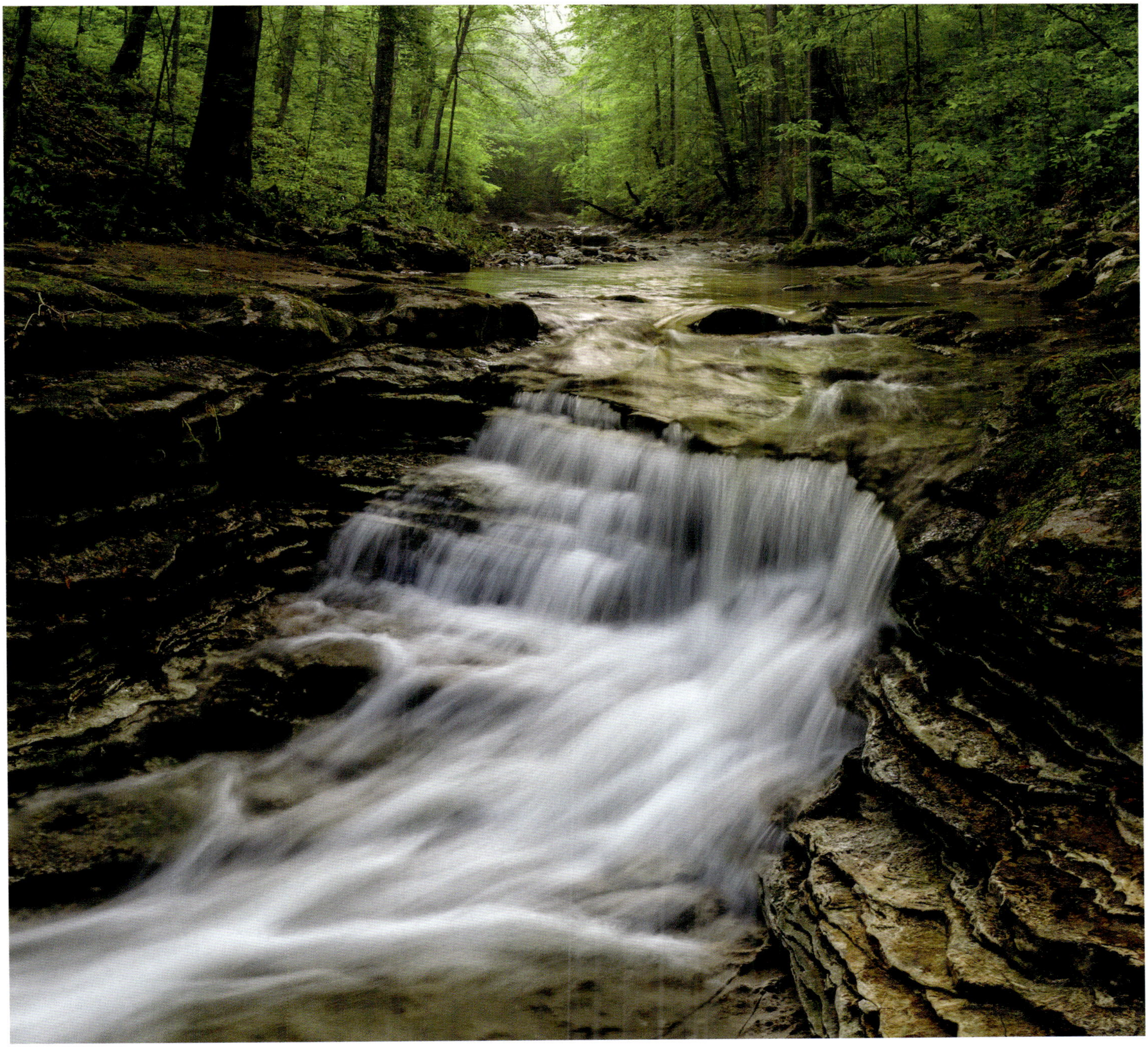

Top Of The Slots Falls on Leatherwood Creek near Ponca

There are a couple of signature waterfalls in this drainage (like Balanced Rock), but there are also several really nice cascades and water slides like this one.

< Maple tree showing off its October color

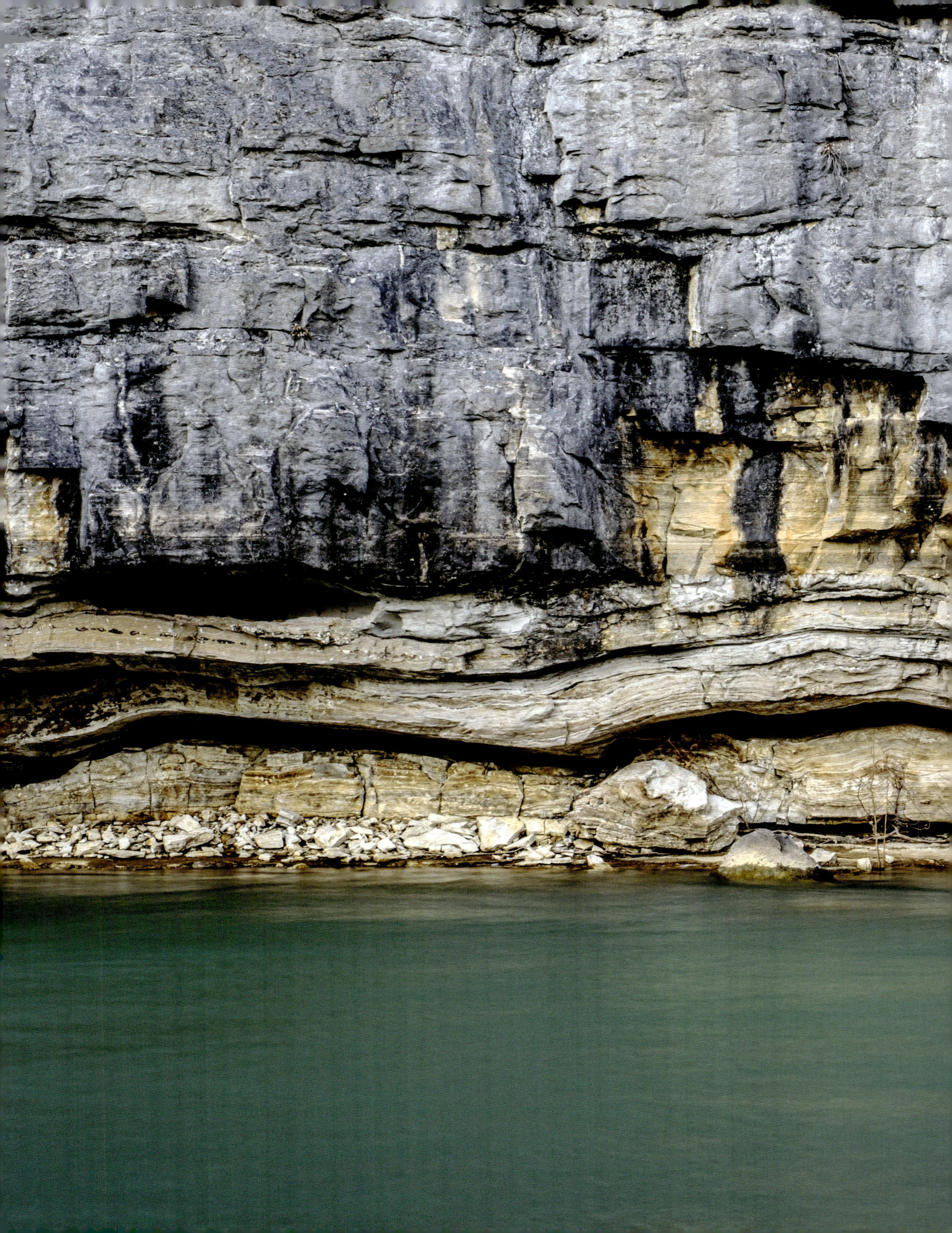

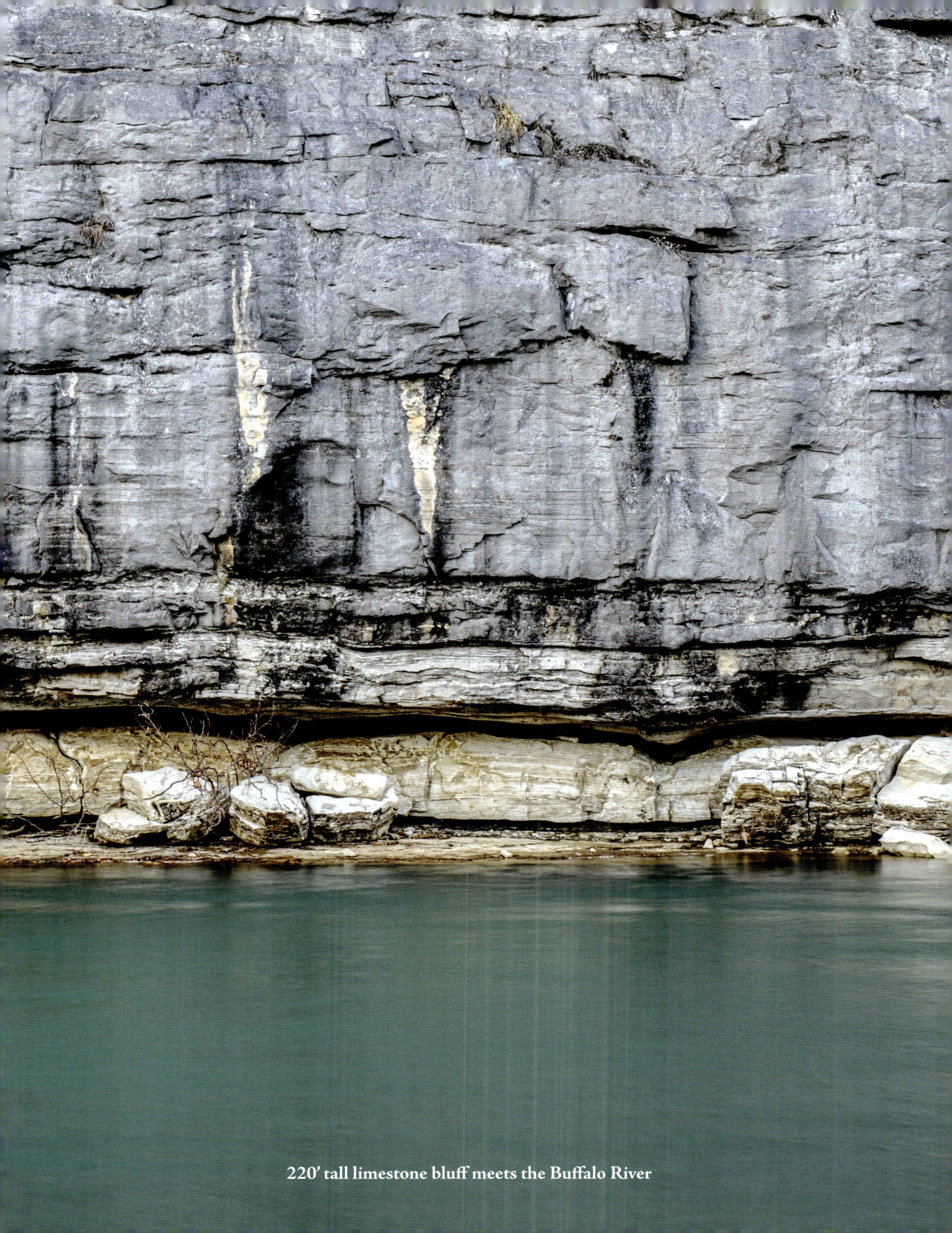

220' tall limestone bluff meets the Buffalo River

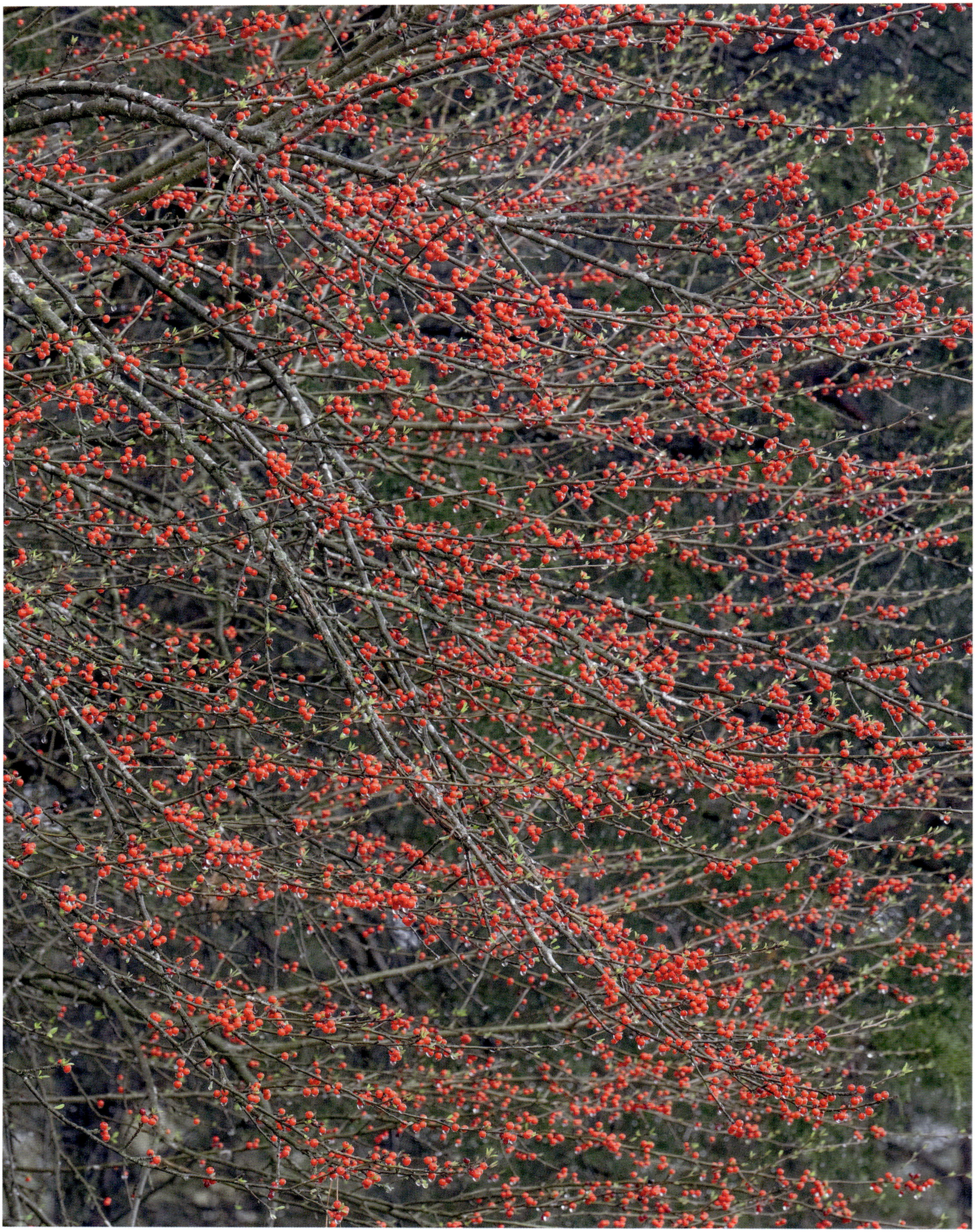

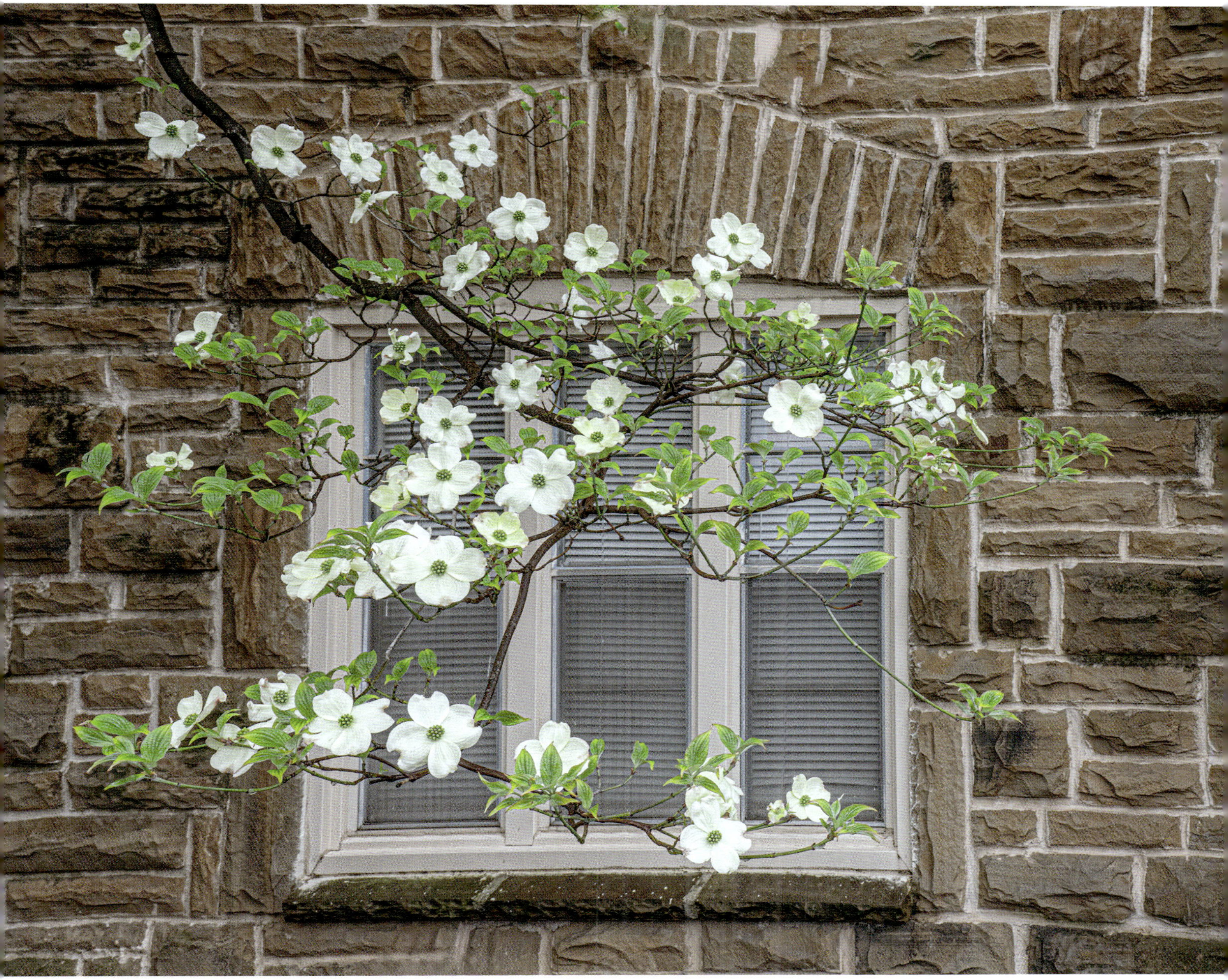

Dogwood: fall berries and spring blooms

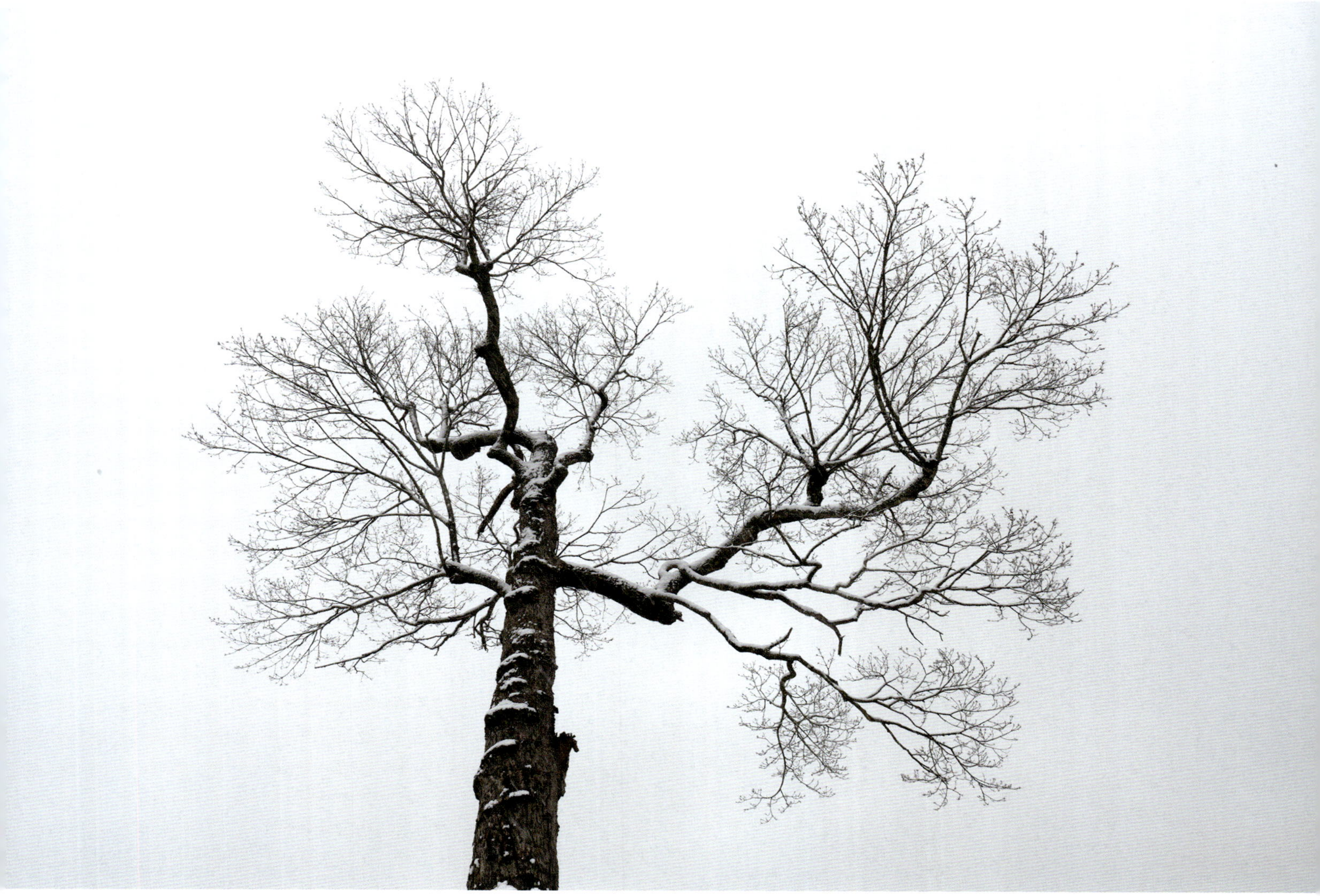

This is the same oak tree as the Blood Moon on page 40—it has so many different personalities!

Flat Rock Falls on Mt. Magazine, Ozark National Forest >

When I first set my tripod up at this waterfall I was overjoyed at the entire scene surrounding it. I took pictures for more than 30 minutes, moving around and changing lenses, zooming in, zooming out, each new composition was like a brand new scene. It was a kid-in-a-candy-store experience. Later on when I was picking out a photo of this for my new ***Arkansas Waterfalls*** guidebook (also for the new ***Arkansas:*** *JUST* ***Waterfalls*** picture book), I zoomed right on in past most of those photos and almost immediately picked this one to publish. The water looks so clean and pure.

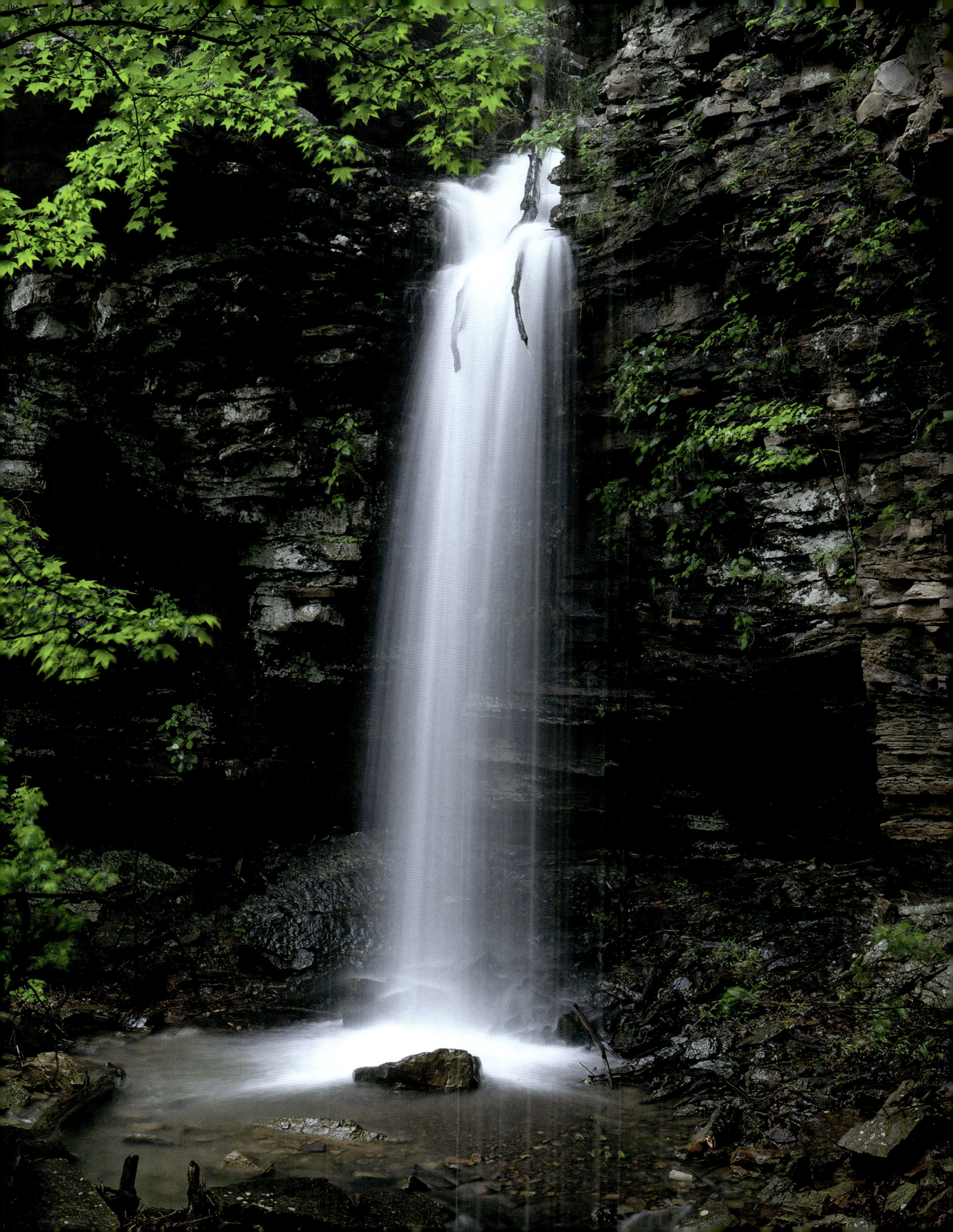

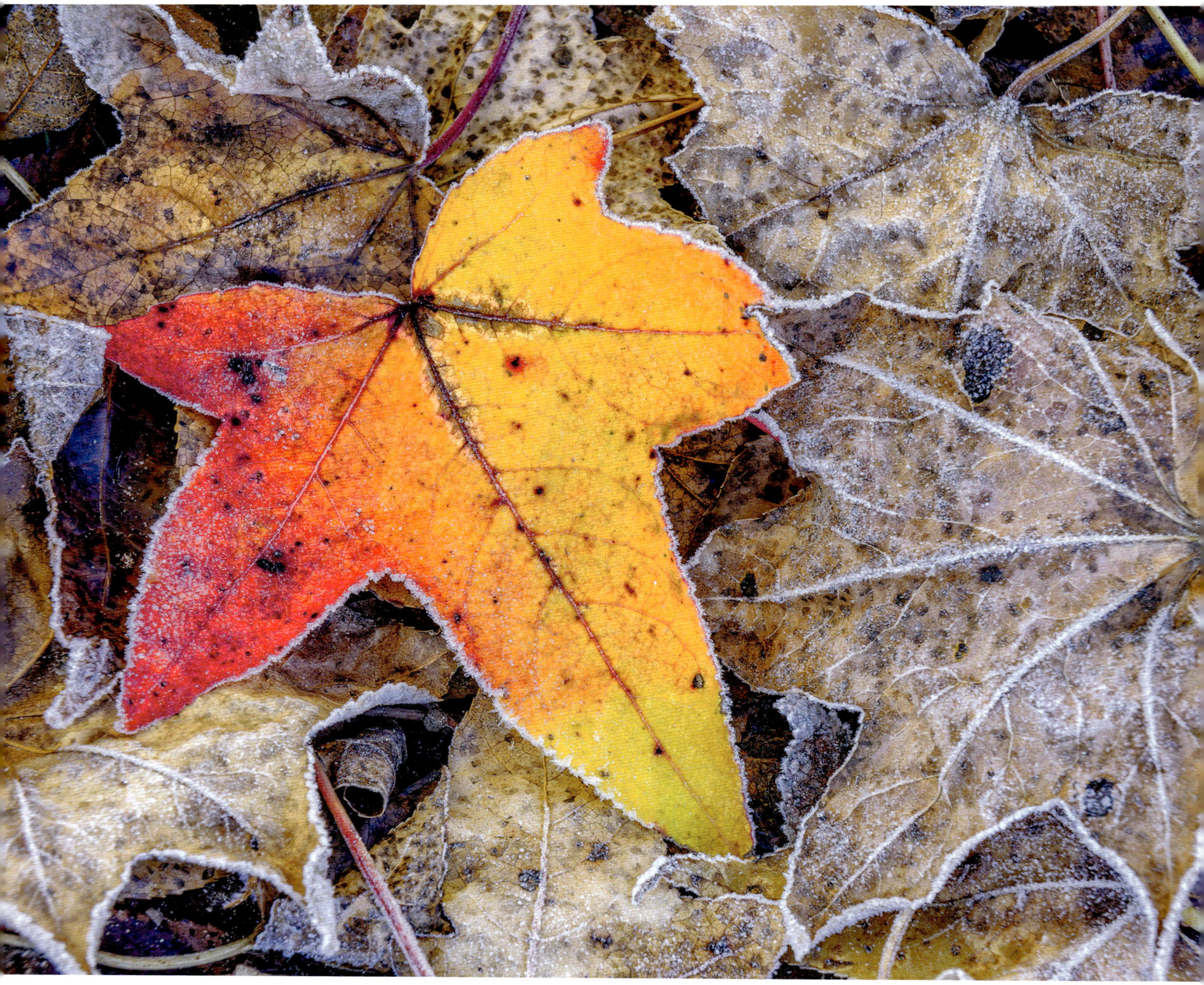

Crawling around on my belly after a heavy frost under a sweetgum tree

Sally Ann Mystic Falls, Ozark National Forest >

My first time to explore this unknown side drainage had me down on all fours, literally clawing my way up the very steep slope, through a jungle of briar bushes and other debris on a very foggy day. The Miley Cyrus song playing inside my head "The Climb" kept me energized and I felt triumphant when I finally reached the top. At one point I could see at least five different waterfalls from the same spot (there are three in this scene, including a 60'+ tall one in the upper part of this photo). I had originally named this group Five Falls View, but after my second trip there—also very foggy—I decided to name it Mystic Falls. It is indeed a *climb* to get to.

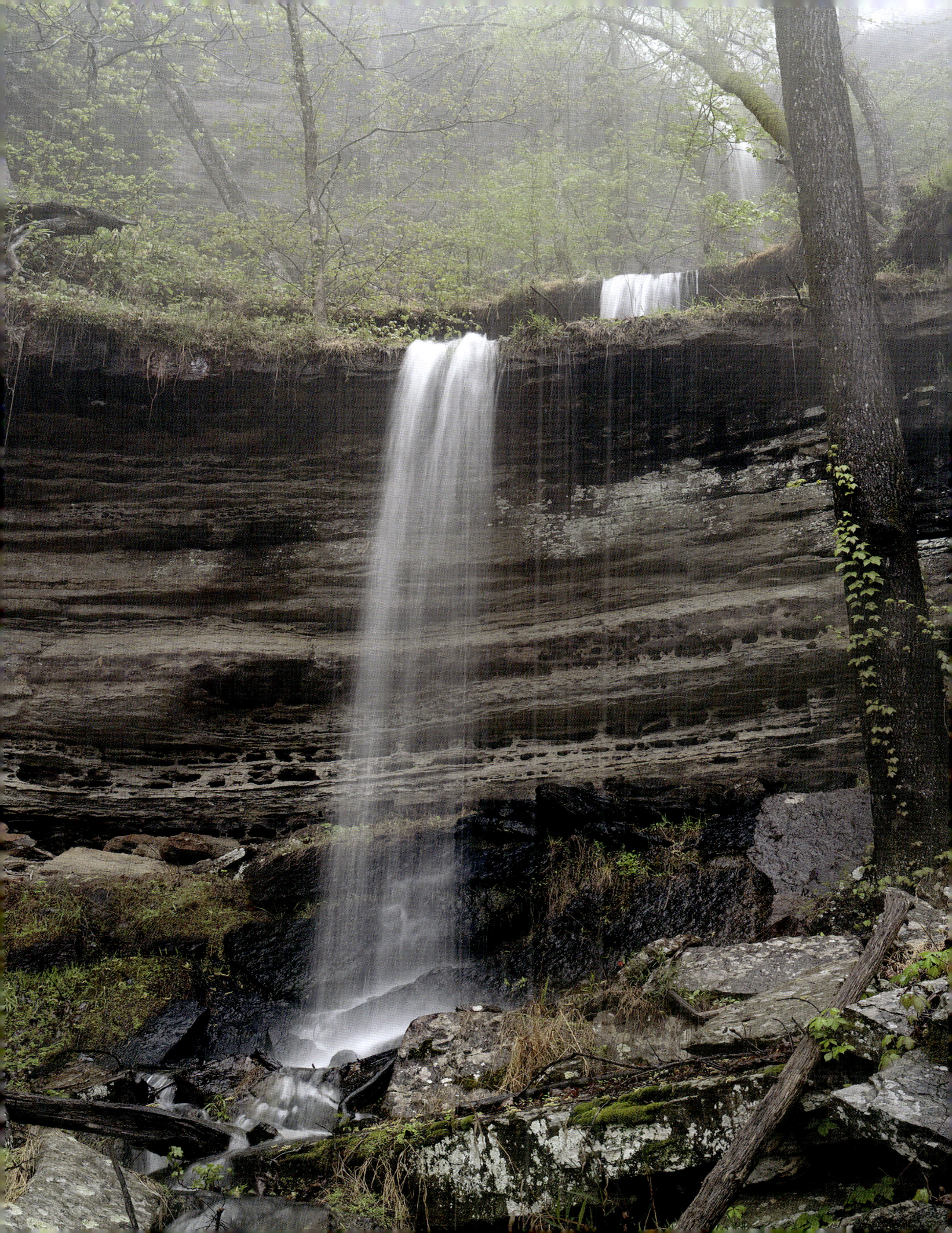

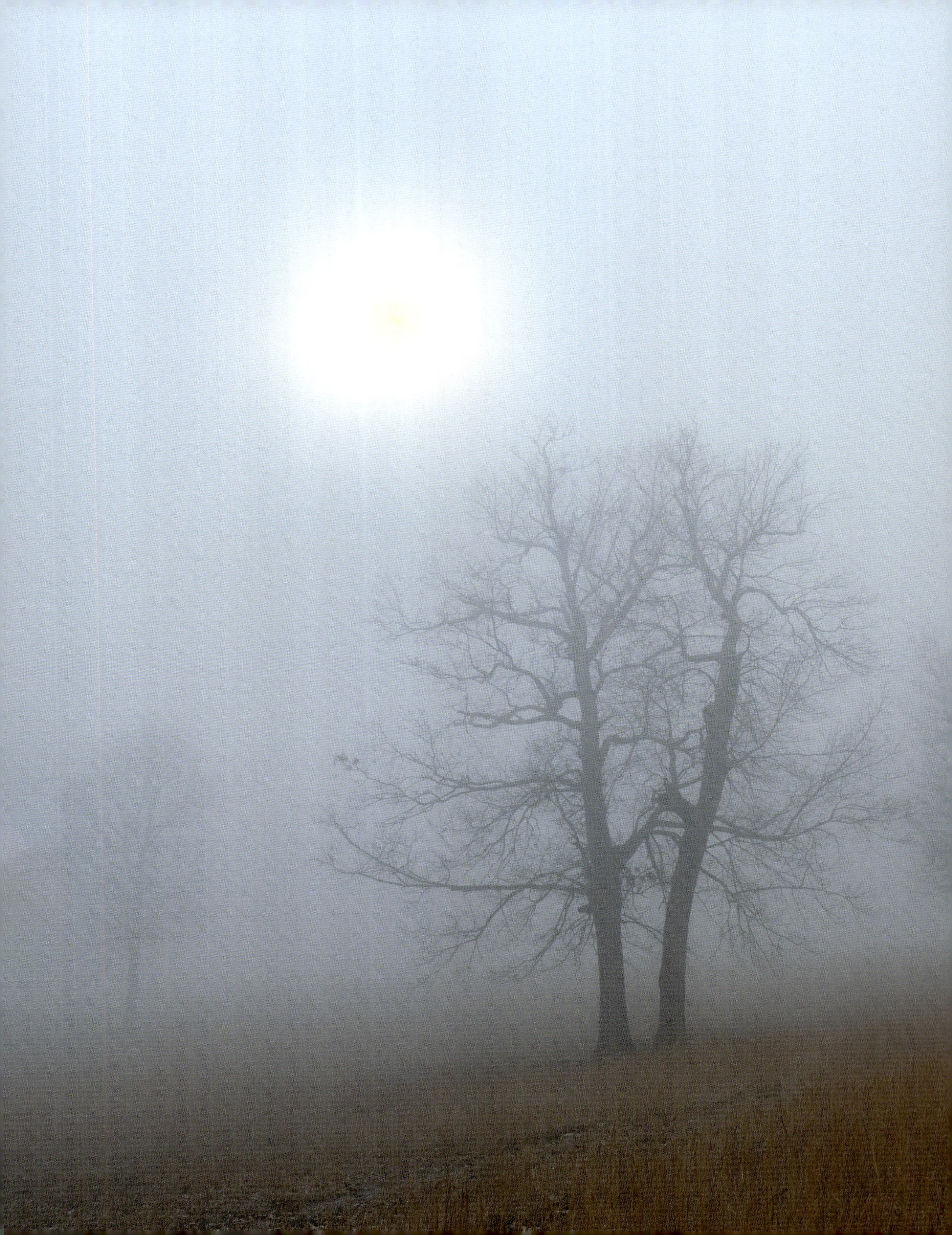

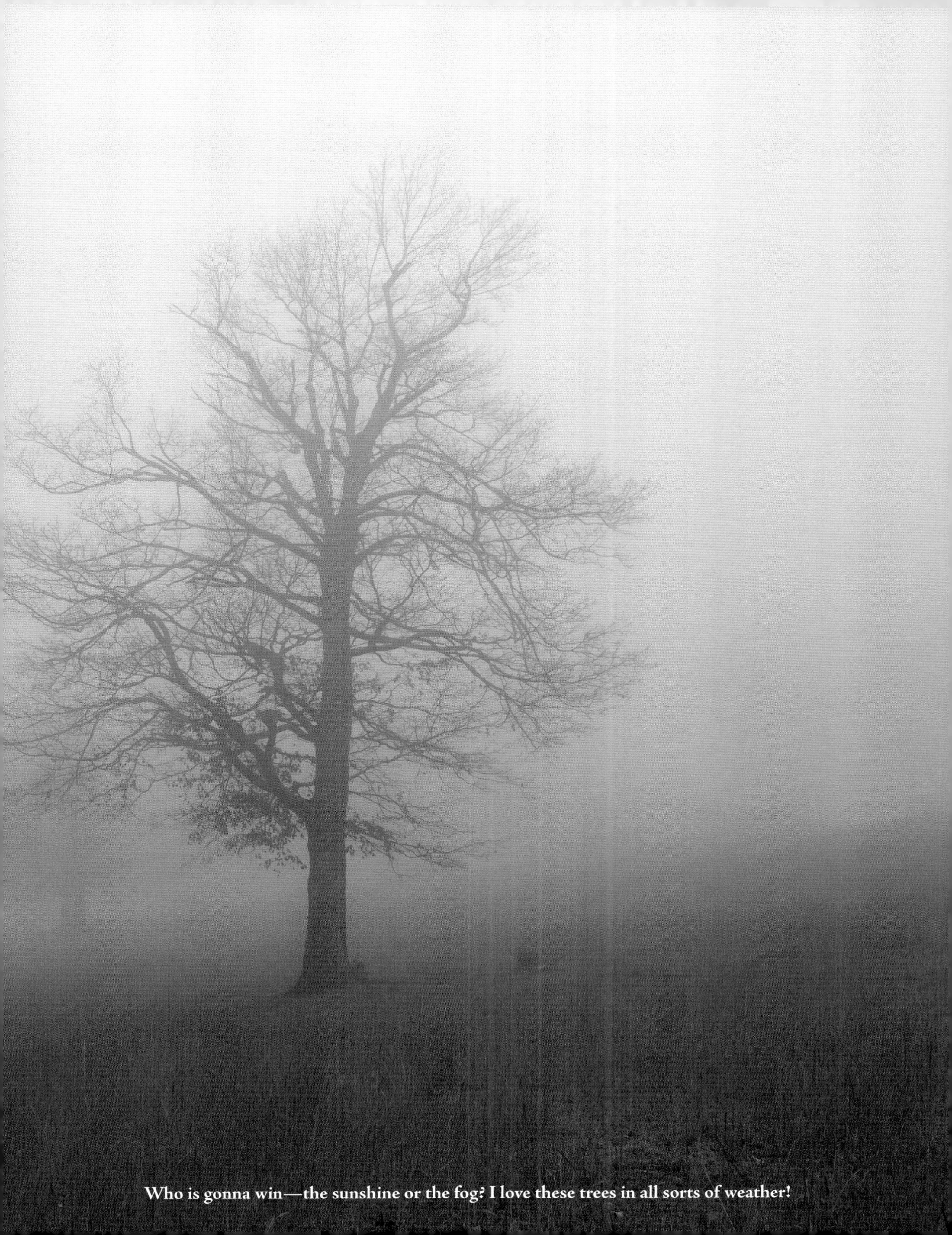

Who is gonna win—the sunshine or the fog? I love these trees in all sorts of weather!

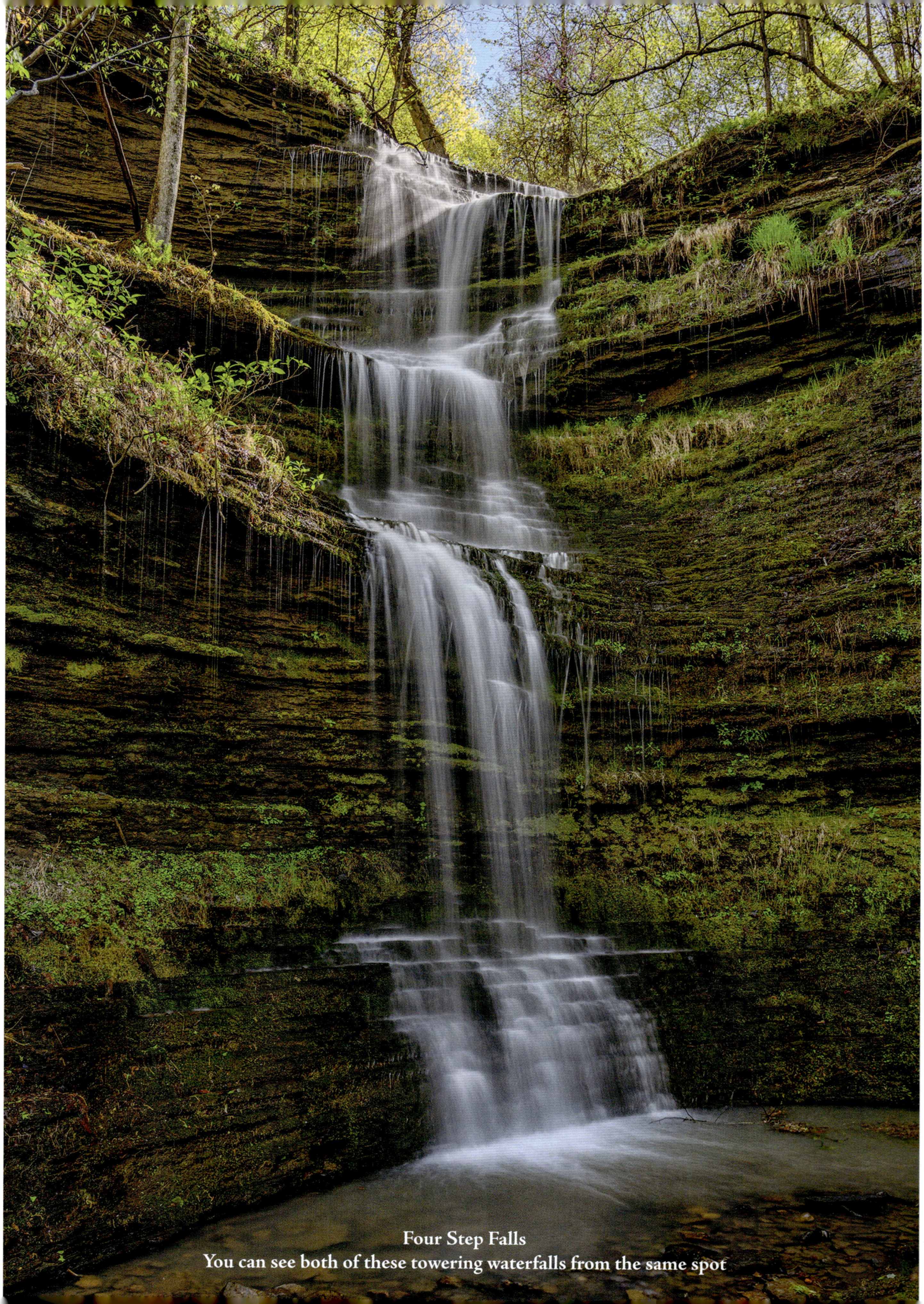

Four Step Falls
You can see both of these towering waterfalls from the same spot

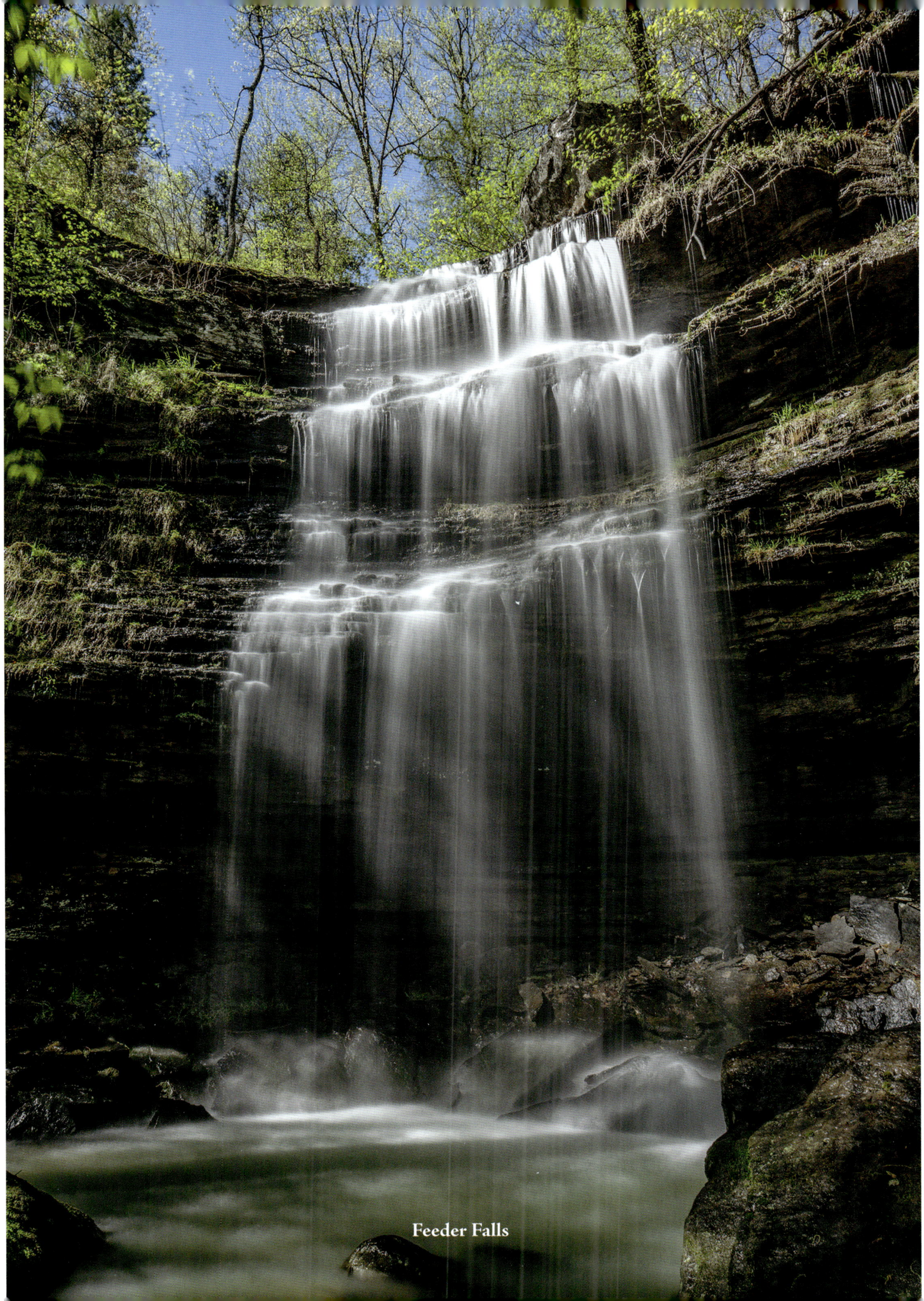

Feeder Falls

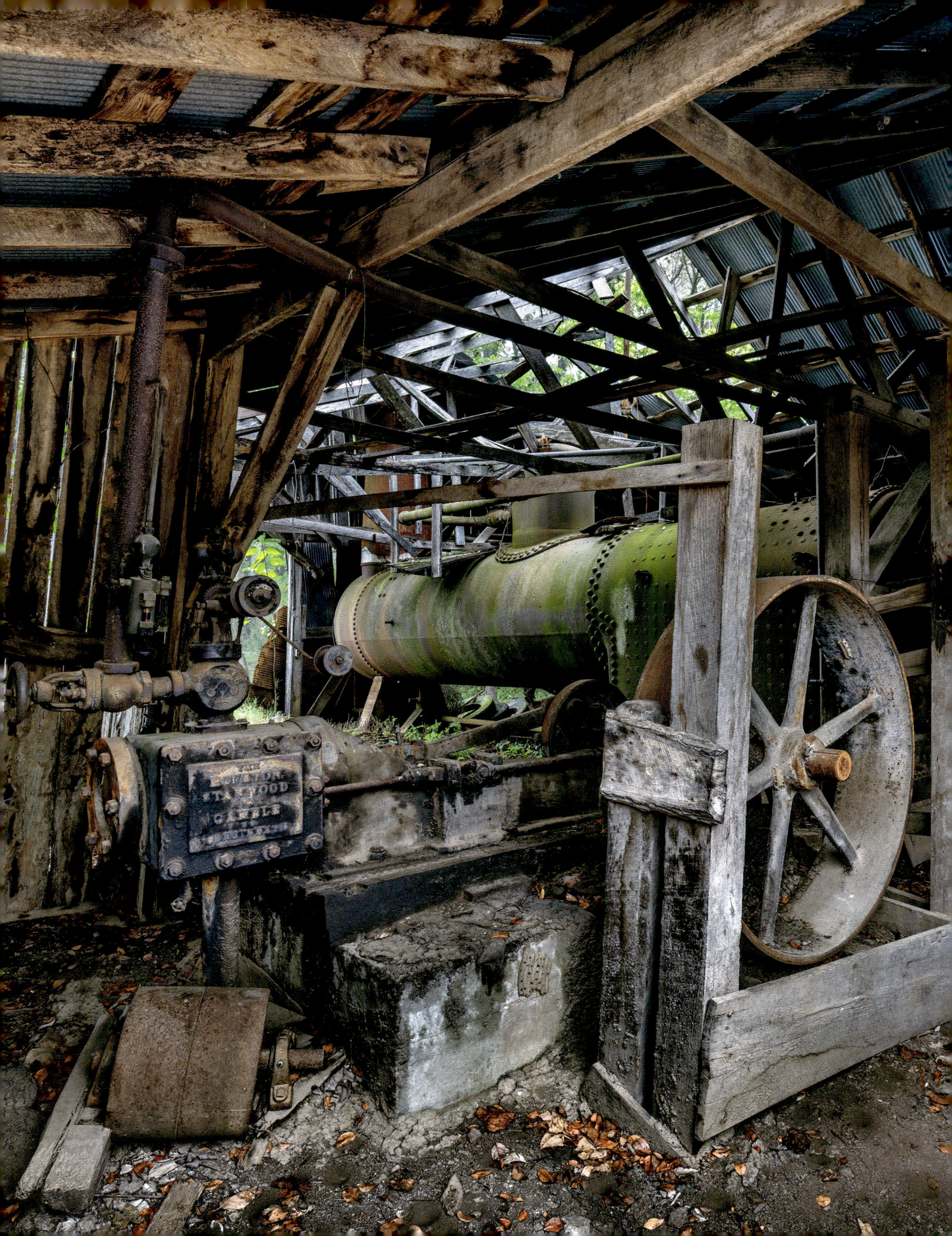

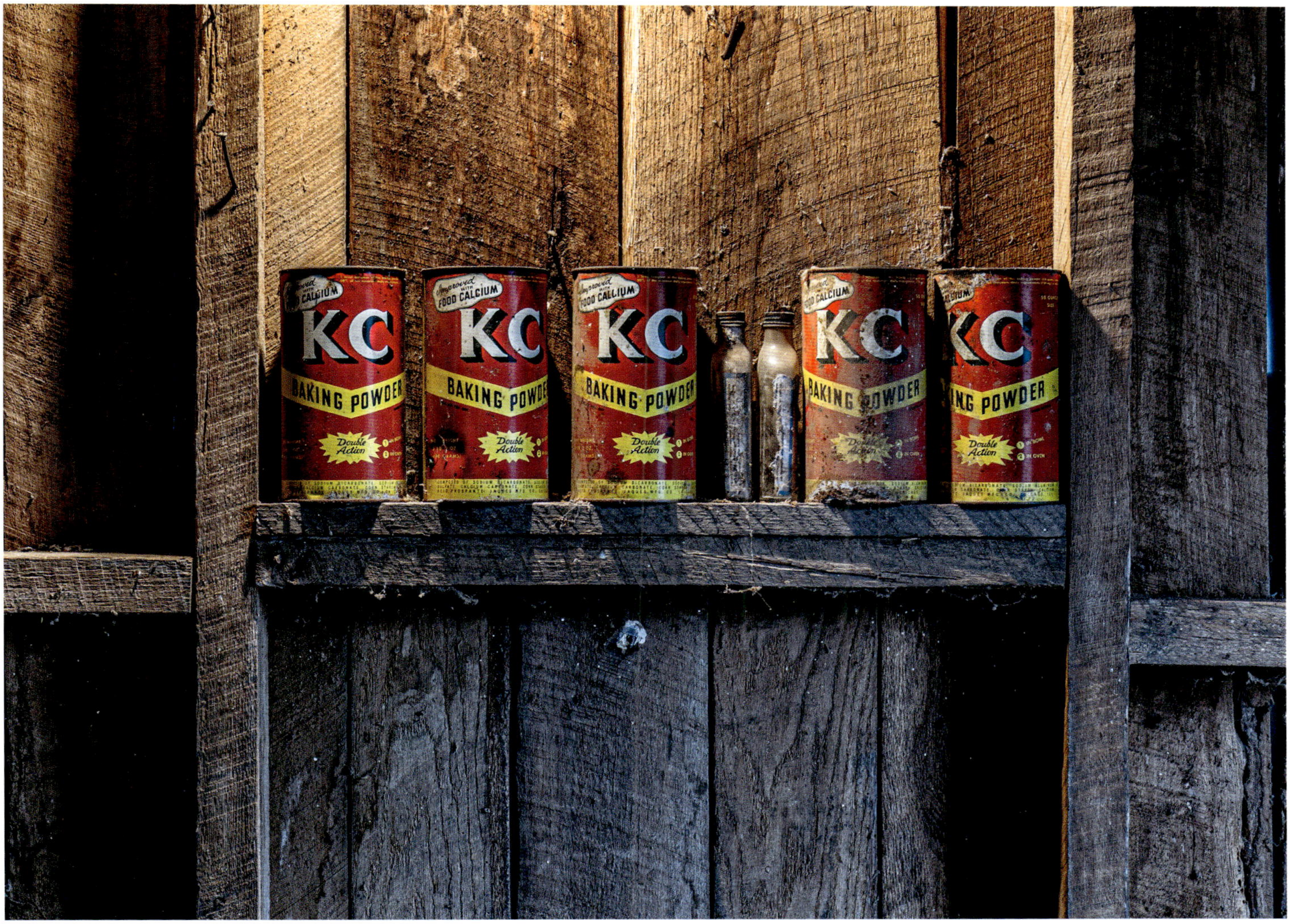

Seems no one wanted the last cans of baking powder in the old store that was next to the sawmill.

< Inside the Arvil and Elsie Casey steam-powered sawmill (in 2025), Boxley Valley Historic District

Known for its towering smoke stack and trademark whistle that could be heard throughout Boxley Valley, would signal the beginning and end of each work day. Trees processed at the mill and at other local sawmills over the years included: hickory for golf clubs, walnut for rifle stocks, hickory and oak (white and red) for furniture, beech, ash, black gum, sweet gum, persimmon, dogwood, cedar, red oak for flooring, hickory for handles, elm for chair parts, maple for chair backs, ash for shovel and hoe handles, and pine for general lumber and log-cabin logs. (this list gathered from Ken Smith's ***Buffalo River Handbook*** and Jim Liles' ***Old Folks Talking,*** both terrific historical resources)

Unfortunately this great historic structure is falling into itself, but I am drawn to such places where time seems to have made the scene even more interesting, photographically speaking. (It's located on private property so no trespassing—I've been asked to stop and take photos by the owners when I can...)

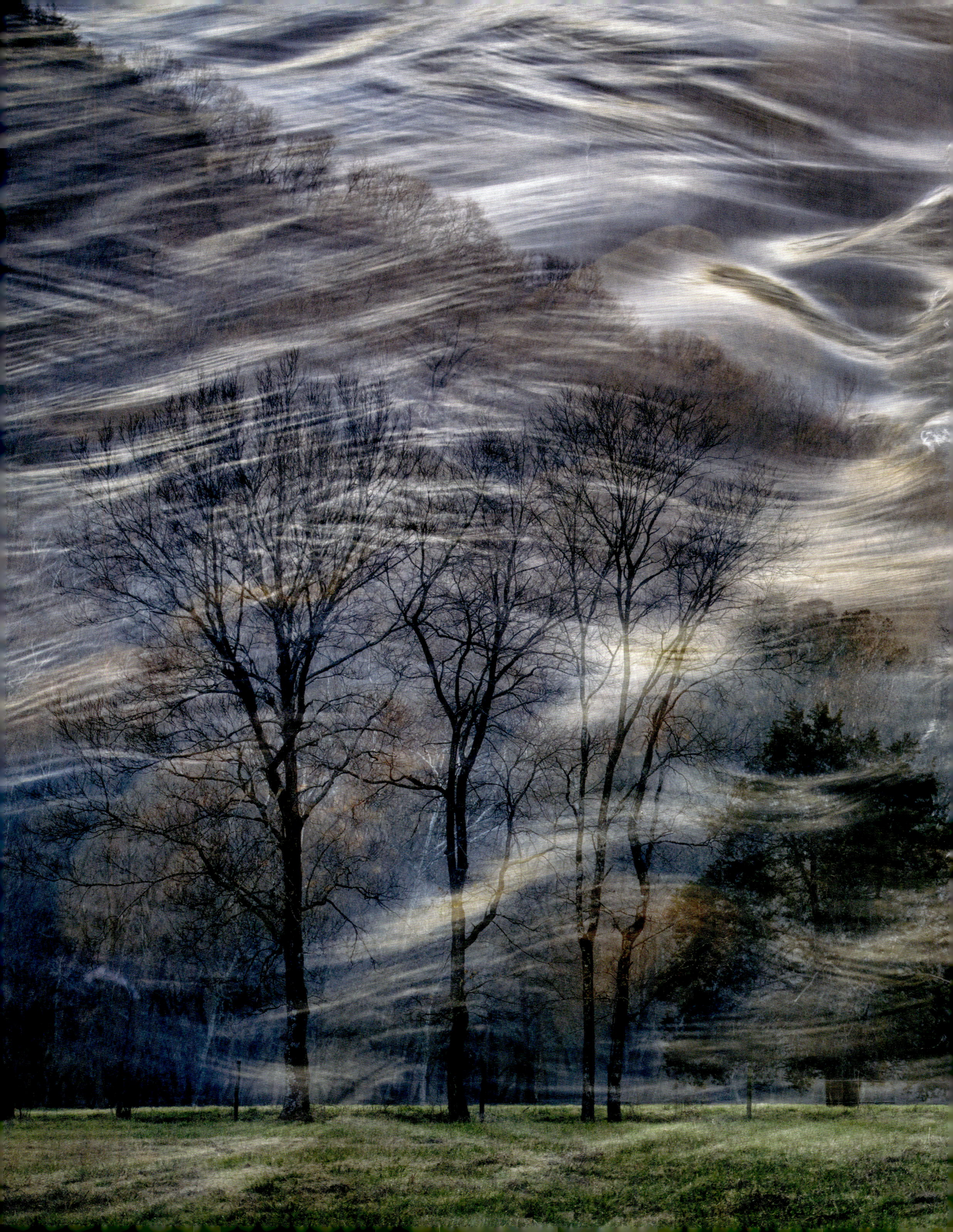

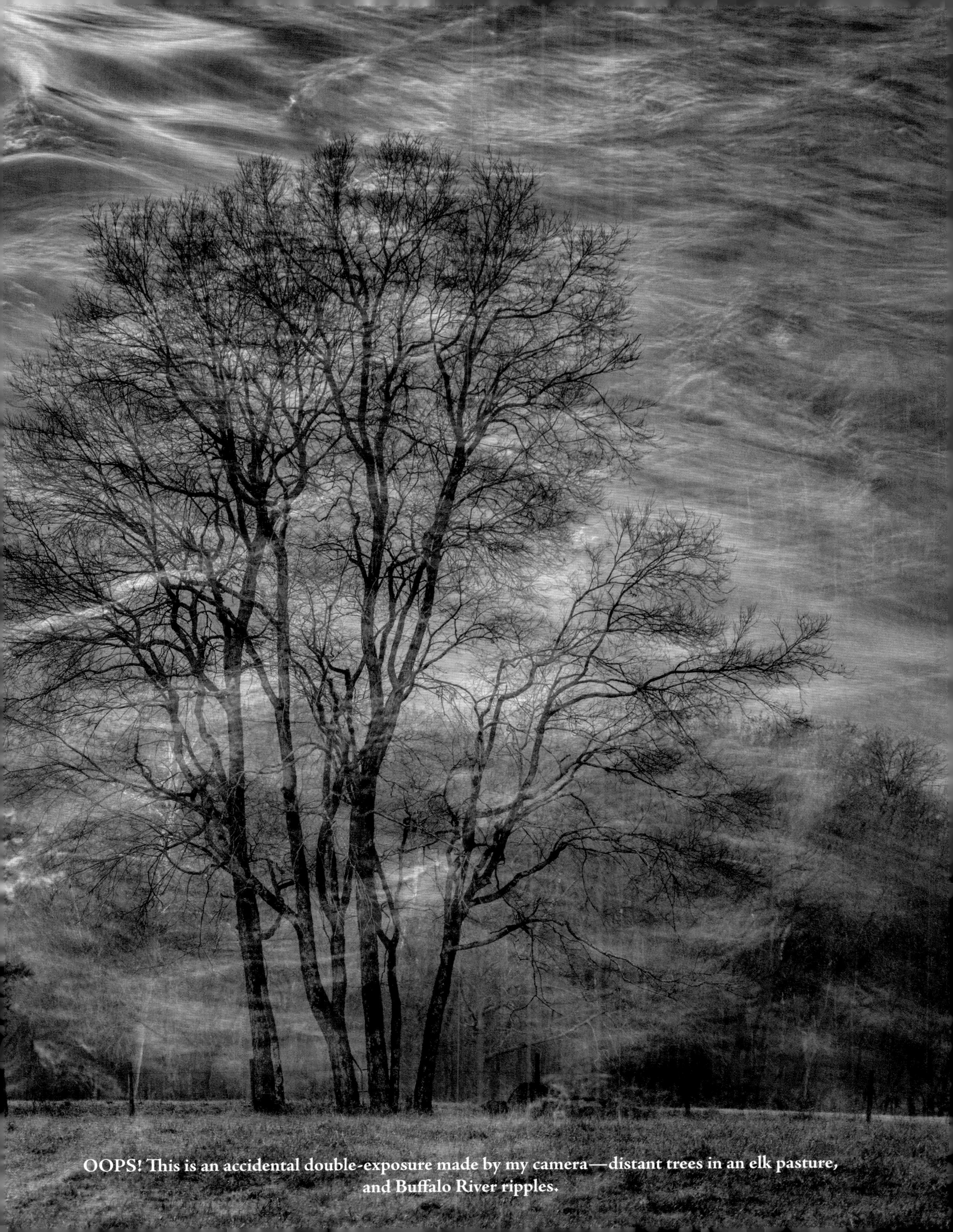

OOPS! This is an accidental double-exposure made by my camera—distant trees in an elk pasture, and Buffalo River ripples.

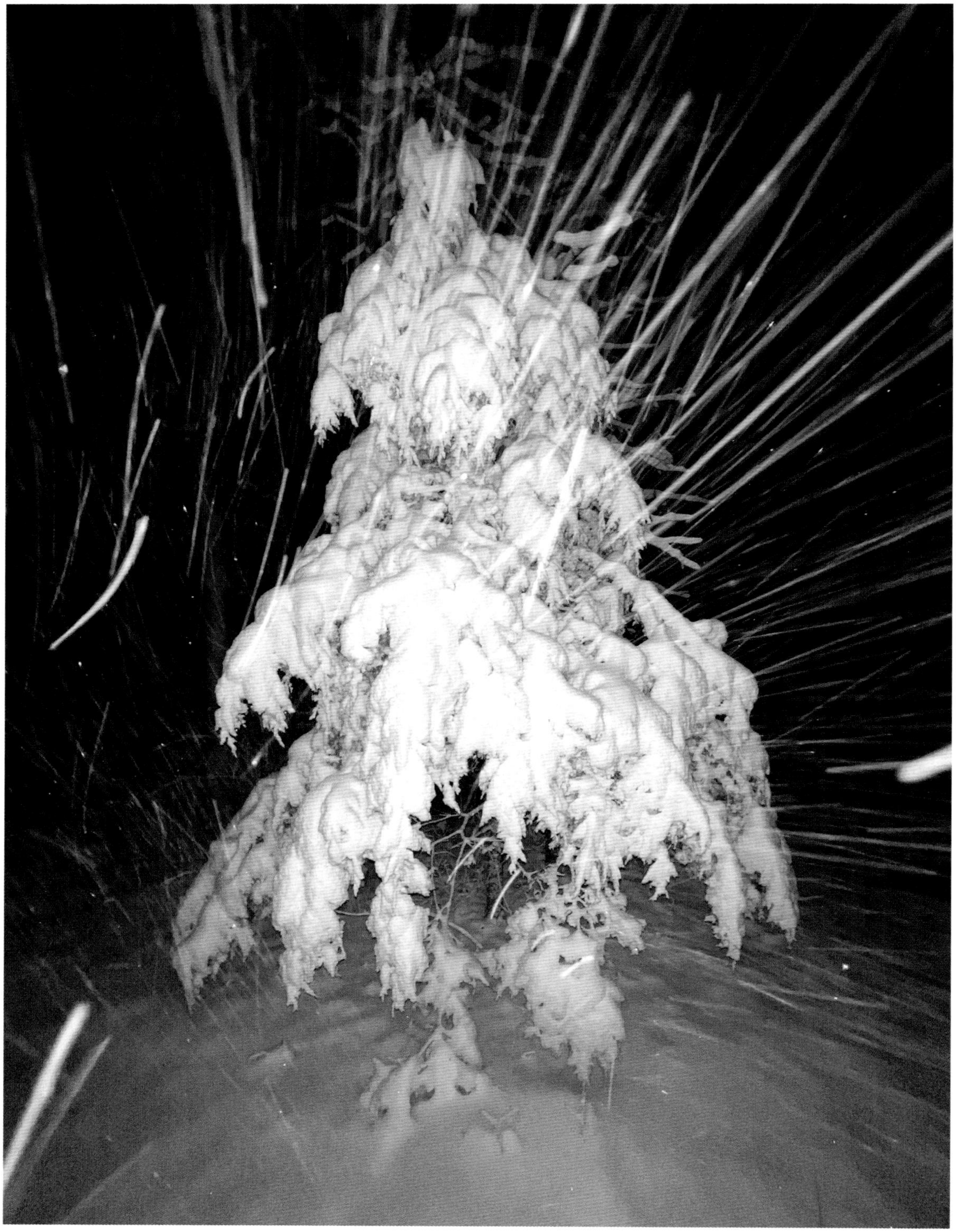

THIS is a reason to use a cell phone instead of an expensive camera—for snapshots in bad weather!

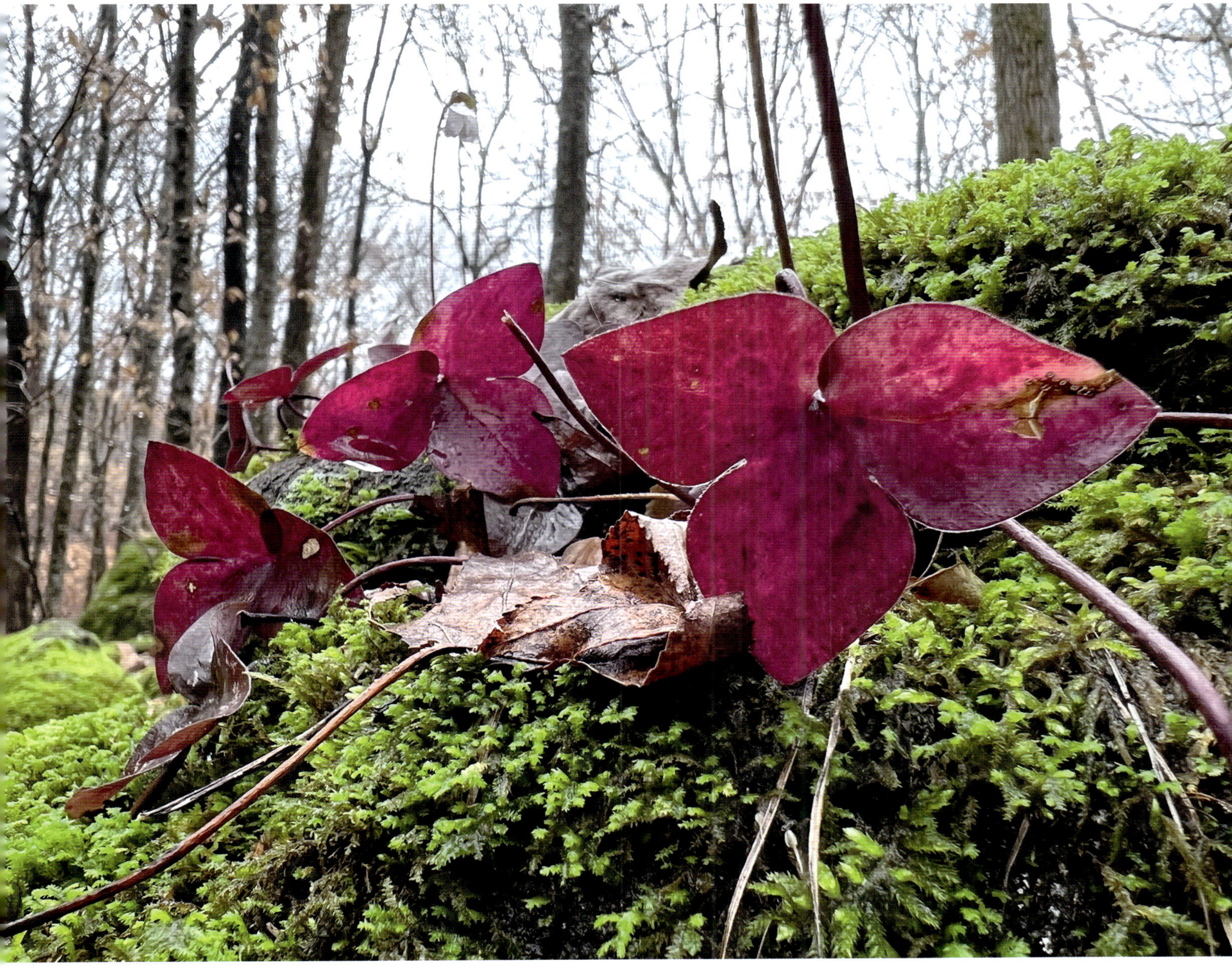

Hepatica or "liverleaf" wildflower—you gotta get down on your belly to get a photo like this.

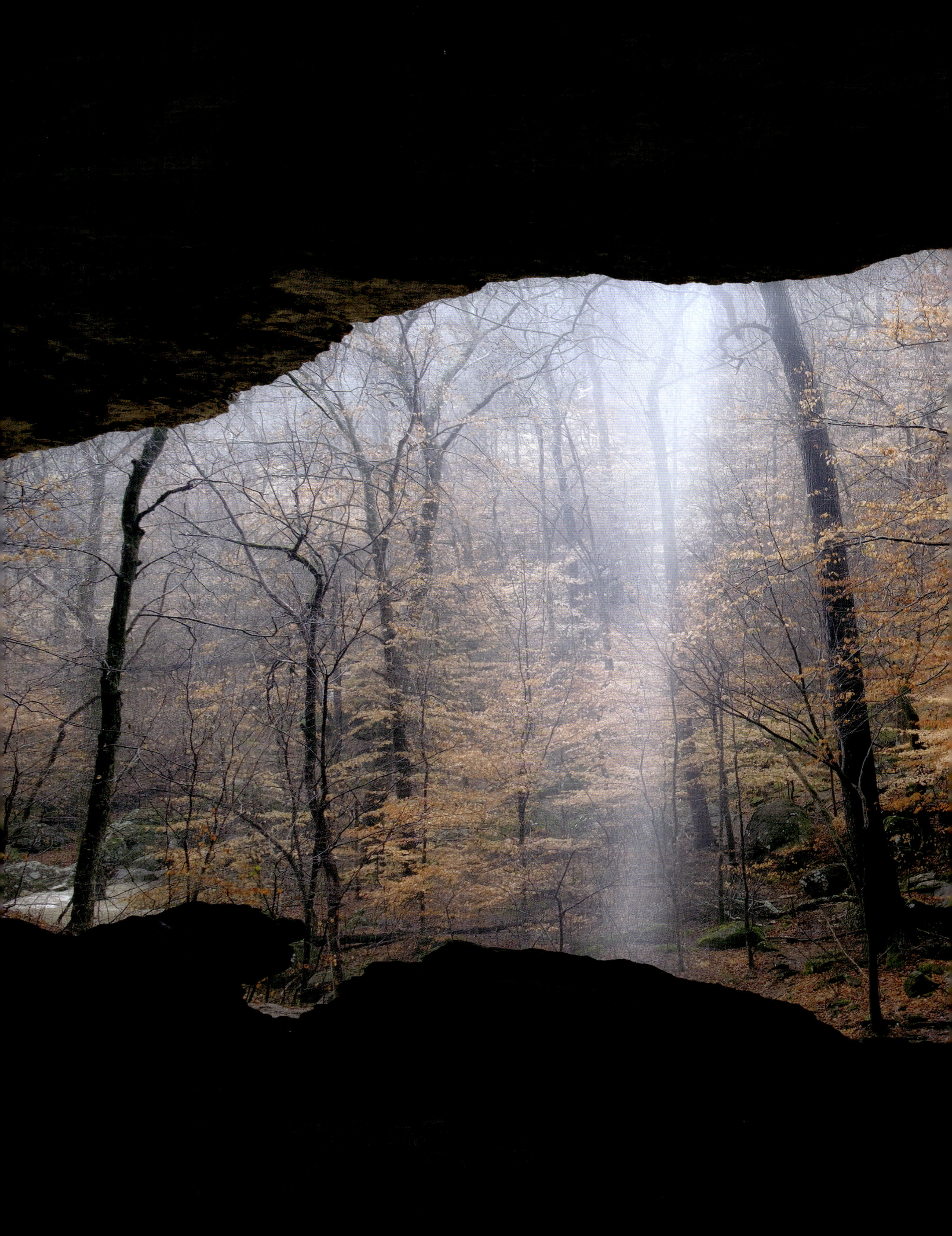

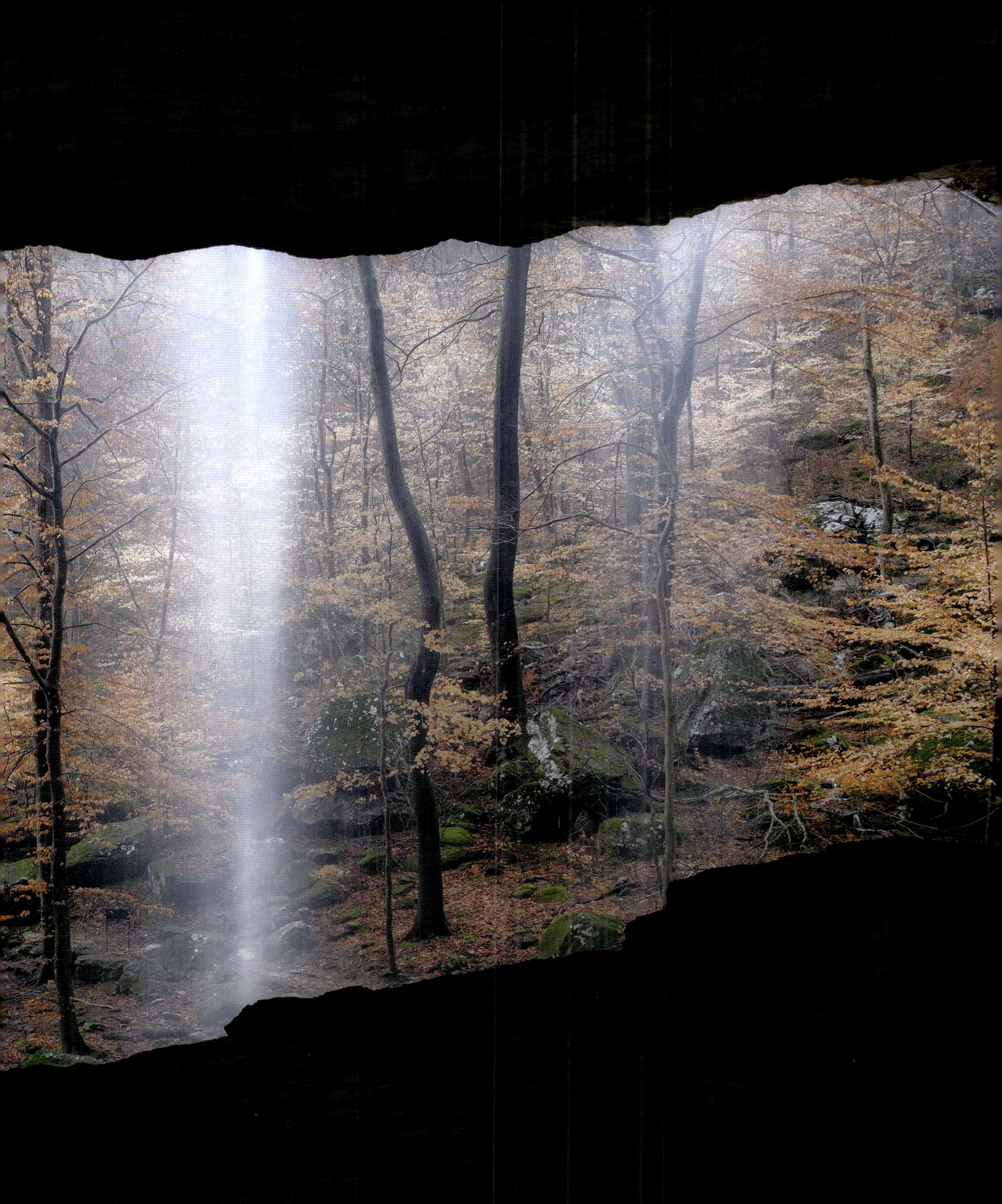

Looking out from the back of Cobb Cave in Lost Valley, with winter beeches showing off their winter color

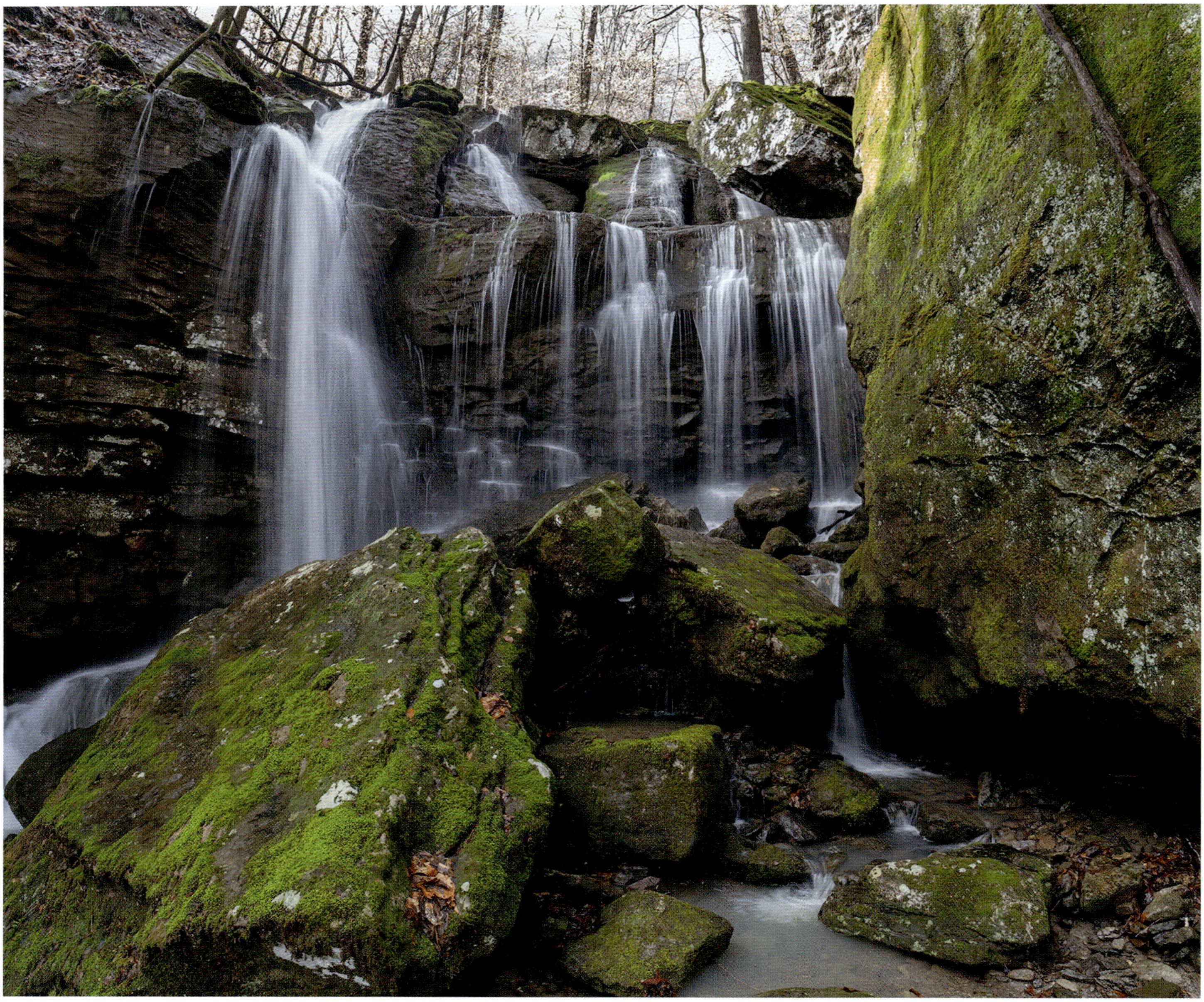

Littishie Falls

After finding this beautiful, mossy 39' tall waterfall I learned there is a small cemetery at the very top of this drainage—with the lonely grave of little Sarah Waterman. She lived along the Big Piney River below, along with at least eight siblings. She was only seven when she died in 1898. Life must have been pretty tough back then, though I have a feeling she also had some happy times growing up with the river and surrounding Ozark Mountains. I like to think she visited this very waterfall a time or two and sat in wonder and smiled. I thought she needed to be remembered somehow, and so choose her unique middle name to be forever associated with this waterfall. (headstone photo by Cheryl Kueker)

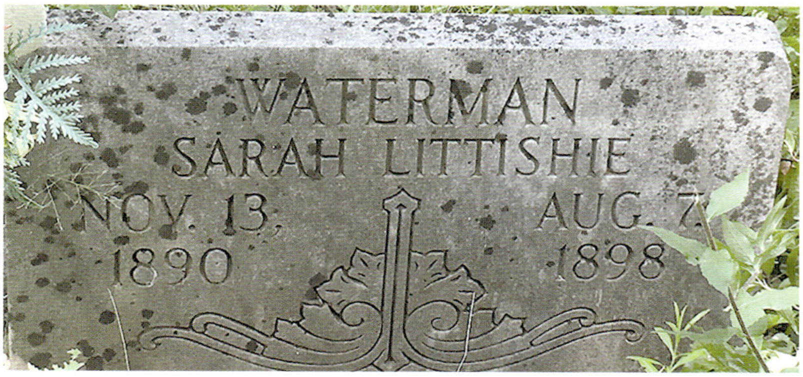

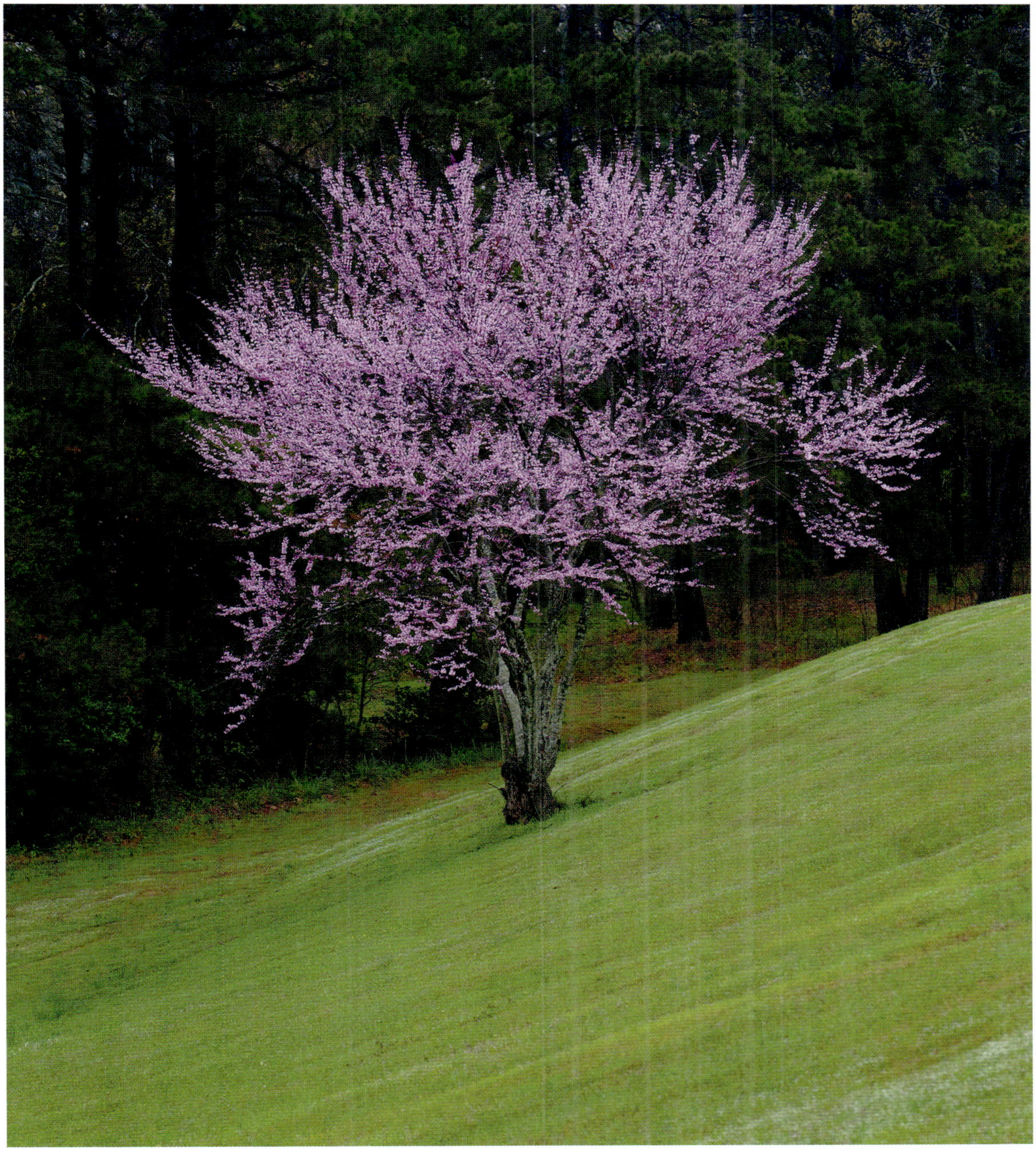

A fresh redbud tree in all it's springtime glory, Arkansas River Valley

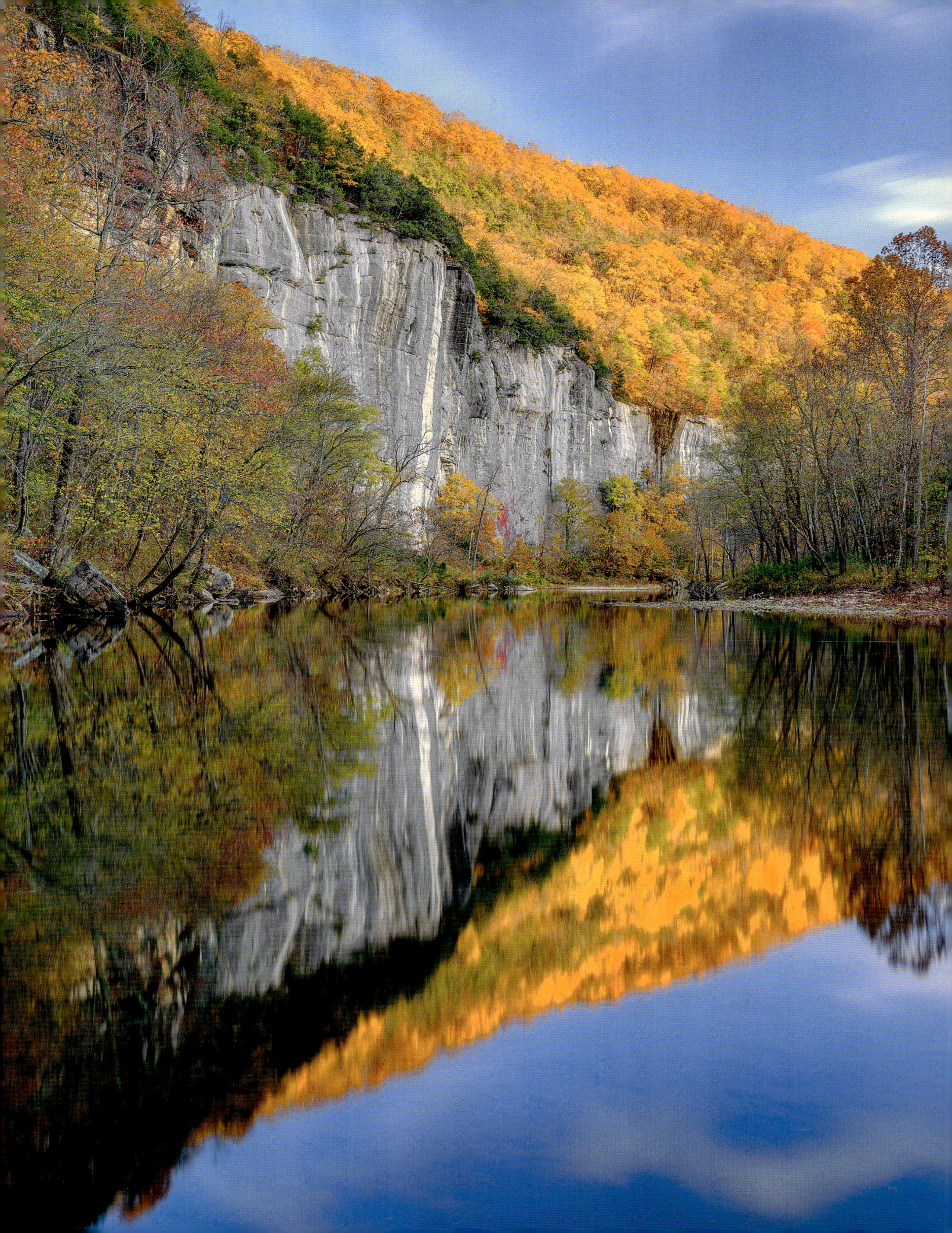

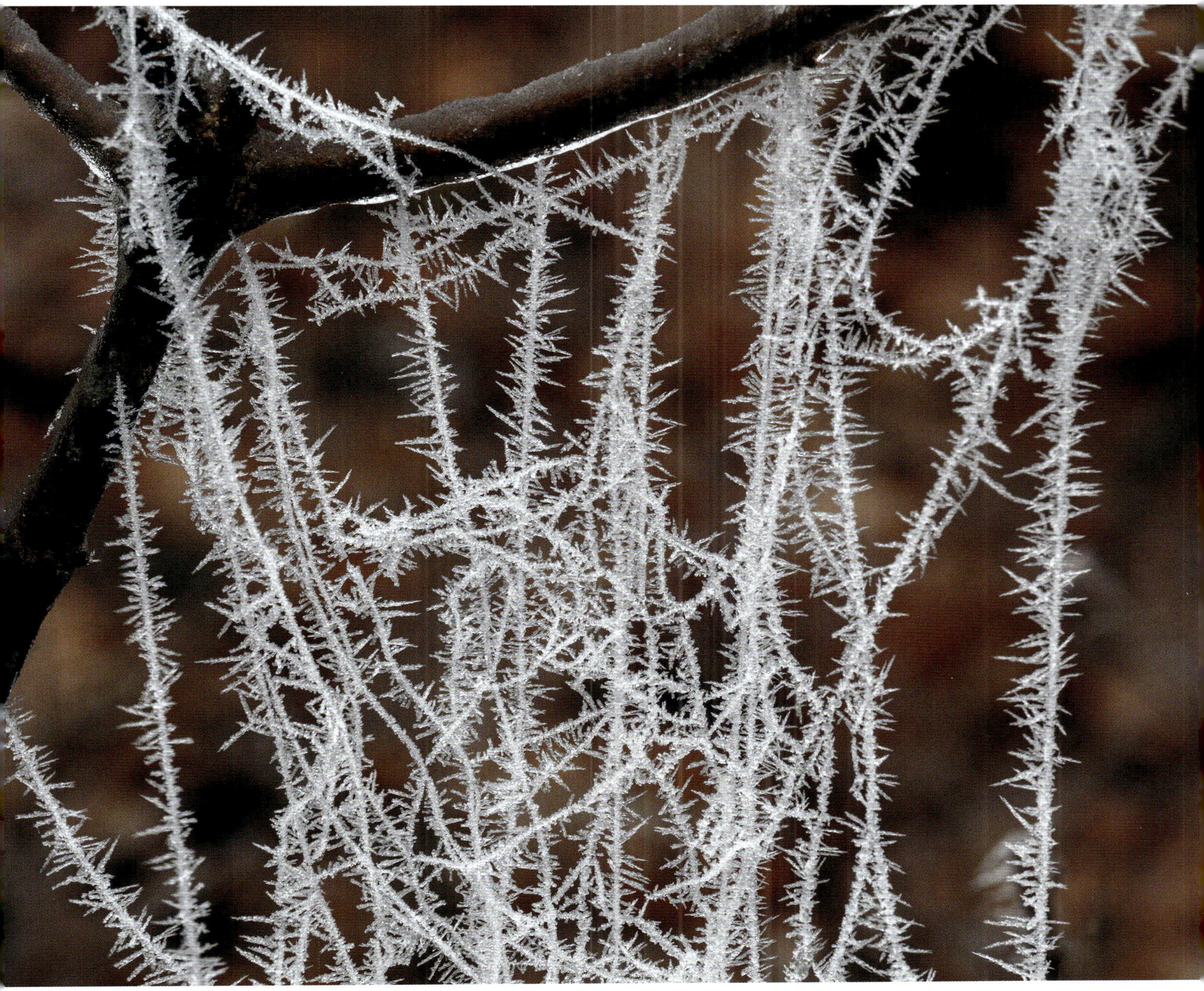

If you were a spider this is what your web would look like when "spiky" frost forms.

< Evening October light on Bee Bluff, upstream from the Steel Creek Recreation area.
This reflection wasn't really there. In fact, I stood in the middle of the river, waist-deep with my camera on a tripod, for nearly an hour as the sun set and lit up this scene. I was waiting for breezes that blurred the water surface to quit, but they never did. Playing around with long exposures, I discovered that a two-minute exposure would average out the ripples and the reflection that wasn't there in real time appeared!

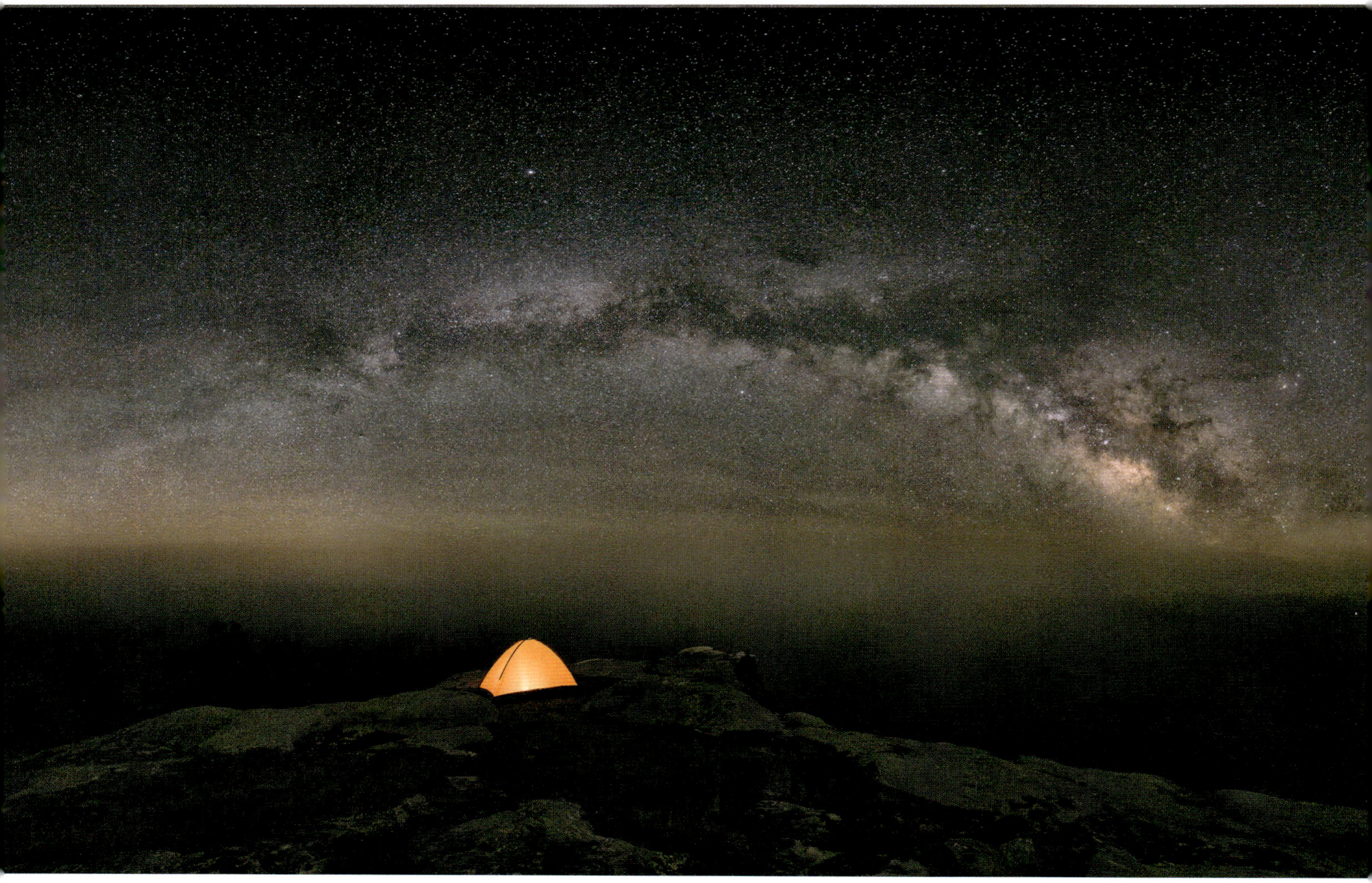

The Milky Way arches over my campsite on top of Ludlow Bluff, Lower Buffalo Wilderness.

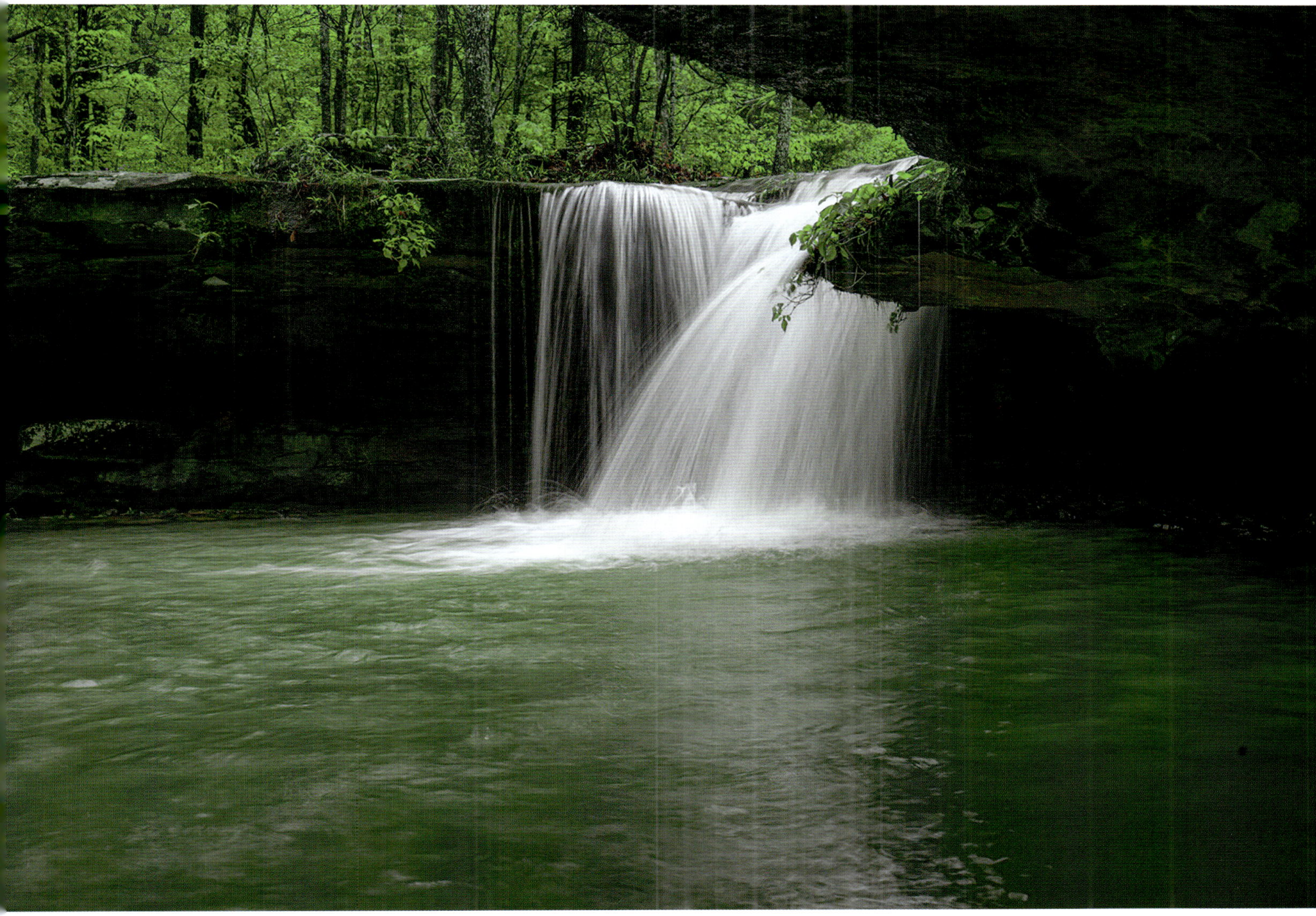

Panther Pool Falls, Wilderness Rider Ranch

You can ride an ATV right to the top of this one, or do like I did here and wade into the water for this view.

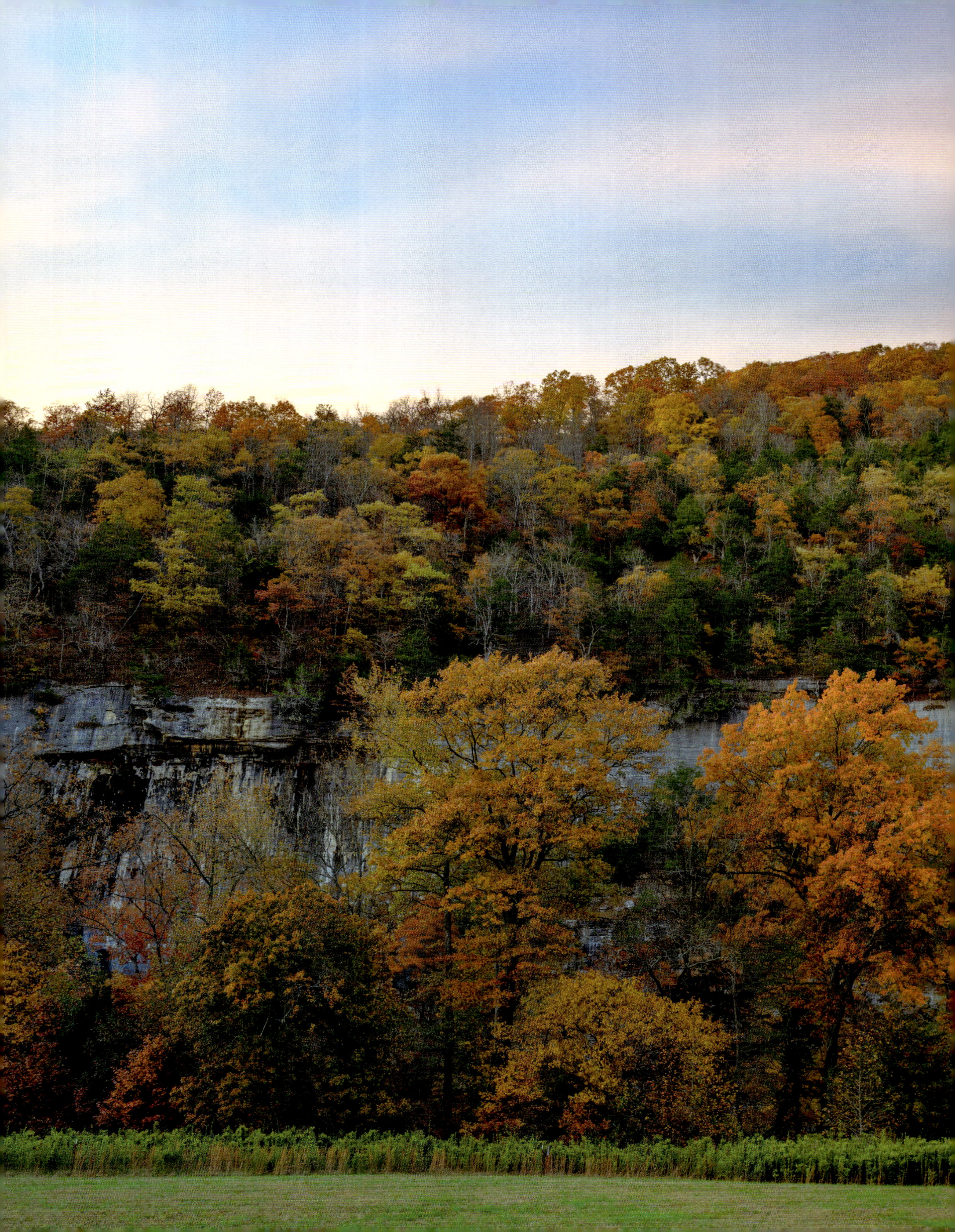

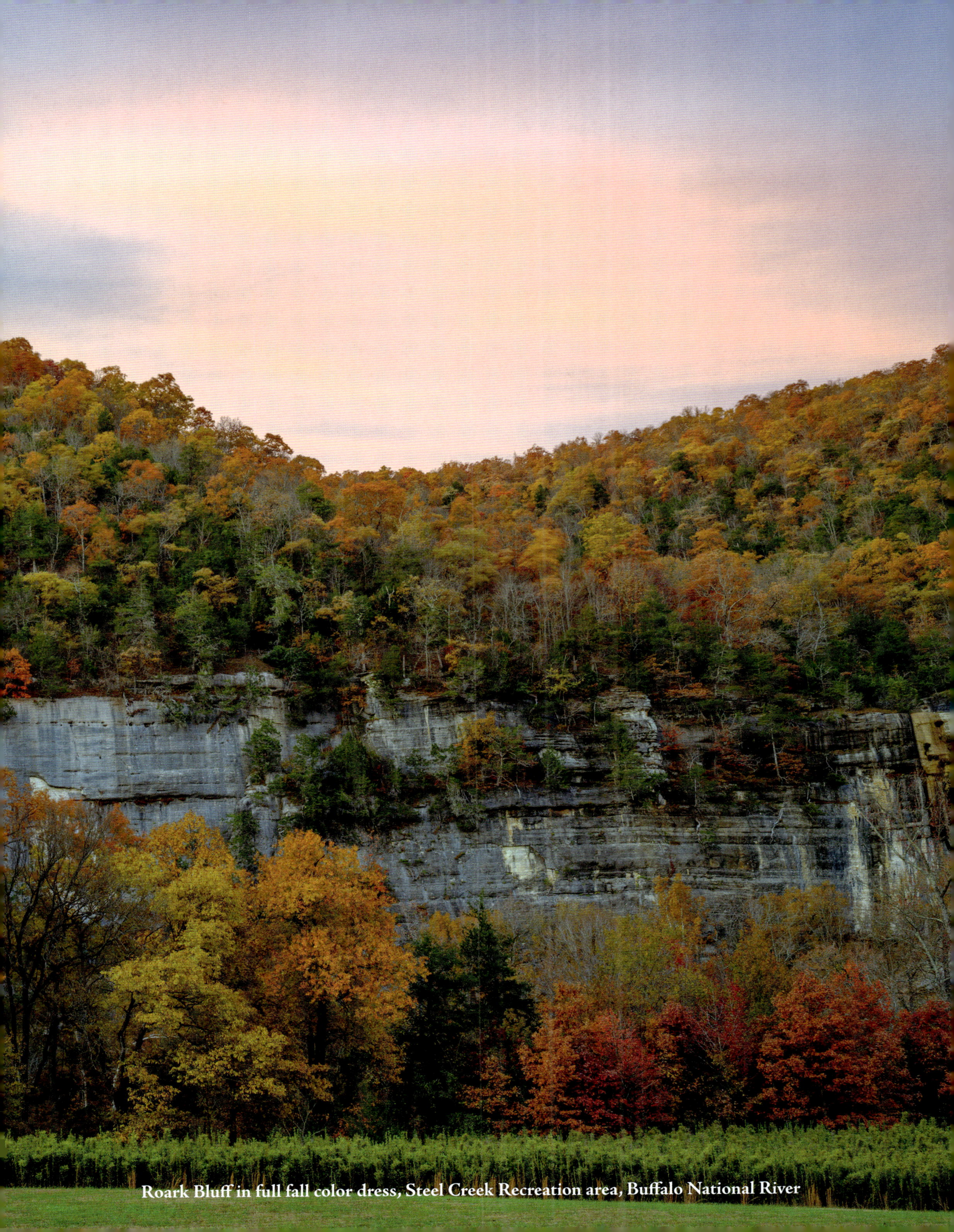

Roark Bluff in full fall color dress, Steel Creek Recreation area, Buffalo National River

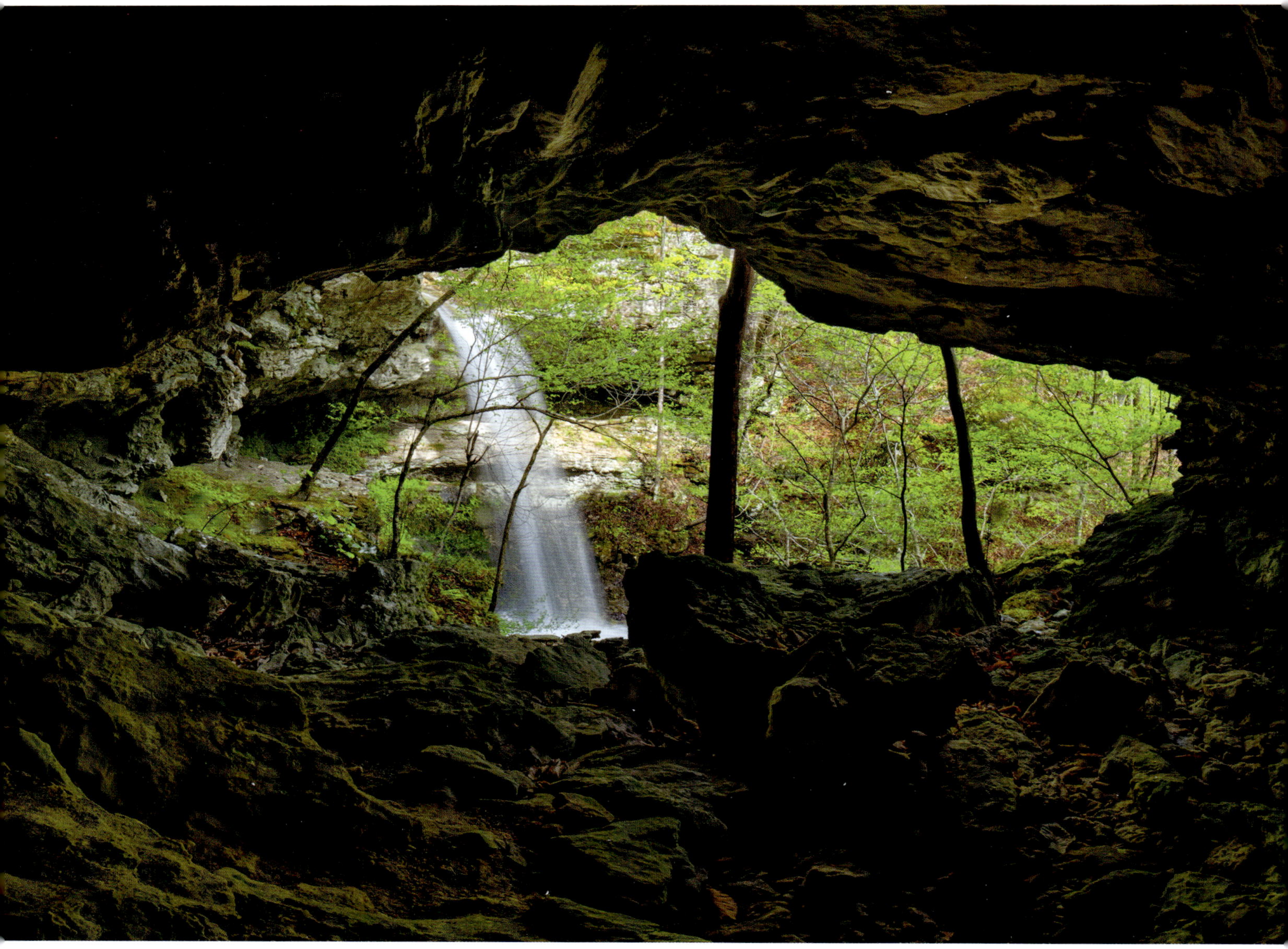

Chimney Rock Mine Falls, Ponca Wilderness

Hole In Rock Falls, Wilderness Rider Ranch >

This is not the Glory Hole Falls, but it was created with the same type of water action—a swirling creek through eons of time drilled a hole through the roof of a bluff overhang. You can drive an ATV (or an easy hike) to the top of this one (or with a little hiking get down below the big bluffline for a great view of this 66' tall falls from the bottom)

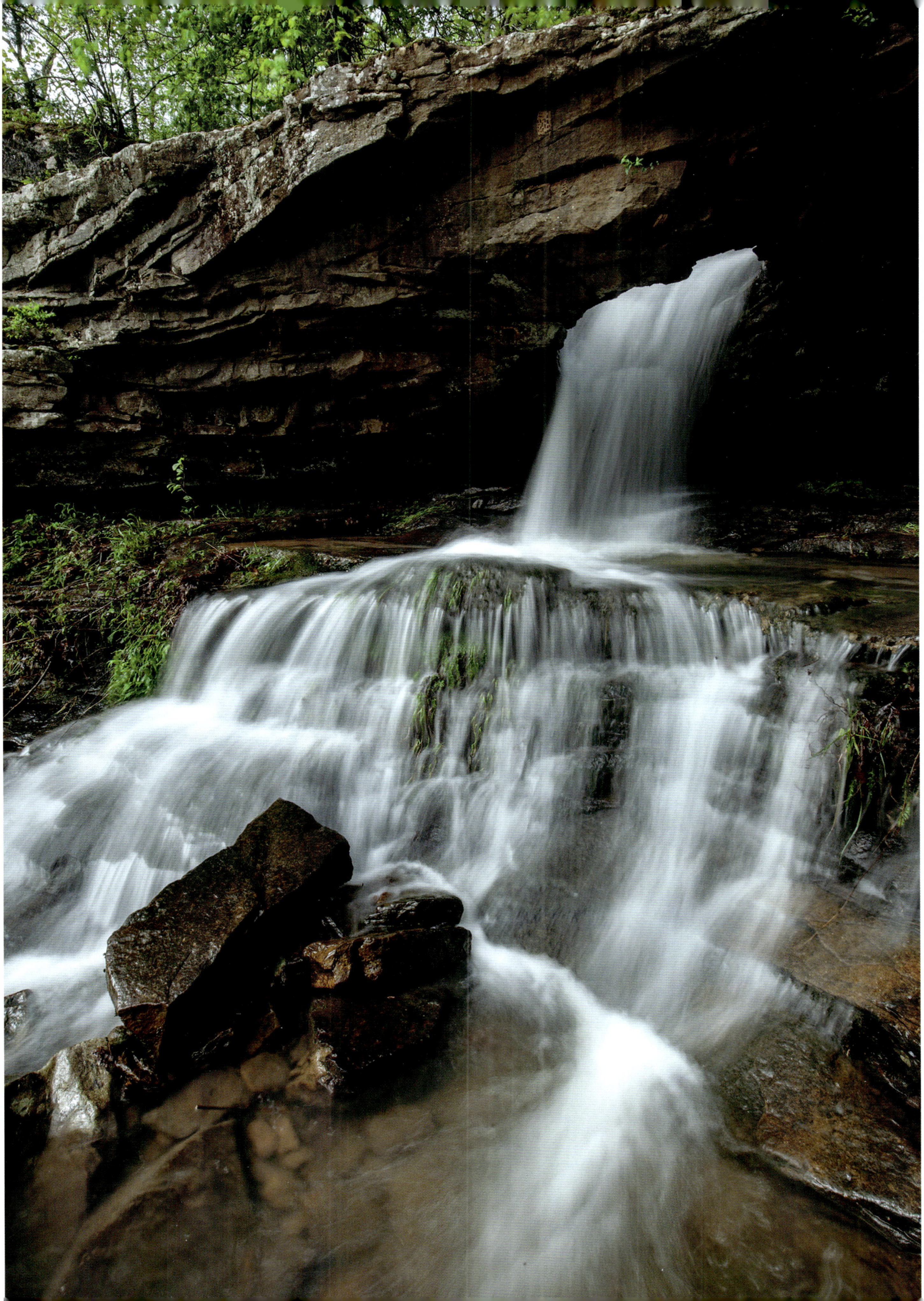

My campsite at the Buffalo River Arch, Lower Buffalo Wilderness >

The glow is from a small lamp inside my tent. The river is just below this arch, but it's almost impossible to see the arch from the river, unless you float past it and look back. I'm a big fan of natural bridges and stone arches. I was up much of the night taking photos of this scene, and when I finally got to bed I discovered my big fat blow-up air mattress did not make the trip with me. Sleeping on the floor of a STONE arch without one is not fun!

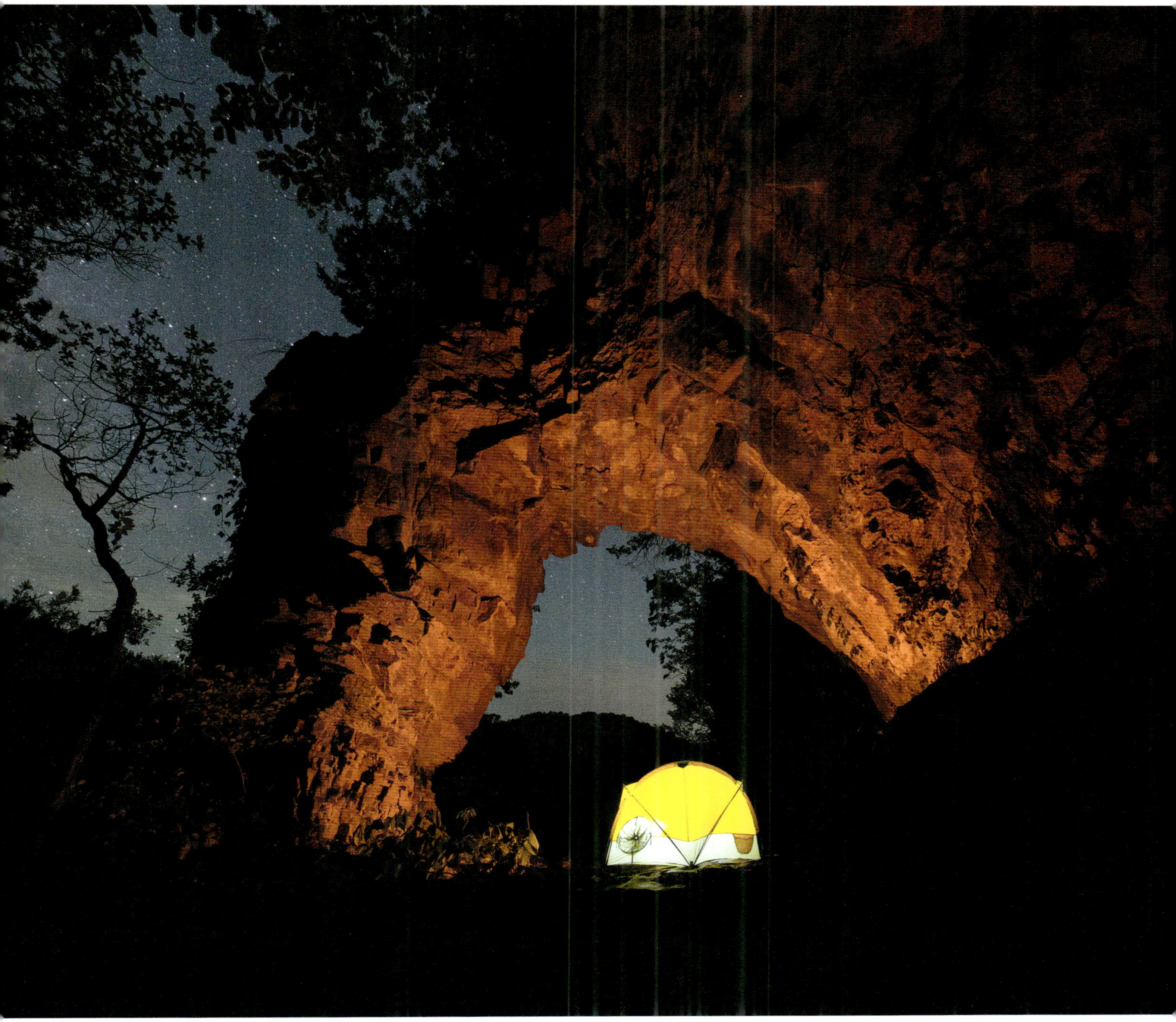

Hidden Falls along the Buffalo River Trail just downstream from the Ponca Low Water Bridge. >
If you hike this popular trail you literally have to step over the top of this waterfall along the way, but most folks don't realize it is there. It's also hidden from view if on the river by the thin fin of bluffline that curves out from the bluff around the falls. It is truly a "hidden" gem. Hint, hint—my new Arkansas Waterfalls guidebook (Third Edition) tells of an easy way to get to this view from below.

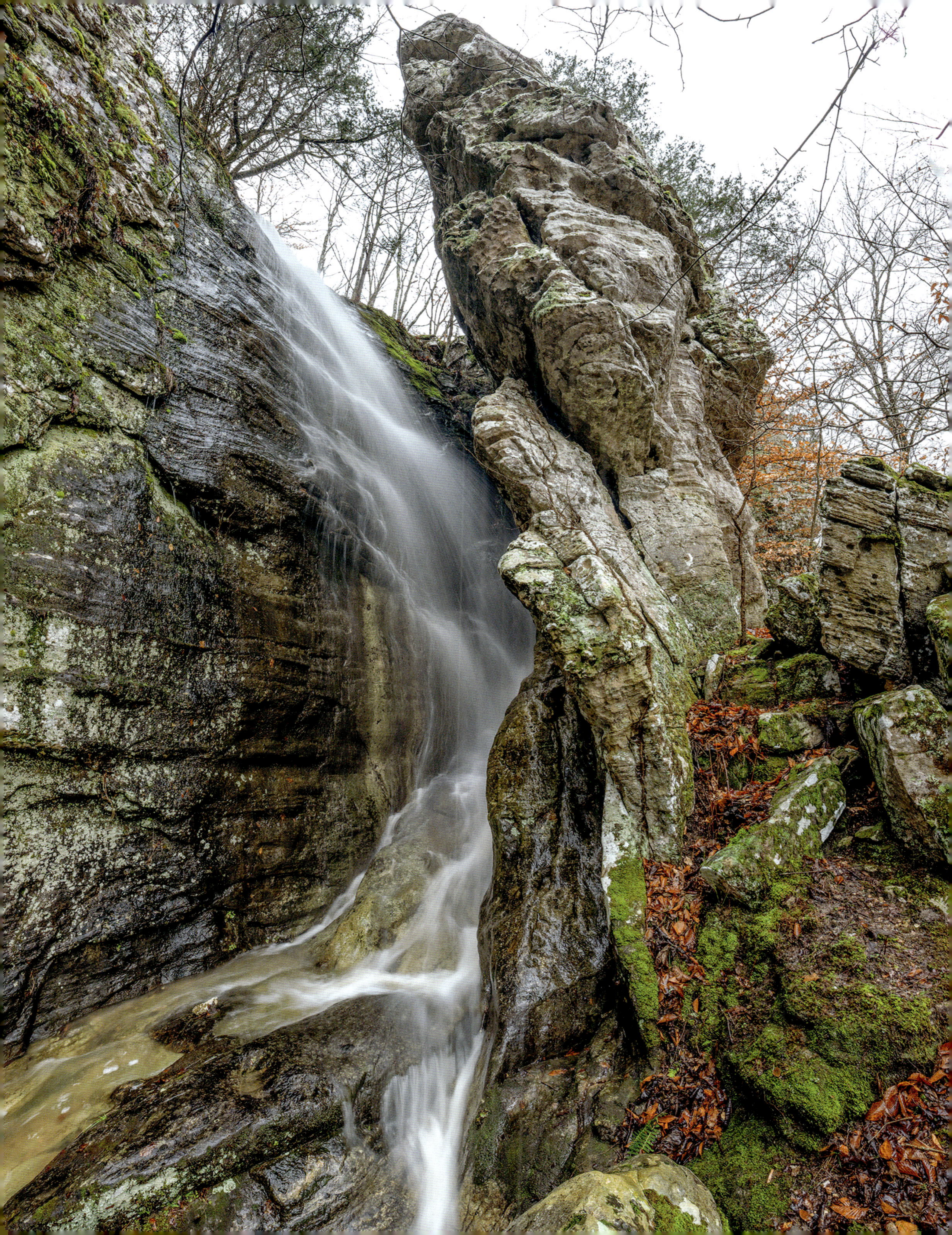

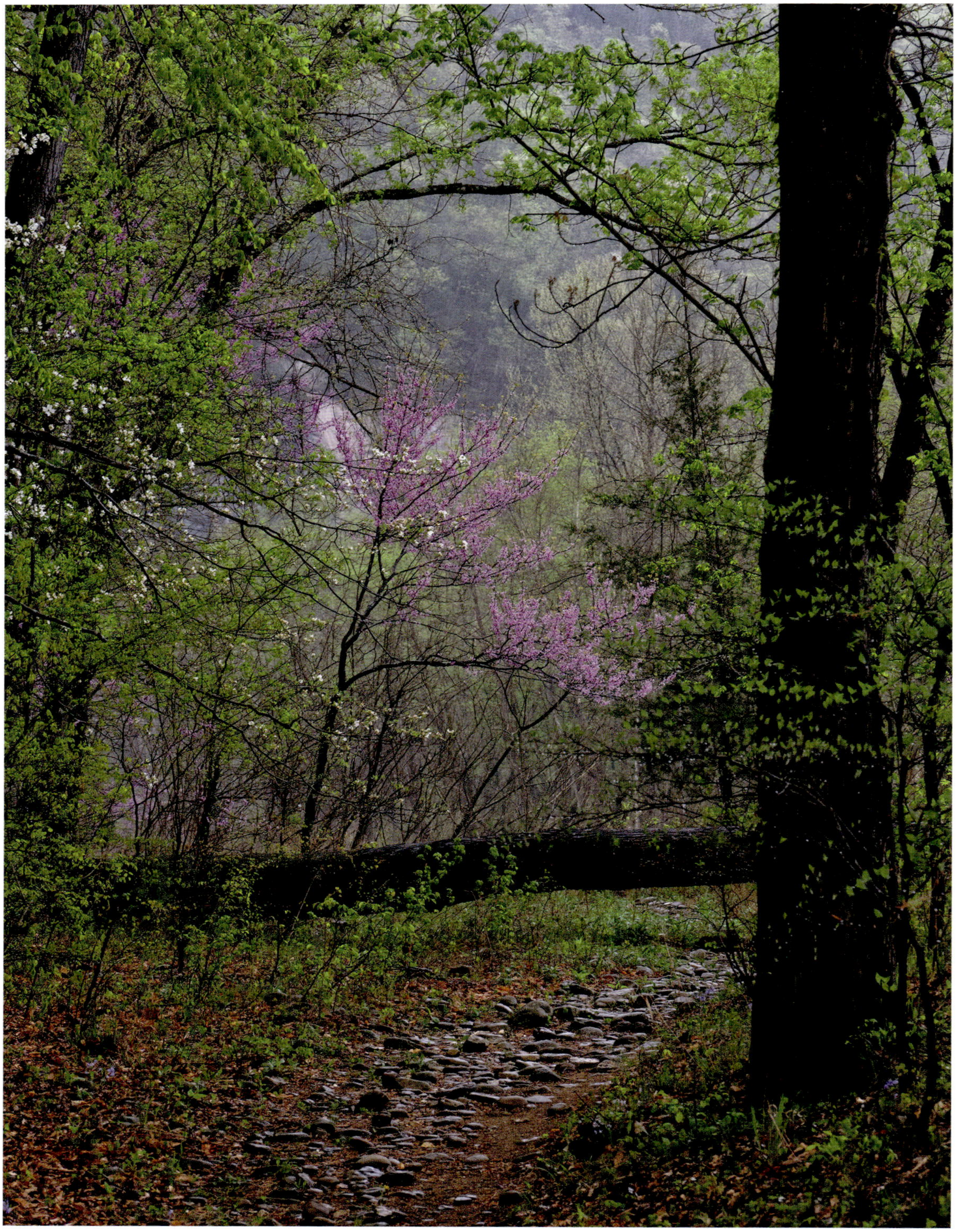

Sometimes you just gotta stop along the trail and enjoy the view.

Cameron Bluff (Savanna Sandstone) and a wild plum tree brace for an incoming storm. Mt. Magazine State Park >

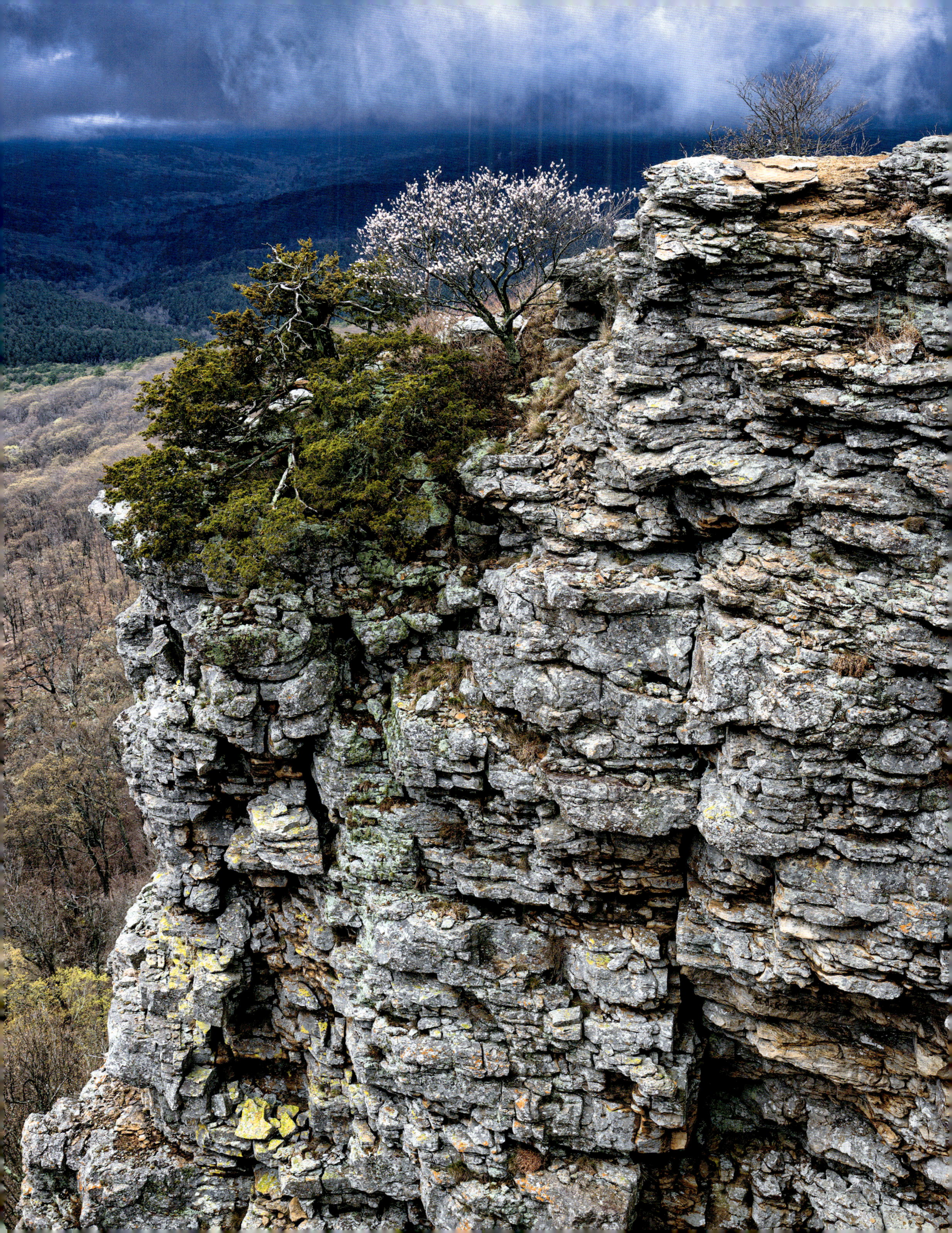

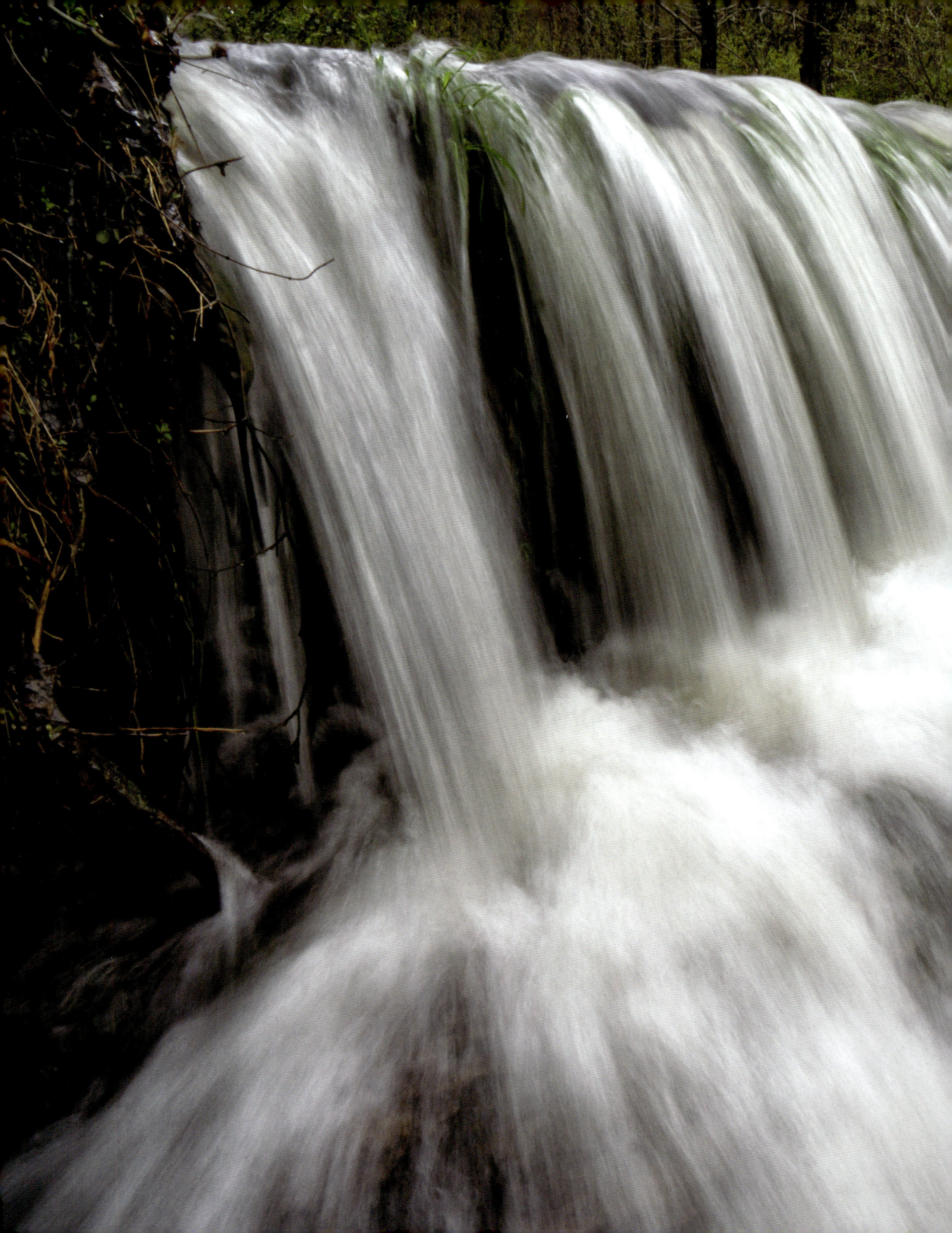

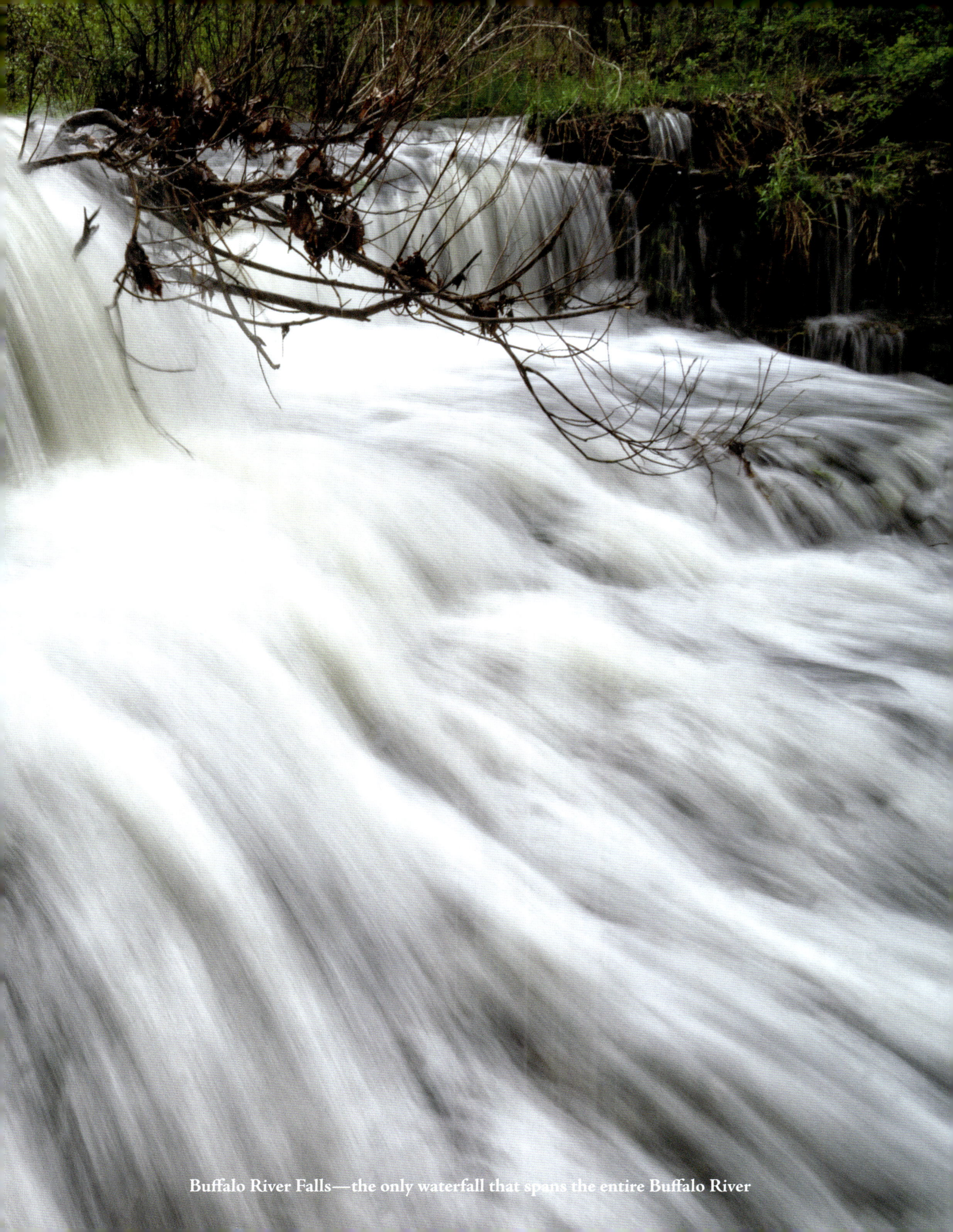

Buffalo River Falls—the only waterfall that spans the entire Buffalo River

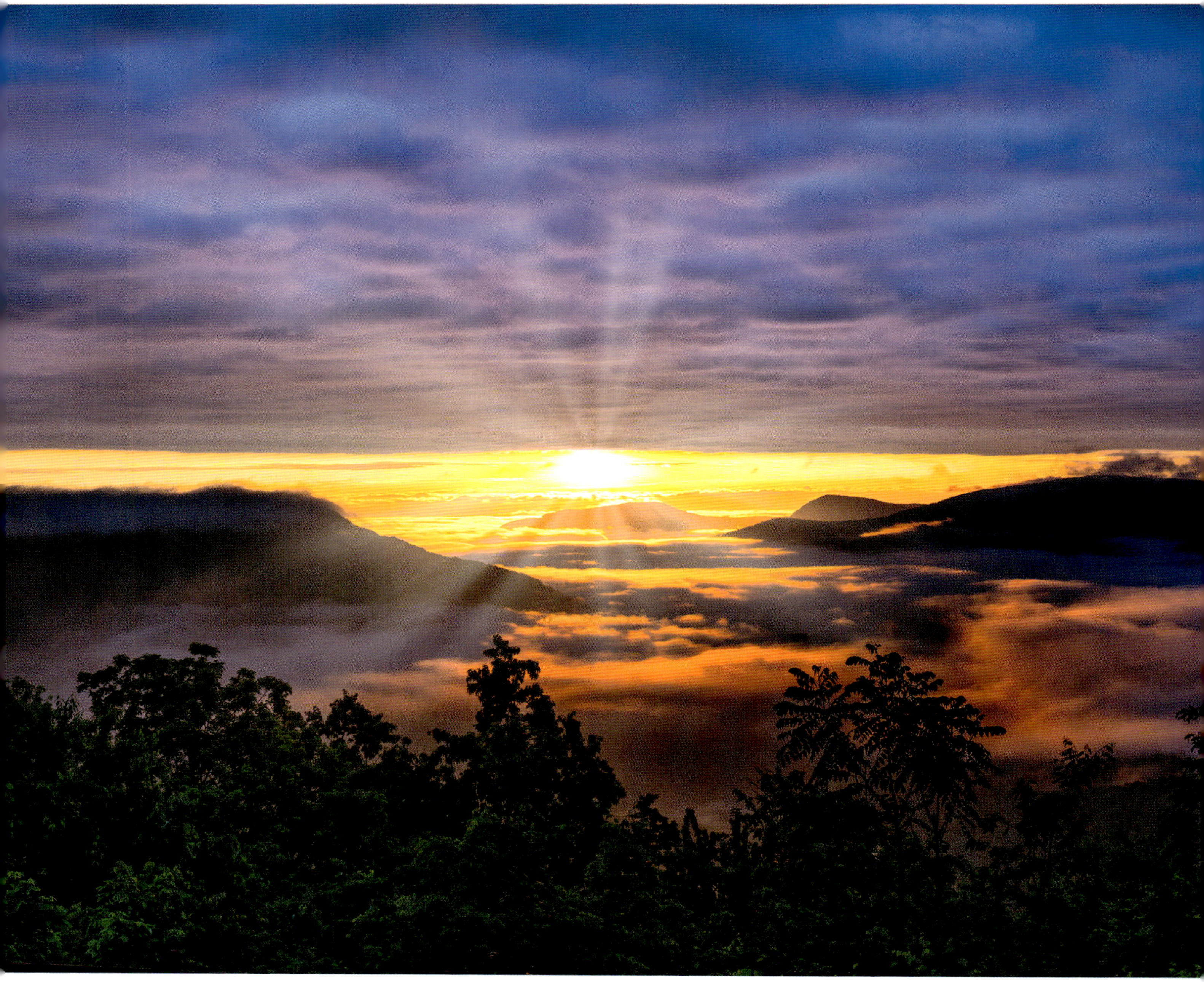

Looking into the Arkansas Grand Canyon (deepest in the Ozarks).

Early one morning I was headed to photograph a waterfall before harsh sunshine lit it up. As I drove like a madman (not *really*) along scenic and curvy Hwy. 7, I saw this amazing scene start to happen—but there are only two spots I know of with an open view, and I'd already passed one. THIS was the second viewpoint, where I jumped out of the car and took a single shot with my big camera, then the sun disappeared into the clouds. Timing is everything.

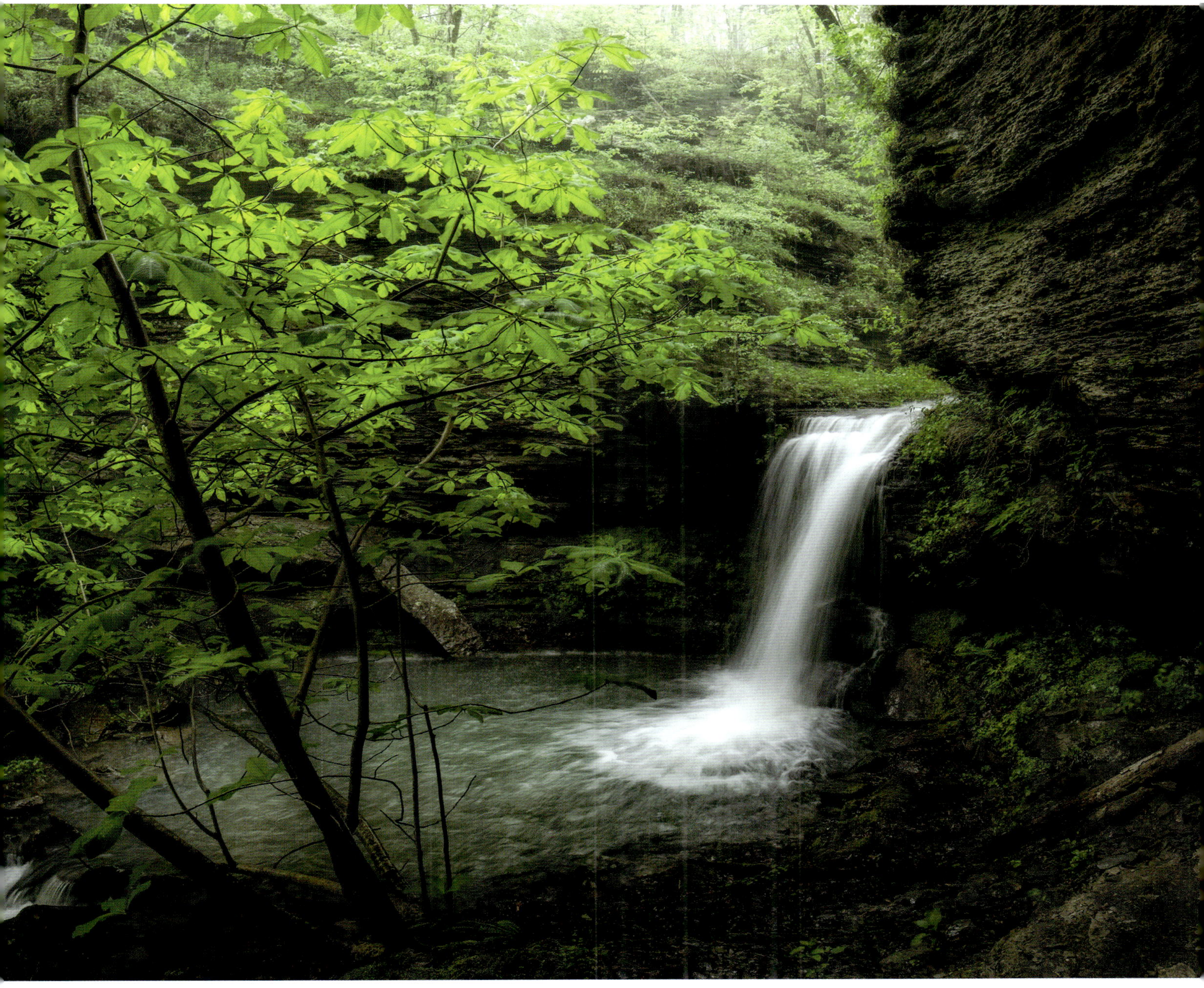

Wild Hollow Grotto, Bearcat Hollow Wildlife Management Area

You probably can't tell from this view, but the reason I happen to get this photo was because a massive thunderstorm had chased me into this little grotto for cover, and while I waited out the storm I had plenty of time to set up my camera and get a little work done.

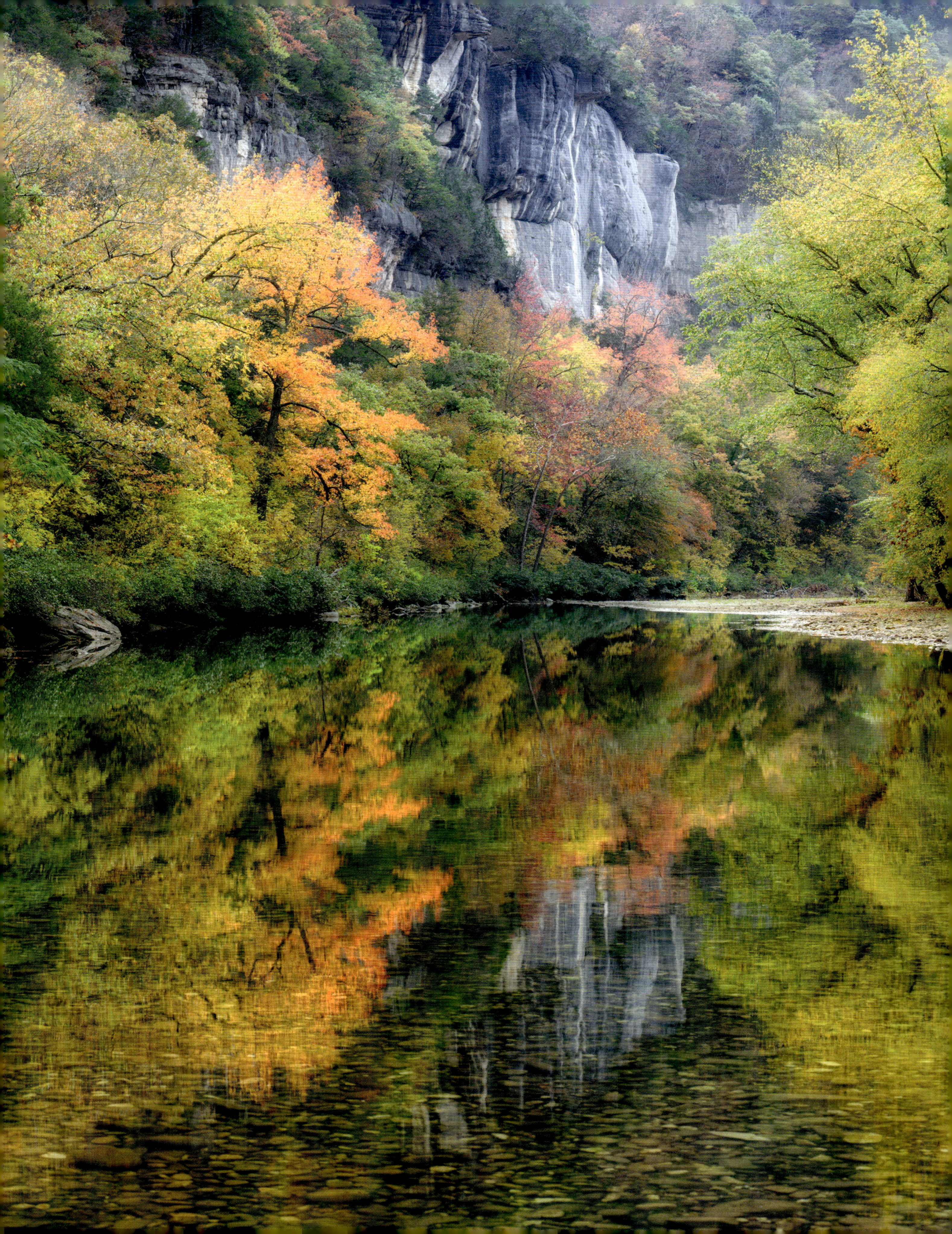

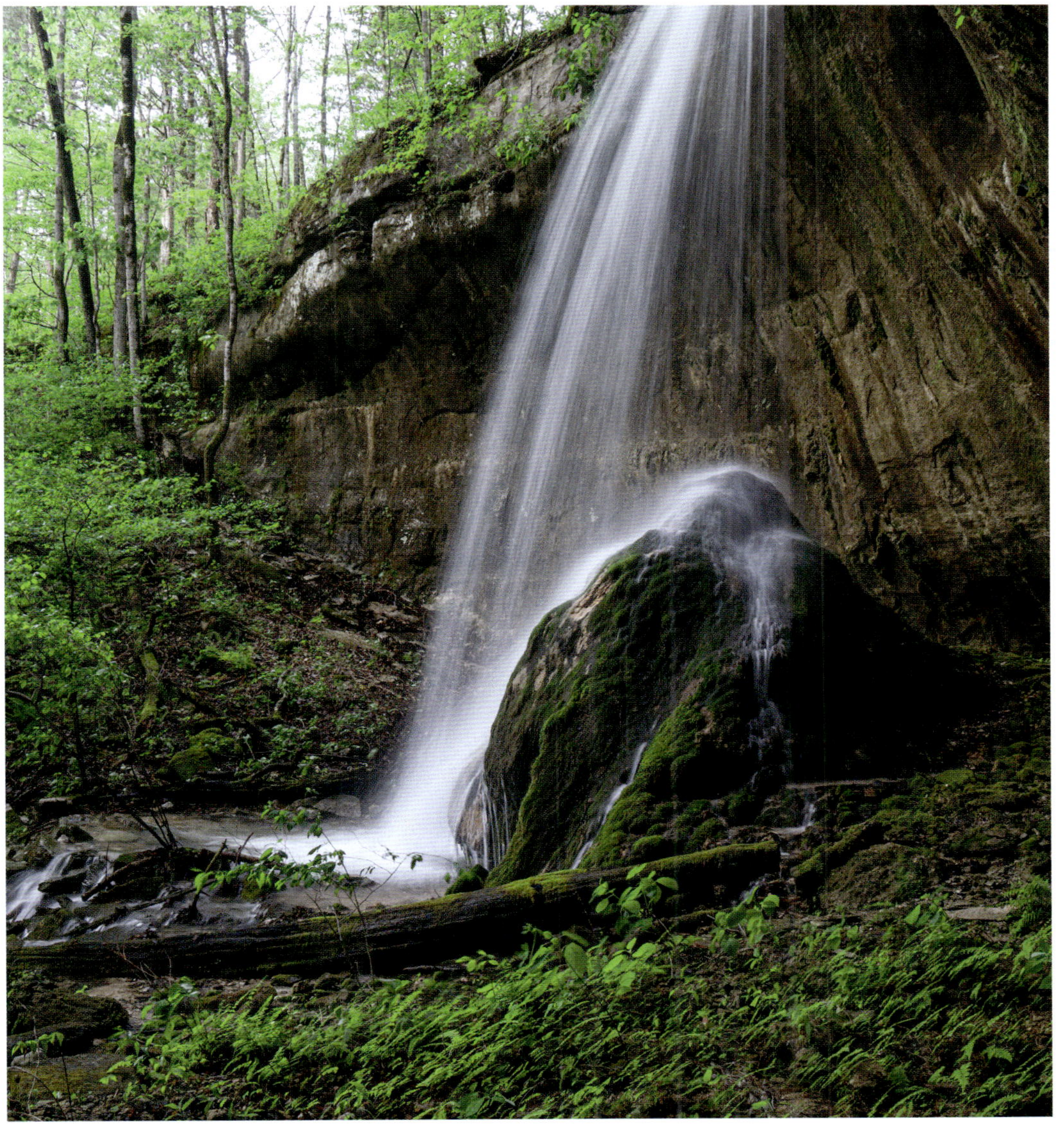

Stalagmite Falls along the Ozark Highlands Trail

That is actually a cave formation at the bottom of this waterfall, a stalagmite that forms when mineral/calcium-rich water splashes on a rock, leaving behind a tiny bit of "calcite" that can slowly build up over thousands, even millions of years. These usually form inside caves, but are also found along the blufflines and waterfalls of the limestone bluffs in the High Ozarks.

< Looking upstream towards Harvest Bluff, Buffalo National River

It took me seven tries to get this photo. It's an easy hike to reach, then just wade out into the river, but each morning I arrived the color was not QUITE as good as I wanted, so I came back the next day, and the next, and the next. And finally I got enough color to my liking. And I hope yours too!

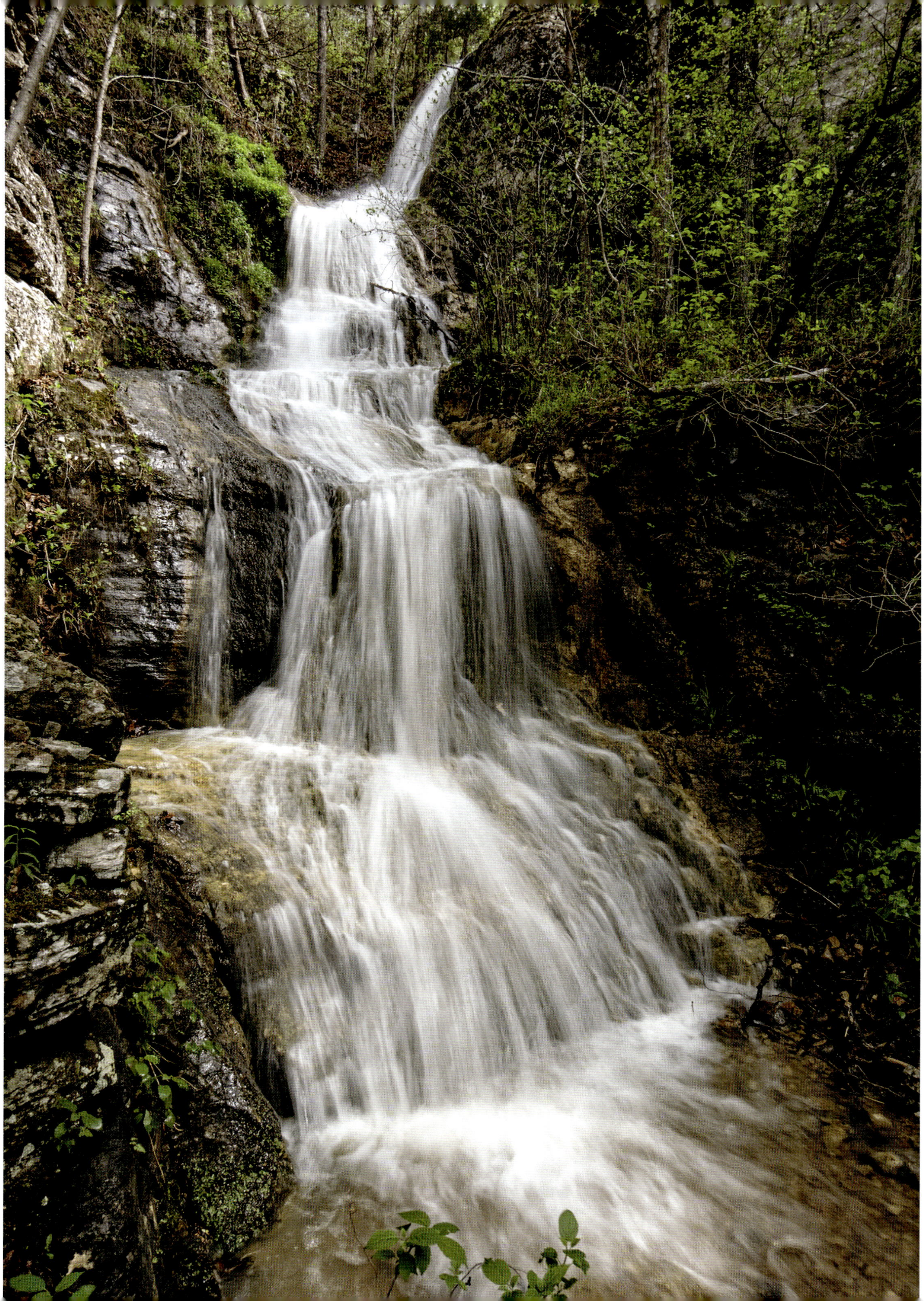

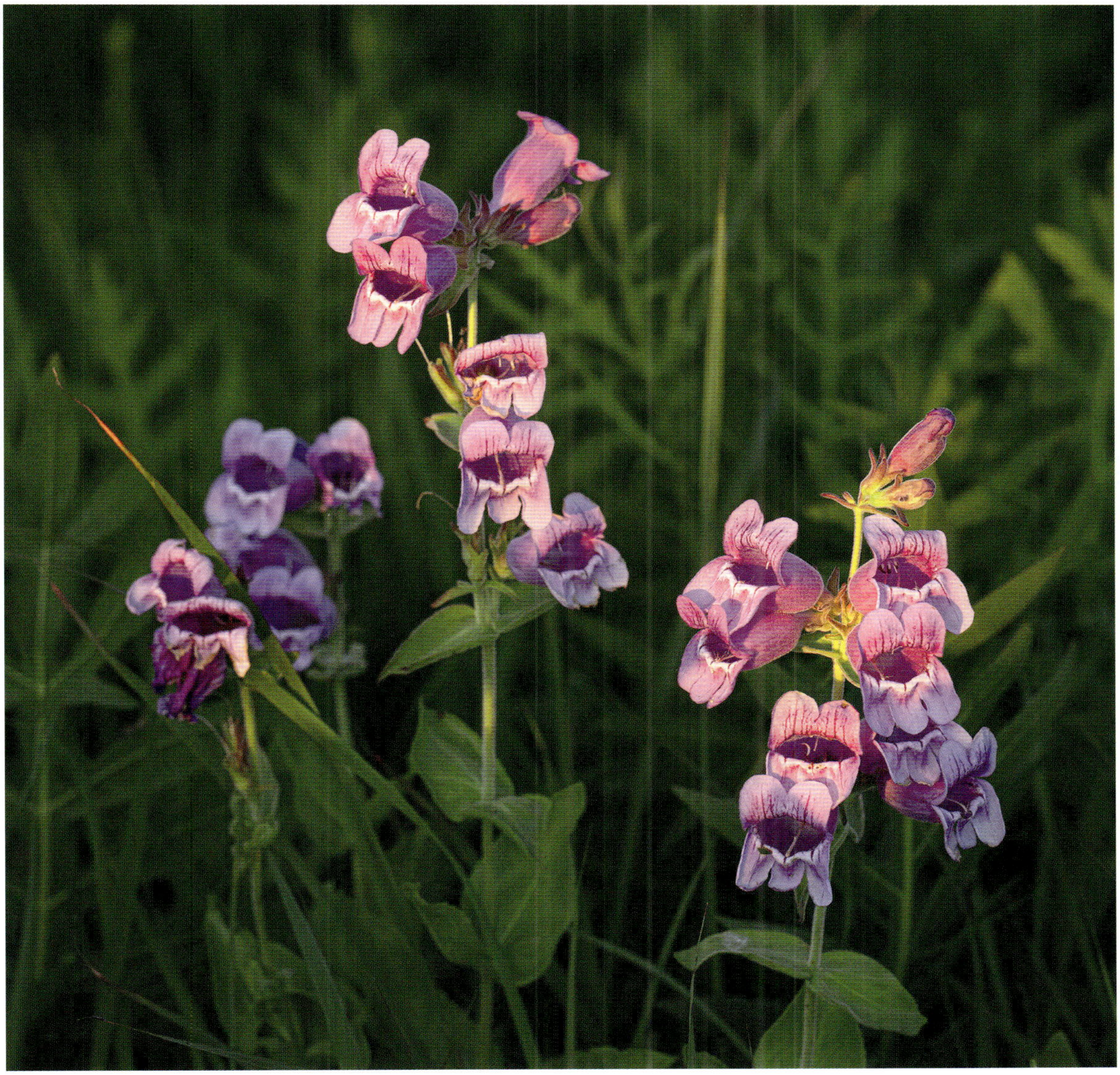

Purple Beardtounge, Rick Evans Grandview Prairie

< Cat Man Falls in Cliff Hollow, Ponca Wilderness

Along the old road down past Big Bluff to Granny Henderson's (now the Center Point hiking trail) lived Frank Little. He was known for always having a herd of cats at home—15-30 at a time! If you follow the stream that feeds this waterfall all the way up to the top of the mountain you would come out near Frank's old home site.

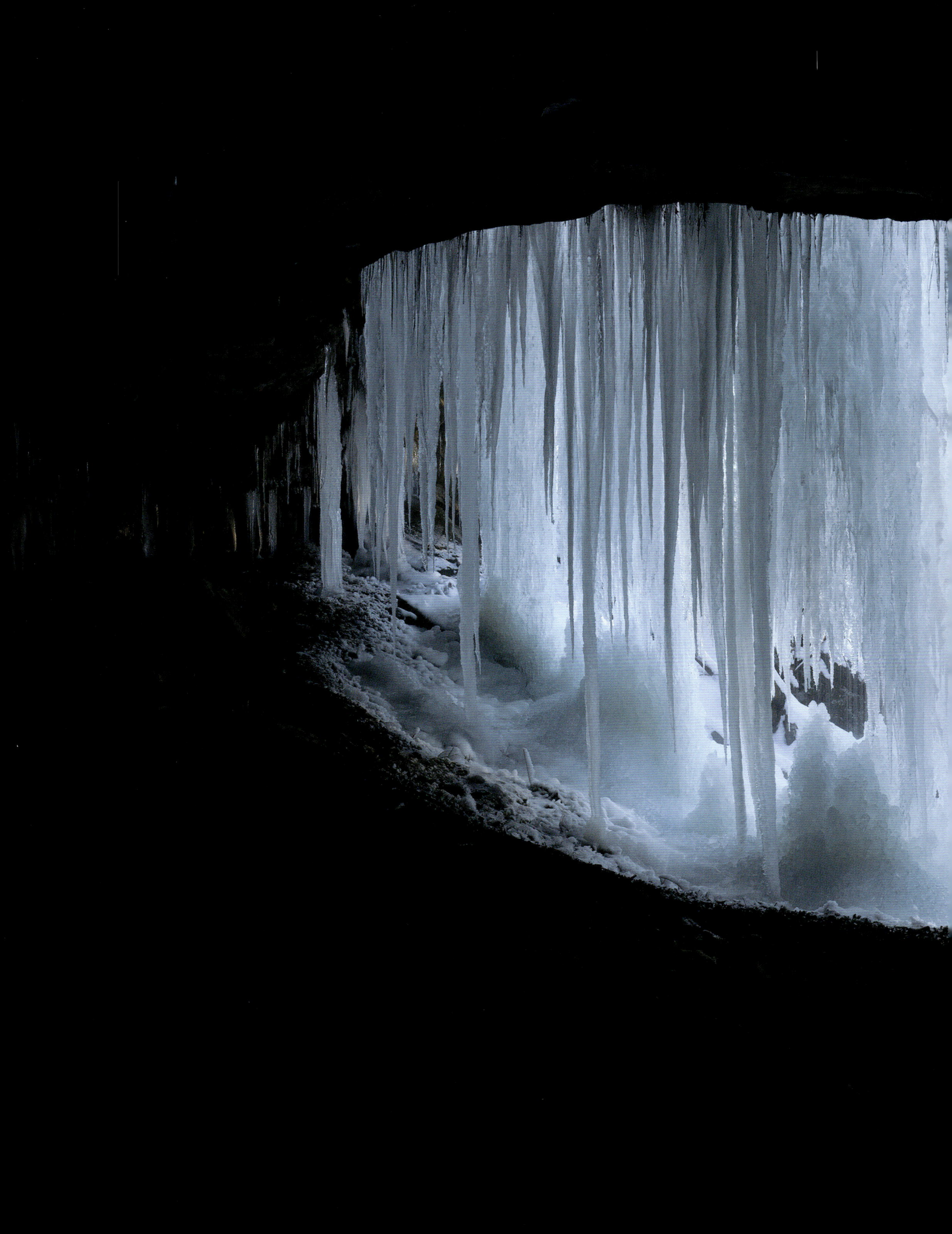

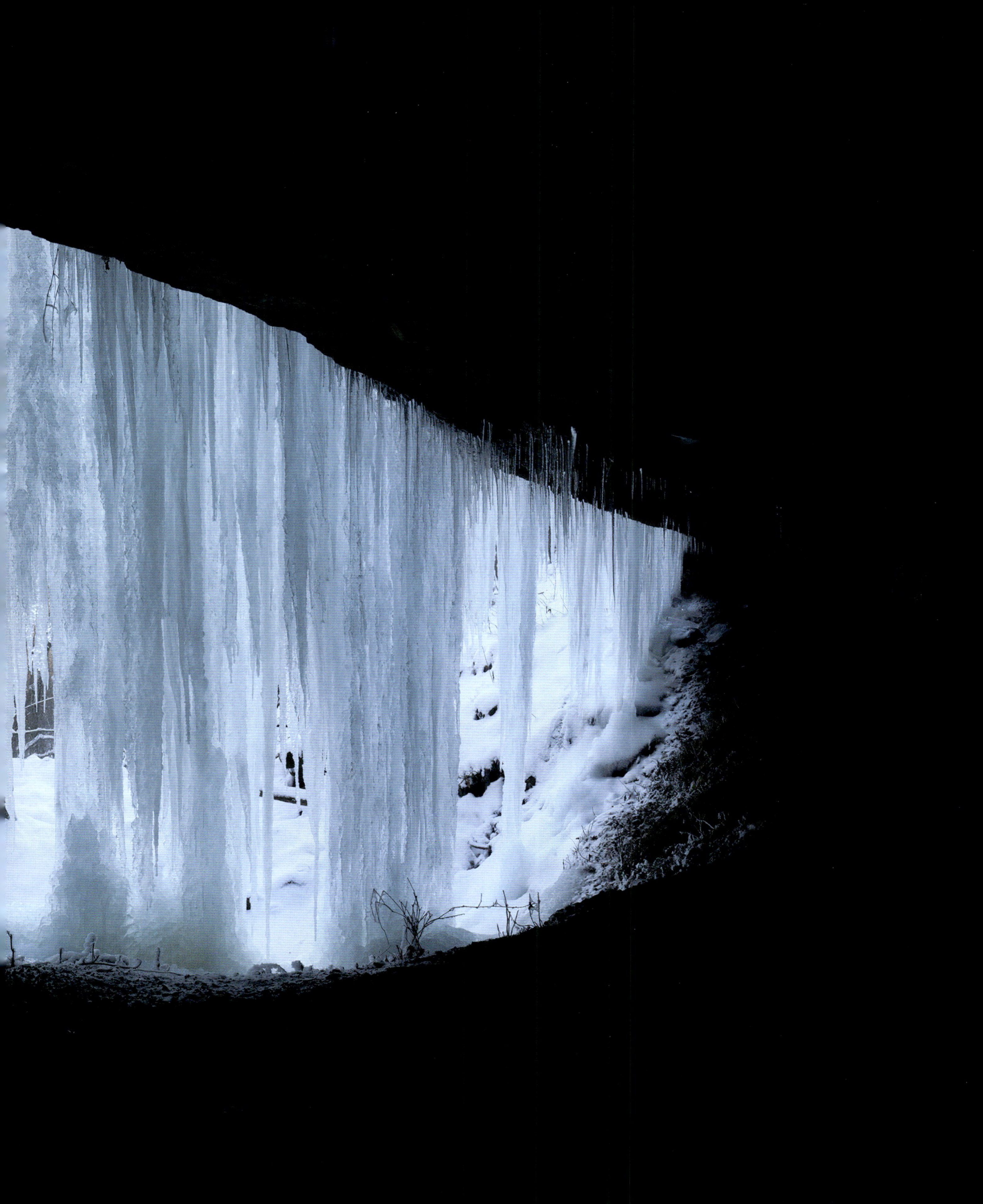

I'm sitting inside this ice cave waiting for the sun to appear and it's 5 below zero (I got a couple good photos).

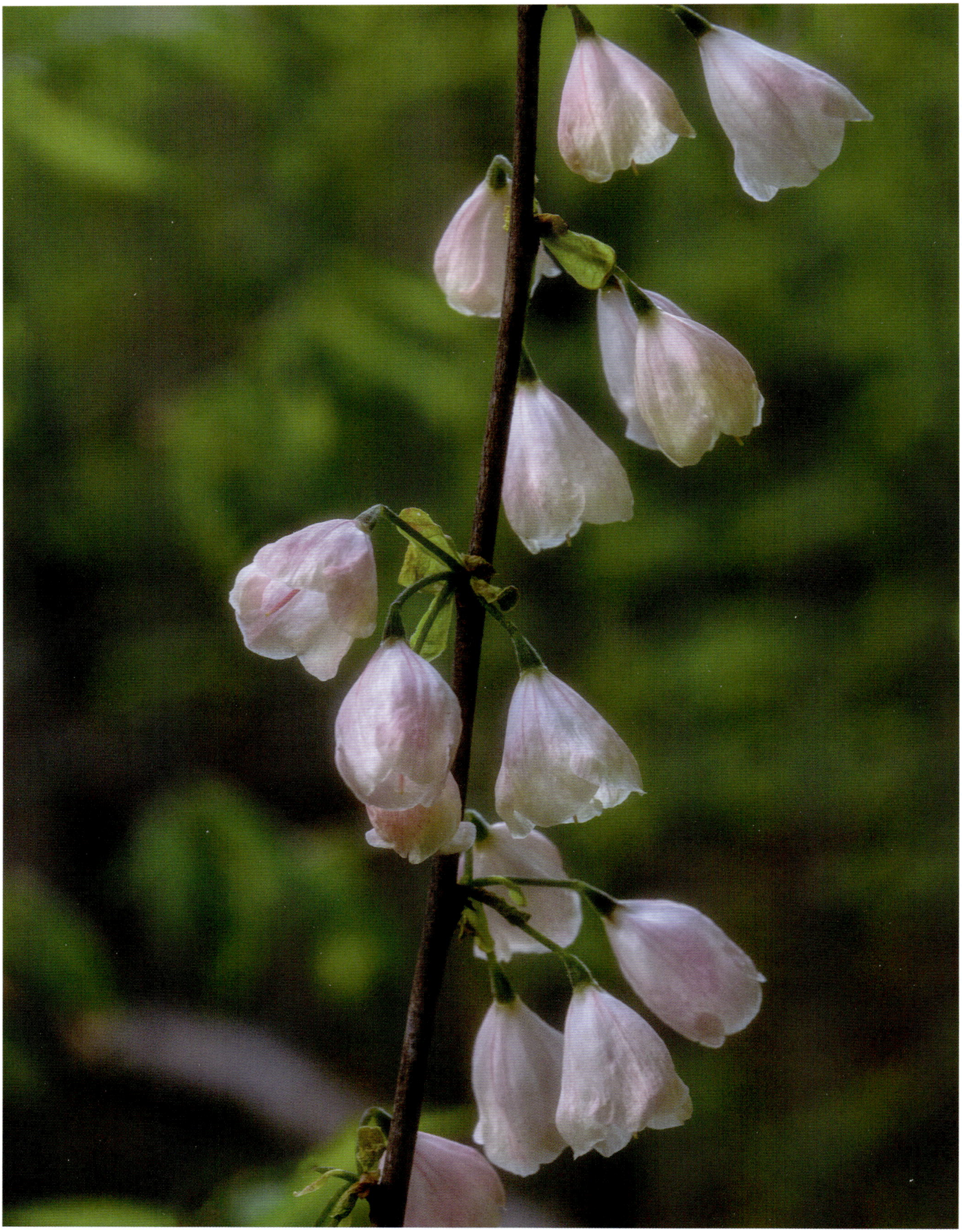

Mountain Silverbell blooms in Sally Ann Hollow, Ozark National Forest
The waterfall on the right was named after this beautiful flowering tree I found growing nearby.

Silverbell Falls, Sally Ann Hollow >

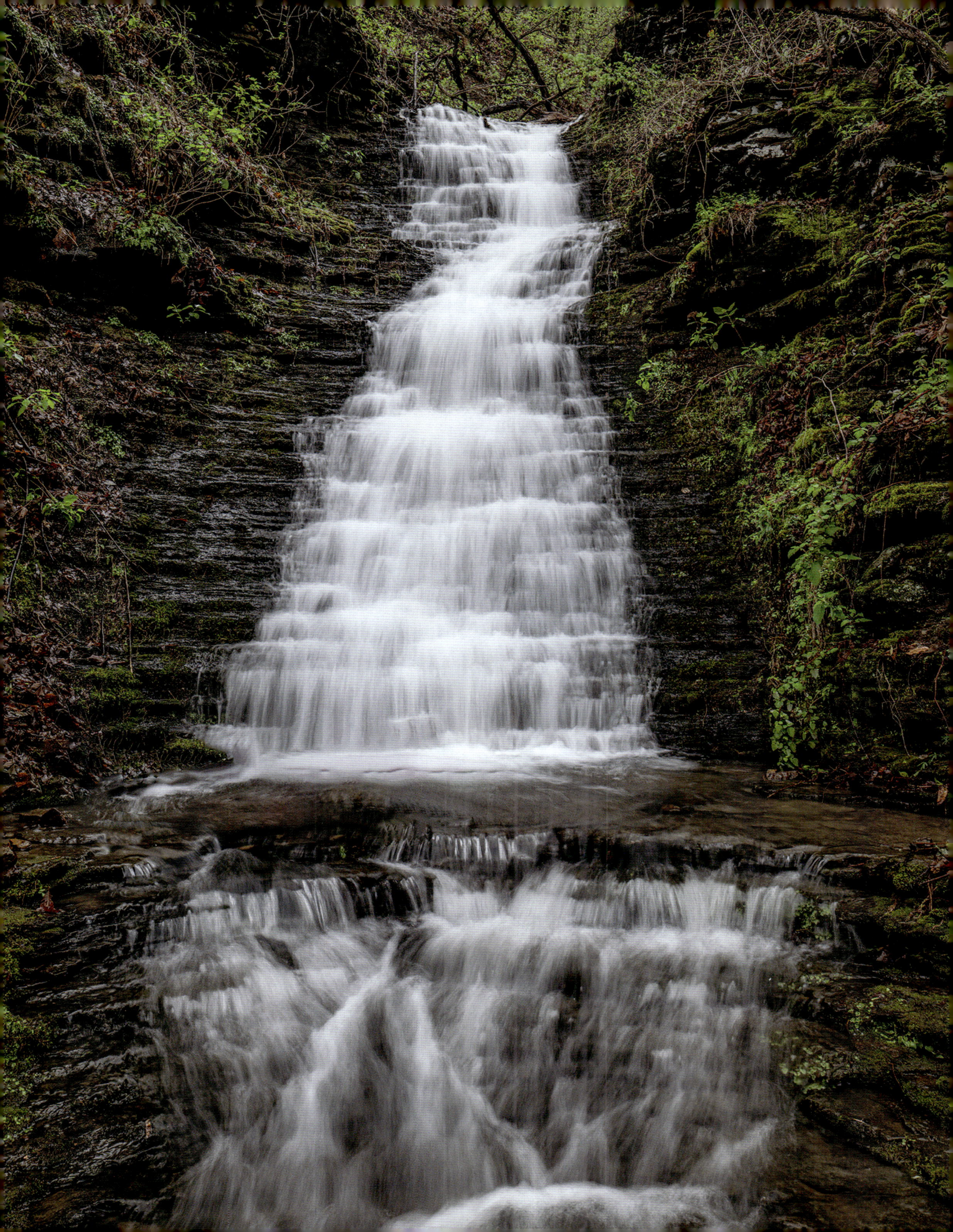

Frosted oak trees after a flash winter storm

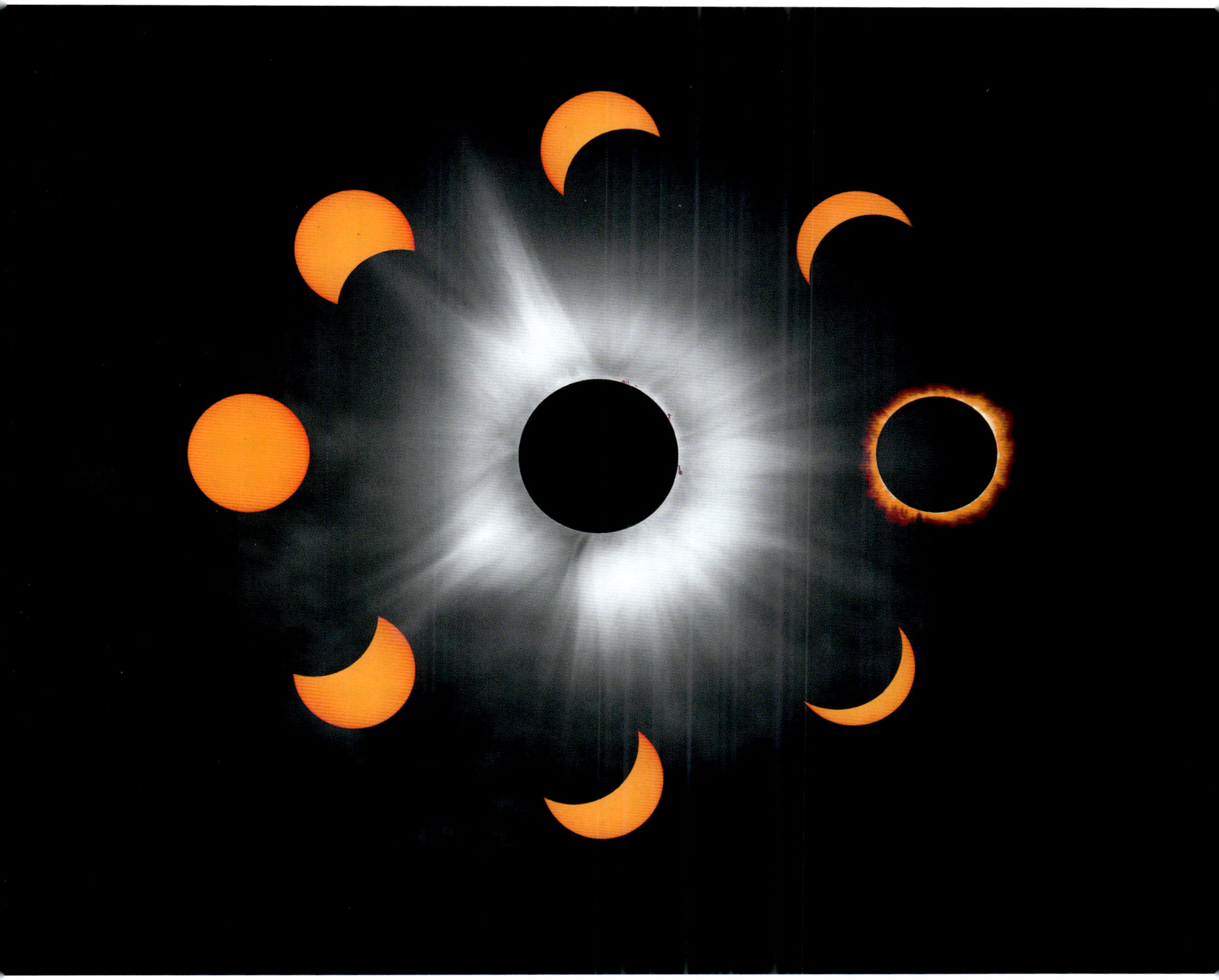

The Great American Eclipse, April 8, 2014

I didn't have to travel far for this one, and set up my big camera and giant telephoto lens in the back yard. Knowing nothing about how to do this sort of thing, I wasn't expecting much. Then a friend loaned me a special solar filter which I used to photograph the different phases of the eclipse, piece of cake! We only had about 2 minutes of totality, and holy cow did that time go FAST as I was making 24 different photos—all at different exposures—in order to capture the detail you see here in the "corona."

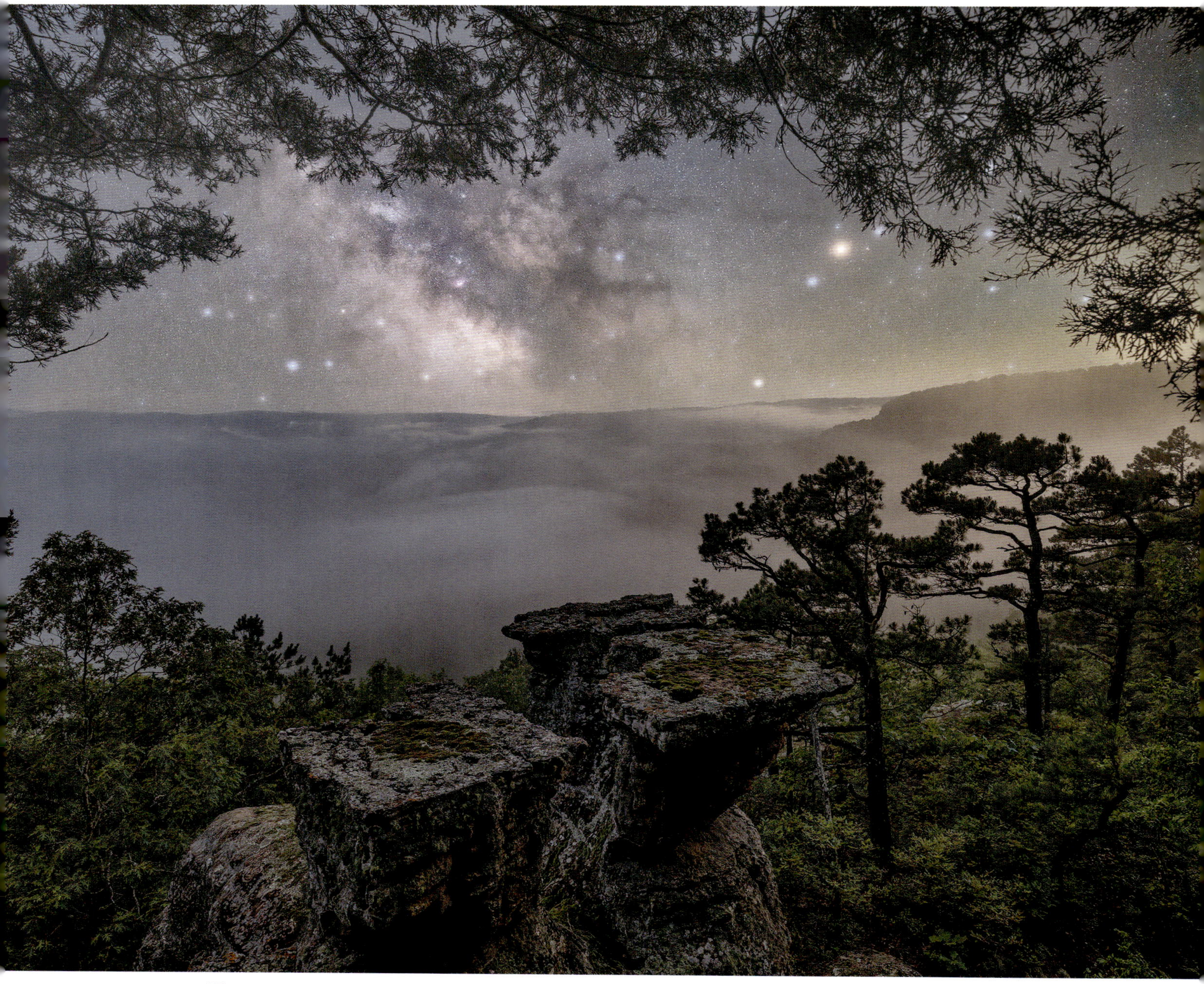

Clearing summer storm and the Milky Way at Tea Table Rocks, Ozark National Forest
FYI, this rock formation is on public land, but is surrounded by private property and permission is required for access.

Cincinnati Freedom Falls, Little Cow Creek, Ozark National Forest
Cincinnati Freedom was a cow that escaped from the slaughter house in the city and became famous while on the run, eventually being bought and named by artist Peter Max. She spent her golden years on a farm sanctuary for cows in New York. There is a large tributary system in the Ozarks with at least three main prongs of Cow Creek. Many dozens of waterfalls there are named after famous cows or other things associated with cows. This particular waterfall has some special power and magic when it's flowing like this, one of my absolute favorites. (It's the front cover of my ***ARKANSAS: JUST WATERFALLS*** picture book.)

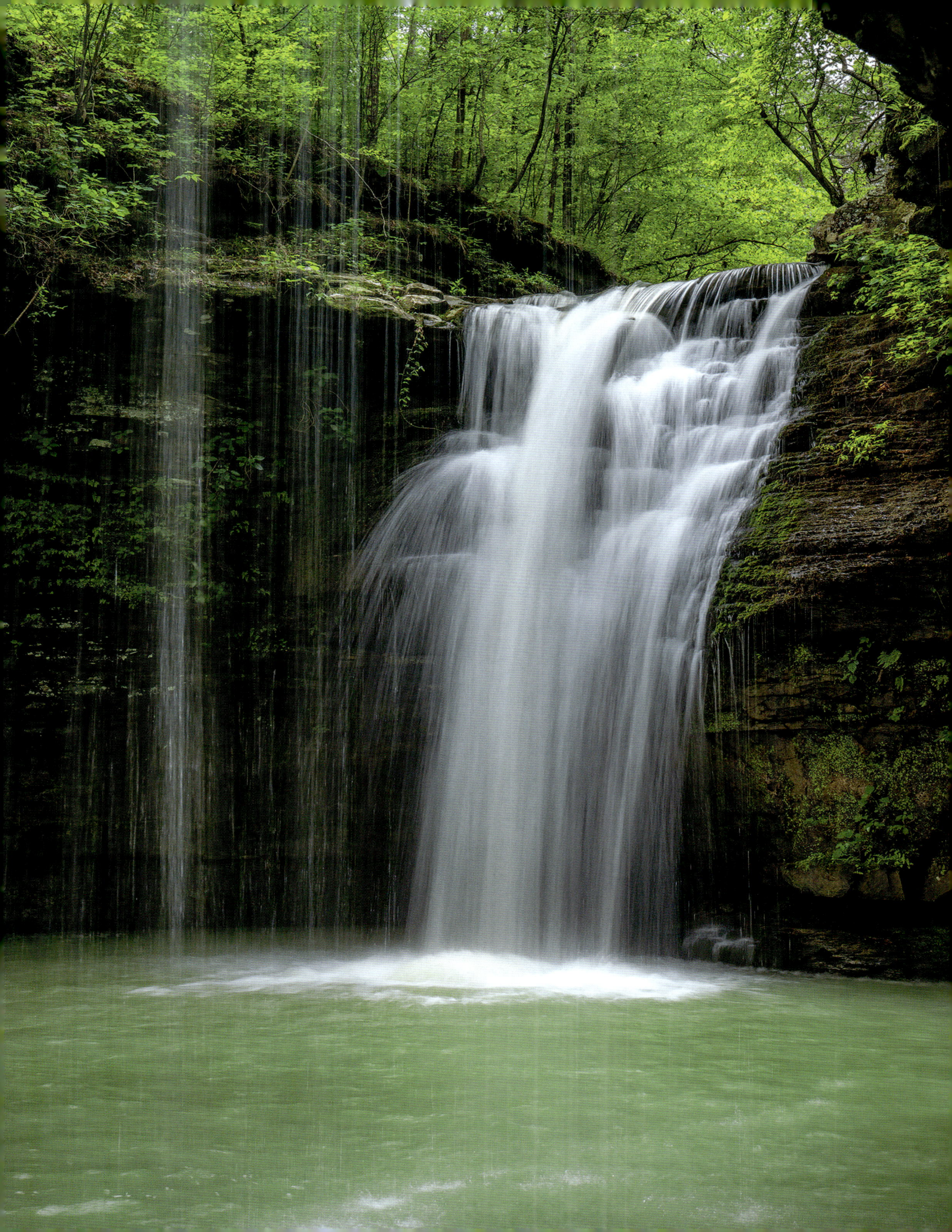

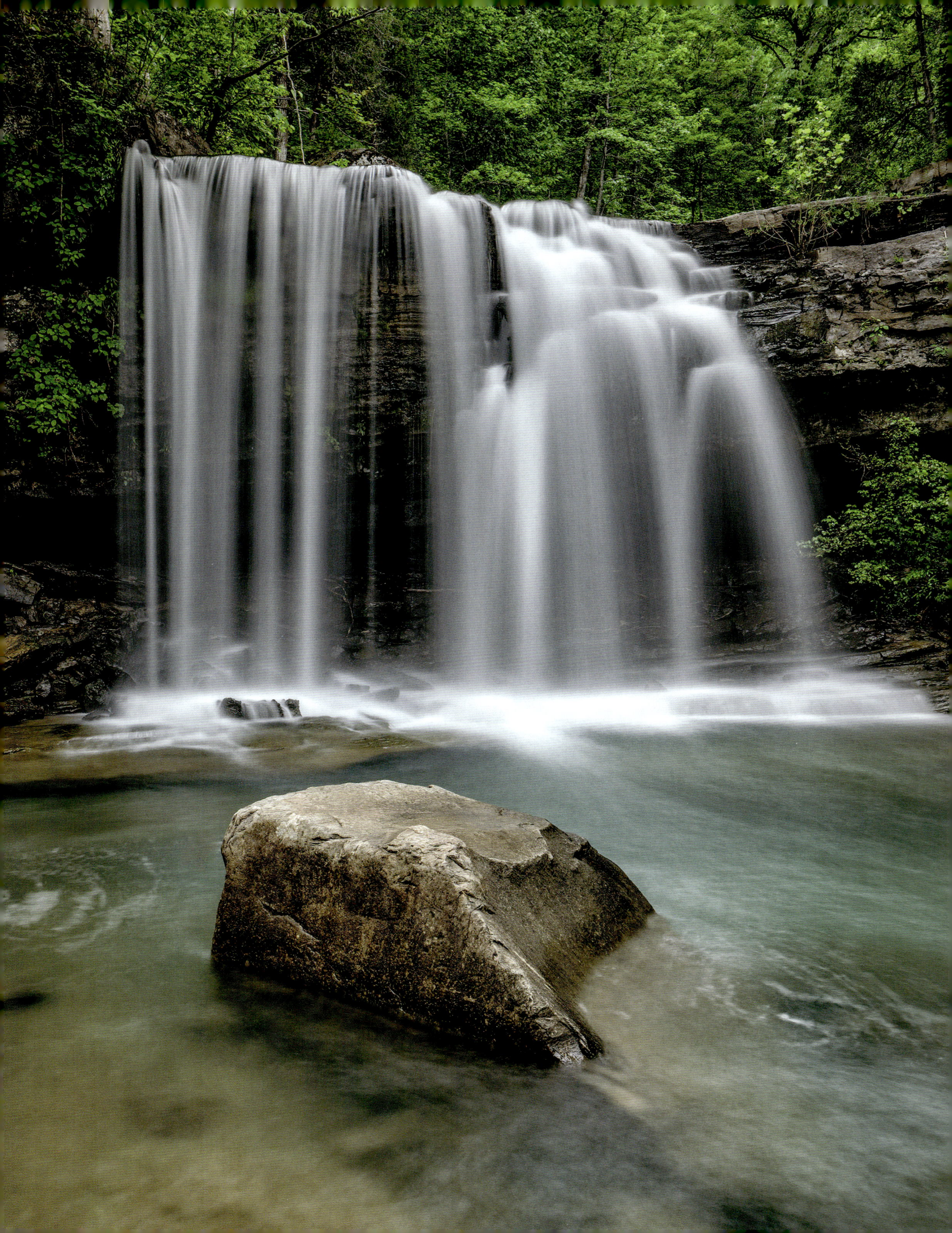

< Big Devil's Fork Falls (part of Twin Falls), Richland Creek Wilderness

THIS is the photo that made it possible for me to complete my lifelong dream of being a Nature Photographer for 50 years! It wasn't so much the actual photo, but rather the camera I was using—and what happened just before I took this photo. Five years ago I pretty much had decided to throw in the towel with the publication of my 20th picture book, ARKANSAS GREATEST HITS. 45 year of work in the woods was enough.

But then it really wasn't. I had sold all of my best camera equipment, but still had the desire to get out and take pictures And I did. But I tried to make due with not very good cameras, and I was not happy with my results. I know, I've preached for decades that it's really NOT the camera, but, well, it doesn't hurt to have really good tools to work with and I wasn't using them.

On a lark I borrowed back some of the expensive camera gear I had sold and kind of went on a test run to see if it really was the camera equipment, or had I just lost whatever skill I may have had. My first hike was into the heart of the Richland Creek Wilderness, to one of my all-time favorite waterfalls, Twin Falls of Richland Creek. Low hanging fruit I figured. And it was beautiful as I expected it to be.

I quickly set up my old camera gear on a tripod and got ready to take my first photo, but was getting in a hurry to get the shot before harsh sunshine blew away the delicate cloud cover. I reached over into my camera bag to grab something, and out of the corner of my eye I saw movement—it was that big old and heavy camera I had just borrowed that somehow decided it needed a bath, and the camera and tripod tipped right on over and into a five-foot-deep pool of water—kerPLUNK!

I was kind of shocked, and didn't really know what to do other than to dive in after it. But what was the use—certainly the electronics inside would have immediately fried. I was devastated, not only for my stupid mistake, but especially for the COST of having to buy my friend a new camera and lens!

Low and behold, somehow, the camera continued to function, and while I only took one photo with it, it DID work and I got the photo you see here. Almost immediately after I clicked the shutter, the lens (and probably the camera body too) filled up with water—sort of a delayed reaction. Let's just say it was a very long hike out and drive home, and then an un-fun phone call to the camera's owner.

Fast forward a year, and I was STILL using the very same camera (though not the lens, it was toast). I ended up buying a new version of that camera with lenses, and that is what most of the photos in this book were shot with (along with a year's worth with my old camera). During the long hike back out that day I decided if I could save the camera I would get back to shooting again and work towards one more picture book. Had that Fuji GFX camera not survived the swim it took, I most likely would not have ever taken pictures again. (And of course, moral of the story is to never loan me any camera equipment!)

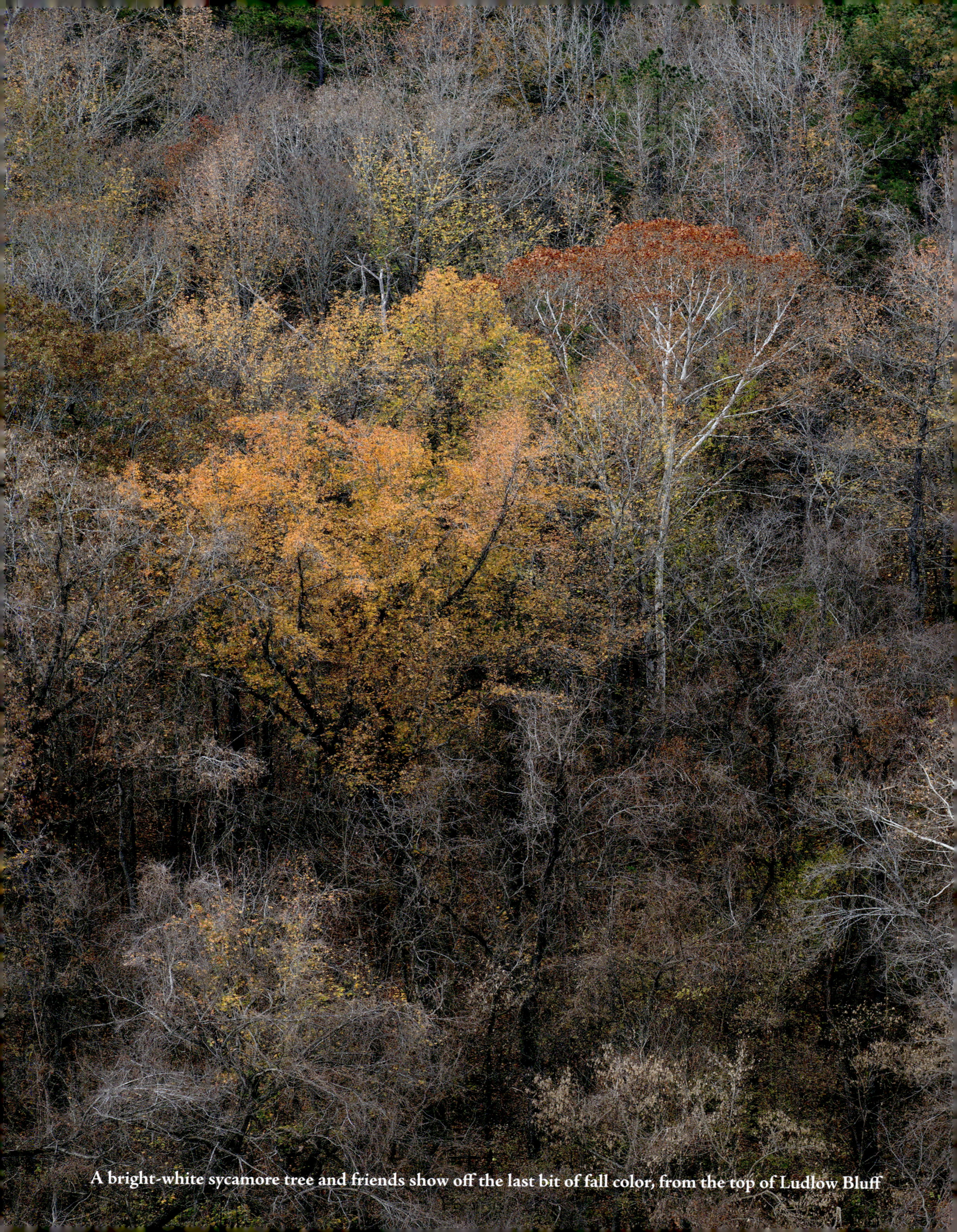

A bright-white sycamore tree and friends show off the last bit of fall color, from the top of Ludlow Bluff

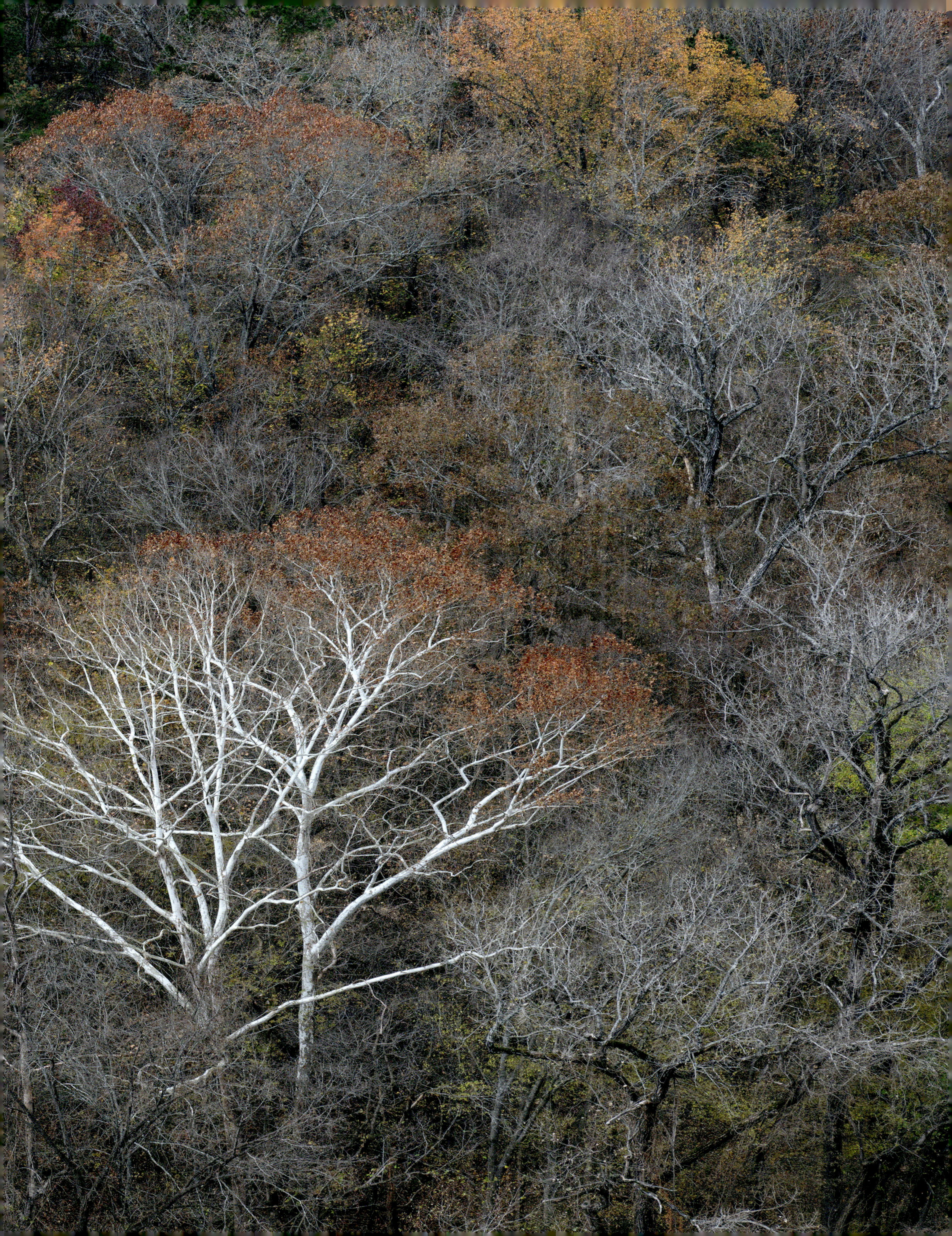

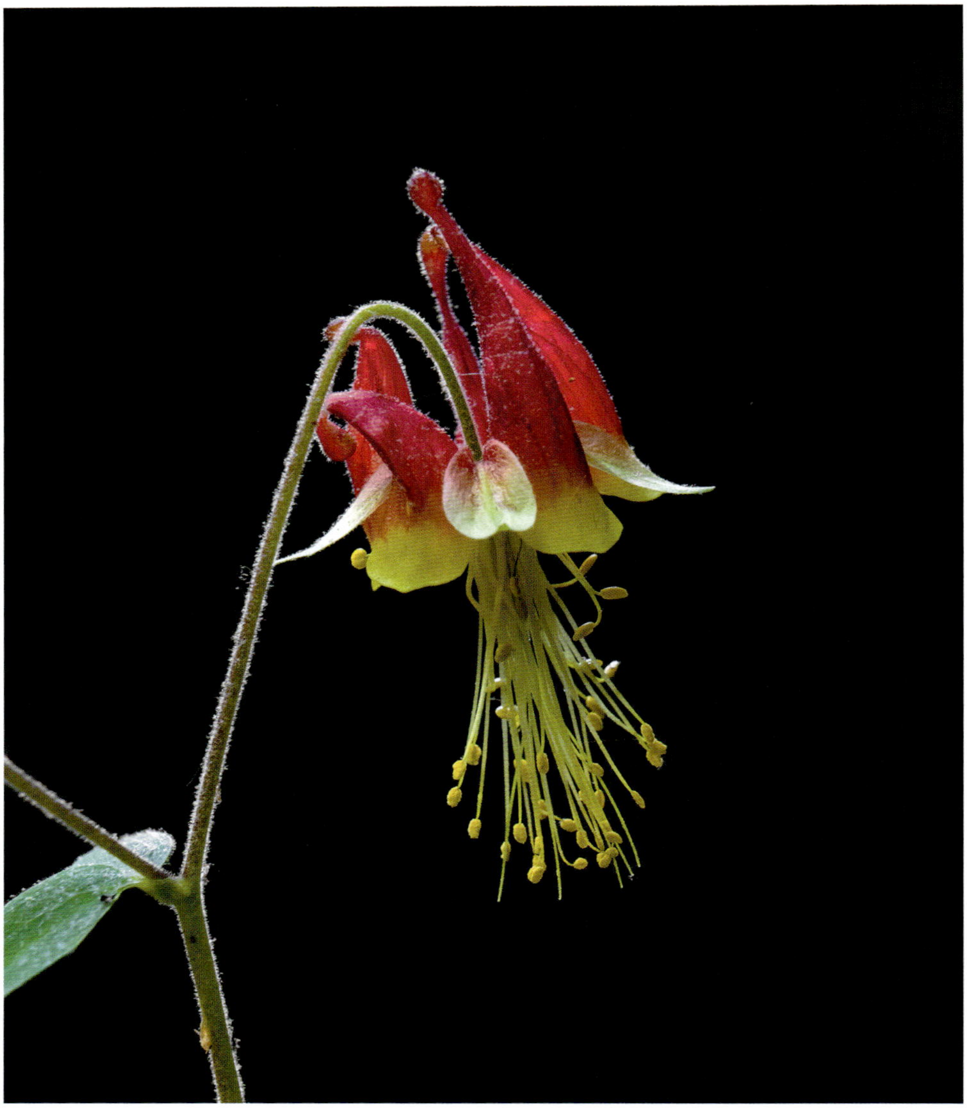

Columbine, Arkansas variety!

Eden Falls at the end of the Lost Valley Trail, in the moonlight (see the stars?) >
See page 23 for what the trail looked like on my hike back out—I LOVE hiking in moonlight

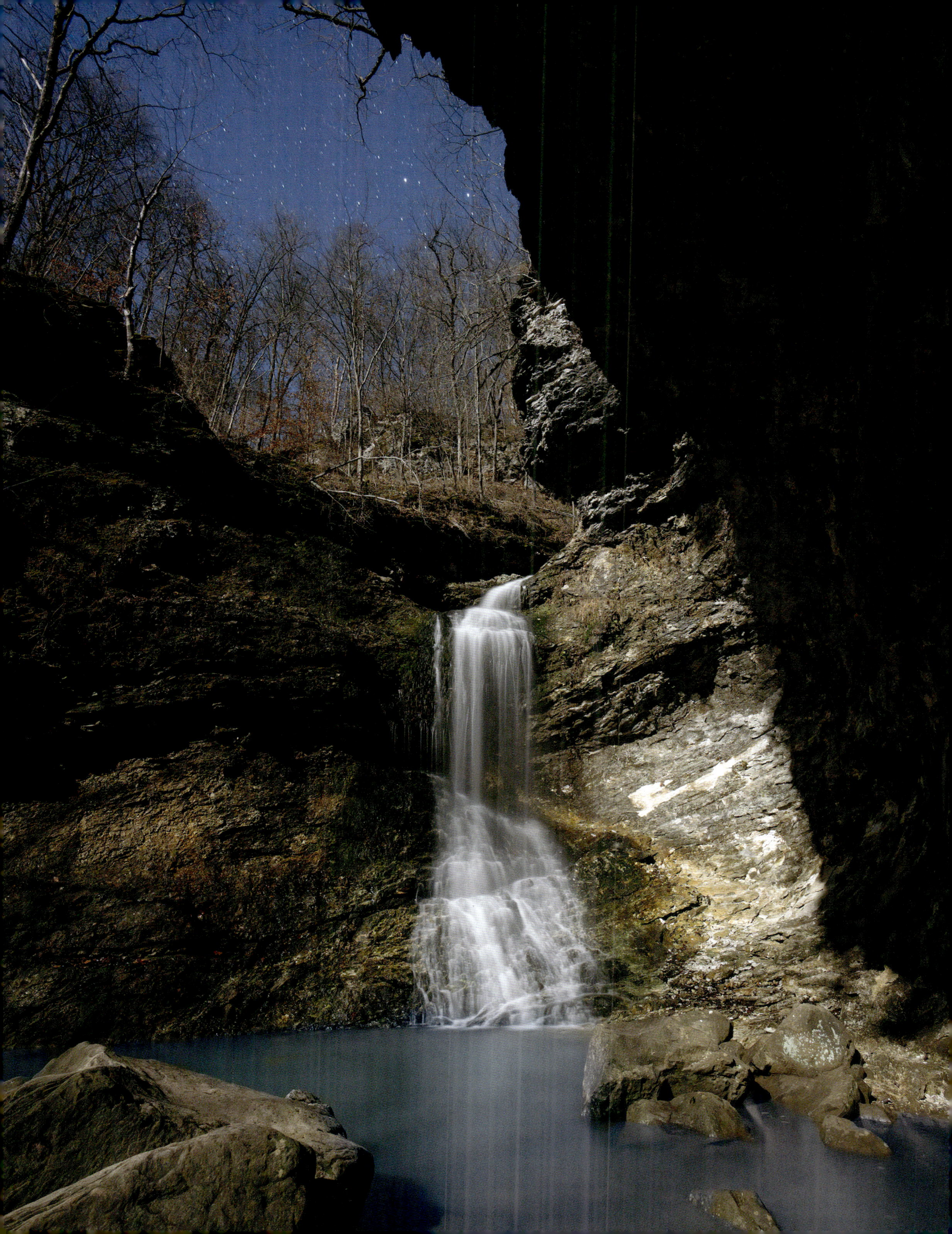

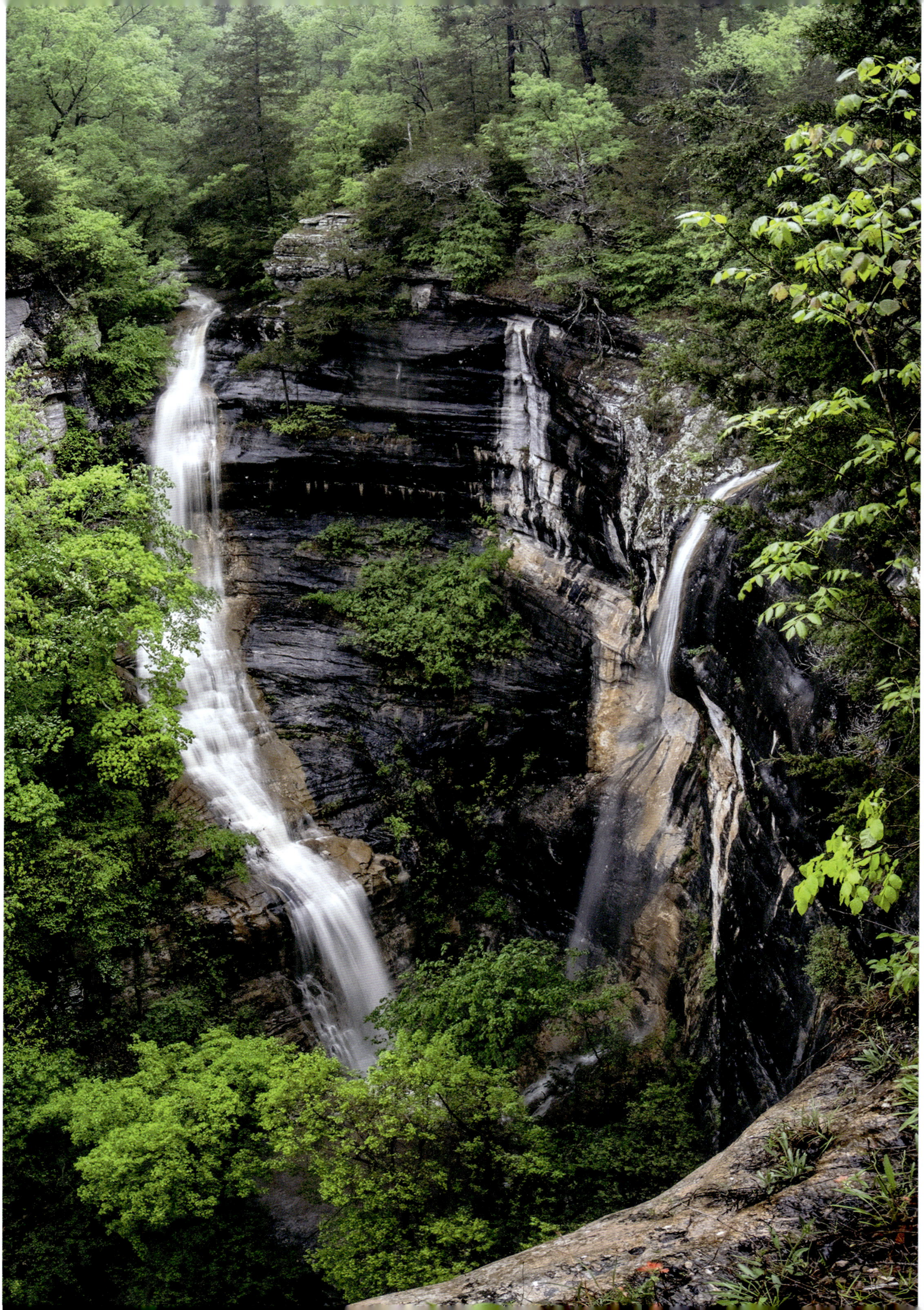

< Cecil Hollow Falls (108' on the left), and Smokey Joe Falls (105' on the right)

This pair of waterfalls pour into the same pool below—the tallest pair like this in all of Arkansas.

While exploring this unknown drainage for the first time I was a little gaga when I came to the bottom of these two monsters. They were quite impressive, though neither was flowing much and I didn't even take any photos. I sat down on a rock to admire and wondered what they looked like when cooking a full boil. Well, just then a LOUD crack of thunder happened, and good grief the sky opened up and it started to pour buckets! I ran for cover and crouched beneath a narrow bluff as the storm raged on all around me.

Finally the deluge ended and oh my both falls roared to life!

Haha, the joke was on me because the water and splash was so powerful that I was unable to take a single photo—in fact, I had to scramble for cover to keep from getting swept away! I managed to climb out of the canyon to safety and decided to head back home (it was almost dark already and a long hike to get back to my car).

< THIS is what I found the next morning, great water and lots of swirling patches of fog. The fog reminded me of the Legend of Smokey Joe I'd heard about as a tenderfoot boy scout across the river at Camp Orr. There are many variations of the story that is still told round the campfire to scouts each summer. I think Ol' Smokey Joe may still be out there...

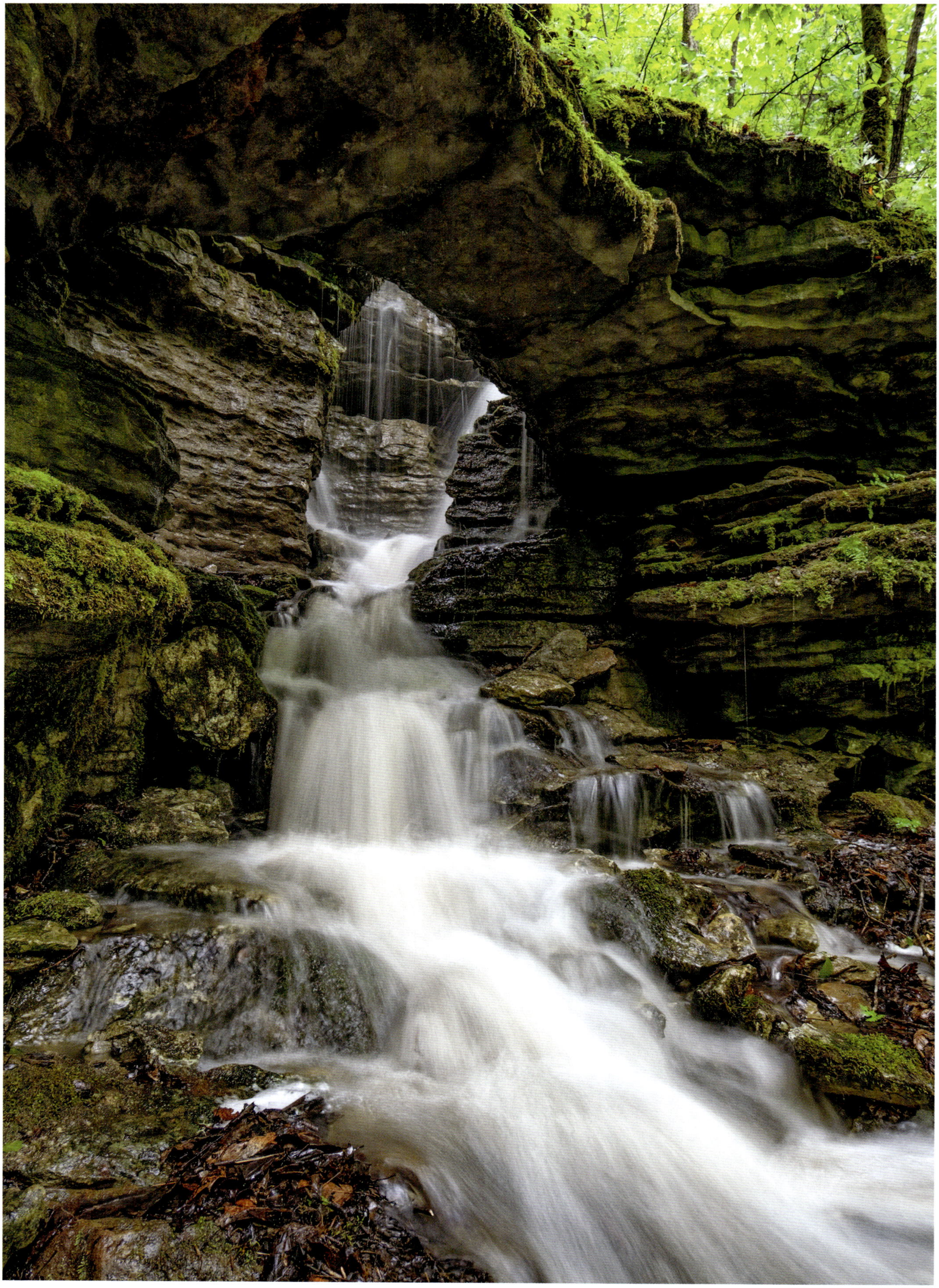

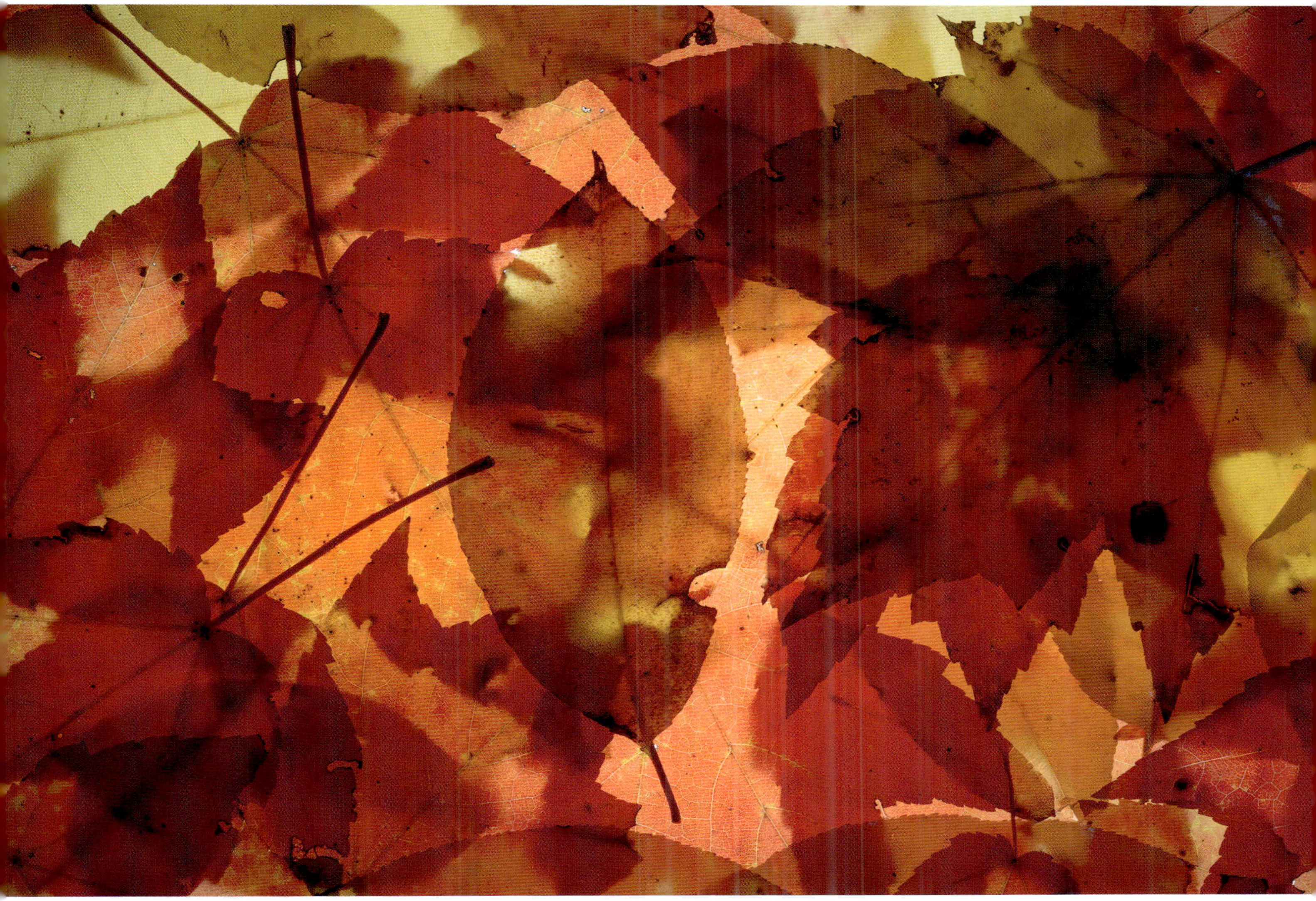

This is just a bunch of fall leaves I picked up and tossed onto a light table

< Natural Bridge Falls, Leatherwood Creek

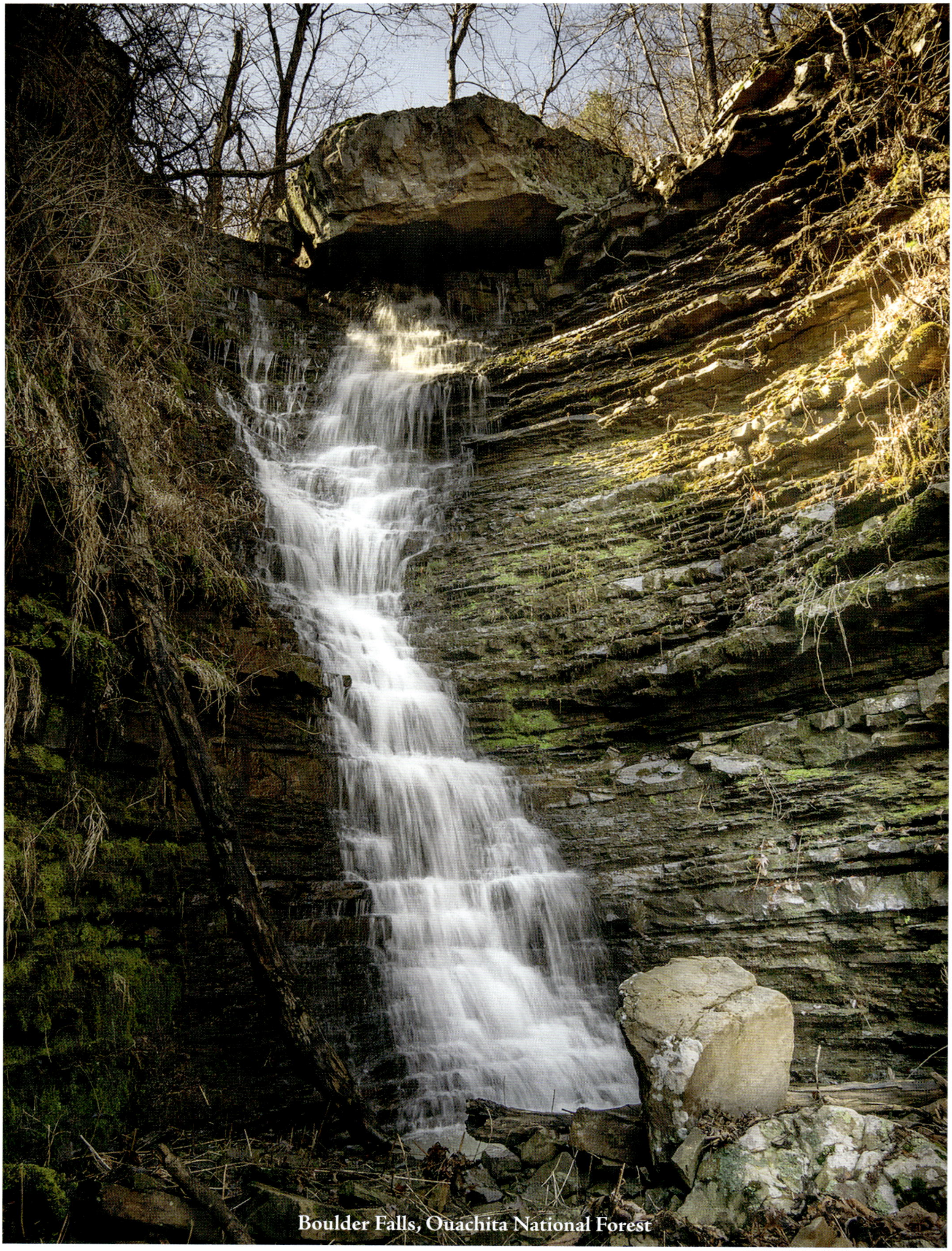

Boulder Falls, Ouachita National Forest

Flood Springs Fall, the tallest waterfall in the Ouachita Mountains (91', and me for scale) >

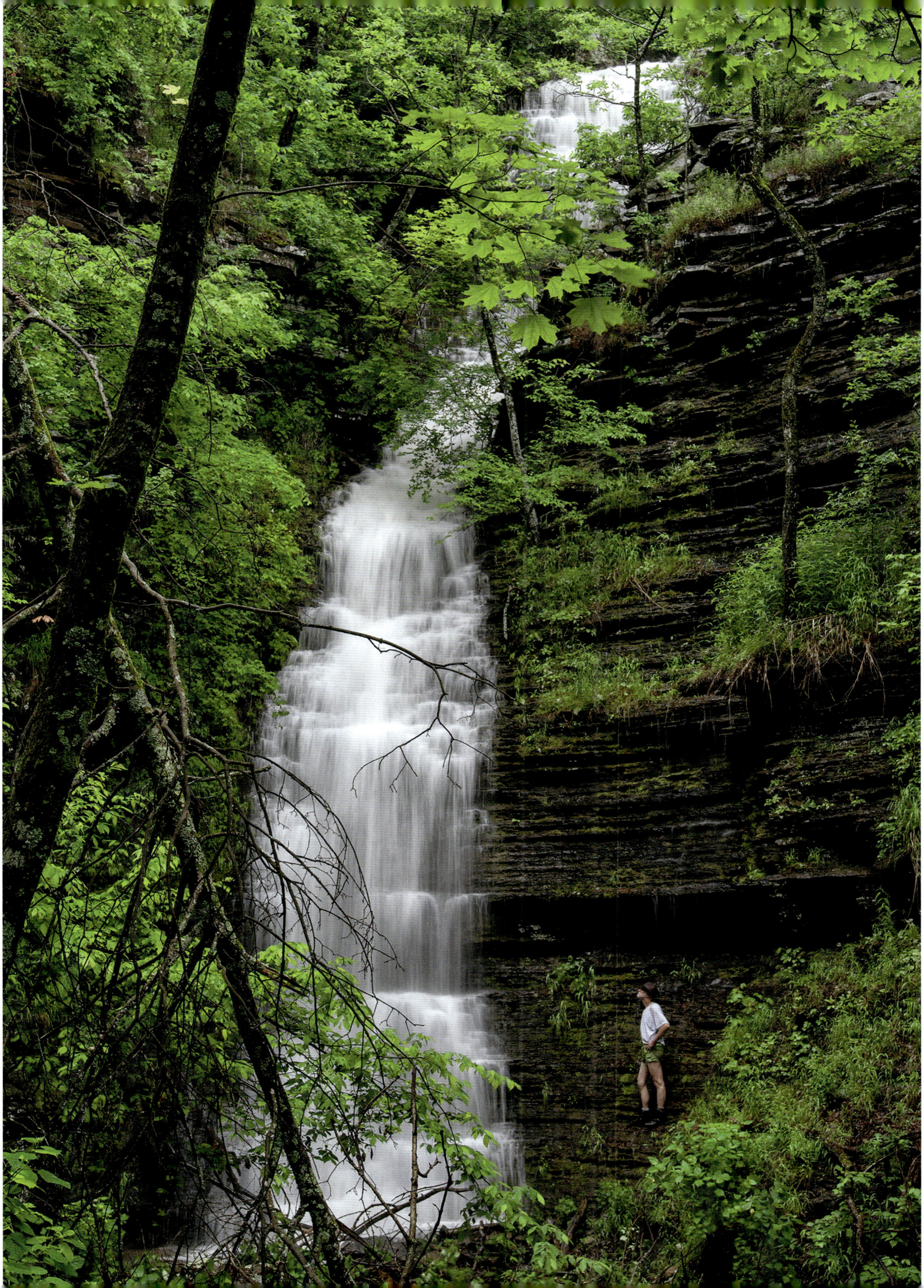

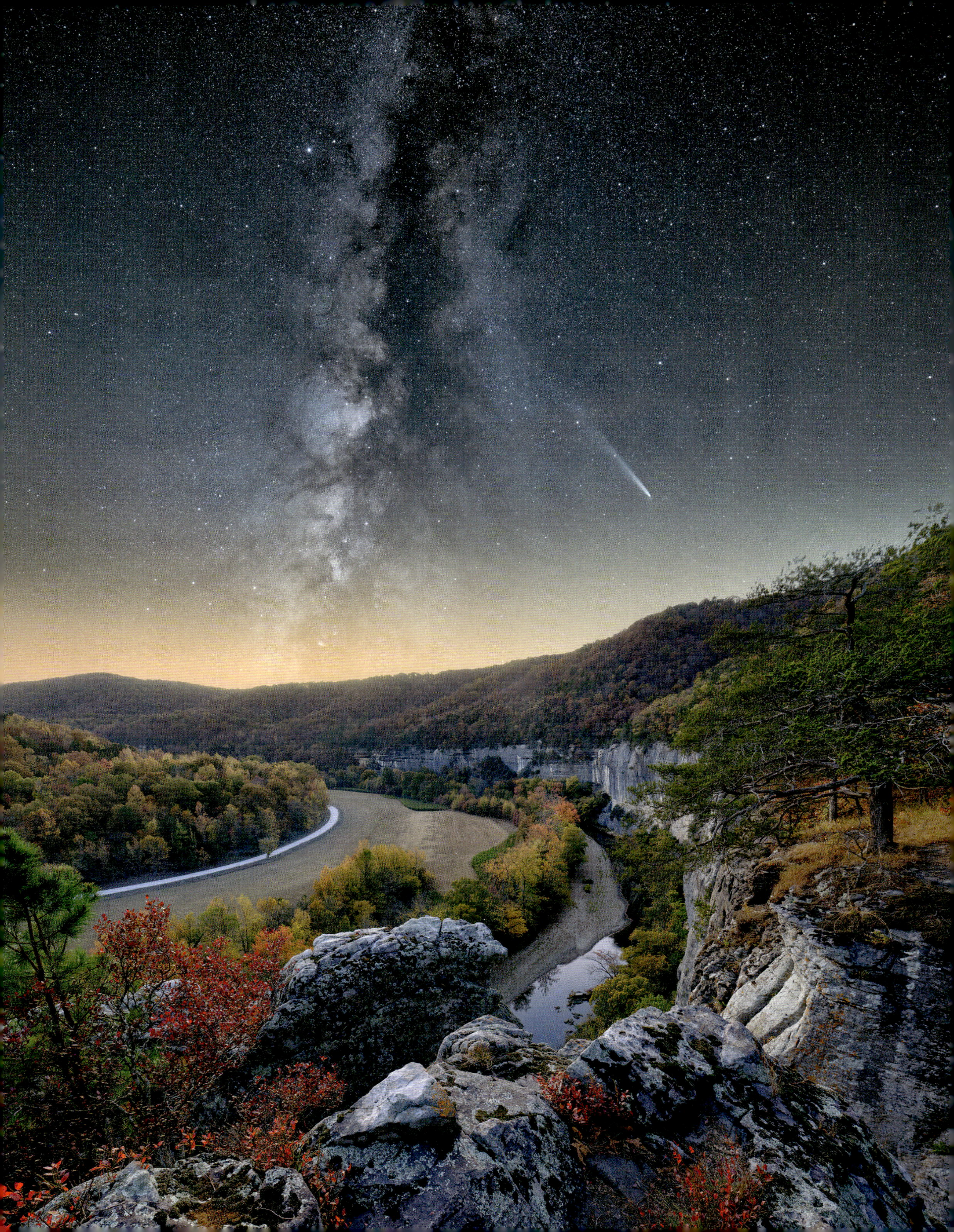

< Roark Buff and the Comet (A3 Tsuchinshan-ATLAS), Ponca Wilderness, Buffalo National River

This was the brightest Comet we've seen in a long time. I'm not a Comet photographer, but the first night I was able to just look up and see it clearly in the sky, I kind of got onto a mission to see if I could get a photo of it.

The very next night I was sitting right there where this photo was taken, and shot the first part of a planned double exposure —the bluff, fall color, and the river at twilight (almost dark). The wind was dead still, it was a very long exposure and the colors really popped. Then I sat down next to my tripod and waited (careful not to move anything). Waited for a couple of hours for it to get completely dark and for the Milky Way and Comet to rotate into the view that you see here. SNAP! The second part of my double exposure was done.

That was the easy part. I'm not much of a computer or photoshop guru, and had to get someone who was an expert to merge the two photos together, which when blended, created the final image.

Not happy with beginner's luck, I went out to different locations every night for the next week or two and shot many more images, but none of them were as good as this. The Milky Way and Comet all looked the same, but to me it's the foreground of the bluff, fall color, and the river that make this work (and I never found a better location). YEA, I got a Comet photo! FYI, they had just spread fresh white gravel on the road into Steel Creek Campground, which is the white trail you see in the photo.

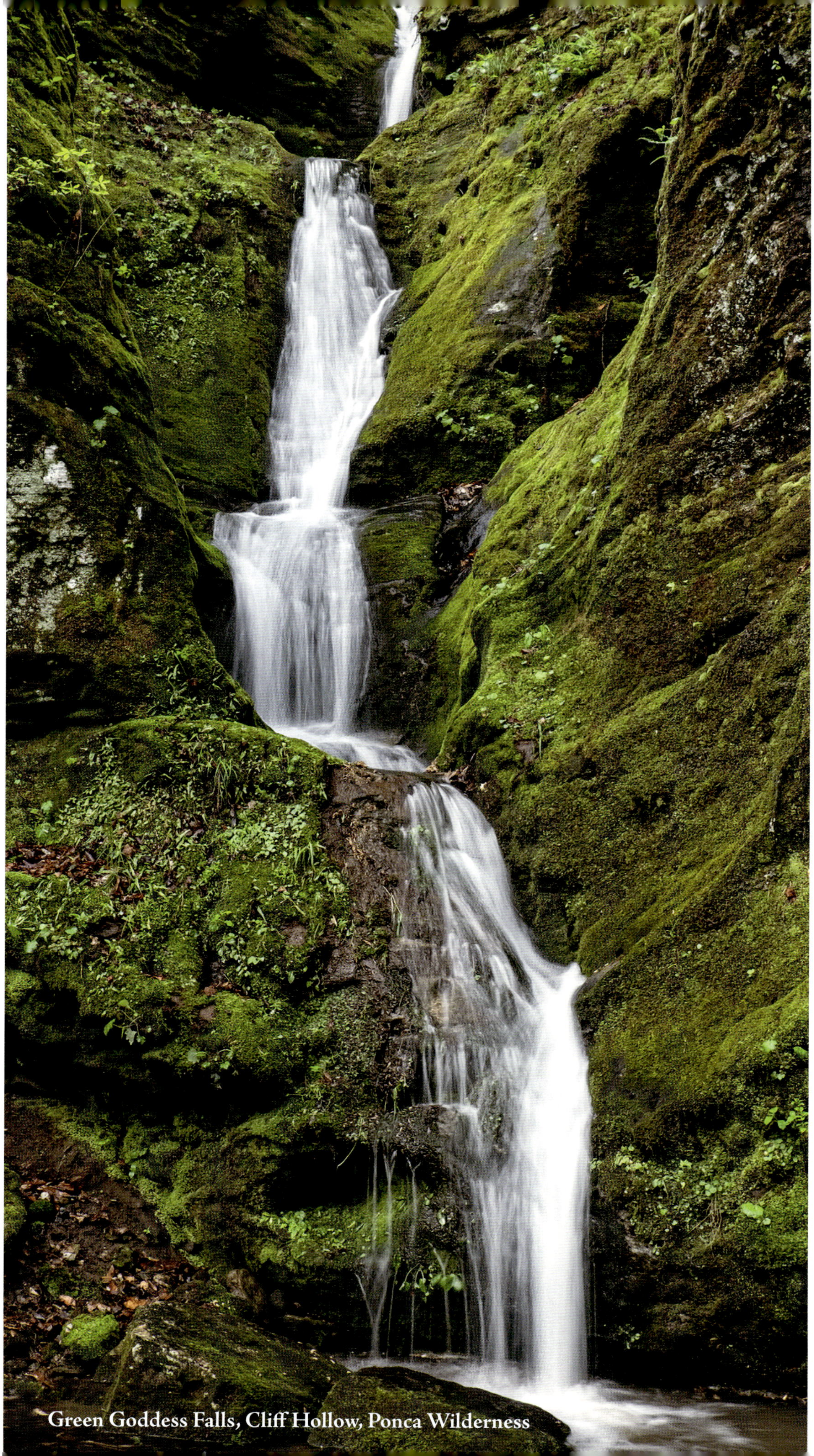

Green Goddess Falls, Cliff Hollow, Ponca Wilderness

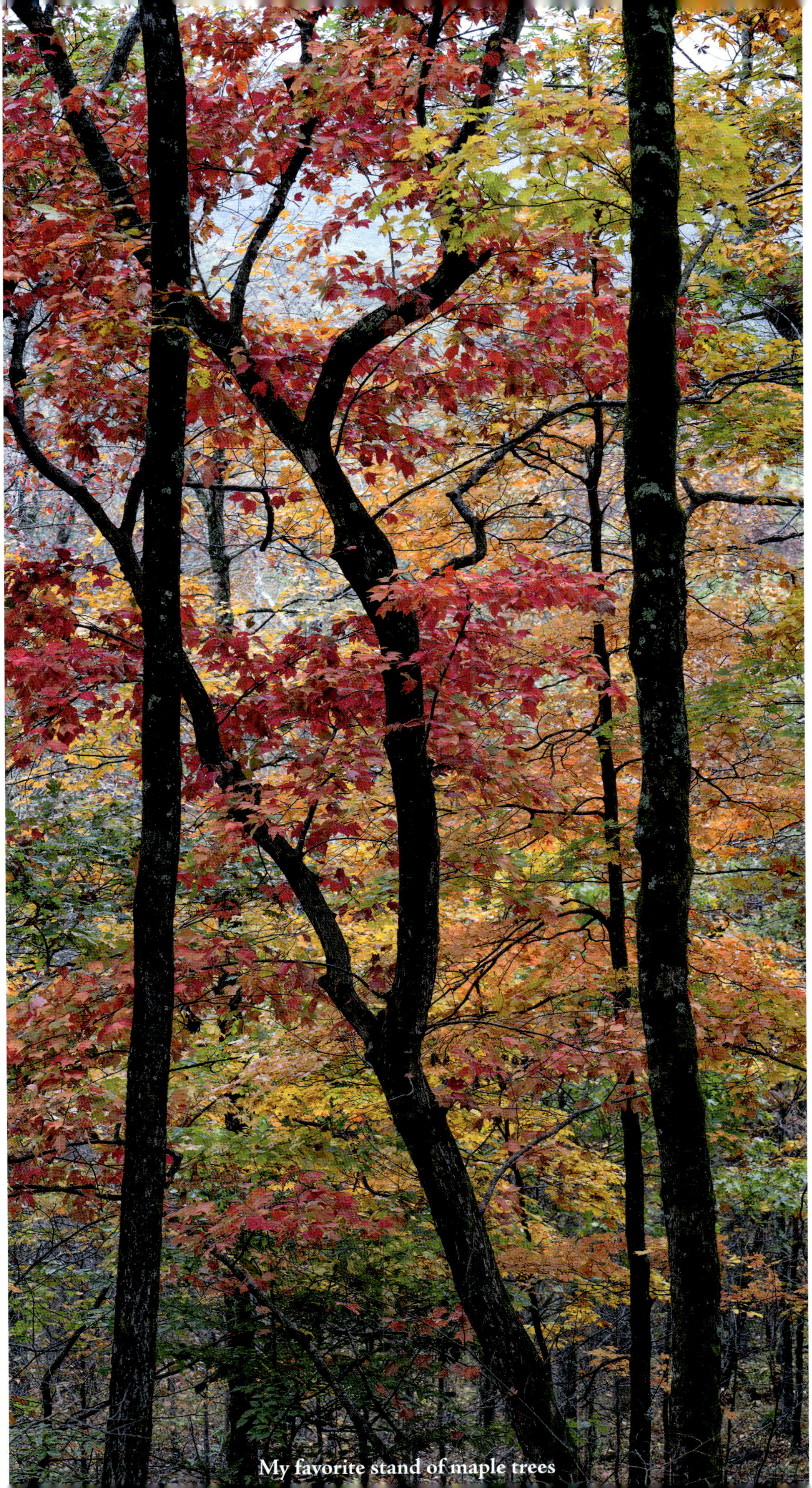

My favorite stand of maple trees

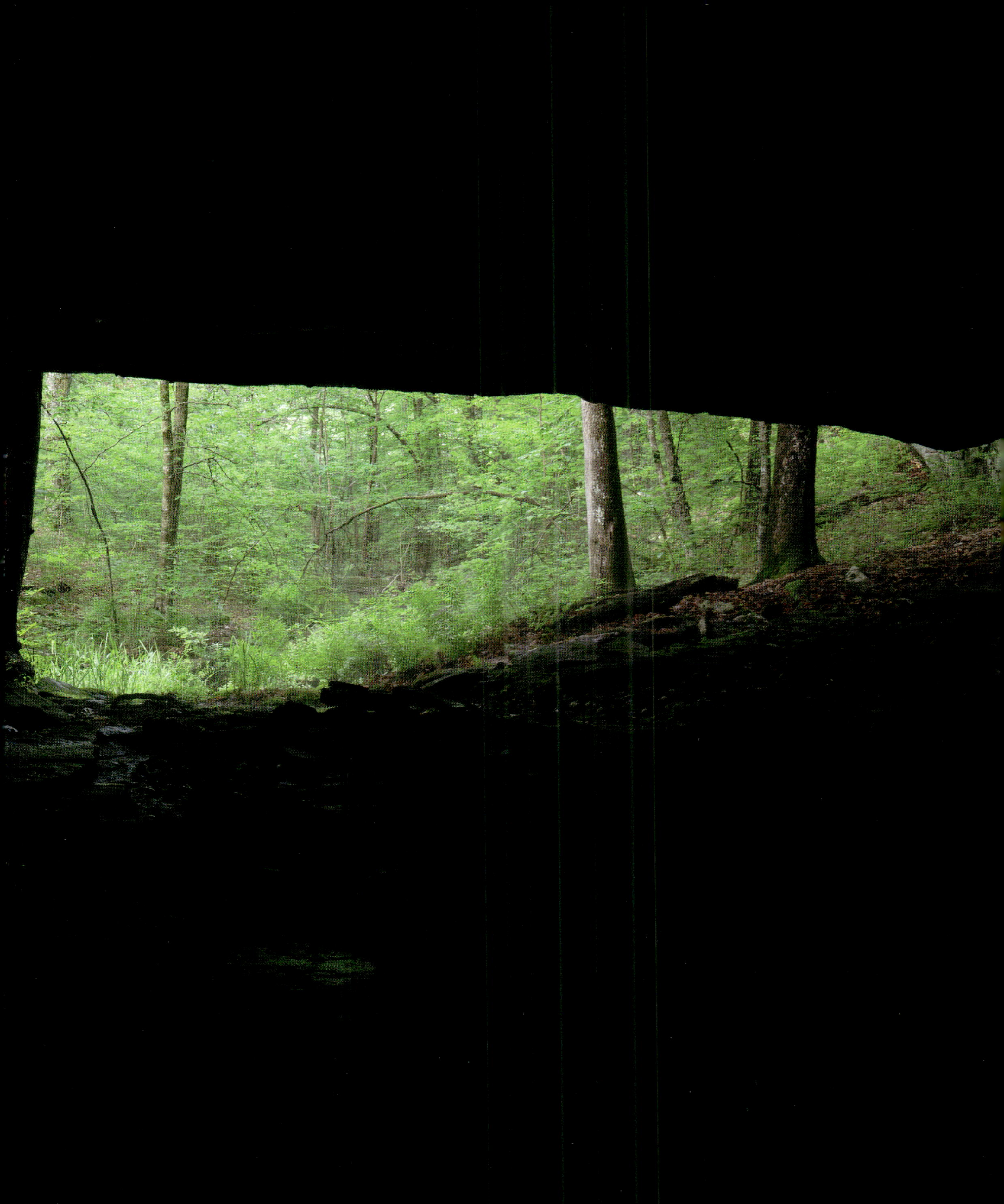

Leonardo Falls, Upper Buffalo Wilderness

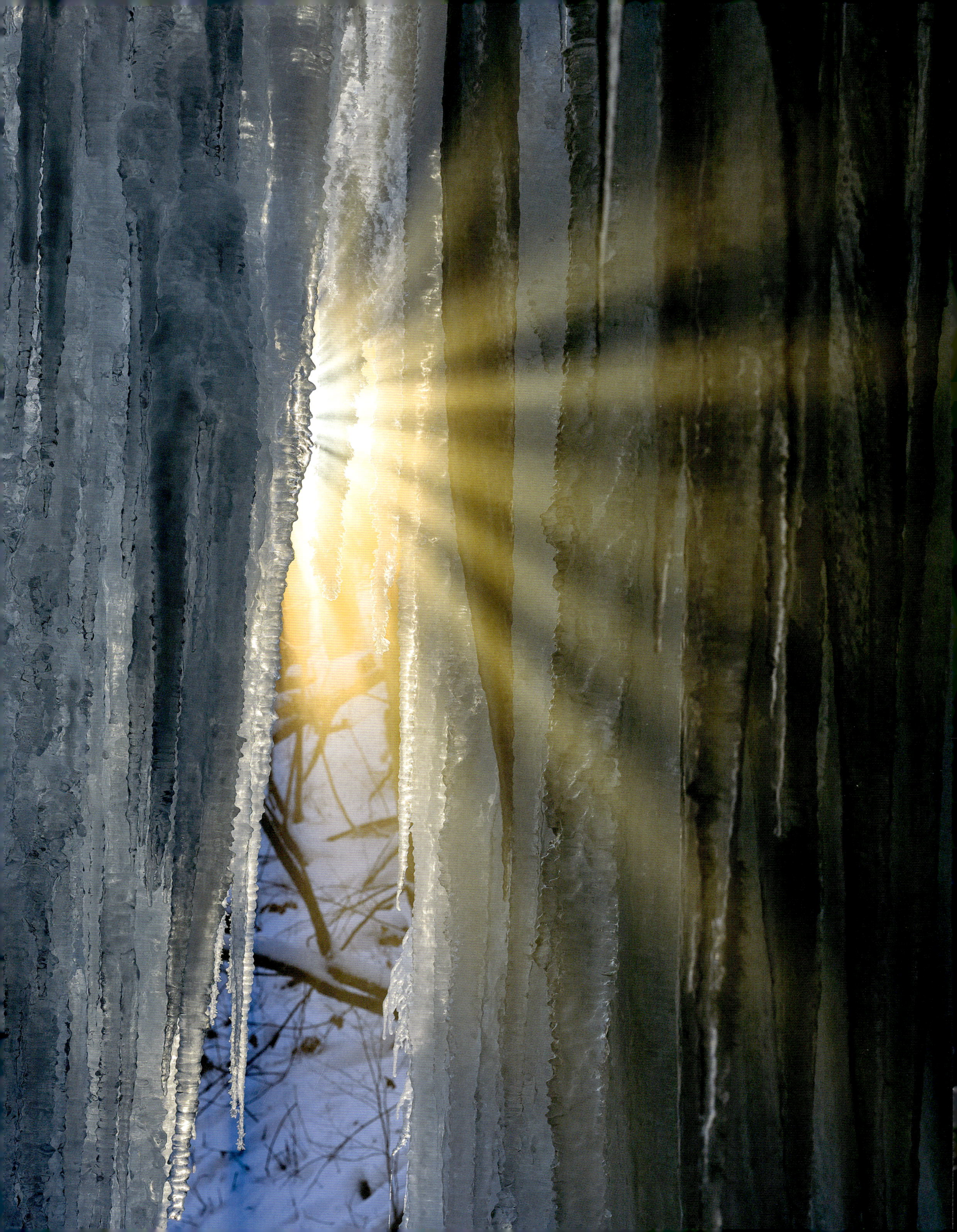

< From the back of our ice cave at 5 below zero, the sun finally breaks through—YEA!
***The following entry is from my online Cloudland Journal, which I've been keeping since 1997**

01/15/24 It was three degrees below zero when I suited up in an old snowmobile suit I got for a trip to Alaska in winter many years ago—it's my ZERO suit which I only get to wear once or twice a year. I had planned to hike down and visit a waterfall on our lower trail—no doubt it would be frozen over with lots of colorful ICE.

It was slow-going as I bushwhacked through the thick brush—all downhill but lots of snow–covered limbs hitting me in the face. Looked like we had received about 8–12" of snow total in the past 24 hours.

When I arrived at the waterfall I found it almost totally iced up all the way across, with no real spot to stand in front of it for photos. So I found a spot on one end where I cold break through enough of the ice for me to slip past the ice wall, kind of tumbling into the cave behind the wall of ice. I MADE IT!

For some reason I had forgot my bike helmet that I would normally wear in a low-ceiling overhang like this, but figured my head was hard enough anyway. Once I duck-walked across to the middle of the ice wall I sat down and had a look around, and it was SPLENDID! Ice flows like this will often be multicolored—blue, white, green, yellow—depending on what the water was like and how the light was shining. Actually it was still overcast so no sunshine, but everything had a blue cast along with the other colors.

I took a couple of quick snapshots with my phone, but was anxious to get out my real camera with a special ultra-wide angle lens I brought for it. SURPRISE—I brought the wrong lens! (I have two of these old-school tiny, but all-manual lenses - and both are the same size and unless I'm wearing my glasses I can't tell them apart).

But no matter, I stood up as best I could and got really close to the ice and started to take pictures with the little lens. Only two shots then BATTERY EXHAUSTED flashed on the camera for a moment, and then it went dark, oh no! I didn't have a backup battery and the frigid temp sapped all the juice from my main battery.

I sat back (the ceiling was too low to stand, I could only sit, kneel, or stand up and bend over, which was not good for my back). I decided to abort and left the ice cave and headed back to the cabin. Note to self—#1, make SURE you have the correct lens with you, especially when headed out to an ice cave at below zero! #2, bring your HELMET! #3, bring a BACKUP battery!
Maybe tomorrow...

01/16/24 This morning was the coldest we've had at 5.1 BELOW ZERO, so naturally I suited up and headed back out and down to our ice cave. Nothing but clear-blue skies and I wanted to be inside the cave when the first rays of sunshine hit the ice.

As I arrived back at the frozen waterfall I discovered the hole in the ice curtain I'd knocked out the day before had formed more ice and was once again a solid wall of ice. Oops. No matter, I used the spiked feet of my trusty tripod to knock out a new opening for me to slip through. When doing this sort of thing—with a steady stream of frigid water pouring down—I remove my camera backpack and toss it and the tripod through the hole so those items don't catch on any ice. I rolled on through the hole and once again found myself in an ice cathedral, only this time there was sunshine approaching!

I set up my camera and got a few shots with my new lens, but I ended up mostly shooting with a couple of other lenses that I'd also brought with me, including a special 70-200 macro lens. Besides frozen fingertips the biggest issue I had was operating while bent over, but I managed to shoot a few nice scenes.

At one point I stopped shooting and just crawled around a bit without the camera to give myself a little time to soak in all the beauty. The sun had appeared, which immediately started melting the wall of ice—even though it was still below zero! And then a shaft of sunshine hit me right in the face. I looked up and saw an amazing scene—brilliant beams were coming in through a crack in the ice and shafts of warm sunshine flooded the cave. QUICK—where's my go—darn CAMERA!?

I crawled back and grabbed my camera and tripod and set up as fast as I could, then took a few frantic shots as the sun beams quickly disappeared. It all happened about that fast and the light drew silent again. I spent the next ten minutes checking each opening in the ice wall for sunbeams but never did get any more. No matter, I got ONE really good frame of this event and it was worth all the pain and suffering.

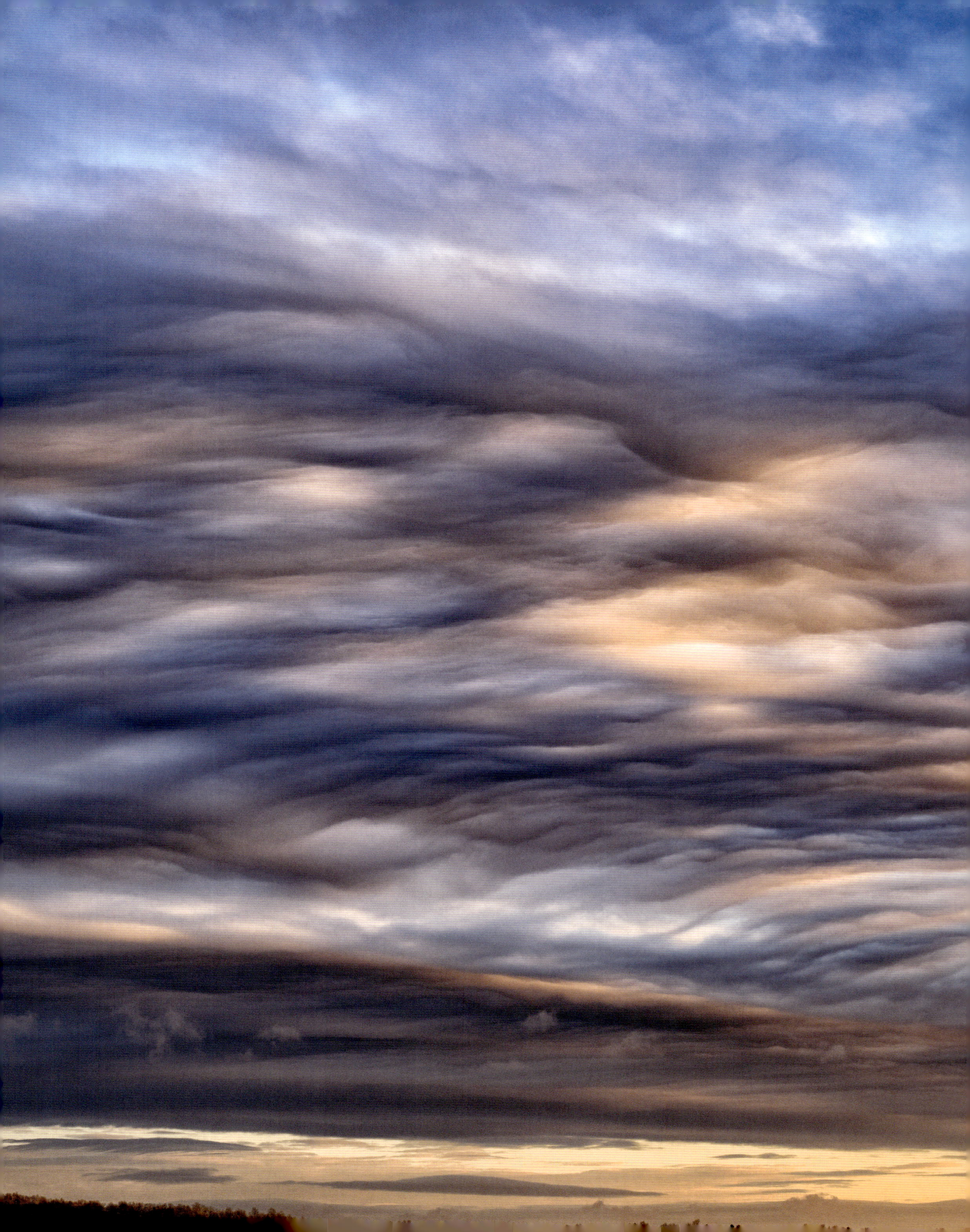

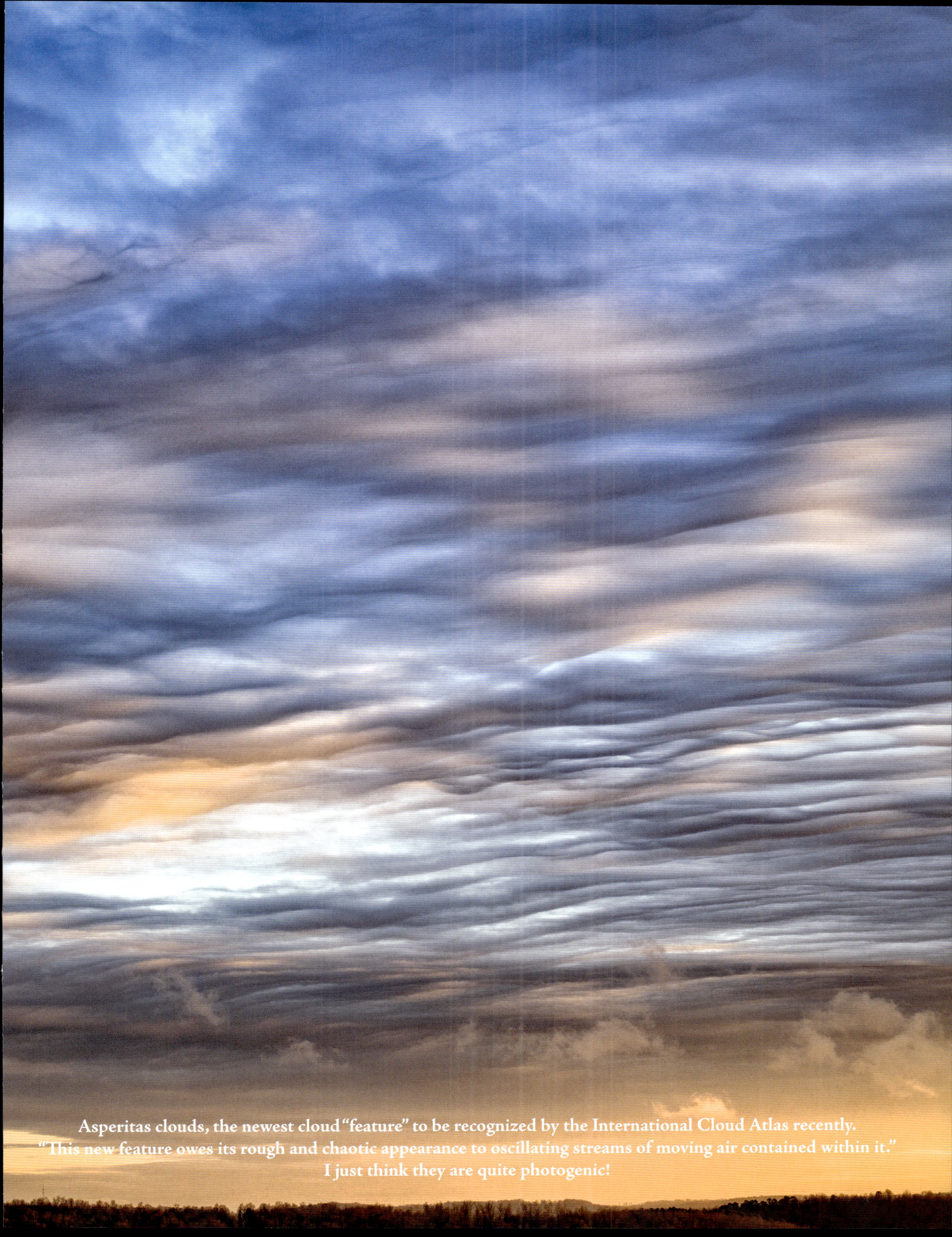

Asperitas clouds, the newest cloud "feature" to be recognized by the International Cloud Atlas recently. "This new feature owes its rough and chaotic appearance to oscillating streams of moving air contained within it." I just think they are quite photogenic!

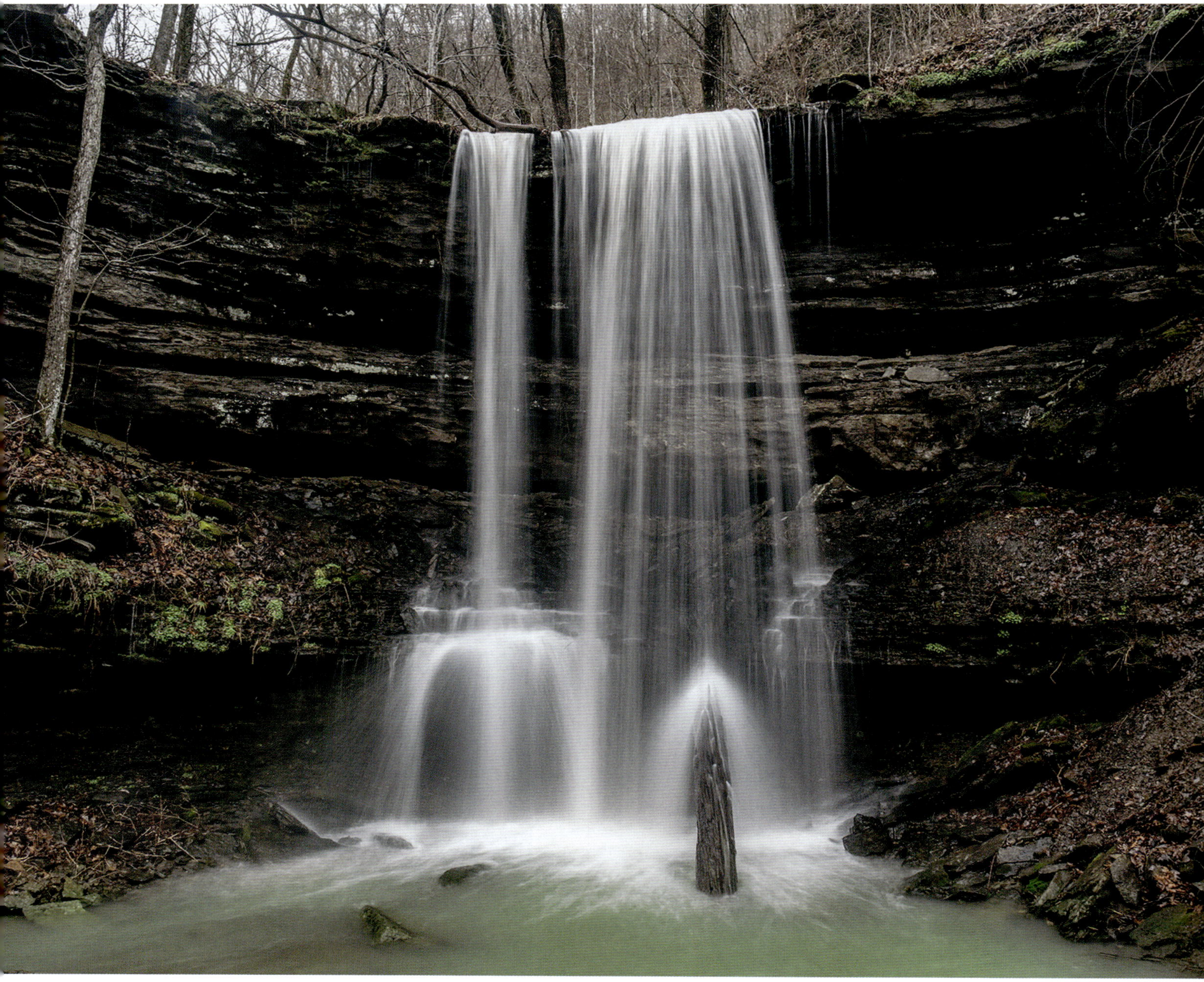

Log In The Way Falls, Ozark National Forest

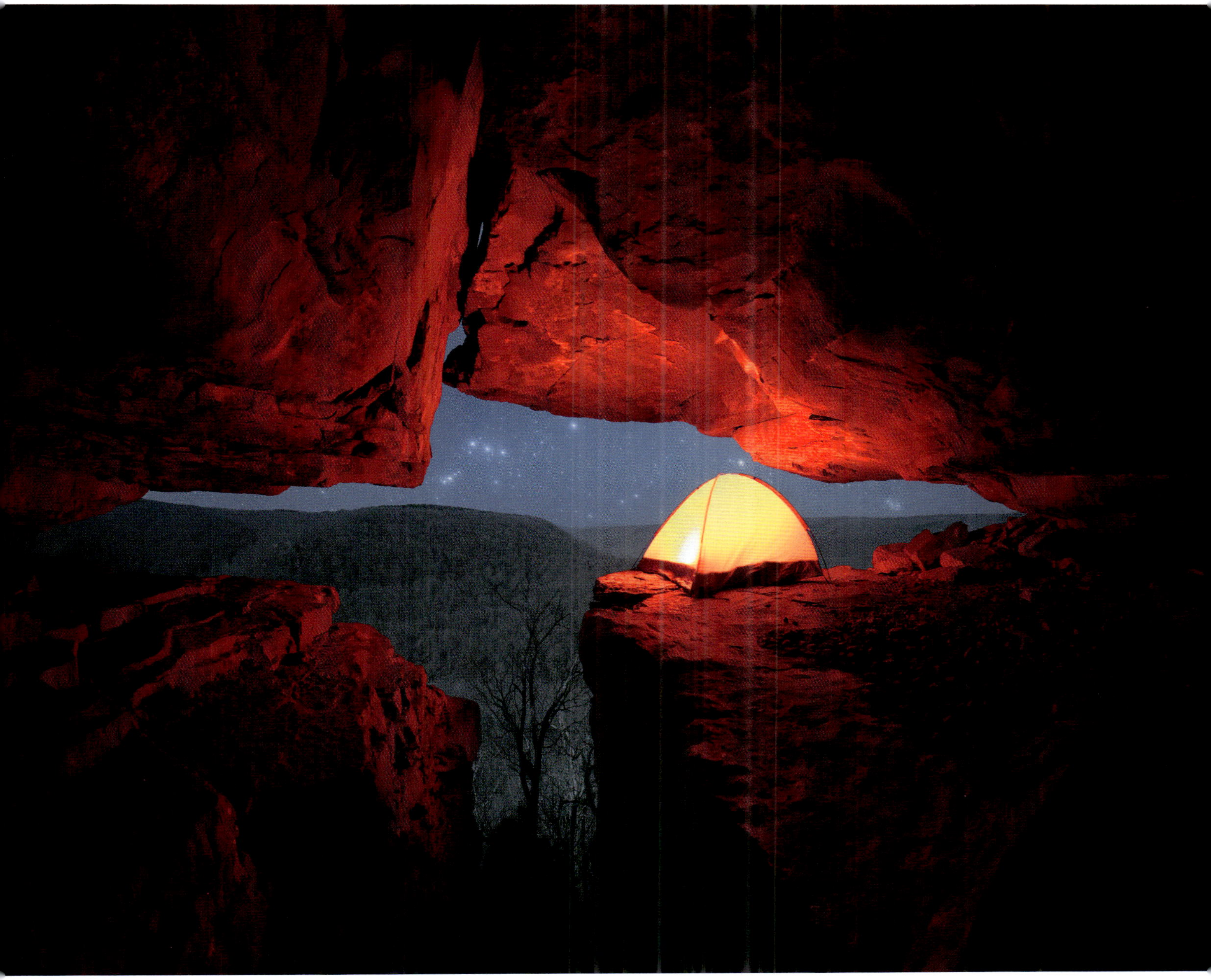

Thunderbird Cave campsite, full moon illuminating the landscape, and Orion setting. Ozark National Forest (The tent was used as a prop—don't try this at home!)

They said it was a really difficult hike/climb to get to this location. Heck I couldn't even get my car to the parking spot. But I did find a place to park, and a bushwhack hike to this location that seemed a little easier than the other described route (and avoided private property). Turned out ***most*** of my new route was easier, except for this little 500' vertical drop down to and across a creek, and then a 500' climb up the other side. Everything else was a piece of cake. (I actually enjoy steep climbs, and these were "down on all fours clawing up the hillside" type of climbs.)

My only issue was that it took me five trips to get the photo I really wanted (above), and four of those trips were in the DARK, bushwhacking, with no trail. One of the night trips I made without a flashlight (don't ask).

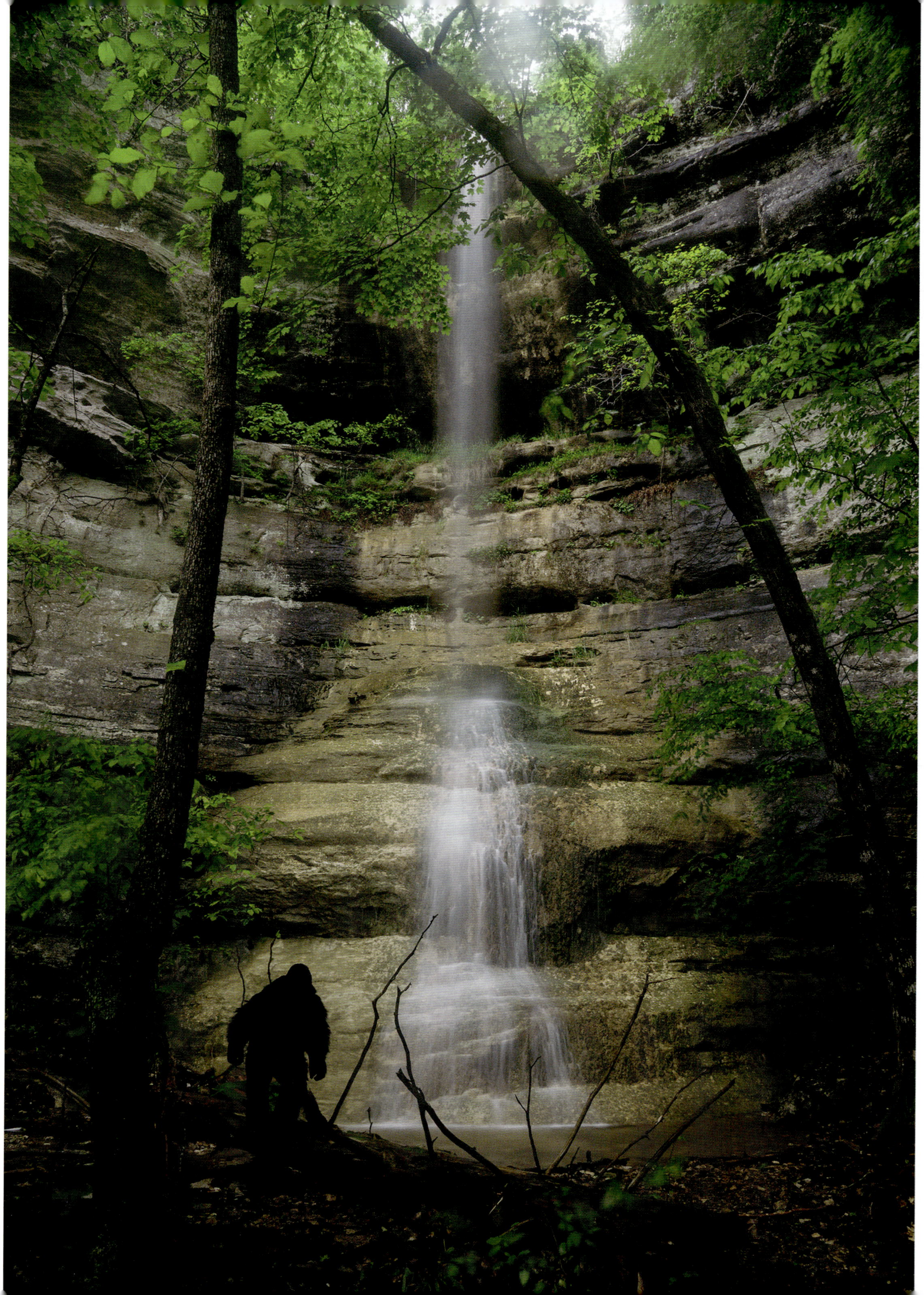

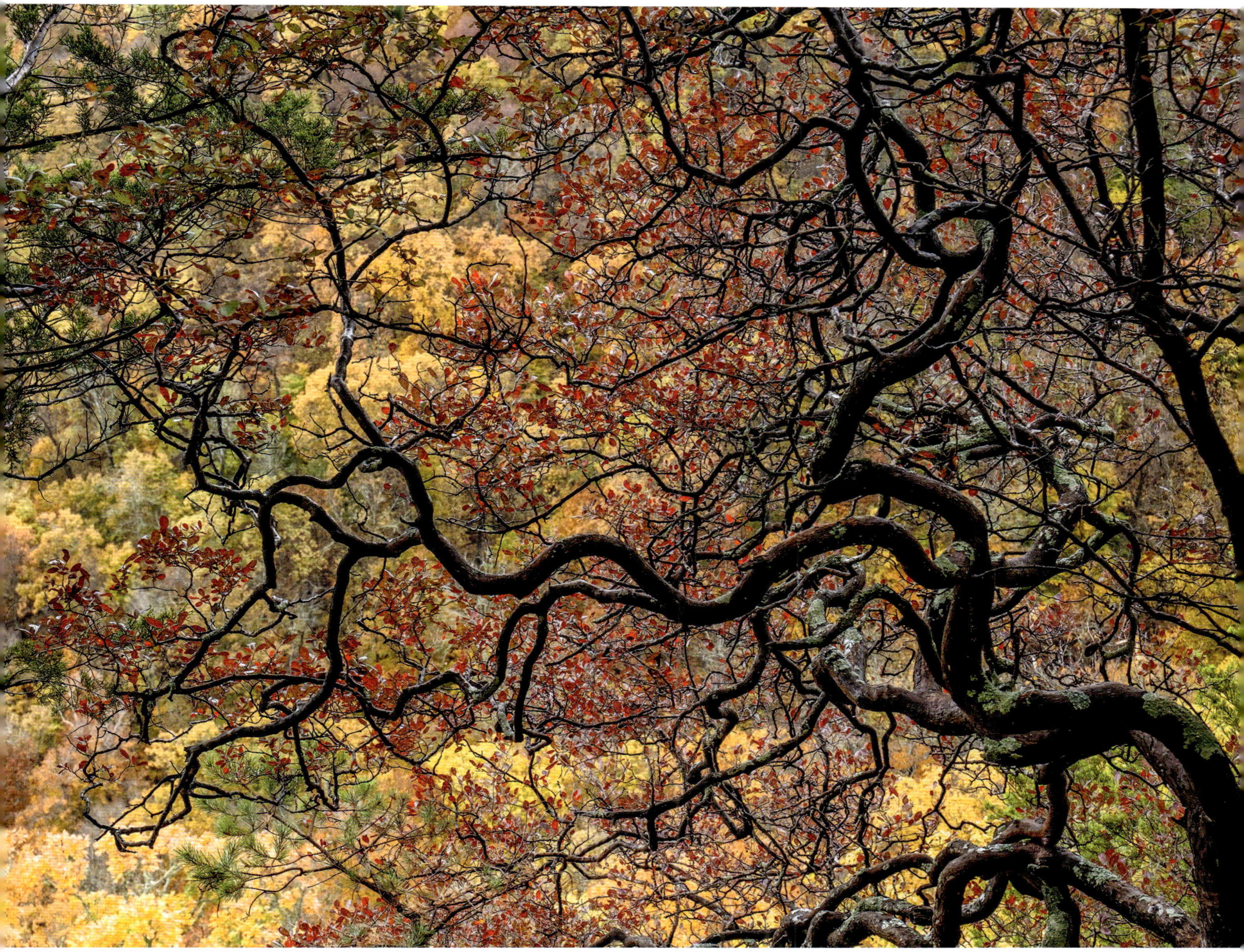

Highbush huckleberry, aka farkleberry bush

These guys live along the tops of bluffs—this one is right next to a very popular hiking trail, yet most folks walk right on by. Reminds me of a Bonsai tree on steroids. This has been my most popular photograph of the past five years.

< Bigfoot Falls, along the Buffalo River Trail

I tend to name waterfalls after things I find there. Hum.......

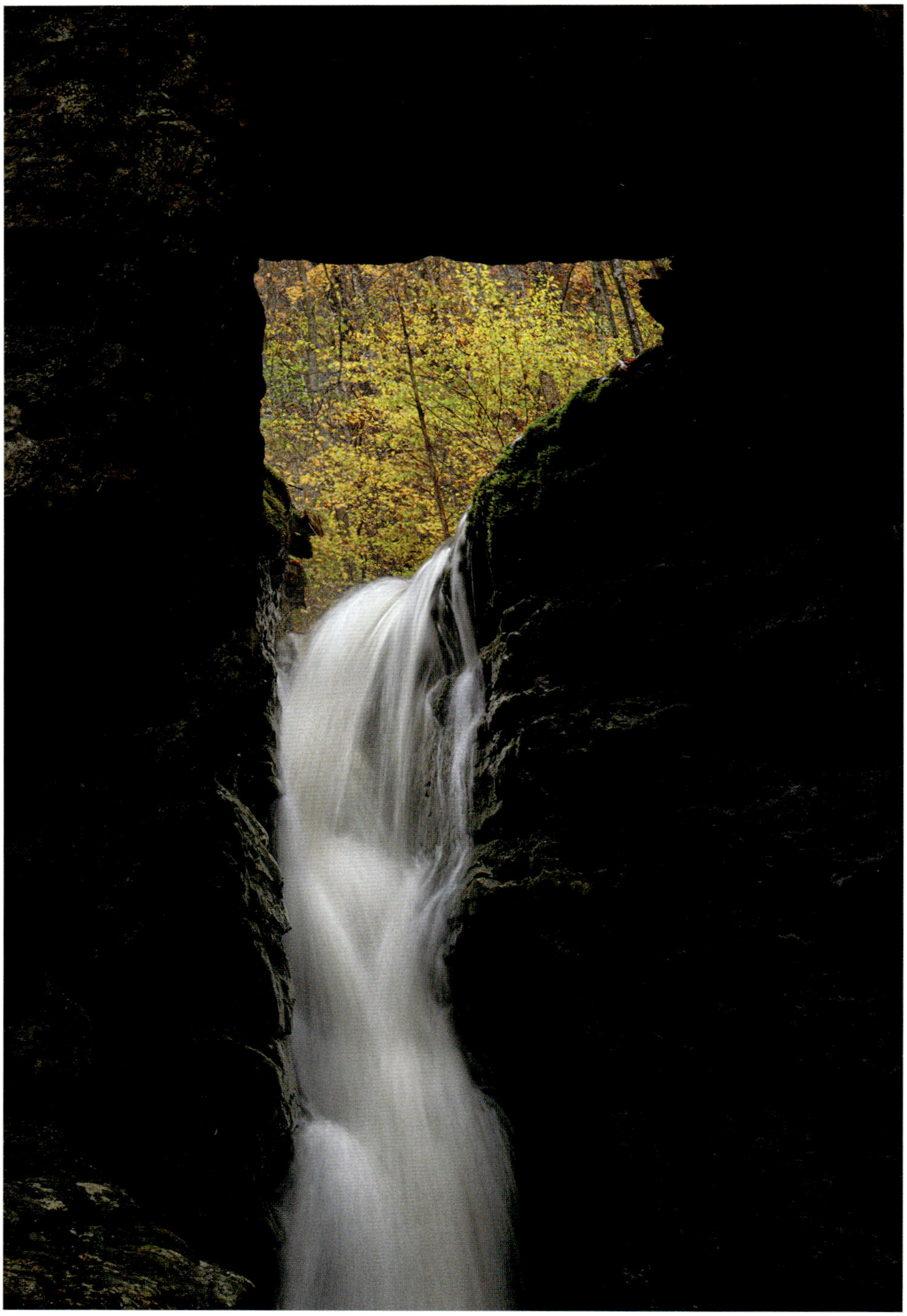

ARKANSAS Falls?

Balanced Rock Falls, Leatherwood Creek drainage near Ponca >

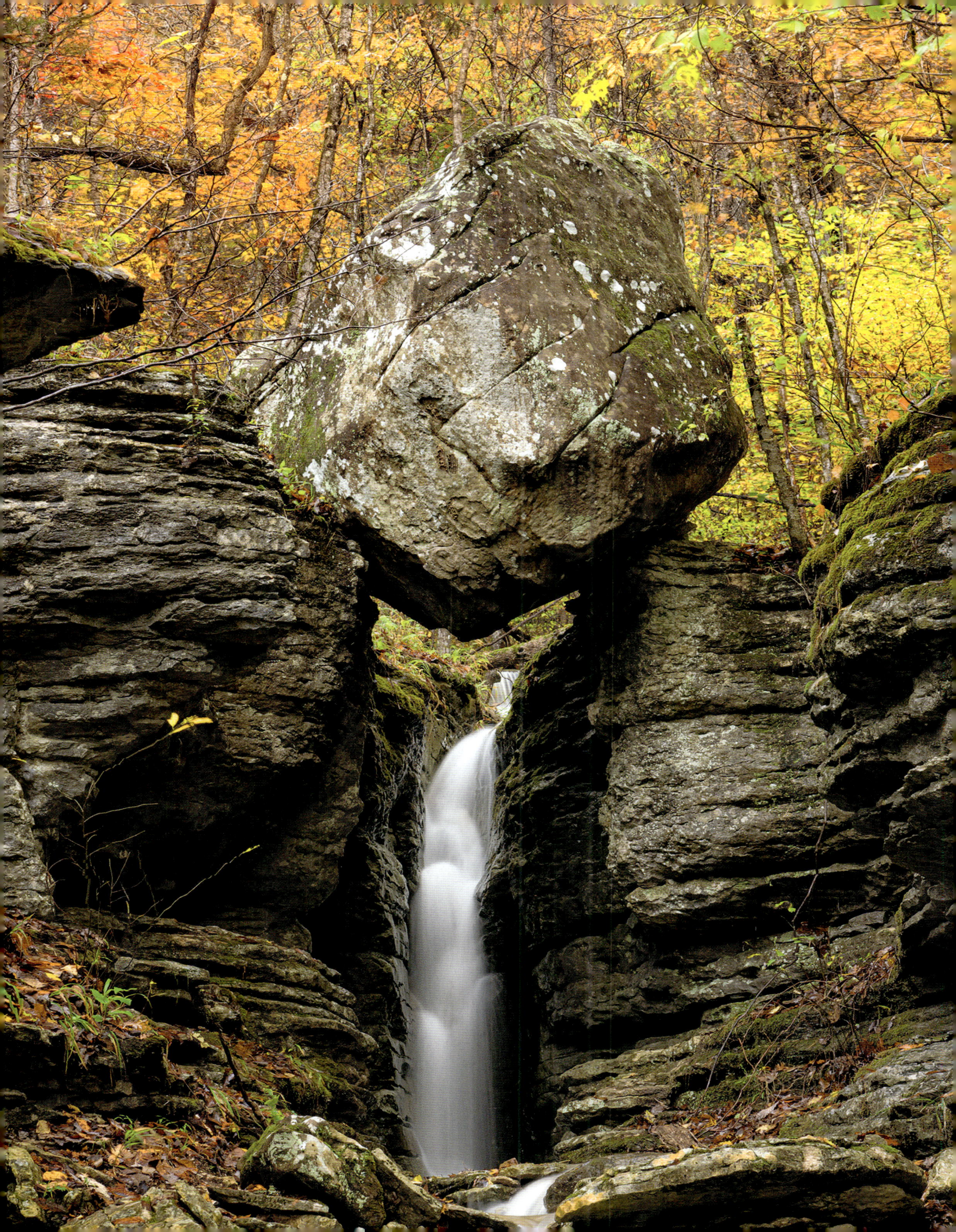

ABOUT THE AUTHOR

Tim Ernst lives in rural Newton County, Arkansas near Jasper with his lovely bride, Pamela, and puppy dogs Mia and Wilson.

I've been a professional nature photographer for 50 years with images published in most of the major nature publications from ***National Geographic*** on down, including hundreds of national, regional, and local magazines, books, calendars, even a U.S. postage stamp. This is my 21st coffee table picture book—see covers of the first 20 on the opposite page. (I have one more in the hopper to be released soon—***ARKANSAS: JUST WATERFALLS.***) I've written a couple dozen guidebooks to outdoor Arkansas destinations that will lead you to waterfalls, hiking trails, and special scenic locations. My lovely bride and I own and operate a small publishing business, Tim Ernst Publishing, since 1981. We also sell fine art prints via online galleries and through our Tim Ernst Photography Canvas Gallery location that serves as gallery, digital darkroom, and print studio (open to the public on special days, and by appointment). My bride is a pastel artist, and has a selection of her original pastels on display at our gallery too (see www.pamspastels.com). www.TimErnst.com.

The most frequent question I get is what camera I use. I switched to digital cameras around the turn of the century, and lately have been using only mirrorless digital cameras. My workhorse cameras for this book included an ancient Sony A6000, Sony A7RV, Fuji X-E4, and Fuji GFX bodies with a variety of lenses. (and of course ***my phone***, haha)

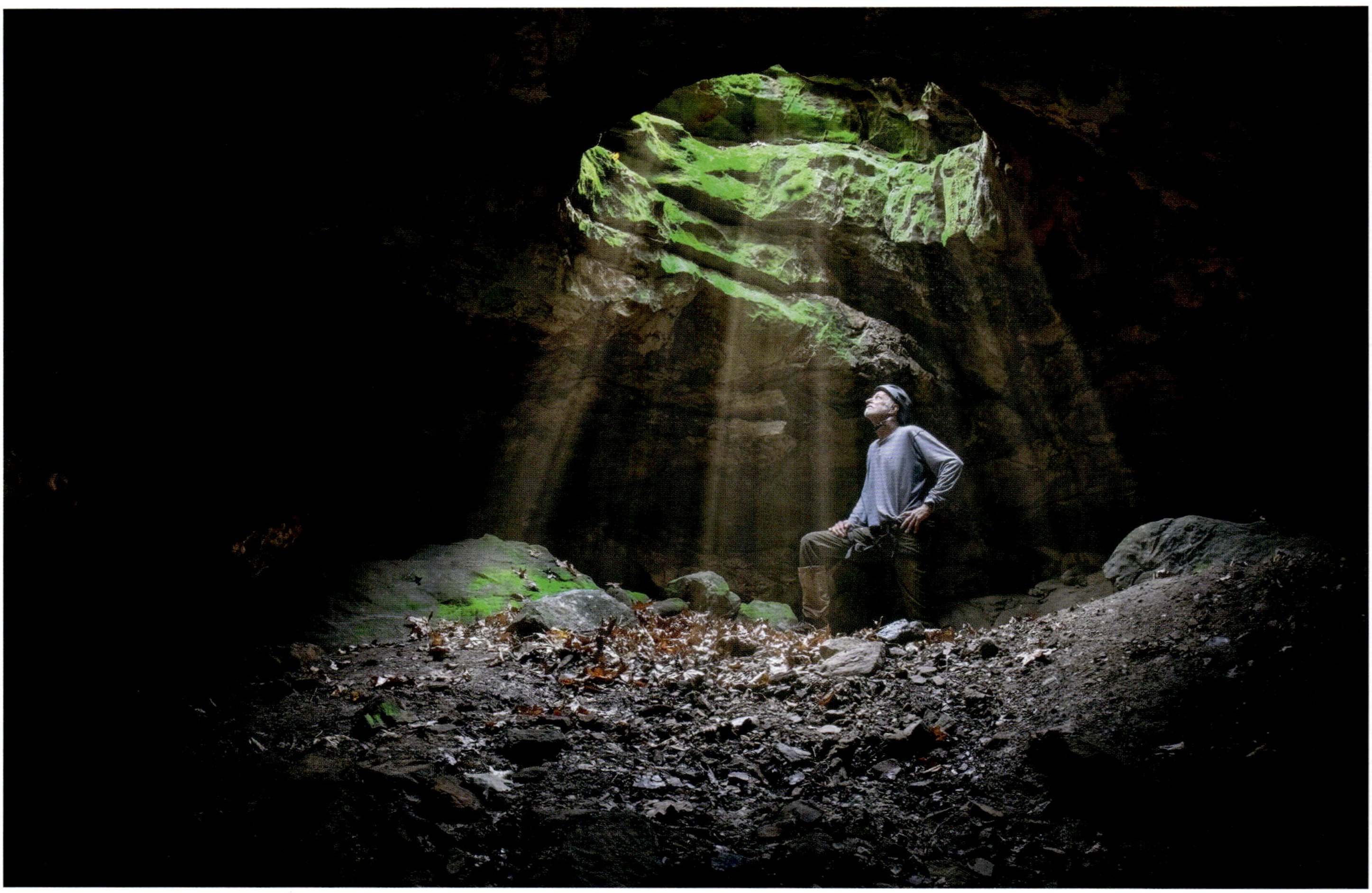

Here's the geezer with his bike helmet and snake gaiters at the Mystic Hole, Lower Buffalo Wilderness Area
(photo by Allen Wilcox)

The Ernst coffee-table book collection—it only took me 45 years and 3 million photos.

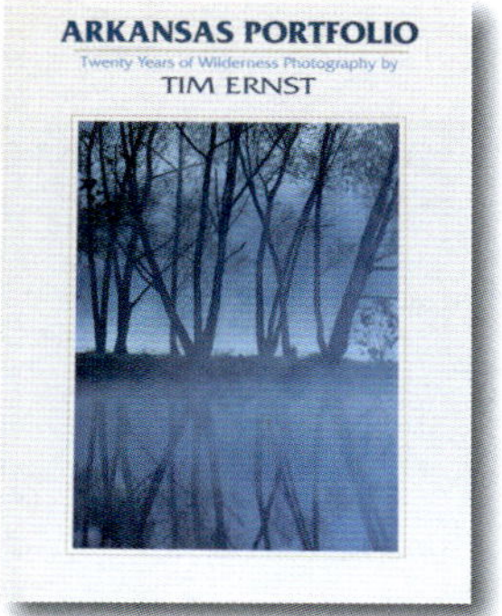

Arkansas Portfolio, 1994

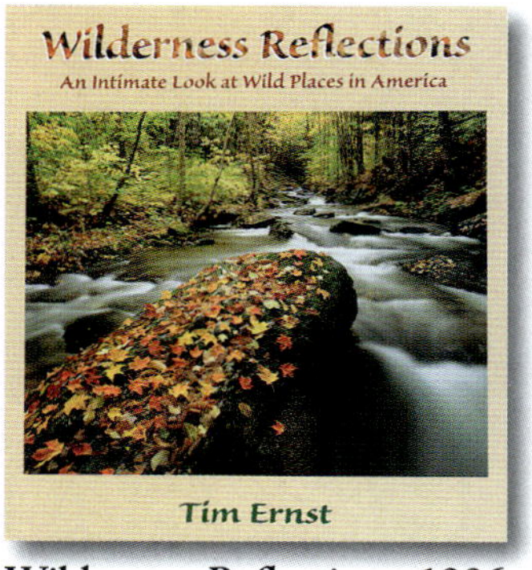

Wilderness Reflections, 1996

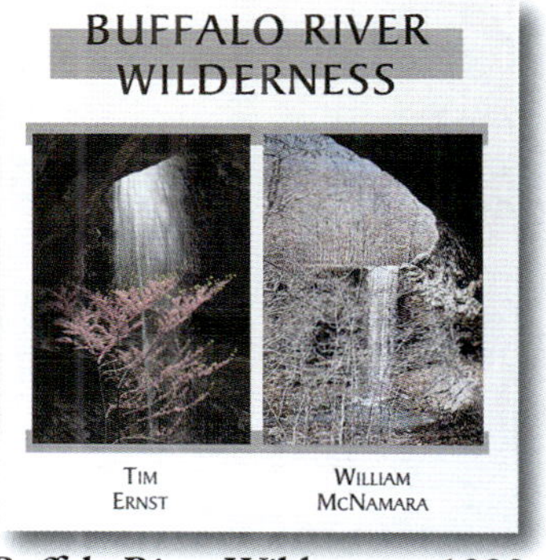

Buffalo River Wilderness, 1998

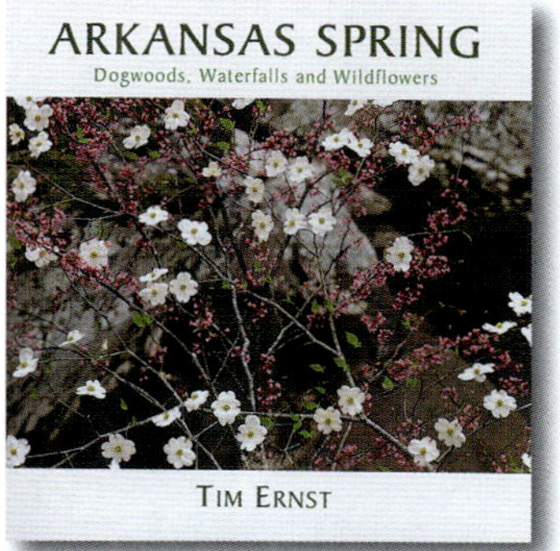

Arkansas Spring, 2000

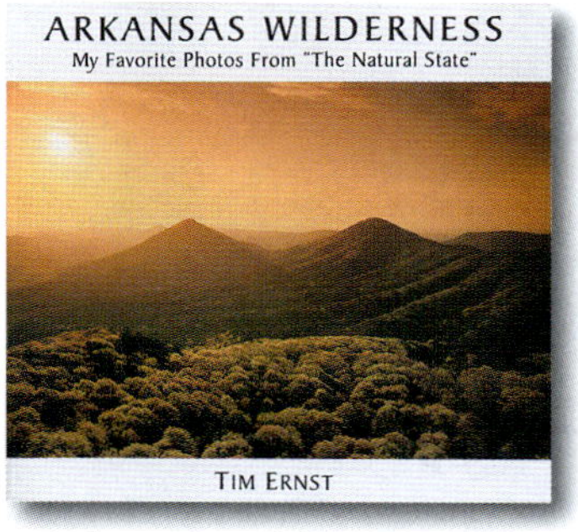

Arkansas Wilderness, 2002

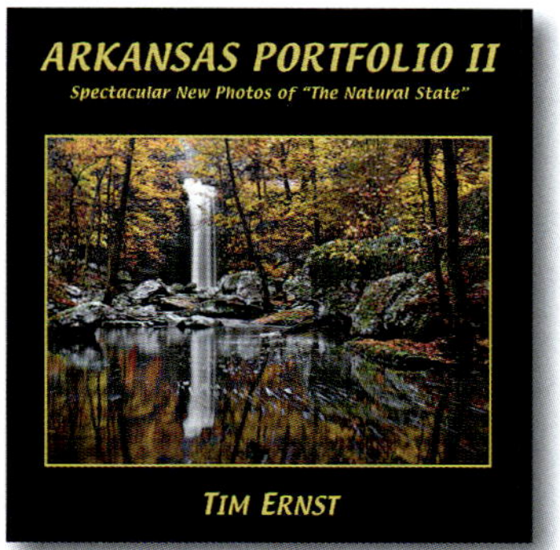

Arkansas Portfolio II, 2004

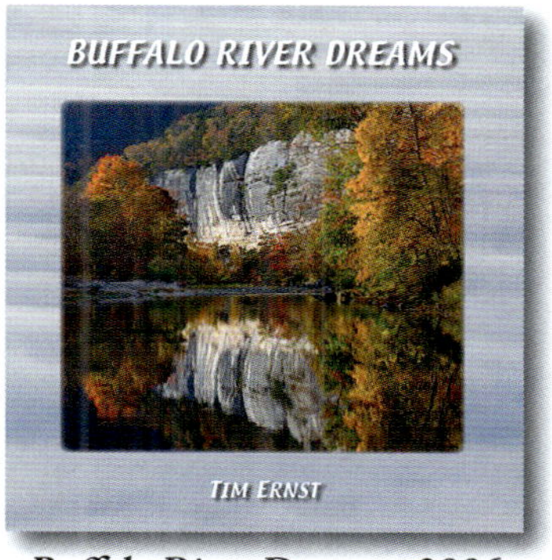

Buffalo River Dreams, 2006

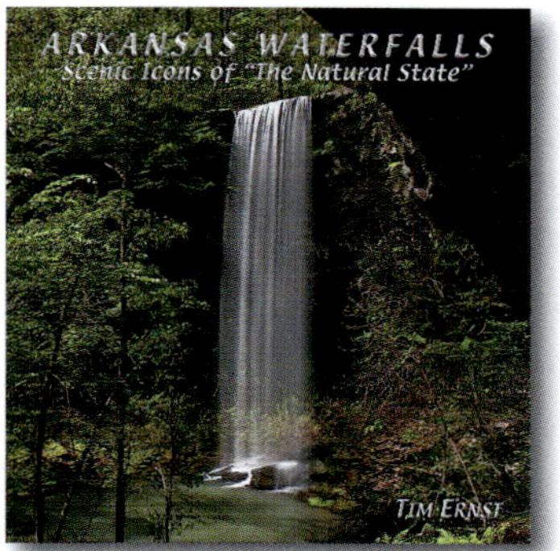

Arkansas Waterfalls, 2007

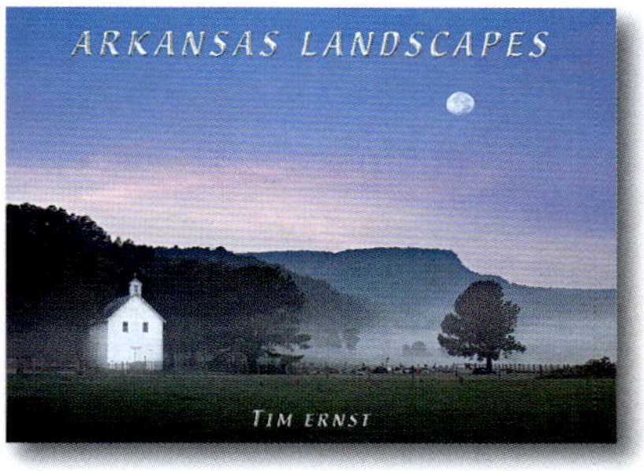

Arkansas Landscapes, 2008

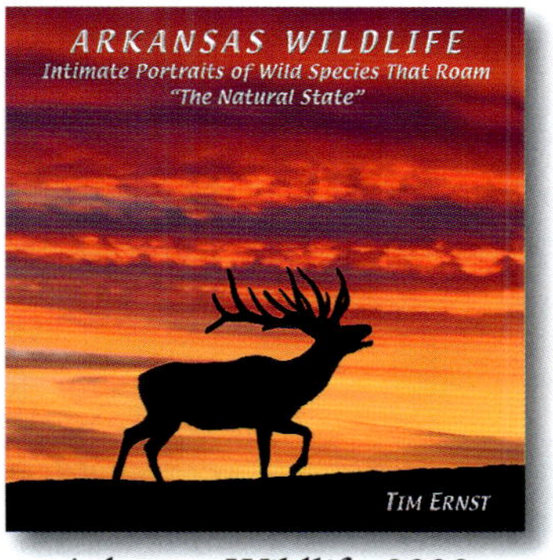

Arkansas Wildlife, 2009

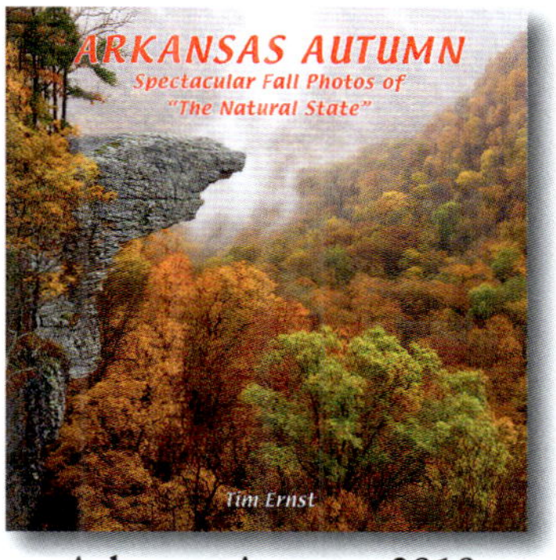

Arkansas Autumn, 2010

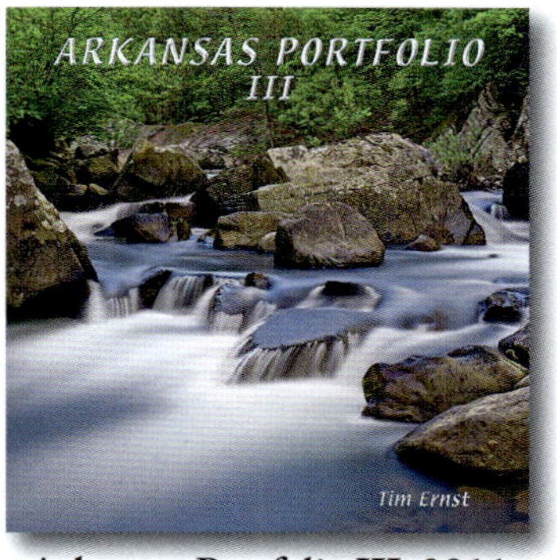

Arkansas Portfolio III, 2011

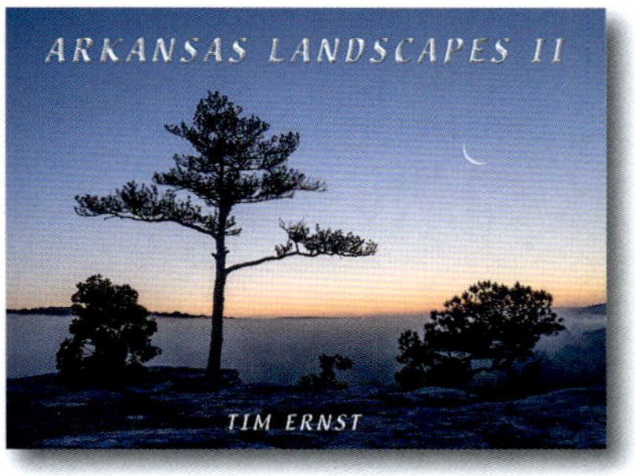

Arkansas Landscapes II, 2012

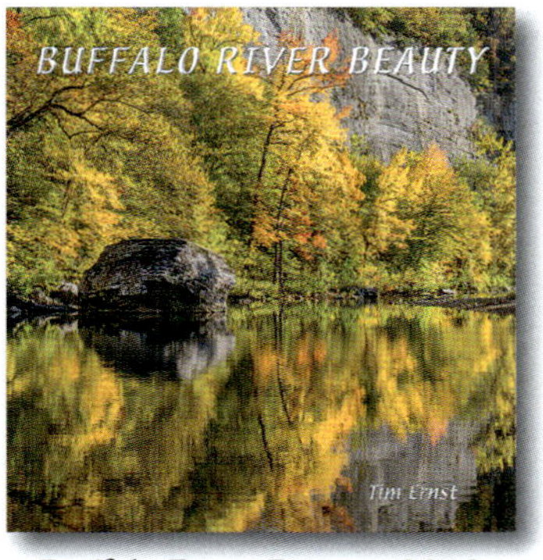

Buffalo River Beauty, 2013

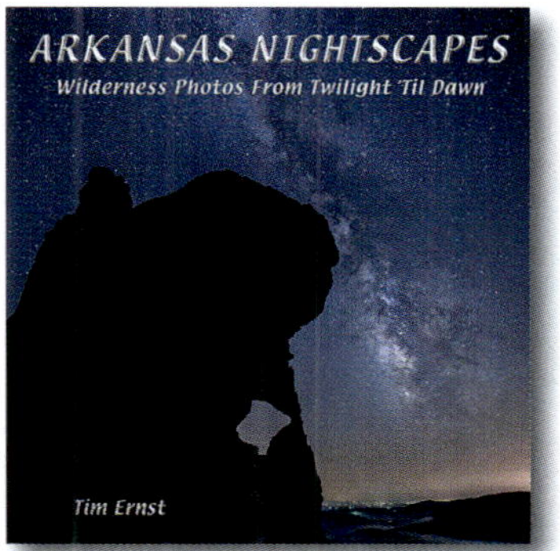

Arkansas Nightscapes, 2014

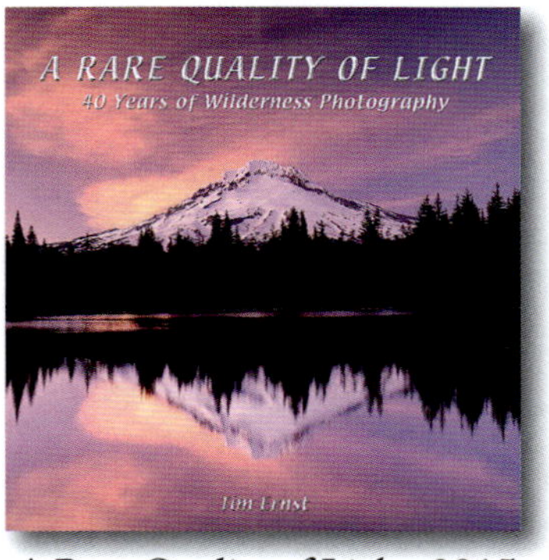

A Rare Quality of Light, 2015

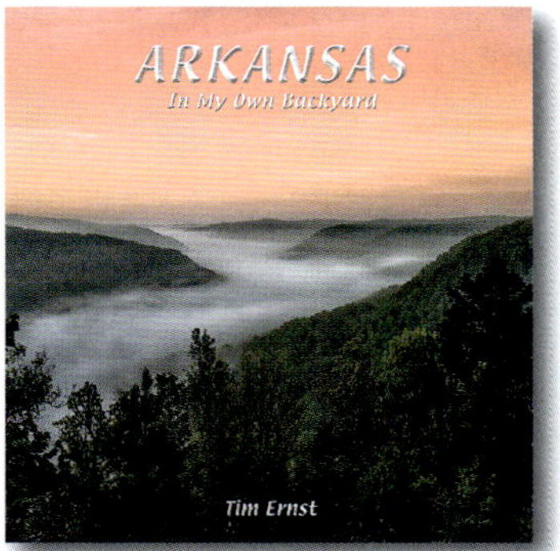

Arkansas In My Own Backyard, 2016

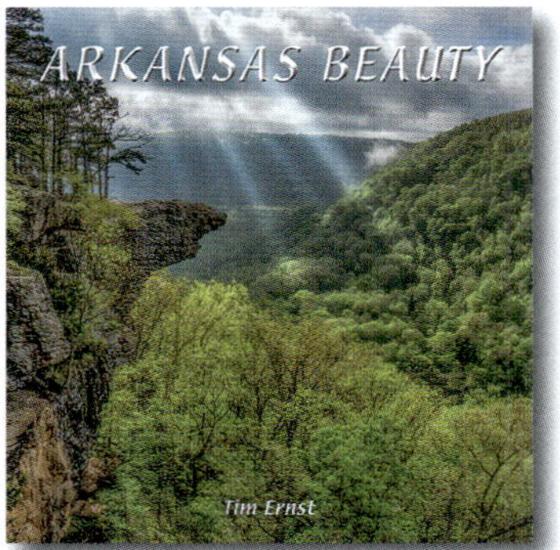

Arkansas Beauty, 2017

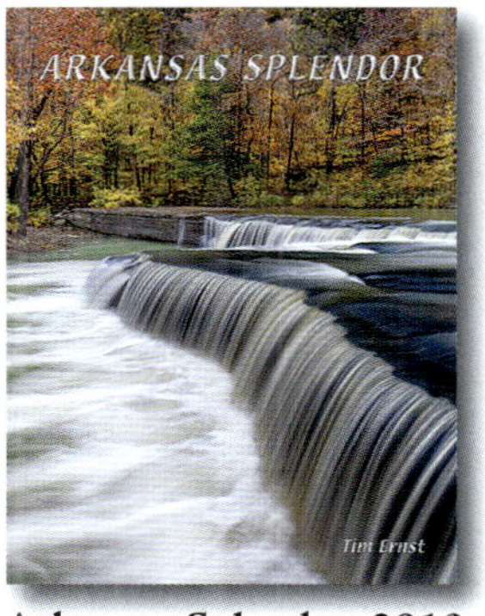

Arkansas Splendor, 2019

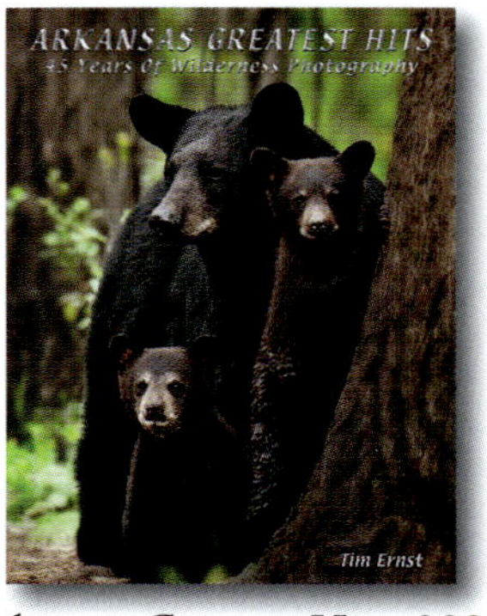

Arkansas Greatest Hits, 2020

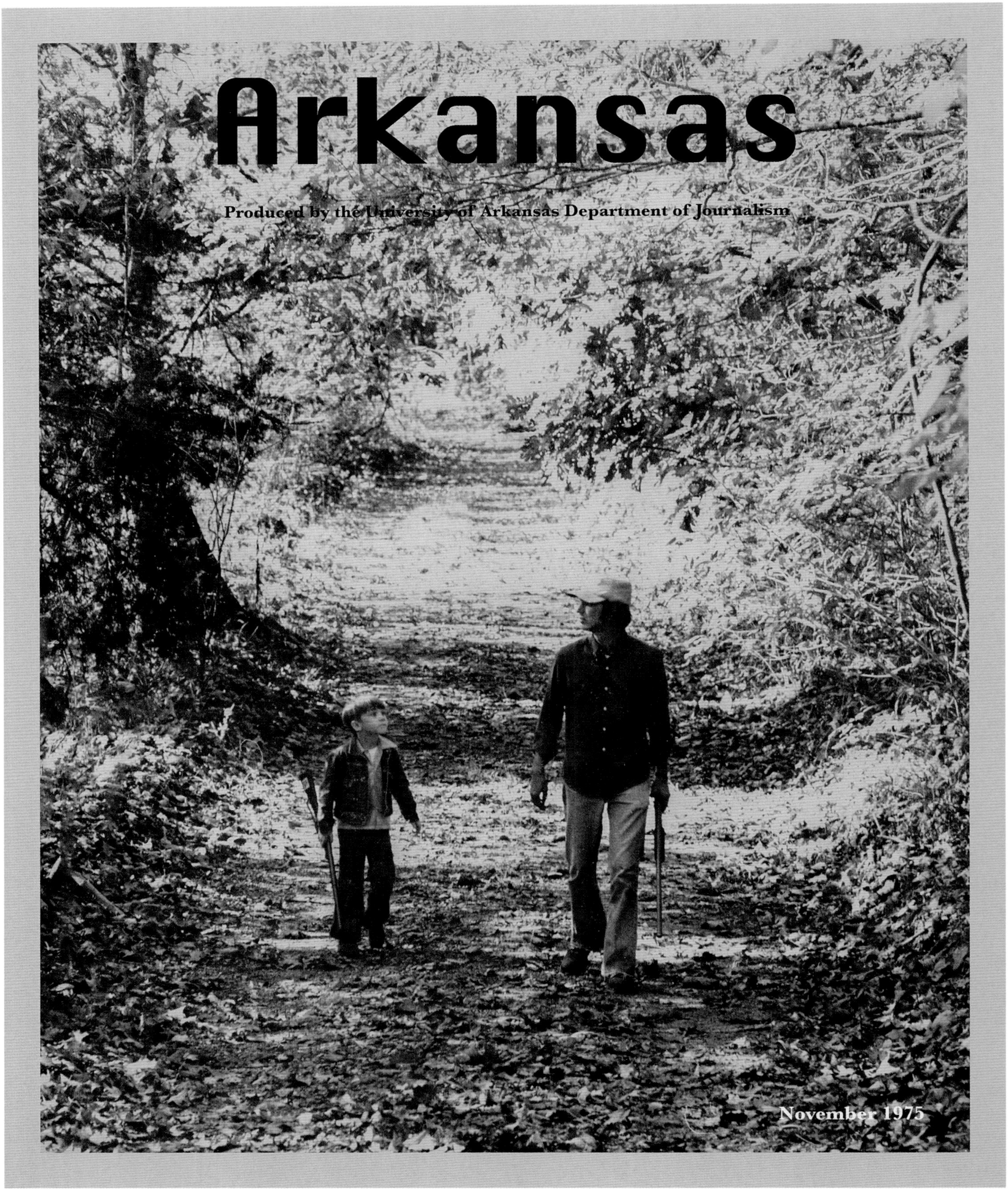

I end with the beginning—this is the FIRST photo of mine that was ever published (1975). The last photo I took for this book is on page 1. **It has been my pleasure** for the past 50 years to capture and share the great natural beauty of my home state of Arkansas. That job is never really complete though until someone on the other end views them. So ***THANK YOU*** for taking the time to look at these pictures—I hope they have brought you joy! ...Tim Ernst, November 2025